AF207781

Luminos is the open access monograph publishing program from UC Press. Luminos provides a framework for preserving and reinvigorating monograph publishing for the future and increases the reach and visibility of important scholarly work. Titles published in the UC Press Luminos model are published with the same high standards for selection, peer review, production, and marketing as those in our traditional program. www.luminosoa.org

A

*Philip E. Lilienthal*

B O O K

The Philip E. Lilienthal imprint
honors special books
in commemoration of a man whose work
at University of California Press from 1954 to 1979
was marked by dedication to young authors
and to high standards in the field of Asian Studies.
Friends, family, authors, and foundations have together
endowed the Lilienthal Fund, which enables UC Press
to publish under this imprint selected books
in a way that reflects the taste and judgment
of a great and beloved editor.

The publisher gratefully acknowledges the generous support of the Philip E. Lilienthal Asian Studies Endowment Fund of the University of California Press Foundation, which was established by a major gift from Sally Lilienthal.

The publisher also gratefully acknowledges that this book has been published with the assistance of the Frederick W. Hilles Publication Fund of Yale University.

Luxury and Rubble

# Luxury and Rubble

*Civility and Dispossession in the New Saigon*

Erik Harms

UNIVERSITY OF CALIFORNIA PRESS

University of California Press, one of the most distinguished university presses in the United States, enriches lives around the world by advancing scholarship in the humanities, social sciences, and natural sciences. Its activities are supported by the UC Press Foundation and by philanthropic contributions from individuals and institutions. For more information, visit www.ucpress.edu.

University of California Press

Oakland, California

Suggested citation: Harms, Erik. *Luxury and Rubble: Civility and Dispossession in the New Saigon*. Oakland: University of California Press, 2016. doi: http://doi.org/10.1525/luminos.20

Cataloguing-in-Publication Data is on file at the Library of Congress.

ISBN 978–0-520–29251–2 (pbk. : alk. paper) | ISBN 978–0-520–96601–7 (ebook)

26   25   24   23   22   21   20   19   18   17
10   9   8   7   6   5   4   3   2   1

*For Isabella*

# CONTENTS

# ILLUSTRATIONS

# Introduction

## Luxury and Rubble

*I seek to show that the pure multiplicity of rubble is the void that haunts modernity.*

—GASTÓN GORDILLO, *RUBBLE: THE AFTERLIFE OF DESTRUCTION*

### THE PHÚ MỸ BRIDGE

The Phú Mỹ suspension bridge rises from a bend in the Saigon River a little more than three and a half miles south by southeast of District One, Ho Chi Minh City's downtown core. From downtown, the bridge can be seen from the city's expensive rooftop bars, at places along the banks of the river, and down recently widened avenues, where breaks in the urban fabric open up views to the edge of the sky. In this former French colony, in the city once (but no longer) called the "Paris of the East" or the "Pearl of the Orient," these broad roads, ripped through dense neighborhoods, evoke memories of the nineteenth-century labors of Baron Haussmann, whose reconstruction of Paris under Napoléon III replaced crooked streets with grand boulevards. Today, as Ho Chi Minh City's neighborhoods are flattened, new vistas emerge, including the view of the bridge stretching across the river in the distance, its elegant spans, two modern towers, and graceful suspension cables framing the southeastern horizon like a gateway to the city (fig. 0.1).

The Phú Mỹ Bridge connects District Two and District Seven, two of the city's newly urbanizing and formerly rural districts (fig. 0.2). On one side of the river, to the east of downtown, in a still partially rural but rapidly urbanizing section of District Two, the bridge rises out of rice fields, which are in turn hemmed in by newly subdivided residential housing and recently constructed apartment complexes built to resettle thousands of residents who have been displaced by the Thủ Thiêm New Urban Zone, a major new urban development project. On the other side of the river, the bridge's hulking cement columns and its massive on- and off-ramps pierce the dense urban fabric of District Seven, cutting through the

1

FIGURE 0.1. The Phú Mỹ Bridge. District 2 is in the foreground; District 7 is on the far side of the bridge. The faintly visible apartment towers in the background rise from the Phú Mỹ Hưng New Urban Zone. Author's photo, July 2012.

working-class neighborhoods that have expanded throughout the district over the past two decades of rapid periurban growth. A sleek flyover connects the bridge to an area of District Seven called Saigon South, bypassing the dense city below, conveying traffic straight into the heart of an upscale residential and commercial development known as Phú Mỹ Hưng.

## LUXURY AND RUBBLE

This book is about Phú Mỹ Hưng and Thủ Thiêm, two master-planned urban development projects located on either side of the Phú Mỹ Bridge. My primary aim is to show how large-scale urban infrastructure projects become entangled with the lives and aspirations of people living in a rapidly growing city, and to show the role these projects play in the complex political and economic dramas taking place in an urban world increasingly driven by the market logics of real estate development. The dramas of urban development described in this book are staged on contested parcels of land and set within a city and country that have endured a tumultuous twentieth century marked by colonialism, devastating warfare, and a postwar period marked first by the utopian ambitions of building socialism, then by the dystopian consequences of that project, and, more recently, by the rampant real estate speculation that followed the introduction of a market economy.

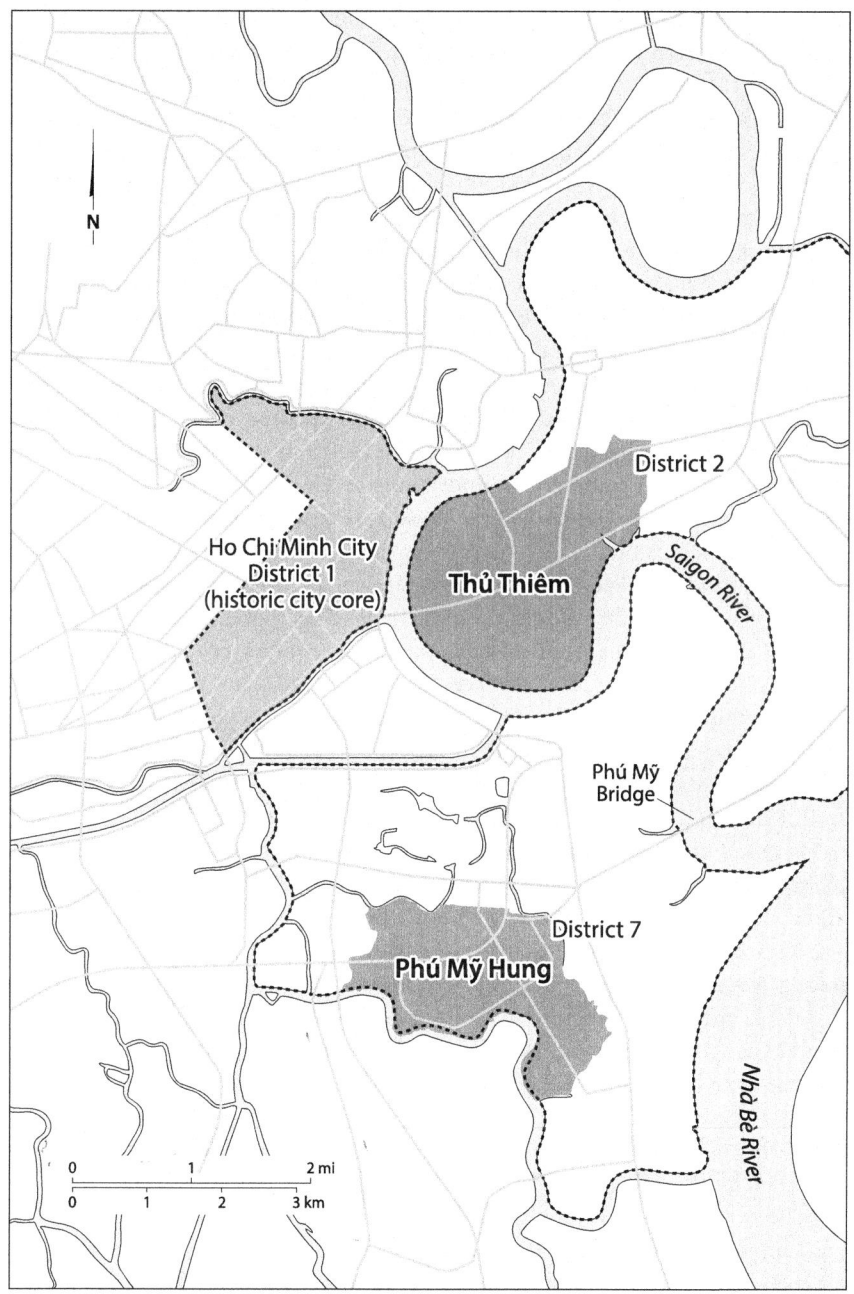

FIGURE 0.2. Map of Ho Chi Minh City indicating the location of Phú Mỹ Hưng and Thủ Thiêm. The boundaries of Districts 1, 2, and 7 are marked by dotted lines.

Ever since 1986, when the Vietnamese Communist Party introduced a political and economic reform policy called Đổi Mới (renovation, literally "the change to the new"), the story of urban development in Ho Chi Minh City has been the story of what happens when market-oriented economic policy reforms butt heads with the single-party state's strictly maintained limits on political freedoms. The postreform era, which really began to gather momentum in the 1990s, has gradually led to an increasingly liberal (and many would say, neoliberal) emphasis on free markets. At the same time, political life in Ho Chi Minh City—which residents increasingly call by its old name, Saigon, and which I sometimes call "the New Saigon"—remains circumscribed by strict limits on free speech, careful restrictions on public assembly, and surveillance of other forms of civic activism and intellectual or artistic expression. In this context, where markets are generally free but speech is mostly not, people living in what is sometimes called the "renovation generation" or the "postreform era" often look less to civic politics than to market-based solutions and commercial innovations as a way to express their sense of urban citizenship. City residents have no formal way to choose elected representatives, and there is no democratic process through which they can express their ideas about the so-called right to the city. Today, their most tangible right to the city is, for better or worse, bound up in their "land use rights."

As I will show, this political and economic context produces a situation where concepts like "civility" are sometimes forced to stand in for the language of citizenship, where "free markets" are often forced to act as an imperfect substitute for political freedom, and where "property rights" (or more precisely, "land use rights") are regularly conflated with rights more broadly construed. In this situation, where neoliberal economics mingle with illiberal politics and free-market expansion coexists with persistent political unfreedoms, master-planned urban development projects become important sites for imagining and contesting new ideas about urban life. Because overtly contentious politics remain impossible, I argue that the agitation over land use rights and civility taking place in these two places operates as a surrogate for the kind of political life citizens in other countries normally enjoy. As I will show, for many people living in the new Saigon, master-planned housing and commercial developments symbolize the exciting potential of remaking the city, and perhaps even rethinking urban governance and reconstructing social life. Many of the people I spoke to even told me that these zones offer a model for a free society governed by the rule of law. Nevertheless, as I will also show, the act of building these kinds of developments rests on the rubble of mass displacement, eviction, and dispossession.

The story of master-planned urban developments in Ho Chi Minh City is thus double-edged. The market in land made possible by economic reforms has both enabled spectacular development (with emphasis on the spectacle) and left a path of extraordinary destruction in its wake. The two sites discussed in this book illustrate the two sides of this story in clear, even stark terms. Phú Mỹ Hưng is a space of luxurious urban living where residents claim to be building a new form of urban consciousness and where they stress the importance of "civilized" political expression founded on an emergent sense of individualistic rights. It is a place where residents insist on living in accordance with the rule of law and other forms of orderly comportment. Meanwhile, the developers of Thủ Thiêm, which is still not completed, have aimed to make it into a place like Phú Mỹ Hưng. In the process of getting there, however, Thủ Thiêm became a site of extensive urban demolition, eviction, and human displacement. A language of rights also emerged among those being evicted in Thủ Thiêm, but those rights arose quite literally from fields of rubble. The rights that emerged in Thủ Thiêm were thus largely expressed in negative terms, as the kind of rights people realized they did not actually have. In both places, the language of rights was intimately bound up with conceptions of land use rights. What soon becomes clear, however, is that—just like land in contemporary Vietnam—some people quite literally have more rights than others.

The luxury and rubble of this book's title refers to the contrast between Phú Mỹ Hưng and Thủ Thiêm. The book itself is divided into two parts, each devoted to the experiences of people living through the social and spatial changes transforming each place. The title of the book is thus meant to form an outline in a phrase. Quite simply, I seek to tell the story of the city's new urban zones from two vantage points. In the most immediate and descriptive sense, I show that the luxury and the rubble scattered about contemporary Ho Chi Minh City's urban landscape are coproduced by the same urban processes that have emerged, roughly speaking, since 1993, when Vietnamese land laws began to allow people to buy and sell land use rights in earnest. As the subtitle of the book indicates, I further argue that civility and dispossession are bound together. In making these claims, I echo the poignant observations of Gastón Gordillo, who has recently argued that capitalism "rules through the production of spectacular places" while simultaneously leaving a path of destruction and vast fields of rubble in its wake.[1] Building on a range of scholars—from Walter Benjamin to David Harvey, Guy Debord to Ann Stoler—Gordillo usefully outlines a process he calls "destructive production" and convincingly shows that "the destruction of space under capitalism is the most devastating ever created."[2] The figure of rubble is, in Gordillo's elegant telling, the quintessential sign of our times. The new Saigon, one of the most rubble-strewn cities I have ever known, can easily be added to Gordillo's list of places where the spectacles of profit-oriented development emerge out of bulldozed landscapes. The city is thoroughly marked by rubble, and its neighborhoods everywhere teem with bulldozers, what Gordillo rightly calls "one of the main machines of spatial destruction under globalized capitalism."[3] In part, this book is an extended attempt to show, as Gordillo has also shown, "that the pure multiplicity of rubble is the void that haunts modernity."[4]

Gordillo, however, focuses almost exclusively on the rubble itself, turning spectacular infrastructure into a void of its own. I depart from this approach by taking spectacle just as seriously as I do rubble. I do this because my friends in Vietnam do. Listening to the residents of the new Saigon, as I have been doing for nearly two decades now, it is clear that the master-planned dreamworlds of places like Phú Mỹ Hưng are as much a part of the contemporary reality within which Vietnamese live as any other part of the city. Furthermore, the city residents I know best have always demanded that I be more sophisticated in my critiques of capitalism than I might otherwise be if left to my own devices. When I complain that certain developments in the city are "neoliberal," for example, the translation always falters, because the root word in the Vietnamese translation of neoliberal is *freedom*. How could I be opposed to that which might deliver a "new freedom" to my friends, especially people who have, as I noted above, endured so many restrictions on their liberty for so long? Although I am at heart a Marxist urbanist, their experiences urge me to engage not just with the perils but also with what they consider to be the many pleasures of capitalism as they have experienced it since the beginning of the reform era. Of course, they cannot help but juxtapose contemporary life against the difficulties of life they faced in the years that followed the end of the Vietnam War in 1975.

Nearly every resident living in Saigon today has lived and continues to live through the consequences of revolutionary socialist critiques of capitalism, and the fact of the matter is that they generally did not like the ensuing results. The Marxist-Leninist experiment in Vietnam produced a great deal of pain, and it is therefore necessary to develop a nuanced perspective for thinking about contemporary urban development in Vietnam that makes space for multiple perspectives, and situates it in relation to the country's recent past. An honest critique of the inequities brought about by the recent emphasis on the market economy is urgently needed, and this book presents such critiques from beginning to end. But such a critique must also take Vietnamese enthusiasm for ostensibly capitalist projects seriously. Projects that we might otherwise be inclined to dismiss as artificial spectacles or neoliberal illusions are in fact quite popular in the country. Instead of dismissing them, scholars need to understand them.

From the perspective of my friends in Vietnam, both those living in Phú Mỹ Hưng and, quite surprisingly, those who have been evicted from Thủ Thiêm, the return of the "market economy" has not only produced rubble and destruction; it has also inspired no small number of dreams and aspirations, as well as future-orientations that fill people with enthusiasm. These grandiose projects often give people a sense of pride that Vietnam has finally emerged from the morass of destruction that resulted from colonialism, extended warfare, postwar reconstruction, and socialist collectivism. People across the country regularly denounce the cronyism that comes with market-oriented socialism, and it is also clear that the rise of spectacular infrastructure leaves much destruction in its wake. But for many Vietnamese, such spectacle also serves as a sign that the country is finally rebuilding itself from the rubble of warfare. For this reason, in this book I insist on looking at luxury and rubble in a single frame, taking both seriously, and showing how they simultaneously negate and infuse each other with meaning. In contemporary Vietnam, the rubble piles that grow in the wake of urban development evoke destruction, of course, and even nostalgia; but they also signal possibility and future-oriented action. More than simply heaps of meaningless detritus, rubble piles have a dualistic capacity to suggest both destruction and possibility. Rubble truly is a kind of "pure multiplicity." To capture this multiplicity, however, requires viewing it alongside the luxurious spectacles of modernity that both give birth to and emerge from the rubble. If, for some, rubble evokes a void, for others the luxury that produces rubble also signifies the forward march of a larger project designed to fill a preexisting void of its own.

In telling this story of luxury and rubble, I make two major arguments. The first is straightforward, perhaps even obvious: I argue that several seemingly countervailing urban processes are in fact intimately entangled with each other—the expansion of luxury housing cannot be separated from the proliferation of rubble, the rise of civility is founded upon rampant and inherently uncivil acts of dispossession, and renewed calls for collective consciousness emerge in tandem with trends toward privatization. By the end of the book, I hope that readers will agree that it is impossible to understand any one side of these different, seemingly opposed, processes without considering the other. This argument runs throughout, and in fact structures the organization of the book. The second argument is more complex, and will only unfold incrementally through the course of reading the book from cover to cover. As the book comes to a close, after telling the story of master-planned development from two very different perspectives, I will demonstrate that the increasingly contentious language of "rights" that is emerging in contemporary Vietnam is itself intimately entangled with the commodification of land. Because of this entanglement, I further argue, much of the rights discourse we see expressed in Vietnam today is tied up in a double bind: on the one hand, the newfound rights many people seem to be asserting in Vietnam embolden them to resist the processes of land accumulation that drive their dispossession; on the other hand, accumulation by dispossession is itself made possible by the advent of land use rights.[5] Land use rights have not only encouraged people to believe that they have something called rights worth fighting for, but they have also enabled a rapacious Vietnamese land market to emerge in ways that have threatened those rights at every turn.

Studies of accumulation by dispossession tend to focus on things like privatization and rapacious land markets and how they enable the disadvantaged to be stripped of their land. Such processes are clearly at play in the stories that will follow. Nevertheless, the idea of property has itself also been central to the formation of new ways of articulating the very notion of "rights" that is currently being mobilized by the disadvantaged in order to contest the terms of such dispossession. Despite the destructive aspects of profit-oriented development imperatives, the rubble of dispossession has become a space in which new forms of political subjectivity are born. At the same time, the fact that emergent notions of rights are born out of such destructive processes should also give pause: political agitation for the right to the city, often heralded as the antidote to dispossession, is itself largely dependent on notions of proprietary rights that are themselves intimately entangled with logics of exclusion. The fact that land use rights, and the rights that are imagined to be born with them, can be both inclusive and exclusionary at once, and that they can enable dispossession as well as offer tools to resist it, becomes immediately apparent when juxtaposing Phú Mỹ Hưng against Thủ Thiêm.

### Phú Mỹ Hưng and Thủ Thiêm

Phú Mỹ Hưng (pronounced, rather roughly, Foo Mee Hoong) is an award-winning urban megaproject, known throughout Vietnam as one of the most desirable housing and commercial developments in the country (fig. 0.3). Located in District Seven, on land that was part of rural Nhà Bè district until district lines were redrawn in 1997, Phú Mỹ Hưng is one section of a larger 3,300-hectare master-planned mixed-used residential and commercial development plan called Saigon South. It was developed by and continues to be run by the Phú Mỹ Hưng Corporation, a Taiwanese and Vietnamese joint venture that was formally established in May 1993, the same year that Vietnam's revised 1992 Land Law went into effect, thus allowing for the gradual introduction of "land use rights," which have since then laid the foundation for new forms of land transfer and ultimately led to a wildly profitable real estate market. Built according to a master plan designed by the international planning firm Skidmore Owings Merrill, Phú Mỹ Hưng is a classic example of what Vietnamese urban planners call "new urban zones" (khu đô thị mới), a term sometimes translated as "new urban areas,"[6] and an urban form similar to urban development styles often called "urban integrated megaprojects" or "new towns" in other Asian cities.[7] Like similar large-scale master-planned urban developments in other countries, Vietnamese new urban zones not only bring together a range of mixed-use housing and retail, but also a host of innovative political and economic arrangements, including novel yet controversial alliances between city or national governments and profit-seeking land developers.[8] The projects are often accompanied by no small amount of hype and hubris. Phú

FIGURE 0.3. Phú Mỹ Hưng, District 7, Ho Chi Minh City. Looking east across Crescent Lake, toward the Crescent District. Author's photo, May 2012.

Mỹ Hưng is no exception: its Sino-Vietnamese name itself means Wealthy (Phú), Beautiful (Mỹ), and Prosperous (Hưng).

Phú Mỹ Hưng's advertisers and its residents, however, insist that the development, with its landscaped grid of villas (some gated, others not), row houses, duplexes, and modern high-rise apartments, is more than a space of luxury living and commerce. Rather, it is portrayed as part transformative urban experiment and part moral project. It aims to rethink urban governance, build a new "urban civilization" and "urban civility" *(văn minh đô thị),* and foster nothing less than a new form of consciousness *(ý thức).* While only a select minority of city residents can afford to live there, Vietnamese people from all walks of life and from around the city come to shop or window-shop at its extensive retail offerings, which include mixed-use shop-houses, a wide array of cafes and restaurants, as well as formal business and commercial districts, including the Crescent Mall, which opened in 2012 as Saigon's largest and most luxurious shopping mall. There is a hospital built to "international standards" and a selection of international schools, sports facilities, parks, and popular pedestrian promenades.

On the other side of the Phú Mỹ Bridge, in District Two, Ho Chi Minh City officials have been planning to build a new master-planned development at a bend in the Saigon River known as Thủ Thiêm (pronounced, roughly, as Too Tee-um).

FIGURE 0.4. Thủ Thiêm, District 2, Ho Chi Minh City. Demolition in progress; looking west from the rubble fields. The 68-story building in the background, known as the Bitexco Tower, is located across the Saigon River in Ho Chi Minh City's District 1. Author's photo, November 2010.

Since the late 2000s this area has been the center of massive site clearance and evictions, where city officials ultimately aim to construct a new central business and financial district for the city (fig. 0.4). Located immediately across the Saigon River from the high-rises, historic edifices, and high-end shopping areas of District One, the project aims to expand the city center across the river using urban design principles that are modeled in many ways on Phú Mỹ Hưng as well as other megaprojects across Asia, most notably Shanghai's Pudong.[9] The Thủ Thiêm New Urban Zone (Khu đô thị mới Thủ Thiêm), as the project is formally called, is part of a wholesale attempt to reconceive the city as a cosmopolitan regional hub for Asian business. Touted by both the national and city government as the most important urban development of twenty-first-century Vietnam, the Thủ Thiêm project also became known throughout the country as a site of displacement and struggle, where over 14,600 households were evicted from their land in order to clear space to build the project. Between 2002 and 2014, thousands of houses there had been reduced to rubble, and many of the residents were enraged by the poor compensation they had received. The ambitious project was continuously mired in controversy and saddled with debt. Throughout the eviction process, cries of injustice and allegations of corruption ran wild. As late as June 2016, groups of residents were still denouncing their eviction.[10] And yet, as I will also show in this book, dreams of the future of Thủ Thiêm also abounded—enthusiastic, noncynical dreams of a city yet to come.[11]

*Crossing the Bridge: Two Stories Told as One*

While the stories of Phú Mỹ Hưng and Thủ Thiêm are typically told separately, this book purposefully brings them together into a single narrative. Doing so allows me to look both microscopically at the stories of real people living in both places and macroscopically at more generalizable social processes associated with building new urban zones and what this reveals about contemporary urban development in Ho Chi Minh City specifically, in Vietnam more generally, and beyond that in cities in Asia and elsewhere in the world. As I will show, Vietnamese new urban zones unabashedly claim to be dedicated to building a modern "civilized" urban order. At the same time, the processes through which these projects are constructed rely on extraordinarily dramatic processes of demolition and extensive acts of dispossession. Telling the story of these two developments together highlights the many positive and negative facets of master-planned development, explicating in one place the aspirations and the dreams these two projects embody while also attending to the politics and social struggles that course through them both. Although the social struggles in these two places take different forms and affect their residents in dramatically different ways, the book also demonstrates that their stories are actually connected, because residents in both places are encountering and engaging with evolving conceptions of private property and new imaginations of collective belonging in a late-socialist context. In addition to framing their economic livelihoods, emergent notions of property and land value color emergent conceptions of civic responsibility and justice in contemporary Vietnam.

Exploring these issues is especially useful in contemporary Ho Chi Minh City, where property and land laws are being reformed alongside rapid urban development and real estate speculation, even as the social implications associated with property rights are still being worked out. On the one hand, comparing these two cases of urban development helps clarify the very real and tangible reasons why so many Vietnamese have come to associate the expansion of property rights with their aspirations for building a better world. On the other hand, juxtaposing them against each other highlights the role those very same property rights have played in projects of eviction and dispossession. As will become clear, emergent property rights have enabled the formation of new forms of urban development, as well as new modes of behavior, civic collectivity, and political agency. But those very same rights are tied to new property relations that are themselves intimately entangled with economic forces that drive urban dispossession. Ultimately, the power to evict is founded on the right to own. At the same time, however, for residents staring down an advancing bulldozer, a belief in the right to own can embolden their will to resist eviction. As the ethnography in this book will show, the logic of property informs both the logic of eviction and the logic of resistance. In fact, as I will argue more forcefully in the conclusion, the very notion of rights in contemporary Vietnam is framed largely in terms that conflate citizen rights with land use rights and property value.

To show the connections between luxury and rubble as well as between property and dispossession, this book is structured conceptually around the way I conducted my fieldwork, making repeated journeys between Thủ Thiêm and Phú Mỹ Hưng, crossing the Phú Mỹ suspension bridge both literally and metaphorically. The book occasionally pauses, as I sometimes would, at the top of the bridge in order to keep both places in view and make both explicit and theoretical connections between them. But more often the book offers a close-up view, written from the vantage point of a person walking or riding a motorbike through the streets of these two very different city districts, as I did together with several of my closest Vietnamese colleagues, day in and day out throughout our fieldwork.[12] The fieldwork involved constantly moving between the two zones, resulting in a sometimes dizzying but always thought-provoking experience of bridging two very different social worlds. During these trips, half of my time was spent with my research colleagues traversing the rubble fields of Thủ Thiêm and visiting with evicted and displaced residents, sitting together with them on low-slung plastic chairs in makeshift cafes built within vacated lots on top of crushed homes, drinking coffee, rice wine, and often too much beer while gathering stories of eviction and loss. The other half involved drinking espressos, green tea, imported wine, and often too much expensive whisky in the private villas and upscale apartments of Phú Mỹ Hưng residents while listening to the ongoing debates about Vietnamese politics that daily rage among them.

In addition to our own extended full-time participant observation, living and sleeping in Phú Mỹ Hưng and every day visiting Thủ Thiêm, the book draws upon ethnographic interviews with 335 informants from across the social and class spectrum, which enabled us to document the competing experiences and conceptions different Vietnamese actors have in relation to these two important new urban zones.[13] Most of the words I quote from people in the body of this book come from transcribed interviews and extensive fieldnotes collected during more than nine months of ethnographic research carried out between 2010 and 2014, distributed over five visits to the city: two months at the end of 2010, five months in 2011, two months in 2012, a week in 2013, and ten days in 2014. All of the names quoted in the text are pseudonyms, with the exception of political figures.

### *Demolition, Property Rights, and New Urban Zones*

This constant movement back and forth between Phú Mỹ Hưng and Thủ Thiêm clearly revealed how much destruction and construction are linked together by the formal, official visions of urban development. The Phú Mỹ suspension bridge binds Thủ Thiêm and Phú Mỹ Hưng together as part of a larger plan to shift the city's center of gravity, steering its course of urban development in a new direction. Suspension bridges do not appear by accident, and the bridge is the center of a development agenda that city planners have framed, like so many of their planning concepts, as a motto: they aim to build the city "in the direction of the sea" *(theo hướng ra biển)*.[14] This plan has very material consequences and is changing the organization of space in the city, all while generating profits for some parties and demanding great sacrifices from others. For the current Ho Chi Minh City master plan to be realized, city planners make no secret that Thủ Thiêm had to be "razed to a blank slate" *(giải tỏa trắng)* and all the people moved. The Ho Chi Minh City government commonly insists it is devoted to building a new "urban civilization" *(văn minh đô thị),* and it is clear that a future filled with new urban zones linked by impressive bridges is part of that vision. Yet even if city planners downplay the sacrifices that must be made in order to build the new cities they promote, the signs of demolition evident everywhere in the urban landscape of Ho Chi Minh City cannot be hidden. It is a city where rubble piles, debris, and the never-ending dust of shattered concrete mingle with the clean glistening lines of freshly laid bitumen roads and the carefully manicured landscaping of new housing developments.

Despite taking a critical perspective, this book is not intended as an attack on urban development or on Vietnamese urban planners; rather, it is a modest attempt to show the multiple perspectives city residents have on these projects, and to show the varied effects these developments have on their lives. Ho Chi Minh City is a Vietnamese city, and it is not my responsibility to tell Vietnamese how to build their cities. In my opinion, the hubris-filled history of foreign know-it-alls telling people in the developing world how to live has been neither pretty nor productive. Instead, by focusing on how residents talk about and explain their experiences living within or being forced to leave their homes in these two projects, their desires to build a "modern" and "civilized" city, and their agitation for property rights, I hope to open a conversation about the complexities and ambivalent relationships Ho Chi Minh City residents have with the changes taking place in the city. City residents simultaneously marvel at and curse urban development, and in the process they often share the planners' desire to bring order to chaos by building utopian projects, even as they often disagree with how the projects are implemented and even as they fight for greater compensation when they are forced to give up land for development projects.

In my view, based on many years of conversations with residents from all walks of life in the city, one of the main reasons why the city leadership is able to displace so many people from Thủ Thiêm without completely losing its legitimacy is that so many people actually agree with the city's ultimate desire to build something modeled on the successes of Phú Mỹ Hưng. The large volume of ethnographic evidence I have collected shows that the difference between the residents of Phú Mỹ Hưng and Thủ Thiêm, and between them and city planners, was not in large part about the kind of city they hoped to see, but about their different positions within society and how they were treated in the process of building that city. For many Phú Mỹ Hưng residents, their frustrations manifested as debates over adequate urban services, cleanliness, noise, resistance to tax burdens they deemed unjust, and a general defense of "urban civility" and disciplined comportment which they felt was necessary for building an orderly and less chaotic city. For Thủ Thiêm residents, the causes of their anger were much more dramatic: they were exasperated because they were being forced from their homes and the compensation they were receiving was rarely enough to find new ones. But the Thủ Thiêm residents were not opposed to development in principle. They just did not want such development to come at the expense of losing everything they had worked so hard in their lives to achieve.

The complex, often ambivalent, and sometimes contradictory perspectives residents in both sites shared with me revealed that urban inequalities are less often the result of overt ill will and greed than the unexpected consequence of aspirational desires for social improvement—good intentions with bad results. For example, my conversations with Phú Mỹ Hưng residents, which I describe in great detail in the first half of the book, revealed surprising complexities about the connections they made between privatization and emerging ideas of collective social responsibility. While they were clearly interested in protecting their own private property and defending their contractual rights to homes they had purchased, and while many of their lifestyle practices depended on emergent forms of privatization, they consistently described themselves as committed to developing what they called a new urban "consciousness" (ý thức) and cultivating an awareness of others. They explicitly linked this idea of consciousness to a renewed commitment to civic life and an ethic of duty to the social collective. For Phú Mỹ Hưng residents, the private was not the opposite of the collective. Rather, they felt that a heightened sense of private rights also fostered a heightened sense of obligation to others, which would form the foundation of a renewed ethic of civic engagement and social consciousness. Another surprising discovery, which I describe in the second half of the book, was the way residents being evicted from their homes in Thủ Thiêm often spoke about their own plight in much more subtle ways than I ever expected: while they were extraordinarily angry about what they considered to be insufficient levels of monetary compensation for their land, they were not opposed to the underlying plan of building a new urban zone. They regularly said that they saw the ideas behind the new urban zone as potentially contributing to the improvement of the city.[15] Their appreciation for the ideas behind the project, however, did not mean they were willing to be cheated. They often stated that they were willing to make sacrifices *(hy sinh)* for urban development, but they were not willing to make such sacrifices in order to line the pockets of self-interested real estate developers or government and city officials who had lost their trust.

These two examples flipped my own assumptions on their head. On the one hand, the victims of evictions, despite their resistance to eviction, were not opposed to the ideas of urban development that drove the evictions. On the other hand, the most privatized elites of Ho Chi Minh City, despite their great love for private property, devoted considerable mental energy to building a renewed sense of collective engagement. Simplistic oppositions—about planners versus people, rich versus poor, or private and public—only get us so far, which is to say, not very far beyond preexisting stereotypes. Despite their obvious differences in income and opportunity, it was clear to me that people in both Phú Mỹ Hưng and Thủ Thiêm, by and large, wanted to improve the city where they lived and saw "modern" master-planned urban developments as a promising way to achieve their goals. Furthermore, the wide variety of actors in this study also vigorously shared a will to defend and fight for an emergent yet limited set of "rights," specifically articulated as the right to private property (in the form of land use rights and the ownership of housing) and the right to "justice" and the rule of law. Their shared belief in the importance of land use rights, however, played out differently for the two different parties in this story, showing how the rights so many Vietnamese are increasingly agitating for are themselves founded on deep forms of exclusion.

Just as building a new urban zone requires demolition, and clearing land requires evicting people, a great number of the seemingly positive processes held sacrosanct by advocates of justice turn out to be based on their negative antithesis. "Rights" for some people are often built on foundational violence. "Opening up" the city entails systematic forms of enclosure and eviction. The development of certain forms of public space depends on exclusivity and privatization. Emergent free-market capitalism thrives off of, and in many ways entrenches, lingering state authoritarianism (masquerading as socialism or communism). Certain forms of inclusion themselves engender and depend on exclusions. The rule of law, which in Vietnam was increasingly emphasized in the 1990s, has in many ways become blurred into rule *by* law, which has long been a central part of Vietnamese conceptions of "socialist law."[16] And the expansion of civil society and civility commonly depends on extraordinarily uncivil behavior toward marginalized populations. These contradictions all come alive when we consider the double-edged aspects of property rights in the context of a densely populated urban landscape inhabited by people seeking to modernize and develop. If, as they say, it is often necessary to fight for one's rights, it is also true that new rights often give people new things to fight about.

In Vietnam today, the will to improve city spaces, expand property rights, and make cities more open to modern master-planned development is inextricably tied to the inequities of capital-intensive urban development and cannot be disentangled from large-scale eviction.[17] This is not always the product of individualized greed and self-interest (although it often is), but can even result from good intentions, not least the will to deliver property rights to people in a context where those rights were once denied. Much of this results from the fact that all property is founded on what Derek Hall, Philip Hirsch, and Tania Murray Li perceptively call "powers of exclusion."[18] This fact, in turn, produces a very real and politically volatile set of contradictory movements, which in the case of Ho Chi Minh City can be summarized as follows: First, the reemergence of legal and popular conceptions of property rights since the early 1990s have transformed land into a valuable commodity. Second, the potential value embedded in this land could only be realized by making it available for sale. Capturing this value through sale thus required "liberating it" through a process of exclusion and enclosure, which itself entailed considerable efforts and enormous investments of capital through which people were evicted in order to reclaim and appropriate land. Third, and this is what makes this whole process such a conundrum, the very same emerging notions of property rights that have spurred land appropriation have also developed into the only viable idiom of justice through which residents can resist their eviction. The very same commodification of land that incentivizes the quest to dispossess people through eviction provides, paradoxically, the language through which evicted people can articulate their rights. In other words, people are being evicted as a consequence of a market in land made possible by new forms of property rights, all at the same time that their resistance to eviction is framed in terms of those very same rights. None of this eviction business would have happened without property rights; but without such rights, nothing could be done to resist it.

This situation ultimately reveals an urban world in which individual agents are struggling to make do in a system in which, for better or worse, their own struggle to defend their rights is founded on the denial of similar rights to others. These acts of denial and exclusion most commonly emerge when there isn't enough land to go around. When there are more claims to parcels of land than there are parcels to distribute, not everyone gets an equal number of parcels. As Annette Kim has noted, in a crowded city like Saigon the noble ideal of fighting for "the right to the city" is often compromised by the spatial limits of urban life—there are sometimes simply so many people living in so little space that one person's claim to the city necessarily comes at the expense of another's.[19] In this system, there are certainly a number of self-interested and unscrupulous actors, especially those involved in the Ho Chi Minh City real estate business. And while profit seeking, land speculation, illegal contract procurement, government corruption, and outright land-grabbing have profoundly negative effects on equitable urban development in the city, I argue that a myopic focus only on illegal and intentionally exploitative activities ignores the elephant in the room, which is the powerful conundrum introduced by property rights in a crowded urban system: where there isn't enough land to go around, one person's right to property may well leave another person feeling wronged. Land use rights and other forms of land title are intimately entangled with the legal regimes that legitimize eviction, and every assertion of one's right to private property is itself an act of exclusion. But such assertions of rights in a limited system are also bound to produce counterassertions. This is because the best way to resist the forces of exclusion often entails staking a claim to property rights. In this way, property rights are simultaneously a form of hegemony and of counterhegemony, an expression of power and resistance both.

## THE VIEW FROM THE BRIDGE, THE VIEW FROM BELOW

Modern infrastructure, like private property, can both liberate and oppress. The Phú Mỹ Bridge is a case in point. On the one hand, it is a charismatic megastructure, conveying inspirational messages about a futuristic city on the horizon and proclaiming the Vietnamese government's role in stimulating urban development. The bridge was opened on September 2, 2009, the anniversary of Ho Chi Minh's death and, not coincidentally, Vietnam's National Day. In the "city that bears the name of the Uncle," as Ho Chi Minh City is often called in patriotic contexts, the bridge communicates messages of state legitimacy through signs and symbols of national progress.[20] During construction and at the opening ceremony for the bridge, city and national newspapers celebrated the structure as one of the proudest monuments to the city's recent urban development. As the bridge rose, the state ceremonies and news media implied, the city and the entire Vietnamese nation would proudly rise along with it.

Regardless of what they think of the party or the government, it is clear that city residents do indeed admire the bridge. When late afternoon comes, young people gather along the railing at its apex, their motorbikes parked in a row along the shoulder.[21] The view here is spectacular; the winds are cool. It is possible to sit side by side on the back of a motorbike, next to a friend or embracing a lover, taking in the city skyline. The bends of the Saigon River snake into the distance, and the changing light reflects on the water. A festive atmosphere prevails—the discarded shells of pumpkin seeds and cast-off snack wrappers dance in the wind as they flutter 148 feet down to the river below. In a city defined in many ways by intensity and density, the bridge offers a place to feel calm and unblocked, to enjoy a sense of release. Soaring above the dense city, crossing the open river, the bridge offers a view few residents can see anywhere else in the city. From atop the bridge, city residents can experience the planner's vision of the city—a clean, orderly vision far away from the chaos of the streets below. It is impressive, and it is pleasant.

On the other hand, looking down at the city from this perch high in the sky clearly shows the very different ways in which residents of places like Phú Mỹ Hưng and Thủ Thiêm experience the rise of urban modernity. While the bridge itself binds them together as part of a larger development scheme, the effects of that scheme are very differently felt. In one place, 14,600 people are being forced to relinquish their homes to make this form of development possible; in the other place, a minority of the city's most well-to-do are able to enjoy the benefits of modern infrastructure and orderly living. The view of the bridge emphasizes spectacular architecture and grand ambitions that most city residents find seductive; but the monumental view from above that the bridge provides also obscures the nitty-gritty experiences of people living on the ground, who sacrificed so much in the process of making these developments possible. The celebratory view of the city gained from the bridge, the view from above, as Michel de Certeau famously called such perspectives, is little more than a planner's view, a "rhetoric of excess."[22]

This book brings the view from the bridge into intimate conversation with a fine-grained, bottom-up ethnographic perspective that attends to the ways the city appears from the perspective of people living in the city. But it is important to recognize that the view from the ground does not in and of itself escape ideology, and it too can obscure important connections at the very moment that it offers new perspectives. A close-up view in one location can obscure the view of the other, and despite an anthropological commitment to getting down on the ground and walking the city, ignoring the big picture can be equally blinding. For example, despite the obvious connection the two zones have in terms of the city plan, residents in Phú Mỹ Hưng and Thủ Thiêm rarely see themselves as connected to each other in any significant way. Even when I discussed my research project with them, Phú Mỹ Hưng residents never connected their own experience with the plight of people in Thủ Thiêm and rarely considered the kinds of sacrifices, inequalities, or exclusions that make new urban zones like Phú Mỹ Hưng possible. Nevertheless, they consistently described themselves as part of an emergent social and intellectual vanguard dedicated to a sense of civic responsibility and mutualistic consciousness. Phú Mỹ Hưng residents did not see themselves as self-interested elites, but largely described themselves as members of a self-disciplining and forward-thinking community dedicated to social justice, community, civic consciousness, and civilized interactions with others. They did not primarily see the development of new urban zones as a case of increasing class differentiation (despite the clear fact that it is), but instead saw it more as an opportunity to develop a community of people dedicated to improving life in the city. In other words, what residents of Phú Mỹ Hưng often ignore is the degree to which their emerging senses of "civility," "consciousness," and "rights" are founded on the deep sacrifices of their fellow citizens, both across town in Thủ Thiêm and everywhere else in the city where land developers are collaborating with city authorities to displace people from their land.

Thus, while on one level Phú Mỹ Hưng may look like a space of pure neoliberal self-interested extraction and capital accumulation, most of its residents see it as a site of extraordinary community formation, a space of a developing "consciousness" of what they imagined to be the collective interests of urban citizens. Acts of urban exclusion simultaneously enable class consolidation while also generating a seemingly sincere, but arguably rather superficial, commitment to inclusion. Anthropologist Li Zhang, describing residents of an upscale housing "paradise" in Kunming, has fruitfully called this kind of process a "double movement" though which increased privatization engenders new forms of civic activism.[23] Notions of the individual and the group are not so much opposites as they are concepts that emerge in tandem with each other. It is thus not a contradiction when new forms of community are framed in terms of the language of private property. This book attends to this double movement throughout, taking the perspectives of people living within specific social settings seriously while also making connections to larger processes that they may or may not consciously refer to on their own.

Similarly, but from a different vantage point, what most residents of Thủ Thiêm don't realize is the degree to which their conception of "rights" to the property from which they are being displaced has been itself "developed" over time by the very same forces of development—and more specifically by the land developers and private property interests—that are causing their displacement. When they express their resistance to eviction by demanding more compensation based on the market value of land, Thủ Thiêm residents inadvertently reproduce a language that conflates "rights" with property value. Ironically, their language of resistance both borrows from and reinforces the market logic that drives their eviction. Property rights are both driving them out and giving them the language to fight for a right to be included in the city.

### Rights, Exclusions, and the Structure of the Book

Property rights—and, one might argue, rights in general—are always founded on forms of exclusion. In the case of contemporary Ho Chi Minh City, many of the exclusions that would seem at first glance to be easily reduced to acts of illegitimate force—decried as land grabs—are in fact founded on discourses of rights, justice, responsible urban citizenship, civility, and other concepts that can't always be dismissed as cynical ploys. In many cases, furthermore, many of the developers involved are not driven only by profit motives, but clearly have very real desires to improve the infrastructure and quality of life in the city: as I show in chapter 1 and then again in chapter 4, urban developers as well as many city residents sincerely believe that these projects are transforming "wasteland" (đất hoang) into something valuable. These improvements, and the alchemy of turning "wasteland" into the "golden land" (đất vàng) of valuable real estate, however, depend on exclusion, which in a dense city essentially translates into eviction.

Subsequent chapters will show that the emergence of a "civilized consciousness" based on private property relations in places like Phú Mỹ Hưng is founded, in ways few residents openly consider, on the deeply uncivilized treatment of less fortunate residents elsewhere in the city. It will become quite clear that building urban civility for some depends literally on crushing the livelihood of others, smashing their homes to rubble, and evicting them to margins of the city where they are left to bear all the risks of rebuilding their lives in inhospitable new surroundings. The Vietnamese term for eviction, giải tỏa, is itself a euphemism that means to clear, to release, to unblock. In a dense urban setting like Ho Chi Minh City, not unlike Baron Haussmann's nineteenth-century Paris, every act of opening up urban space is of course founded on forms of exclusion. However, these chapters will also show how the language of civility is connected to emerging conceptions of rights, justice, and citizenship and thus poses a very real critique of the social and political status quo. Civility is not just an idiom of power, but it often speaks in the language of resistance as well. The same can be said about rights, and the book shows how the emergent language of rights being used by Thủ Thiêm residents to resist their eviction or improve their compensation is itself deeply connected to the forces that have brought them to the point of eviction in the first place.

The first part of the book, "Luxury," shows how concepts of property, civility, and discourses of urban improvement intermingle in Phú Mỹ Hưng, which might be called an "actually existing new urban zone." Chapter 1, "Civilizing the Wastelands," offers a conceptual history of urban development in Phú Mỹ Hưng, focusing specifically on how the development of the new urban zone is commonly described as part of a larger effort to develop "wastelands" and bring "civilized" urban life to Vietnamese cities. This chapter also situates the history of these developments in a longer historical tradition of "clearing land" in order to civilize it, which has precedents in precolonial Vietnamese concepts of "clearing the wasteland" and postcolonial notions of building socialism and developing urban civility (văn minh đô thị). To improve the land, it turns out, requires clearing it first, demarcating who has a right to it, and then alienating it in the form of valuable property.

Chapter 2, "Civilization City," highlights the ways in which project developers as well as current residents describe the Phú Mỹ Hưng development as part of a grand experiment in building "urban civilization." People's explanations of what "civility" means to them show how this new conception of urban space blurs into a thinly veiled commentary on social and political organization in Vietnam. For many residents, Phú Mỹ Hưng promises not only profit and a sound investment, but also a reordering of social relations and construction of what residents see as more transparent urban governance. Urban civility offers a veiled conception of urban citizenship, but it is a form of citizenship founded on exclusion.

Chapter 3, "Exercising Consciousness," continues this discussion by showing how a development that to an outside observer appears to be nothing more than a space of luxury living for well-heeled elites becomes, in the eyes of Phú Mỹ Hưng residents, nothing less than a political project, a place to redefine governance and articulate a developing sense of collective rights and responsibilities. I describe an emergent notion of "consciousness" that is growing within this extremely privatized urban development. The chapter explains how well-to-do Vietnamese people living in Phú Mỹ Hưng maintain a deeply rooted belief in modernist logics of planning, efficiency, order, and "urban civility," as well as how these residents simultaneously fight for new kinds of rights and reinforce a world of class exclusion. All three of these chapters show that rights and exclusion emerge from the same place.

The second part of the book, "Rubble," describes the contested development of the Thủ Thiêm New Urban Zone, focusing both on the way it embodies certain aspirations and on the way it demands great sacrifices from residents. Chapter 4, "Thủ Thiêm Futures Past," explores the history of the Thủ Thiêm development and some of the many idealistic visions developers have had for building on that same site over the course of the twentieth century. I show how these plans have contributed to a sense that the space there is empty and in need of development, and how this obscures the vibrant lifestyles of people living in the area. Historical documents also show that visions of developing Thủ Thiêm existed long before the current project began, during the French colonial period and during the period of the United States' intervention in Vietnam. Nevertheless, despite the recurring assertions in all of these periods that Thủ Thiêm was an unoccupied "wasteland," I show that Thủ Thiêm has had a long history of habitation, albeit with a form of settlement and village morphology quite different from that seen elsewhere in Saigon.

Chapter 5, "Building a Civilized, Modern, and Sentimental City," describes how people being evicted from Thủ Thiêm were angry about being displaced but also enthusiastic about some of the plan's core concepts. Residents forced from their homes loudly complained that they were unfairly undercompensated for their lands. While they were dissatisfied with the terms of their monetary compensation, they were often very supportive of the underlying development goals of the project. To explain this, I take the promises of the plan seriously and show how the plan's ideals became tied both to a nationalist vision of Vietnam's advance into modernity and to forces that required transforming land into value by clearing it. Readings of urban plans, historical and newspaper source materials, as well as interviews with project developers and other actors involved in the project, show the sincere vision planners had for the development of this project and the important role they believed and still believe it will play in improving life in the city. At the same time, descriptions of the demolition in the district also show the ways that building this vision of an urban civilization rested on profound acts of "infrastructural violence."[24]

Chapter 6, "From the Rubble," describes contestations over land and compensation from the perspective of Thủ Thiêm's evicted residents. Here we see how residents undergoing eviction were drawn into a language of "rights" and "rule of law" and how this became entangled with a focus on monetary compensation, which simultaneously empowered them and reinforced the notion that land should be understood as a commodity best understood in terms of its market value. I show how, in the process of contesting their displacement, they became drawn further and further into a language of "rights" that was articulated in very specific, quantifiable terms as property value, calculated in terms of square meters of land. Through this process, residents both found an empowering voice to express their anger and inadvertently reinforced the assumptions and terms of the debate in ways that supported the agenda of those seeking to evict them. In the final instance, despite fighting for "rights," they still ended up displaced to distant margins of the city.

In moving between these two ethnographic sites, I show that very different actors in both Phú Mỹ Hưng and Thủ Thiêm were increasingly engaged in a quest for something called "rights." In the conclusion, I bring these two cases together again to show how this quest for rights played out differently. In some ways, this emerging "rights consciousness" inspired new forms of agency and collective action. But the emphasis on rights did not prevent the dispossession of Thủ Thiêm residents from house and home. I suggest that the new conception of rights emerging on the edges of Vietnamese cities cannot be disentangled from the very inequalities that are fueling dispossession. Rights, in this case, are not so much a product of citizenship—equally distributed to all members of the nation—but are increasingly linked to the value of one's land. As a result, in substantive terms, the more land one has, the more rights one enjoys. Accordingly, fights over land use rights have become conflated with fighting for rights more broadly construed.

New urban zones are not just modern places to live and work, but are considered to be political experiments in how to live in and organize society. From the perspective of residents, these zones become a means to rethink the role the state plays in urban governance, and from the perspective of the state, the zones, through their emphasis on civilized lifestyles, become a means to govern. The contradictions and ambivalent experiences these experiments have produced, in turn, should inform the way we study master-planned mixed-use urban developments across the globe. Critically engaged scholars cannot stand back and study these zones from an armchair or by looking at plans alone, but must interact seriously with the people living in these zones, seeking to learn what the developments purport to offer their residents and what sacrifices they demand. To learn all of these things, of course, requires getting down into the city, where the movement of bodies through space itself enacts the urban experience, and where streets of the city carve a path through the history of the new Saigon.

## INTO THE CITY

Descending toward the city from the top of the Phú Mỹ Bridge, motorbike riders and automobile drivers must choose between two off-ramps, one leading to the right and one to the left. To the right—the off-ramp most often chosen by motorbikes—the road descends steeply and suddenly, quickly bringing vehicles to a sharp grinding halt in the belly of the working-class city, not far from the city's first export processing zone at Tân Thuận. Here in the dense web of alleyways and mixed-use commercial and residential streets, heavy traffic and motorbike fumes, industrial exhaust, and surface-level dust mingle with the smell of grilled meats and stir-fried delights, and busy combinations of informal and formal commerce blur the boundaries between industry, shop-house, restaurant, and street.

The ramp to the left is dramatically different: a long elevated flyover carries vehicles in a gently inclined, uncrowded lane for more than a mile above the dense city. From this vantage point, looking out the windows of an air-conditioned car, gliding over the working-class neighborhoods below, one has the sensation of being in a jet airplane as it smoothly descends into the heart of the city. This path, taken mostly by automobiles, eventually touches down in the center lanes of a manicured, tree-lined, ten-lane road known as Nguyễn Văn Linh Parkway, named after the eighth general secretary of the Communist Party of Vietnam, a man most famous for ushering in the country's Đổi Mới reform policies at the party's 6th National Congress, in 1986. The road bearing Secretary Linh's name leads straight into the heart of Phú Mỹ Hưng, itself the heart of a larger area called Saigon South. The Phú Mỹ Hưng property development, a Taiwanese-Vietnamese joint venture that capitalized on real estate reforms introduced in the 1990s, would have been inconceivable before the Đổi Mới reforms began shifting Vietnam's state ideology toward a hybrid policy of "socialism with a market-orientation."

Across town, another brand new multilane road bears the name of another postwar Vietnamese leader, former prime minister Võ Văn Kiệt, who was eulogized upon his death as a key "architect of Đổi Mới."[25] Part of a much longer road called the East-West Highway, the Võ Văn Kiệt Parkway curls through the heart of old Saigon, running along the banks of the Bến Nghé Canal—once known to the French as the Arroyo Chinois—and enters the mouth of a tunnel, opened in November 2011, under the Saigon River. The road and tunnel link District One with the razed neighborhoods of District Two, where the Thủ Thiêm New Urban Zone will someday rise. Like the Phú Mỹ Bridge, the Thủ Thiêm Tunnel is part of a large-scale physical transformation depicted in the city's master plan.

While the Võ Văn Kiệt Parkway leads directly to Thủ Thiêm, it is also linked to Phú Mỹ Hưng. Before and after becoming prime minister, a post he held from 1992 to 1997, Võ Văn Kiệt held unofficial think-tank sessions with reform-minded advisors. The "Friday Group" (Nhóm Thứ Sáu), as these weekly strategy sessions were called, helped create the political conditions necessary for engaging foreign investors and for developing the very concept of new urban zones.[26] It was Kiệt who signed the prime ministerial decree in 1994 that formally approved Phú Mỹ Hưng's master plan, and it was members of the Friday Group who first engaged the Taiwanese developers who were then looking for land, sending them out to then seemingly distant Nhà Bè and reserving Thủ Thiêm for their own future projects. The two parkways named after Võ Văn Kiệt and Nguyễn Văn Linh can thus be read as material artifacts of reform-era Vietnam, monuments to renovation inscribed on the face of the city. A source of great pride to city residents, these spectacular construction projects—bridges, major roads, and master-planned developments— evoke a history of market-oriented, yet state-led, economic development and hint at the future urban growth direction of the city. They also offer subtle clues about whom the future growth of the city will serve and at whose expense it will come. The rest of this book will follow these bridges and roads into these two new urban zones, as we speak with the residents there and learn about the new worlds these zones promise to build and the old ones they reduce to rubble.

PART I

# Luxury

# 1

## Civilizing the Wastelands

### *A Short History of Urban Development in Phú Mỹ Hưng*

*Trong đầm gì đẹp bằng sen,*
*Lá xanh, bông trắng, lại chen nhị vàng.*
*Nhị vàng, bông trắng lá xanh,*
*Gần bùn mà chẳng hôi tanh mùi bùn.*

*In swamps the lotus shines,*
*Green leaves, white flowers, fine stamens.*
*Blooms, leaves, and stamens gold,*
*Near mud without the moldy stink.*

—VIETNAMESE FOLK POEM (AUTHOR'S TRANSLATION)

### FROM A WASTELAND TO A NEW URBAN ZONE

One mid-February afternoon in 2011, four Vietnamese students dressed in white school uniforms with blue trim approached me to ask if I'd be willing to answer some questions for a school project. I had been standing on Nguyễn Đức Cảnh Street, in the heart of Ho Chi Minh City's Phú Mỹ Hưng New Urban Zone, immediately across the street from the Saigon South International School and its neighbor the Lawrence S. Ting School (where, I soon learned, the students were all enrolled in the same eighth-grade class). The lunar New Year celebrations had recently ended, the spring weather was still mild, and people were out and about, walking along the sidewalks and among the storefronts and restaurants that line the base of the Grandview apartment building, an upscale residential complex where I was living, together with my wife and two young daughters, in order to conduct an ethnographic study of everyday life in this new urban zone. With notepads drawn and pens pressed to paper, the enthusiastic group of students cornered me in front of a Korean bakery and quickly explained, in fluent English, that they were conducting a series of interviews for a class project about people's perceptions of Phú Mỹ Hưng.

It was a stroke of good luck. These bright young students were researching exactly the same topic I had flown across the world to study. After answering their questions, I gave them my business card and told them I would like to learn more about the results of their project. They smiled politely, thanked me for the interview, and then walked away, disappearing past the recently shuttered Espressamente café (which still advertised but no longer sold its famous Italian Illy coffee), past the Lion City restaurant (advertising its famous Singaporean frog porridge), and past Gà nướng Pháp—L'Etoile, a French-Vietnamese grilled-chicken restaurant (advertising famous sauces prepared by its chef, who had studied in France). Then they disappeared beyond the yellow awnings of Phở Hùng, a popular Vietnamese noodle shop where I had conducted some of my own initial interviews with local families. As I watched the students walk away, I chided myself for not asking them any questions of my own. Then they were gone.

Gone for the day, but not lost forever. The next week, one of the students, whose name I have changed, sent me the following email:

*From: Lucy [mailto:lucy1997@gmail.com]*
*Sent: Monday, February 21, 2011 6:36 PM*
*To: erik.harms@yale.edu*
*Subject: Mr. Erik!*

Dear Mr. Erik!

Hi, I'm Lucy—the 8th grader that you met last Thursday, you were my interviewee, remember? ^_^

I was so excited when I found out that you are the professor of anthropology in Yale university! (I searched on Google about your school).

We are still doing the project and the survey. Our plan is to do an E-book about the development of Phu My Hung—from a wasteland to an new urban city! We are writing articles about Phu My Hung with many small contents such as Education in Phu My Hung; An new urban city from a wasteland; Phu My Hung's future; The difficulties in developing Phu My Hung; why choose south saigon, Vietnam?;. . . . and also about the survey we did—what do residents think about Phu My Hung. We will put some pictures and videos in it, too. Do you have any other suggestions for our project?

I am trying to finish the article that I have the responsibility to write and would you mind giving me some advice when I have finished it? Thanks a lot!

I will also send you our project when it is done.

Nice to meet you and your family!

See you soon,

*Lucy*

This email caught my attention because it showed that I was not the only one interested in Phú Mỹ Hưng. Even a group of eighth-graders knew it was important. Furthermore, I had been googled! I had become an "observer observed."[1] With a kind of double vision, my anthropological gaze was being returned, my reflections were meeting the reflections of the very people I had hoped to learn about, and I was pleased to know that our interest in each other's perspectives proved mutual. But something else in Lucy's email captured my attention.

I was particularly struck by the phrasing Lucy used to refer to Phú Mỹ Hưng as a city rising "from a wasteland." This notion—which appeared twice in her short message—had already become familiar to me, because I had come to hear it over and over during my research, especially during my reading of Phú Mỹ Hưng's own internal company history, which juxtaposed pictures of inundated agricultural lands against colorful photos of the development's swimming pools, high-rise apartment buildings, roads, and modern infrastructure. That company history was titled *Rising from the Swamps* (*Vươn lên từ đầm lầy*, 2005) and clearly presented a "before and after" narrative of urban development.[2] It was certainly no surprise to read such a triumphalist story from a land developer, but seeing the phrase in Lucy's email showed just how pervasive this notion was among everyday Vietnamese. What I had until then dismissed as the scripted language of corporate brochures extended into daily life; the idea of building a city from the wasteland was clearly a "key symbol," reproduced without prompting by an eighth-grader in her email to me.[3] Where was this idea coming from, and why did it resonate with so many of the people I was meeting?

The students soon invited me, with the permission of their teacher, to their classroom at the Lawrence S. Ting School, where they gave a presentation about their research project and presented me with a DVD copy of the e-book they had created. The e-book and the presentation made one thing unmistakably clear: the students were deeply enthralled by Phú Mỹ Hưng—not simply interested in it but gushingly proud of it. They saw Phú Mỹ Hưng as a triumph of the human will. It offered them evidence for Vietnam's socio-economic emergence and gave them hope for the country's development potential. Their e-book linked Phú Mỹ Hưng's development to that of the city and the nation as a whole. It began like this:

As Vietnam steps into the stages of growth and renewal, as Vietnamese, we are more than delighted to introduce to the world a set of community changes in the location of our school in Phu My Hung, district 7, Ho Chi Minh City, as the example to prove the change of this community has brought Vietnam to glory, today.

We, [as 8th-grade students] in Lawrence S. Ting School, would like to present a story of dedication, contribution, and success. It covers the whole process of South Saigon, the Phu My Hung's urban development. It's the case that we believe is a typical and exceptional example for community change. Phu My Hung project included a group of excellent people who have changed this area, from a barren swamp land to a vital economic area.

[ . . . ]

Through the entire project, we recorded man's unbelievable ability in overcoming impossibility as well as foreseeing the fine future of Vietnam with this community change, in this specially-made e-book.[4]

When reproduced here, this text appears exaggerated, even hyperbolic, with its strong adjectives, and its mention of glory, "excellent people," and turning swamps into spaces of economic vitality. But in person, the students (and their teachers) conveyed these sentiments with deep earnestness. They sincerely saw the Phú Mỹ Hưng project as an example of successful urban development for the rest of Vietnam to follow.

The story of development the students told with such sincere praise was further tied together with the same story of urban civility rising from a wasteland that I had noticed in Lucy's email. In a section of their e-book entitled "Phu My Hung—A New Urban from a Swampland," the students juxtaposed the "modern" urban amenities of the present-day city against what they depicted as the "outdated" features of agrarian life, which they consigned to a glum past marked by poverty, deprivation, and political stagnation. Their text provides a relatively succinct description of Phú Mỹ Hưng, hints at its history, and also offers a sense of what impresses them most about the project:

Phu My Hung (PMH), a civilized, modern and international-standard city area, is located in the South of Ho Chi Minh city. It has a large parkway called Nguyen Van Linh, which goes across the PMH and was built in the need of a new traffic network. This parkway has ten lanes with six fast traffic lanes. If you go along this parkway, you will see lots of high buildings and apartments that form the Phu My Hung New City Center. There is also a fascinating bridge called Starlight Bridge. It is a very special bridge made up of sophisticated technologies that self-assist the bridge with solar energy to operate an array of LED lights. At night, the bridge shines with various-color. People come to enjoy the spectacular view with a beautiful illuminated waterfall. Another side of the bridge is the Crescent Mall. It will soon become the largest shopping and entertainment destination in Vietnam with an area of two hundred thousand square meters. PMH is so attractive, but does anyone know [ . . . ] where it started from? [ . . . ]

Let's go back to the period between 1989 and 2004. Phu My Hung was a piece of swamp land. It was a very poor area with a low income from outdated agricultural production. Trees could not grow because of the alum contaminated in the soil. Unlike other areas in the city, Phu My Hung and Nha Be (a nearby area) were not densely populated. As a matter of fact, South Saigon was incredibly empty. Vietnam government considered this place was hopeless. There was no investment from any companies, domestic and foreign as well. At the same time, in Taiwan, Mr. Lawrence S. Ting and the Central Trading & Development (CT&D Group) were finding a place to invest. They spent two years looking for the right place. They went to Russia, China, Cambodia, etc. Finally, they landed in Vietnam.

Mr. Ting thought that Taiwan has a similar background like Vietnam thirty years ago. He felt Vietnam was alike his beloved hometown. This made Mr. Ting questioned the government: "What does Vietnam want?" The answer was clear that Vietnamese wanted more jobs when there was nothing to do better than waiting for government supplies. Vietnam wanted to change.[5]

This passage and the origin story it tells, like much of the students' e-book, deserves the extended attention I have given it here because it hits all the major points that most people tend to emphasize when describing what they find most impressive about Phú Mỹ Hưng: it mentions the broad Nguyễn Văn Linh Parkway, the modern buildings, the Starlight Bridge, the Crescent Mall, the attractive landscaping (fig. 1.1). It also repeats the standard story of development I heard over and over again whenever people recounted the story of Phú Mỹ Hưng. The details of this history are largely accurate: the history of Phú Mỹ Hưng can indeed be traced back to 1989; and the late Lawrence Ting, the Taiwanese businessman and real estate developer after whom the students' school was named, is indeed credited by most sources as the founder of the project. In this way, the e-book offers a useful snapshot history of the Phú Mỹ Hưng development.

But serious attention must also be paid to the way the story embellishes history with aspirational claims; for there is more at stake in the telling than the simple description of a place and the recounting of its history. The story of Phú Mỹ Hưng is also told as a parable of hope that conveys the importance of believing in the future. "Phu My Hung has grown up from mud and swamp," the students write ten pages later. This, they add, is not just an observation, but actually "proves" something about the human will: "It proves that it's not impossible to change a hopeless land into an extremely-developed urban center. It proves to people that with faith, courage, unyielding mind, determination and enthusiasm, we can do anything. [ . . . ] This urban center will always remain as our great pride . . ."[6]

## PHÚ MỸ HƯNG'S HISTORY AND THE "STORY OF CLEARING THE WASTELAND"

The students at the Lawrence S. Ting School clearly worked very hard on their e-book, which showed great creativity and thoughtfulness. But they did not invent this narrative about Phú Mỹ Hưng entirely on their own. I repeatedly heard versions of this story during my research—retold during interviews by the adult residents who live in the New Urban Zone, and also by developers, planners, and architects. It appeared frequently in company documents and came up in formal interviews I had with people aware of the history of the development, including both knowledgeable residents and corporate officials associated with the Phú Mỹ Hưng Corporation. In one of my first formal interviews, one of the most active

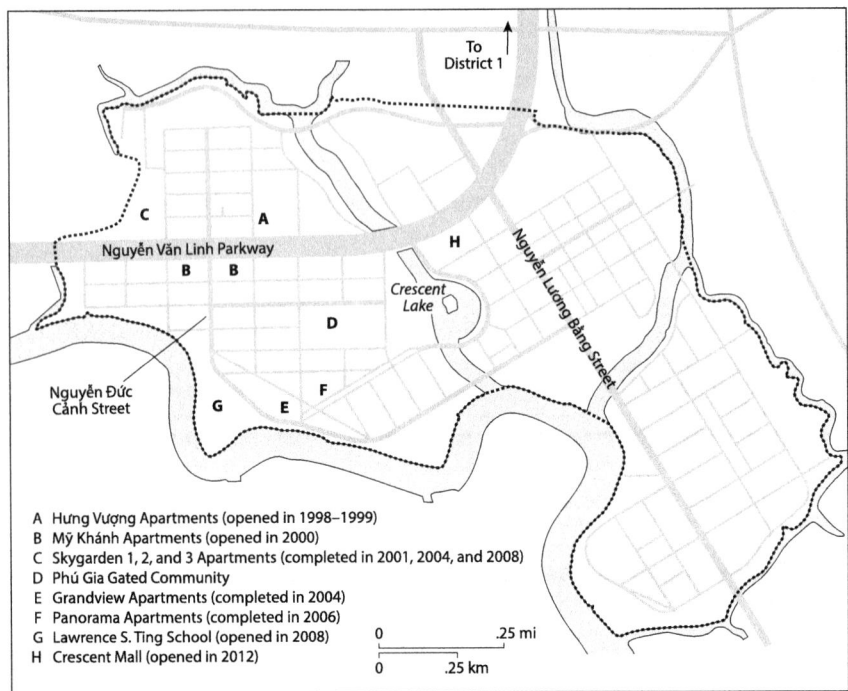

A  Hưng Vượng Apartments (opened in 1998–1999)
B  Mỹ Khánh Apartments (opened in 2000)
C  Skygarden 1, 2, and 3 Apartments (completed in 2001, 2004, and 2008)
D  Phú Gia Gated Community
E  Grandview Apartments (completed in 2004)
F  Panorama Apartments (completed in 2006)
G  Lawrence S. Ting School (opened in 2008)
H  Crescent Mall (opened in 2012)

FIGURE 1.1. Map of Phú Mỹ Hưng.

architects in the project explained, while reflecting on the early days of the project, "Basically, Saigon South was a wasteland." Then he showed me images taken of the district from a helicopter in 1993, which he juxtaposed against the built landscape as it appeared in 2011. The modern development stood in striking contrast to the rural landscape that had existed there less than two decades earlier. As mentioned above, the official company history of Phú Mỹ Hưng is called *Rising from the Swamps.*[7]

In sketch form, this is a valid story to tell. It might be seen as little more than an attempt to account for the undeniably rapid transformation of the built environment that has taken place in the district. But it also carried a message of hope. When telling me about Phú Mỹ Hưng's rapid urbanization, even residents with no stake in the company often adopted a tone of awe-stricken enthusiasm—their voices picked up with the expression of sheer astonishment and wonder. They conveyed honest fascination with the human capacity for change and development, and sincere respect for the accomplishments of the Phú Mỹ Hưng Corporation. No one ever forced anyone to tell the story in this way, and there is no reason to believe that people in any sense doubted what they were saying. Phú Mỹ Hưng is, after all, an impressive project, and it is not surprising that people would marvel at its many accomplishments. In 1997, even the American Institute of Architects was sufficiently impressed to give the Saigon South master plan its Honor Award for suburban design. Describing this award, *Architectural Record* insisted that "the Big Plan is making a comeback," adding that the project in Saigon could be seen as signaling a turn away from the "distrust of big ideas" that had by then become prevalent in contemporary urban design. The article then added, however, that "the fact that the three boldest planning efforts are outside the continental U.S. suggests that vision is more welcome abroad" than it was in the United States.[8] The enthusiasm I encountered for Phú Mỹ Hưng while conducting research there was palpable and nearly omnipresent. Virtually all the Vietnamese people I encountered in my research truly did appreciate the Big Plan, and their appreciation for Phú Mỹ Hưng was a clear example of that.

Despite such enthusiasm, the story of clearing the wasteland must also be recognized as at least partly a manufactured history, constructed and repeated over and over again by planners, developers, teachers, and others who control the way the history of the development is told by printing brochures, publishing books, organizing events, running schools, and much more. The student project here is itself a case in point: the late Lawrence S. Ting, the namesake of their school, is commonly celebrated as the founder of Phú Mỹ Hưng, and the corporation Mr. Ting helped found has been actively involved in concerted efforts to manage his image and preserve his legacy. The students' school project had been assigned by their teachers, and in the process of helping the students conduct their research, Lawrence Ting's own daughter had given a lecture to the students about the project's history and also gave them materials to aid their research. In other words, the sources for all the information about the "excellent people" involved in the project were those very excellent people themselves.[9] It is thus not unfair to say that the students' conception of the triumphant history of Phú Mỹ Hưng had itself been at least partially taught to them by agents of the Phú Mỹ Hưng Corporation.

The corporation, furthermore, has expended no small degree of effort in telling this story. Here, for example, is another version of the "wasteland story," taken from Phú Mỹ Hưng's own internal history, printed in 2005:

> **Rising from the Swamps:** Looking back at the past 10 years of clearing the wasteland *[khai phá]* and building, the Phú Mỹ Hưng joint venture company has achieved some small accomplishments. In these impoverished, neglected *[hoang sơ]*, and inundated mangroves of northern Nhà Bè rural district, it has now become transformed into the Phú Mỹ Hưng Urban Zone, a modern urban zone integrated into nature, full of green, a place with many schools, hospitals, supermarkets, parks, playgrounds, and sports fields.[10]

The parallels between this story and the one in the students' e-book are plain to see.

Vietnamese "Wasteland Narratives"

It is tempting to stop here—to insist that the students and other awe-struck observers were merely piping a story fed to them by corporate advertisers. But the Phú Mỹ Hưng story, and the particular wasteland narrative it builds from, cannot be attributed only to clever marketing by the Phú Mỹ Hưng Corporation. The structure of the passage noted above, and by extension the structure of the story told by the students, itself neatly parallels the stories Vietnamese regularly tell about the founding of Saigon, which is also typically described as the clearing of a wasteland. In this way, while it is clear that the students learned much of the history they told in their e-book from the Phú Mỹ Hưng Corporation's stories about itself, the corporation's history itself is also clearly influenced by Vietnamese modes of historical storytelling.

Compare, for example, Phú Mỹ Hưng's internally produced history with a well-known account by the Vietnamese historian Trần Văn Giàu, in which the founding of Saigon is summarized with the subtitle: "Vietnamese people arriving to clear the wasteland and establish villages in the Saigon region." Trần Văn Giàu's text then goes on to explain that "from the late 16th century and early 17th century, up until the end of the 17th century, many Vietnamese people had conquered nature [*chinh phục thiên niên*], become land masters, opened and cleared with jungle-clearing axes, cut the grasses with scythes, and tilled the fields with buffalos and plows; it is because of this that a work of unshakable stability gradually emerged; it is because of this that the people became completely and tightly connected to the fields and gardens, where who knows how much sweat and tears have been spilled".[11] This essential storyline is so often repeated in Vietnamese historical works (and other contexts as well) that it might be assigned a folklorist's tale-type: "the story of clearing the wasteland."[12] This tale-type itself forms the core plot around which almost all Vietnamese stories of the founding of Saigon are organized, and it quite closely parallels the story told about Phú Mỹ Hưng.

This "clearing the wasteland" tale-type proliferates in Vietnamese historical narratives of expansion. One clear example appears in the foreword to the historian Nguyễn Đình Đầu's book *From Saigon to HoChiMinh City: 300-Year History*, published on the occasion of the city's 300th anniversary celebrations in 1998. In that foreword, Huỳnh Phú Sang, "director of the Ho Chi Minh City Service of Land," described the Gia Định region surrounding Saigon as "the wild woods," which were only sparsely occupied by "strewn villages," which in turn were occupied by Vietnamese coming from places in central Vietnam "to claim virgin land." The foreword goes on to insist that it was only though Vietnamese occupation and administration that so-called underutilized land could be made valuable, noting that Vietnamese "policies have enlarged the Gia Dinh area, turning it into a prosperous area, a strategic place, a key gateway for exchanges, and an administrative hub for the entire southern Vietnam." Integrating this account directly into the story of clearing the wasteland, Huỳnh Phú Sang added: "Such a development also reflected the industriousness and creativity of the migrants, of those 'land openers' who had surmounted numerous difficulties to survive the harsh conditions of the wilderness."[13] In these and countless other Vietnamese histories, the story of Saigon is commonly told as the history of "opening the land" *(mở đất)*, "clearing the wasteland" *(khai phá đất hoang; khẩn hoang; khai hoang)*, or otherwise civilizing and creating value out of lands described as wasted or uncultivated *(bỏ hoang, hoang địa)*, neglected *(hoang sơ)*, and deserted or wild *(hoang vu)*.[14]

Of course, Vietnamese people did historically move from points to the north into southern lands. And surely, this was difficult work. There were tigers, snakes, and an unfamiliar watery landscape. And of course the precolonial landscape in the region now occupied by the city of Saigon—Ho Chi Minh City—was very different than it is today. The environmental historian David Biggs has carefully documented the ways in which Vietnamese, French, and American occupiers radically transformed the environmental landscape of the south through their civilizing efforts.[15] But as Biggs and other scholars have also shown, these lands were never empty, despite the way the story of clearing the wasteland rests on and perpetuates imaginary constructions of the southern lands as such. The rhetorical force of the narrative itself commonly obscures or at best downplays the presence of non-Vietnamese peoples, even though readily available evidence underscores the long-standing complexity of preconquest lifeways and civilizations.[16] The story of clearing the wasteland obscures all that was there then, and in the process of becoming the standard mode of telling the history of Saigon and of Vietnam's south as a whole, it has come to color the way the history of this land has been imagined by the Vietnamese. Philip Taylor's recent ethnography of the region now politically incorporated into the southern part of Vietnam supports this point, showing in particular how Vietnamese narratives commonly ignore the vibrancy of Khmer lifeways.[17]

Today, just as nationalist Vietnamese histories constructed southern lands as wastelands, contemporary urban developers and city planners claim to have done the same thing to Ho Chi Minh City's periurban fringe. But the lands on the outskirts of Vietnamese cities were never empty. In fact, they were populated by vibrant, cash-poor but culturally rich agricultural communities, the same bearers of Vietnamese wet-rice "civilization" who had displaced earlier peoples from lands that were depicted as empty but were in fact not so.[18] The main difference today is that those who have been civilized out of existence by periurban expansion are the descendants of previous civilizers—if Vietnamese agrarian pioneers pushed out

Khmers and others in the past, in more recent years Vietnamese urban pioneers have joined with foreign developers and mobilized a similar civilizing rhetoric to push out their own countrymen, all using a language that resonates with the proud history of Vietnamese manifest destiny.

This story of clearing the wasteland on the periurban fringes of Ho Chi Minh City is nothing less than a subgenre of Vietnamese historical narratives of civilizational conquest.[19] For example, the following statement, from the internal corporate history of Phú Mỹ Hưng cited above, explicitly integrates what is essentially a massive real estate project into the city's civilizational history:

> The city has now been developing for over 300 years, counting from 1698, when the Nguyễn Lord sent Lễ Thành Hầu Nguyễn Hữu Cảnh into the southern capital to establish Gia Định prefecture (Phủ), thus bringing all the settlers together to come and clear the wastelands *[khai khẩn]* in this region. Three hundred years old is young for a city, and the period of 12 years so far spent establishing and developing the Saigon South New Urban Zone is only a first step. But with all the things that have been done in that short period, it is possible to acknowledge that this has been the right path, and that the feasible goals and open future of Ho Chi Minh City is lifting us in the direction of the Eastern Sea.[20] We are connected to the pathways of our ancestors, who cleared the wastelands, intent on transforming the low-lying saline mangrove lands in the south and southwest of the city into modern urban zones. These zones carry the spirit inherited from those people who went before us and are also full of the innovative spirit of the children of the contemporary city.[21]

Just like the students' e-book, the story told here of clearing the wasteland on the edge of the city draws the development of Phú Mỹ Hưng into a narrative of civilization and uplift. What might look to some outside observers as a "foreign" model of development—just another high-end housing and shopping development like those to be found in any urban margin of the world—manages to become deeply integrated into common historical fables about the long march of Vietnamese history.

## OUTER-CITY GROWTH AND THE BIRTH
## OF PHÚ MỸ HƯNG

The fact that there is a narrative structure at work in the story of Phú Mỹ Hưng's development does not mean that there has not been rapid urbanization in the area. By all accounts, the rapid transformations on the edges of Saigon over the past two decades have been bewildering, especially for city natives who have (or at one time thought they had) clear maps in their heads of the area before it was urbanized. On one memorable occasion, for example, a friend of mine from downtown Saigon became completely lost when trying to visit me in Phú Mỹ Hưng. After arriving over an hour later than expected to our appointment, he explained that he had not been to Phú Mỹ Hưng in several years and had remembered it as being located just beyond the edge of the city, "in the middle of nowhere." But in the intervening years the area had changed so rapidly that the edge of the city had literally shifted, and he rode at least five kilometers past the development, disoriented by all the new construction in and around it.

It is no surprise that my friend got lost. The residential and commercial center of the Saigon South New Urban Zone has developed so rapidly that many people find themselves bewildered. Commonly referred to as Phú Mỹ Hưng, and technically known by the development's planners as "Zone A," the center of the development is today a mixed-use master-planned residential and commercial development built on 433 hectares of land, planned to accommodate 100,000 permanent residents and 500,000 temporary daily visitors. And this is just the beginning. Zone A is itself only one sector of the much larger 3,300-hectare Saigon South Urban Development Project urban master plan, which planners hope will someday also include zones B, C, D, and E, as well as dedicated zones for sports complexes, two university campuses, a zoological waterpark, a golf course, botanical garden, a fairgrounds, and several science-based industrial parks. In Zone A alone, the amount of construction is astounding. In less than ten years—between 1998 and 2007—the Phú Mỹ Hưng Corporation constructed more than a million square meters of built space there, comprising 6,042 residential units. By the time of my fieldwork, they were well into the process of building an additional 491,000 square meters, including 2,696 units.[22] The pace of this construction is even more dramatic when one recalls that the land where Phú Mỹ Hưng now sits was once part of a rural "outer-city district" *(huyện)* called Nhà Bè, which was only redistricted and incorporated as a new urban "inner-city district" *(quận)* called District Seven in 1997.[23] In 1997, the official population for all of newly formed District Seven was 90,958.[24] By 2006 the population had more than doubled, reaching 187,326 persons.[25] In 2011, the year when my visiting friend got lost, the population of the district was 265,997.[26] Bewildering indeed.

The population growth of District Seven, however, has not been confined to Phú Mỹ Hưng, and has in fact increased even more rapidly in nearby wards located outside the New Urban Zone. In 2008, approximately 12,000 residents lived in Phú Mỹ Hưng, and by 2012 that number had risen to approximately 20,000.[27] These numbers, however, are only a small fraction of the more than 175,000 new residents added to the district since 1997. While some of this growth can surely be linked directly to the "pull" of a major development like Phú Mỹ Hưng, most of the development in District Seven has taken place in nearby working-class neighborhoods, which have grown even faster than Phú Mỹ Hưng. Although local real estate developers commonly say that nearby apartment complexes and smaller-scale master-planned developments "feed off of" *(ăn theo)* Phú Mỹ Hưng's infrastructure and prestige, other periurban spaces in other Ho Chi Minh City districts have also seen similar rapid population growth, and it is clear that growth in District Seven has been stimulated in many ways by the same rural-to-urban population movements experienced elsewhere in the city, as well as by internal movement within the city itself. Some of this urban-to-urban growth of course includes people moving to Phú Mỹ Hưng in search of modern apartments or the privacy and space to be found in villas, but most of it takes place in surrounding wards, where affordable middle-class housing is constructed directly next to "auto-constructed" working-class housing in less formally planned developments.[28] Thus, although the New Urban Zone's apartment towers and housing tracts give the impression that Phú Mỹ Hưng has been the center of growth, population density figures tell a different story. In 2006, the population density of wards immediately surrounding Phú Mỹ Hưng all exceeded 21,000 persons per square kilometer, while the density of Phú Mỹ Hưng, at 2,155 persons per square kilometer, was barely more than one tenth as dense. While the act of "clearing the wasteland" is commonly attributed to Phú Mỹ Hưng, the forces of urbanization are in fact proceeding more intensely through the independent actions of hundreds of thousands of new residents living beyond the official boundaries of the development. Quantitatively speaking, the real "land-clearers" and spatial pioneers are living on the edges of Phú Mỹ Hưng, not within it.

The formal and iconic nature of architecture within Phú Mỹ Hưng itself, however, easily captures the popular imagination, making it understandable that people imagine the development to be the primary force driving urbanization in the area. Within the development itself there are new roads, golf courses, hospitals, shopping malls, an international convention center, a university campus, international schools, bridges, broad boulevards, extensive infrastructure, landscaped promenades, and thousands of units of residential housing. While Phú Mỹ Hung is often misrepresented as a "gated community," the residential housing itself is quite diverse, and includes not only single-family villas (both inside and outside of security gates) but also town house–style villas with shared walls, row houses with street-level shopfronts, and a wide variety of mixed-use apartment buildings with commercial space on the ground floor (see figures 1.2–4). In 2011, there were at least ninety-three separate housing developments within the Phú Mỹ Hưng development, ranging from blocks of villas to upscale mixed-use high-rise apartment buildings, and from rows of shop-houses to mid-range walk-up apartment buildings. None of this existed before construction of the first apartment buildings began in 1997.

Construction in Phú Mỹ Hưng has been fast and continuous, and a new center with a distinctly modern urban character has indeed emerged here in less than two decades. The first two apartment blocks went on the market in 1997 and were opened for occupation in 1998. The first of these two, called Hưng Vượng I (marked with an "A" on fig. 1.1), consisted of five-story buildings built along Nguyễn Văn

FIGURE 1.2. A typical villa, viewed from the side. The plot of land in the foreground is available for development. The sign reads: "Land for sale." Phú Mỹ Hưng, District 7, Ho Chi Minh City. Author's photo, July 2012.

FIGURE 1.3. A semidetached villa zoned for mixed-use residential and commercial use. The unit on the left is a private residence; the unit on the right is a private tutoring center called "Super Mind," which promises to develop "intelligence" (Trí Tuệ) via foreign-language training and something called "Speed Math." Phú Mỹ Hưng, District 7, Ho Chi Minh City. Author's photo, May 2012.

FIGURE 1.4. Housing plots with private home construction built to owner specifications. Luxury apartment towers are visible in the background, and cleared and graded plots are ready for construction in the foreground. Phú Mỹ Hưng, District 7, Ho Chi Minh City. Author's photo, May 2012.

Linh Boulevard with apartments ranging in size from 69 to 147 square meters; the second, Hưng Vượng III, had nine stories and apartment sizes ranging from 71 to 223 square meters. Hưng Vượng II (which despite the name was built third in the sequence) was built in a similar style, but with eight floors, and was completed in 1999. Soon after, across Nguyễn Văn Linh Boulevard, another row of twelve-story apartment buildings, Mỹ Khánh I, II, III, and IV, was completed in 2000 (see fig. 1.1, item B). These developments included street-level commercial storefronts, which contributed to the planned emergence of an urban corridor lined with shops and broad tree-lined sidewalks. Together, these rectilinear apartment complexes combined to define the intersection of Nguyễn Văn Linh and Nguyễn Đức Cảnh boulevards, thereby outlining the first material, physical, and spatial relations of a new urban center. Indeed, while the Phú Mỹ Hưng project was "conceived" as early as 1989, and while the formal master plan was designed by Skidmore Ownings & Merrill in 1993, the sense of place associated with urban space really only emerged at this intersection around the turn of the millennium (see fig. 1.5). In both a poetic and literal sense, the birth of Phú Mỹ Hưng (Rich, Beautiful, Prosperity) as an actually existing urban space can be traced to the moment when Thriving Prosperity (Hưng Vượng) joined with Festive Beauty (Mỹ Khánh). It may be no accident that in Vietnamese the name Hưng is gendered male and Mỹ is gendered female.[29]

In subsequent years, Phú Mỹ Hưng's designers, carefully following the master plan, extended the urban corridor along Nguyễn Văn Linh street by encouraging the construction of multistory rowhouses, all with shopfronts on the bottom. These buildings, part of the Mỹ Toàn development, went on the market in 2000, and were built by individual owners in accordance with basic guidelines to keep them in line with the master plan while also allowing for some minor architectural diversity, which intentionally encouraged a mixed-use form that would combine residential housing with commercial space in order to foster street-level activity and promote walkability. Soon after, in 2001, the eighteen-floor Skygarden 1 complex of buildings was completed, adding density to the new urban city center by bringing more residents, expanding walking spaces, and further defining the urban corridors (see fig. 1.1, item C). Meanwhile, ground-level residential neighborhoods were being constructed behind the main boulevards, effectively filling in those spaces with a range of housing styles. For example, the Mỹ An (Beautiful Peace) and Mỹ Cảnh (Beautiful View) developments, which went on the market in 2000 and were completed in 2001, consisted of six- and seven-story walk-up apartments that sold for prices between US$41,379 and US$55,172, for apartments ranging in size from 85 to 150 square meters (in 2012, the same apartments had a market value between US$134,100 and US$239,464). Meanwhile, Phú Gia (Rich Family), the only truly gated community in the development, went on the market in 2001, with single-family villas selling for between

FIGURE 1.5. The intersection of Nguyễn Văn Linh and Nguyễn Đức Cảnh streets, looking south. The luxury apartment towers at the corners are part of the Mỹ Khánh development, completed in 2000. Phú Mỹ Hưng, District 7, Ho Chi Minh City. Author's photo, July 2009.

US$1,469,605 and US$3,072,812 (see fig. 1.1, item D). When the Phú Gia houses were completed in 2002, they were known as perhaps the most exclusive new homes in all of Ho Chi Minh City, whereas the price of apartments in Mỹ An were well within reach of many families and attracted a number of young professionals, especially families with two working parents employed in secure office jobs with regular work hours, such as lawyers, office managers, university professors, and some small business owners.

Ever since the early years of the new millennium, the development continued to densify by building up around the primary axis at the Nguyễn Văn Linh and Nguyễn Đức Cảnh intersection. After reaching a critical density there, new construction expanded into and then filled in the areas surrounding subsidiary transport axes. The nineteen-floor Skygarden 2 tower complex and the Grandview apartment building were both completed in 2004 (fig. 1.1, item E), the upscale Panorama apartment was completed in 2006 (fig. 1.1, item F), and the first phase of the twenty-floor Skygarden 3 towers was completed in 2008. Between 2008 and 2011, major new projects completed included the Crescent Residences, the Riverside

FIGURE 1.6. View of Phú Mỹ Hưng looking north toward District 1. The first row of houses in the foreground consists of shop-houses with street-level commercial spaces and multilevel private residences above. The subsequent rows form a neighborhood of mixed-use semidetached villas. Author's photo, October 2010.

Residences, and a number of mid-sized apartment complexes, all with street-front commerce, which began to fill in and densify a new urban corridor along Nguyễn Lương Bằng Street. At this point, the urban footprint of Zone A was largely defined by an extensive grid of built-up roads and buildings.

Thus, by 2011, when the students from the Lawrence S. Ting School interviewed me for their project and told me about the city rising from a wasteland, we were indeed standing in the middle of what clearly looked and felt like an urban space (fig. 1.1, item G). In addition to all the developments described above, the street where I met the students, Nguyễn Đức Cảnh, was a bustling commercial road lined by the Saigon South International School and the Lawrence Ting School, as well as the Mỹ Phúc, Mỹ Phát, Mỹ Đức, Park View, Grandview, and Panorama apartment buildings. The neighborhoods behind this street, furthermore, were filled with neatly aligned streets, laid out in blocks of row houses, stand-alone villas, and the Phú Gia gated community (see fig. 1.6). Two parks, one following the riverfront and another leading to a man-made lake, framed the other edge of this, the residential heart of Phú Mỹ Hưng. Given such a rapid and extensive transformation of the physical space of Phú Mỹ Hưng, it is no surprise that residents and developers might assert that this development had risen out of a wasteland.

Vietnam, however, is one of the most densely populated countries in the world, especially in the region immediately surrounding Ho Chi Minh City. Even a cursory glance at the "before" images of Phú Mỹ Hưng immediately reveals that, already back in the early 1990s, this landscape on the edge of the city was anything but empty. Careful inspection of the before images presented in Phú Mỹ Hưng's own company history confirms that every meter of the landscape was marked by the clear imprint of Vietnamese agriculture. Such photos plainly show tree-lined berms, which indicate semipermanent boundaries between individually cultivated plots of land. All of these plots of land would have been part of a Vietnamese agricultural order and as such represented neither emptiness nor waste.

If the lands where Phú Mỹ Hưng was built were never empty, what were they? They were agrarian "outer-city" districts, which have been systematically devalued in the postreform era.[30] In order to capture the latent value seen to be resting in such agrarian lands, new laws had to be passed to remove people from the land. In Phú Mỹ Hưng's case, a special legal basis for land clearance was specifically established for the area in 1994, immediately following the prime minister's approval of the master plan for the project. At that time, a company called Sadeco (the Saigon Development Corporation)[31] was charged with developing the project; it was given specific authorization to carry out evictions needed to clear land for the construction of the Tân Thuận Export Processing Zone (EPZ) and the Phú Mỹ Hưng New Urban Zone.[32] While it has not been possible to obtain a forthright statement from any official sources about the exact number of people ultimately displaced for the Phú Mỹ Hưng project, cadastral records indicate that the area was populated since at least the Nguyễn dynasty.[33] An additional contemporary source reveals that five hundred households were removed from the ward of Tân Thuận Đông to clear part of the land for the project. At 300 hectares, this ward was only about one-eleventh of the 3,300 total hectares planned for the project. This was the site of the first land clearance operations in the area that would later become the Tân Thuận Export Processing Zone.[34] At that time, compensation for the displaced households was set at the equivalent of about one dollar per square meter.[35] In other words, while the land was not actually empty of people, it was certainly undervalued, and the stories of people who once lived on the land have been largely erased from history. Dispersed from the land by the project, there is no record of where they have gone. Or if there is one, it has been excised from both the official records and popular stories told of Phú Mỹ Hưng, which would have us believe that all of the land was empty wasteland waiting to be brought into value.

## PHÚ MỸ HƯNG'S PLACE IN VIETNAM'S
## POSTWAR HISTORY

The theme of "clearing the wasteland" that guides stories about Phú Mỹ Hưng is only partially about the actual act of clearing parcels of land. Generally speaking, few people today give much thought to whether there were people there or not. Instead, the wasteland story they tell has mainly become a convenient narrative arc around which to weave a story of social and political change. This was plainly evident in the e-book written by the eight-graders from Lawrence S. Ting School, who linked the success of Phú Mỹ Hưng to the political will of the Vietnamese people: recall, for example, how they connected the emergence of the new city rising out of swamps with the idea that "Vietnam wanted to change." A similar connection appears in a sprawling three-volume informal history and personal memoir of Phú Mỹ Hưng written by Nguyễn Văn Kích, a former functionary at the Ho Chi Minh City People's Committee, who was involved with many of the key actors in the project. At one point in his history, for example, Kích explains that the New Urban Zone is nothing less than a resolution of the long-standing antinomies of socialism and capitalism. As he puts it, Phú Mỹ Hưng has thrived by using the "market mechanism" *(cơ chế thị trường)* to enact the ideals of collective responsibility that were themselves the core of socialist idealism in the first place.[36] His explanation deserves quoting at length because it captures a central theme in the way Phú Mỹ Hưng planners and many of its residents commonly describe the private development as a mechanism for enhancing collective responsibility, while also celebrating the emergence of rights to private property it is founded upon:

> The space surrounding the house is common property; it is really a socialist property *[đúng là tài sản XHCN]* that no one person has the right to infringe upon. Meanwhile, the space inside the home can be arranged according to one's decorating preferences and their own aesthetic needs. But one cannot change the structure. *The sense of social equity in the Phú Mỹ Hưng New Urban Zone is established right from conceptualization and carries through to planning, design, and construction. It is especially found in the legal framework and self-governing organization that emphasizes social and communal sustainability, community benefits, the environment, public conveniences, and the rules. This is the source of the sense of human dignity, and the humanity of the residents, and in the modern, comfortable, and charming architectural spaces, built spaces, and living spaces.*[37]

While Phú Mỹ Hưng is clearly a profit-seeking development, this passage, like others throughout Kích's memoir, focuses on the lofty ideals behind the project, even claiming that a socialist spirit of collectivity could be reconciled with capitalist privatization in ways that maximize "dignity" and "humanity." Throughout the book, in fact, Kích regularly describes Phú Mỹ Hưng as the ideal expression of Vietnam's postreform-era political project of developing a "market economy with a socialist orientation." If, as was sometimes quipped in Eastern Europe, socialism was the most painful path from capitalism to capitalism, Kích describes market capitalism as a pleasant walk along manicured pathways from socialism to socialism. The old socialism was blinded by ideology and a fear of private property; the new socialism, epitomized by Phú Mỹ Hưng, is pragmatic, willing to tap into the power of capital and the market economy to realize its objectives.

Nguyễn Văn Kích's memoir is just one example of how the Phú Mỹ Hưng story is told as an allegory of the Vietnamese reform policies known as Đổi Mới, officially instituted in 1986 but continually tinkered with ever since. The basic story of Đổi Mới has been a delicate attempt to introduce capitalist market mechanisms to boost economic productivity, all while trying to preserve the legacy of the socialist revolution by framing market reform as a truer path to socialism. An important part of this story has been the introduction of land policy reforms that gradually made it possible to buy and sell land-use right permits. Because Phú Mỹ Hưng's success is itself driven by land markets made possible by such legal reforms, it illustrates the story well. Phú Mỹ Hưng's boosters commonly claim that the development would not have been possible without the political changes of Đổi Mới; but also, in a kind of mutually enhancing feedback loop, they commonly cite Phú Mỹ Hưng as a model for how Đổi Mới should proceed. For this reason, Phú Mỹ Hưng acquires a symbolic force as both a model of and a model for the connection between economic renovation and political change. What are in many ways strictly material acts—building parks and apartment buildings and laying down wide, open avenues—become infused with symbolic and political meaning linked to the story of recent Vietnamese history. The breezy boulevards and modern buildings one encounters in the master-planned development not only promise to deliver wealth, beauty, and prosperity to the Vietnamese people but also evoke a history of reform.[38]

### Opening the Land in Phú Mỹ Hưng during the Open Door Period

Many scholars have rightly questioned the depth of real political reform brought on by Đổi Mới.[39] The essence of some of these critiques, which echo well-known critiques from other postsocialist contexts, is that "market socialism" is just another way to use the heavy-handed force of a strong Communist Party to direct the economic advantages of free-market capitalism to connected elites. While the story of Đổi Mới is commonly rendered in bluntly simplified terms as a postsocialist "transition," it is far from clear what the country is transitioning to. To borrow from the scholar of postsocialist Romania Katherine Verdery, it is as much a transition from socialism to feudalism as anything else.[40] As in Eastern Europe, changes in economic policy have not always been accompanied by political changes, and in some cases have arguably further entrenched power holders associated with the Communist Party of Vietnam. Verdery's observations about what happened to the state in Eastern Europe clearly resonate with regard to Vietnam: "Even as entrepratchiks drain the state's assets, thus debilitating the state and changing both its capacities and its nature, they also support its continuing existence for the resources and subsidies it provides."[41]

In Vietnam generally, and in Ho Chi Minh City in particular, business has thrived with the introduction of both market mechanisms and the introduction of land use rights for landed property, but this has not necessarily changed the lines of authority. For example, the political scientist Martin Gainsborough's observations about Vietnamese "reform" could be ripped from the pages of Verdery's observations about Romania: "In Vietnam, the reform years have certainly seen the emergence of a new business elite. However, while this elite is new in terms of its business interests, it is in fact rather old in terms of its political ties. That is, many of the new entrepreneurs have emerged from within the existing system, are currently serving or former officials, or are the children of the political elite."[42] As Gainsborough's work shows, the incremental emergence of Đổi Mới cannot be understood as a slow march to political liberalism. Instead, it should also be seen as an incremental process through which connected actors struggle to divide resources among themselves, experimenting with reforms that continue to consolidate power while increasing the opportunities for accumulation. Furthermore, Đổi Mới did not immediately bring prosperity. It took the politically connected actors Gainsborough describes time to develop new projects, finesse their connections, and gradually test the limits of the emerging system.

Given the enormous profits that have accrued to the Phú Mỹ Hưng joint venture, Gainsborough's critique is certainly valid. But for observers like Nguyễn Văn Kích, the physical changes in Phú Mỹ Hưng seem to offer concrete evidence about how the embrace of markets and the development of private property have spurred both economic and social development. Early in his narrative, for example, Kích asks readers to imagine their surprise if they were to come back to Nhà Bè District (now the site of Phú Mỹ Hưng) after a fifteen- or twenty-year absence. In place of rivers and channels, he notes, the broad Nguyễn Văn Linh parkway has risen; in place of swamps, the most modern architecture in the city. This, he explains, is part of the general path of Ho Chi Minh City's development, but it is also a product of the hard work of planners, businessmen, and developers.[43] The result, according to Kích, is a triumph of human ingenuity:

> Today, the Phú Mỹ Hưng Urban Zone is regarded as the first modern, clean, green, and beautiful urban zone in Vietnam, an urban area that has been planned with the utmost synchrony, in harmony with natural beauty and the environment, with a wide open and completely unclogged traffic system, with architecturally modern and glamorous buildings and villas that have all the conveniences within walking distance of all the residents yet remains wide ranging and multifarious, including a complete set of cultural and educational projects, hospitals, as well as recreation and

leisure . . . giving a set of invisible yet extraordinarily important values in relation to the new urban lifestyle.[44]

Although the passage begins with the built landscape, it culminates in the gift of "extraordinarily important values." Indeed, throughout Nguyễn Văn Kích's book, a clear argument is being made about the way Phú Mỹ Hưng stands for something much bigger than itself. The book is thus not only a history of the development; it also reads as a triumphant narrative about Đổi Mới. By linking these changes to moral stories of development, these kinds of stories also insist that these kinds of developments have in fact been driving a more fundamental change in the country's political and economic landscape since the late 1980s.

In my conversations with the leaders involved in the Phú Mỹ Hưng project, I was struck by how often they emphasized how hard they needed to fight against ideological resistance to make the project happen. Their efforts to make the project possible were always linked to the larger story of Vietnam's emergence out of prereform socialism. In this way, just as wasteland narratives are often told as civilizing stories, the story of building the New Urban Zone was itself often depicted as a story that was made possible by the efforts of pioneers cutting through thickets of ideological overgrowth and clearing the way for the "open door" *(mở cửa)* policies of the 1990s and beyond. Phú Mỹ Hưng plays this role especially well because some of the early architects of Đổi Mới were also involved in the project. It also helps that the timing of the project directly parallels the generally accepted timeline of Đổi Mới itself—like Vietnam's reform project, Phú Mỹ Hưng was first conceived in the late 1980s, and then, despite ideological, legal, political, and economic difficulties, it was largely implemented in the 1990s, before emerging as a success story in the 2000s.

Like the wasteland stories, these allegories of development as political struggle stressed connections to historical events. During the years immediately following the introduction of Đổi Mới in 1986 and the early 1990s, Ho Chi Minh City, like the country as a whole, faced serious shortages and economic challenges, and many of the city's most talented economists and experienced businesspeople had either fled the country or were treated with suspicion because of their ties to the former Saigon regime.[45] In the late 1980s, with the state facing a serious legitimacy crisis, former Ho Chi Minh City People's Committee chairman Võ Văn Kiệt, then a rising politburo member who would go on to become prime minister in 1992, secretly and cautiously allowed some business actors with connections to the previous regime to conduct what the economist and planning scholar Du Huynh has called "limited assignments," which allowed them to mobilize external business connections to help the impoverished city economy.[46] Thus, in the late 1980s and early 1990s some of Ho Chi Minh City's business leaders, including ethnic Chinese leaders who had until then been particularly subject to repression by postwar policies, once again found it possible to begin courting their overseas networks, primarily in Hong Kong, Singapore, and Taiwan.[47] In this respect, while critics like Gainsborough might insist that reform was nothing but old wine in new bottles, the actors who were actually involved in this period can point to significant and quite real differences in the way business was allowed to operate. And for those associated with the development of Phú Mỹ Hưng, they often point to the changes of the physical landscape as material evidence of what these changes could bring.

One important new leader in this early reform period was a man named Phan Chánh Dưỡng, an ethnic Chinese but proudly Vietnamese physics teacher who had extensive connections to Chinese businesses but no formal business experience himself. His story and his connections to Phú Mỹ Hưng and early business reforms in Ho Chi Minh City epitomize the links between building new kinds of buildings and building new political structures. Before the reform period, an ethnic Chinese leader like Phan Chánh Dưỡng would have been subjected to close surveillance and suspicion. With the launch of reform, however, he was actively encouraged to experiment with market forces when he was appointed the director of the Chợ Lớn Investment and Import Export Corporation (Cholimex).[48] Created in 1981, Cholimex was one of the first "proto–joint stock" experiments in postwar Saigon, and included representatives of the People's Committee from District Five (site of Chợ Lớn, the city's well-known Chinatown) as well as Chinese-Vietnamese entrepreneurs whom the city allowed to engage with their private Chinese business connections in order to mobilize limited foreign trade.[49] With Phan Chánh Dưỡng as a catalyst, an informal group of friends, most of whom had once held leadership positions in the old wartime Saigon regime, would meet on Fridays to catch up with each other and also to think about the state of Vietnam. As they continued to meet, these specialists, unofficially known as the "Friday Group" (Nhóm Thứ Sáu), gradually caught the attention of the city leadership, particularly Võ Văn Kiệt, who formed them into a "special economic research unit" *(nhóm chuyện viên nghiên cứu kinh tế)* and encouraged them to study the economy and banking systems and devise potential strategies for attracting foreign investment.[50]

Meanwhile, in Taiwan, the Kuomintang (KMT) government, increasingly nervous about tensions across the straits with China, formed a company called the Central Trading and Development Corporation (CD&T) as an overseas investment unit to establish economic interests outside of the country in order to mitigate the effects of feared Chinese attacks on Taiwanese industry.[51] Writing with a wonderful sense of understatement about this period, Du Huynh notes that "the political context in Vietnam at the time was complicated."[52] It was so complicated, in fact, that the virulently anticommunist KMT, in its efforts to seek out safe investment alternatives, was willing to work with the still deeply communist leadership of Vietnam. It was also sufficiently complicated that the Vietnamese were finally loosening their tight control over ethnic Chinese business interests in order to mobilize new economic opportunities, and in doing so were authorizing them to deal directly with anticommunist interests. The importance—and complexities—of these early connections help explain why the real estate and infrastructure developments associated with Phú Mỹ Hưng are so often depicted with an almost hyperbolic sense of political and economic significance. For those involved in these developments, especially people like Phan Chánh Dưỡng, the story of "clearing the wasteland" on the margins of the city was not only about cutting through the marshes and overgrowth of the city's fringe; rather, it has come to be described as a pioneering act of cutting through socialist bureaucracy and red tape. As they describe their work, opening the land *(mở đất)* on the edge of the city and the struggle to push for more open door *(mở cửa)* policies were deeply intertwined.

Although the idea behind Phú Mỹ Hưng is often said to have been wholly conceived by "the Taiwanese," or more specifically by Lawrence Ting, key aspects of the concept had already been floated within Vietnam. In fact, by the time Lawrence Ting arrived in Vietnam seeking investment opportunities for CD&T in 1989, Phan Chánh Dưỡng and members of the Friday Group and Special Economic Research Unit had already developed a proposal called the *Study of Building EPZs in HCMC* (in 1988), which was accepted by the city leadership and listed as one of "Ho Chi Minh City's foreign economic development projects for the 1989–1995 period."[53] By October 24, 1989, Phan Chánh Dưỡng had been appointed the director of a newly approved "Tân Thuận EPZ Program."[54] At this time, however, the Vietnamese leaders, by their own account, had a lot to learn about how to negotiate with foreign businesses; the stories they often tell of this period emphasize the degree to which they were fumbling through new, uncharted territory, often bumbling but nevertheless willing to take risks and, above all, persevere in the face of adversity.[55]

Phan Chánh Dưỡng first came into contact with Lawrence Ting's CD&T Corporation during a layover in Malaysia, when he shared a hotel room with a low-level employee, who agreed to take informational materials about Ho Chi Minh City's investment priorities back to Taiwan on Dưỡng's behalf. After this introduction, Ting and Dưỡng had a series of meetings in 1990 at the Cholimex offices and at the Saigon Floating Hotel, which eventually led to a formal agreement.[56] On July 31, 1991, Phan Chánh Dưỡng's group signed an official agreement with Ting's CD&T and another company called PanViet to establish the Tân Thuận Export Processing Zone Joint Venture (known in Vietnamese as the Công ty Liên doanh Xây Dựng và Kinh Doanh Khu Chế xuất Tân Thuận, or more simply as the Công ty Liên doanh Tân Thuận).[57] In 1993 the Tân Thuận EPZ program was renamed the Industrial Promotion Company (IPC).[58] Everything was a negotiation; even the constantly changing names of the businesses involved reveal the ever-changing nature of this regulatory landscape: sometimes new companies had to be formed simply to make deals possible. Each deal, in turn, often required new laws, some of which were issued specifically as exceptions for Phú Mỹ Hưng, which was treated as an experiment in the newly emerging landscape of property investment made possible by the 1992 Land Law.

The stories I was told of the early negotiations commonly featured missteps and difficulties, and aspects of the telling often made them seem like scenes from spy novels. There was no legal basis for private property in socialist Vietnam at the time of the first negotiations, and the 1992 Land Law, which came into effect in 1993, granted only "land use rights," which appeared to resemble property rights, but there was enough ambiguity to always leave doubt in any investor's mind. Mingled amid great hope was also great trepidation. No one knew how far they could push forward with the idea. Nevertheless, when speaking of these early meetings so filled with uncertainty, it becomes evident that those who laid the groundwork for collaboration between 1989 and 1993 have come to see themselves, and have also come to be seen by many other Vietnamese observers, as people whose great perseverance and tenacity created new possibilities for the country.[59] They saw themselves as pioneers opening up a new political and legal landscape, full of risk but also full of possibility.

Retrospectively, these initial acts of "fence breaking"—as these kinds of rule-testing economic practices are often called in the literature on Vietnamese economic and political reform—have all been folded into a narrative of transition much like those Verdery has described in postsocialist Eastern Europe. In Phú Mỹ Hưng's case, this forward movement is commonly depicted as a series of milestones and achievements, all of which are proudly displayed on the Phú Mỹ Hưng website, in nearly all the company's literature, and in the stories people recount of the development's history.[60] This history of successive triumphs, when juxtaposed against the difficulties investors faced in the early years of development, further adds to the symbolic potency of the Phú Mỹ Hưng development, and is often folded into the stories people themselves recount of the project's history as proof of their visionary quest to bring reform to the Vietnamese people. Indeed, Phú Mỹ Hưng developers seem to revel in the way their early "vision" *(tầm nhìn)* for the development triumphed in spite of various forms of resistance. In a 2011 conversation, a vice director of Phú Mỹ Hưng Corporation told my research assistant and me that the plans to develop the Phú Mỹ Hưng New Urban Zone were conceived at "the same time" as the plan to develop the Thủ Thiêm New Urban Zone, in concept around 1989, and officially around 1993. At that time, he explained, Thủ Thiêm was the most sought after plot of undeveloped land in Ho Chi Minh City, while Nhà Bè, where Phú Mỹ Hưng was built, was seen as highly undesirable.[61] But by the time of our interview, the prestigious, award-winning first phases of Phú

Mỹ Hưng had already been inhabited by Saigon's elite for many years, while Thủ Thiêm remained mired in conflicts over compensation and resettlement (see part 2 of this book).[62] The message was clear: Phú Mỹ Hưng's way of doing business was indisputably superior to the inefficient leadership of the state-led project in Thủ Thiêm. On another occasion, when telling me about the history of Phú Mỹ Hưng, Phan Chánh Dưỡng repeated this exact story using similar language.

One of the central themes in these stories is the way in which Phú Mỹ Hưng's developers were able to transform a perceived wasteland into golden land, despite the ideological blinders imposed on them by earlier versions of Vietnamese socialism. It is told as a story of visionaries and pioneers who were opening up not just the land but the very eyes of the country's leadership. One of the most commonly reproduced pictures in the company's internal histories shows Phú Mỹ Hưng officials holding up a map for the prime minister to see, while pointing out across the not-yet-urbanized expanses of periurban agriculture. These themes of "vision," clearing wasteland, economic renovation, and political change permeate the language people use when they talk about Phú Mỹ Hưng. They are also themes that appear in the reverential tones used to describe Mr. Lawrence S. Ting.

## LAWRENCE S. TING'S HEROIC VISION

Lawrence Ting is universally recognized as the founder or, as his many admirers call him, the "mastermind" or "the visionary" behind the Phú Mỹ Hưng project.[63] His suicide in 2004, during lawsuits and legal prosecution on corruption charges in Taiwan, makes it difficult to assess the true nature of his business dealings, but the stories told about him in Vietnam are universally positive. Something of a reverential cult has emerged around his memory, and he has been transformed into someone on par with the founding ancestors commonly described in Vietnamese wasteland narratives—someone who gave everything to the selfless and courageous act of clearing the wasteland (có công khai phá).[64] An idea of this cult is conveyed in an article from the *China Post*, ostensibly about Ting's sons Albert and Arthur, though inevitably it turns to their father's legacy (while also repeating the wasteland narrative):

> In order to explain PMH's miraculous development of Saigon South, we need to tell the story of its mastermind . . . Lawrence S. Ting.
>
> In 1989 the area was nothing but a desolate marsh. Back then Lawrence Ting had just become chairman of CT&D Group, run by Taiwan's then ruling Kuomintang (KMT), following long careers in the military and the plastics industry. Lawrence Ting personally led a large "construction force" to Vietnam, building the Hiep Phuoc Power Plant and the Tan Thuan Export Processing Zone, and handling the land reclamation project for Saigon South. Over the following decade Lawrence Ting suffered a severe setback when the KMT pulled out its stake from CT&D Group. However,

together with his business partner Ferdinand Tsien Peng-lun, a former director of Swire Trading of Taiwan, he poured in over US$10 billion in investments to build a new municipality from the ground up, with state-of-the-art infrastructure and facilities based on the Taiwanese experience. To date no other Taiwanese entrepreneur can boast achievements of such a scale in Vietnam.

In 2004 when Lawrence Ting had already earned himself the admiring moniker "King of Vietnam," a battle for control of the company erupted with another major shareholder, shipping magnate Chen Ching Chih, the owner of Wan Hai Lines.

Eventually, Chen sued Lawrence Ting on charges of breach of trust and embezzlement. As investigations were underway, Lawrence Ting took his life by jumping from an office building, sending shock waves through the Taiwanese and Vietnamese business communities.[65]

While the merits of the legal proceedings against Ting are beyond the scope of this book, and while his legacy in Taiwan remains contested, the effect of his death within Vietnam was to intensify the respect accorded him. As an article in *Forbes* (written by a Vietnamese author) put it: "To this day the family won't discuss the circumstances of Ting's demise, only his achievements."[66] The same can be said of his Vietnamese collaborators. His reputation is carefully preserved, and within Vietnam he is almost universally celebrated for the role he had in clearing wastelands and making them fit for civilized habitation. Even Phú Mỹ Hưng residents, few of whom had ever actually met him, often spoke glowingly of Lawrence Ting, referencing his "vision" as a source of the project's success.

Today, Lawrence Ting's name is everywhere visible in the development, and the corporation itself has been quite active in the preservation of his memory. On November 4, 2004, less than two months after his death (on September 23), the Phú Mỹ Hưng Corporation renamed their central office building the Lawrence Ting Building.[67] In September 2005, in honor of the one-year anniversary of Ting's death, the corporation published a memorial volume, entitled *Let Me Make This Place My Homeland (Xin nhận nơi này làm quê hương),* which consisted of quotes from Mr. Ting as well as short essays by sixty-five individuals who knew him, including family members, friends, and his Vietnamese, Taiwanese, and American business associates. On November 25, 2005, a charity named the Lawrence S. Ting Memorial Fund was established through a formal decision by the Ho Chi Minh City People's Committee.[68] In 2006, the corporation decided to establish a nonprofit school carrying Ting's name in order to "realize the love he had reserved for the Vietnamese nation and the interest he had in Vietnam's youth generation."[69] In September 2008, the first class of students began their studies at Lawrence S. Ting Memorial School—among them were some of the authors of the e-book described at the beginning of this chapter.

The 2005 memorial volume, in particular, offers a telling window into the ways in which people remember Mr. Ting. Here, the moniker "king of Vietnam" is never used, as it was in Taiwan. Instead, in addition to professions of love, the memorial essays repeatedly emphasize three of Mr. Ting's core characteristics: his pioneering spirit and vision; his dedication and persistence in the face of skepticism and financial and political obstacles; and his love for Vietnam. The first words of the volume are Mr. Ting's own: "In the past 15 years, a group of pioneers have dedicated their lives and efforts to create today's Phu My Hung New Urban Area from salted marshlands. Based on this solid foundation, more people are now continuing the development of Hochiminh City toward the East Sea."[70]

This pioneer story echoes the story of clearing the wasteland, and many of the commentators, both Taiwanese and Vietnamese, specifically mention Ting's "vision" and his "forward-thinking" spirit as a way to secure his place in history as the leader of a larger group of pioneers. According to his Taiwanese partner, Ferdinand Tsien, he had "the attitude of a military man" and "gave all his energy to the project in Ho Chi Minh City.[71] In his recollections, Phan Chánh Dưỡng explained that "Mr. Ting really was a world-class businessman with a long-range vision and a broad perspective *[nhìn xa trông rộng].*" From the very beginning of his work in Vietnam, he notes, Ting "was able to recognize that the inundated, salty and poor lands of the Nhà Bè area held a hidden potential to develop in grand ways. And it was precisely the decision to invest in the Nhà Bè area that tied his destiny and his career to the great undertaking of Đổi Mới and the economic development of Ho Chi Minh City in particular and of Vietnam more generally."[72] According to Võ Trần Chí, the former secretary of the Ho Chi Minh City Communist Party Committtee, Ting was faced by doubters and naysayers who scoffed at his idea of building a new urban zone in such a distant place on the outskirts of the city; but Ting perservered, because he "was not only an investor looking for a profit, but also played an important part in helping lay down the Đổi Mới policies" and by thinking creatively. Instead of chasing immediate profit, Chí claimed that Ting took the difficult but ultimately more sustainable path to development.[73] Nguyễn Văn Huấn, former vice chairman of the Ho Chi Minh City People's Committee, explained that Ting was one of the first to work in Vietnam at a time when the legal system was not yet clear, and that he was on the "vanguard of clearing the wasteland" *(là một người tiên phong khai phá).*[74] Others, like Nguyễn Mại, spoke of his "correct vision,"[75] or as Trần Thiện Tứ put it, his "long-term vision" *(có tầm nhìn xa),*[76] which, according to Trịnh Công Lý, enabled him to "see a problem correctly."[77]

These messages of admiration often took pains to highlight how Mr. Ting was not just a builder, but a civilizer who directed his talents to developing the Vietnamese nation as well. As Bùi Thành Sơn, vice director of the Phú Mỹ Hưng Corporation, put it, Ting conducted "business not just for profit" *(kinh doanh không chỉ để tìm lợi nhuận).*[78] All of this was born out of what was commonly described as Ting's "love" for the Vietnamese people. These stories are striking for the way they integrate the ambitions of a foreign real estate prospector into the story of the Vietnamese nation. They recast elements that could otherwise be interpreted as a standard form of profit-seeking ambition into a story of selfless dedication to the cause of civilizational advancement.

Though martial at times, the recollections of Ting are also often quite sentimental. In one emotion-laden story, Phan Chánh Dưỡng, probably his closest friend in Vietnam, described a trip they took in 1994 to Hòn Đất District in Kiên Giang Province to observe a forest planting project. On the way, their entourage stopped to rest in a small hamlet where they met a group of barefoot young children who were "so poor that some of the kids wore pants with no shirts, while others wore shirts with no pants." But Ting saw that their poverty had not robbed them of their energy and joy. Phan Chánh Dưỡng described how Mr. Ting grabbed his hand and said, "Look at them, brother, just look at the bright eyes and the happy faces of the young ones and you will see that your country will develop very quickly in the future." And then Ting handed out candies to the children and shared a smile with them.[79] The sentimental connection, here juxtaposed against Ting's image as a nation-builder, evokes uncanny similarities with the official modes for memorializing some of Vietnam's most famous leaders, not least among them Ho Chi Minh himself. All the features of the standard Vietnamese leadership cult are present in these modes of telling Lawrence Ting's story—the language of developmentalism, the expressed love of country, the stories of vision, the subordination of self-interest to a greater cause, the images of the benevolent leader earning the smiles of innocent youth, and of course, the story of a visionary vanguard clearing wastelands and making them productive. Photographs of Ting—often standing alongside then–Prime Minister Võ Văn Kiệt and other national and city leaders, poring over maps and slashing through scrub forests—recall some of the most famous images of the Vietnam War–era leaders as well.

## CONCLUSION: ALLEGORIES OF PERIURBAN DEVELOPMENT

The story of Phú Mỹ Hưng rising out of swamps recalls a well-known Vietnamese folk poem about the lotus flower rising out of mud, an image that is often said to stand for the Vietnamese people, who have suffered great hardship and yet still stand tall with dignity despite adverse circumstances. In similar ways, the story of Phú Mỹ Hưng's rapid development is commonly told as a tale of uplift that manages to speak to the nationalist pride of the Vietnamese people. Although the story of rising from the wasteland resonates with Vietnamese historical narratives of civilizational conquest, the practice of linking urban development to larger ideological or political agendas is by no means uniquely Vietnamese. Describing master-planned developments across Asia, the planning scholar Gavin Shatkin perceptively notes that the stories told about these large-scale urban developments are often constructed as "allegories—as idealized visions intended to illustrate a possible urban future."[80] This is certainly true in the case of Phú Mỹ Hưng, where the development story depicts a certain kind of civilizational alchemy, of turning wasteland into land more valuable than gold and of bringing pride to Ho Chi Minh City and the Vietnamese people. Within the specific context of postreform-era Vietnam, thirty years after the famous Sixth Congress of the Vietnamese Communist Party initiated the market reforms known as Đổi Mới in 1986, this alchemy is also commonly linked to a narrative of political and economic enlightenment or "reawakening," or a movement from darkness to light.[81]

The story told about Phú Mỹ Hưng rising out of the swamps and becoming a quintessentially modern urban development (with buildings constructed largely out of bright white cement) fits this enlightenment storyline perfectly, and the timeline of the project's history, traced to 1989, even further enhances the way the development can be told as a tale of political emergence linked to the early history of renovation. It is no accident, for example, that the main boulevard running through the New Urban Zone is named after Nguyễn Văn Linh, who was general secretary of the Communist Party of Vietnam when the renovation policies were introduced in 1986. For those who built it, and for most of those who live there, the development is not just a smart investment or a fancy place to live, but is touted as a model of and a model for urban governance in the age of market-oriented socialism. The Đổi Mới story of lightness emerging out of darkness finds its symbolic expression in Phú Mỹ Hưng's story of beauty rising out of the mud, and the dualistic themes of Manichean struggle are well served by the triumphant story of large-scale urban development turning waste into economic gold.

But the story of Phú Mỹ Hưng does something even more complex. While it clearly marks a rupture with select aspects of the socialist past, it also manages to emphasize a sense of continuity with a longer nationalist history of Vietnamese development that supersedes dichotomies of capitalism and socialism, speaking instead to a more transcendent Vietnamese logic of a people constantly marching toward civilization. The story of Phú Mỹ Hưng rising out of a wasteland does not completely forsake the past, but it does so selectively, and links its own success to a traditional Vietnamese trope about the way wonderful things can result from adversity, and how beauty can emerge from the most inhospitable conditions, like a lotus flower rising from the muddy swamps without the stink.

It is true that the schools, the boulevards, and apartments like Grandview, Skygarden, and Happy Valley did not exist before the Phú Mỹ Hưng Corporation built them. And many of the city's residents are happy to see these new developments being built, sharing in the belief that building a new city is not just a form of real estate development but part of a plan to remake the city, remake society, and remake the people who make the city up. The next two chapters will look more closely at some of these people living in Phú Mỹ Hưng and listen to the reasons why they find this vision of civility so compelling. In the private spaces and mani-cured gardens of Phú Mỹ Hưng, many of these people claim to have discovered what they call new forms of civility (the subject of chapter 2) and even conscious-ness (the subject of chapter 3). In the process, they are also writing themselves into the longer Vietnamese story, so commonly told, of civilizing the wastelands.

# Civilization City

*Eventually, he married a rich wife and adopted the surname Văn Minh, meaning "civilization"—a fact suspiciously noted by the Security Office. Through intensified surveillance they discovered that he had added his wife's surname, Văn (literature), to his own name, Minh (light), hence creating the new name. He saw the placement of his wife's name before his own as a simple act of gallantry and not, as others had surmised, as a protest against patriarchy or an attempt to spearhead some sort of national or international reform movement. In fact, it signified nothing at all.*

— VŨ TRỌNG PHỤNG, *DUMB LUCK*

### FANTASY, AND BEAUTIFUL, AND CIVILIZE . . . ATION. CIVILIZED

Lucy and Jake study at the Lawrence S. Ting School in Phú Mỹ Hưng. Neither Lucy nor Jake lives in Phú Mỹ Hưng, but they commute there daily for school. Their friend Tom, who is also in their class, recently moved into a Phú Mỹ Hưng apartment complex called Skygarden with his parents and younger brother. All three students are in the same English class and have given themselves American names (not the same ones I have given them here). During my time living and conducting research in Phú Mỹ Hưng, we developed a friendly relationship. They would sometimes ask me about life in the United States (and how to get into college), and I would ask them about their impressions of the New Urban Zone. On one such occasion, I asked them if I could record their answers to the following question: "What do you think about Phú Mỹ Hưng?" This is how they replied, in English:

*Lucy:* Fantasy, expensive.

*Jake:* Expensive, luxurious.

*Lucy:* Fantasy . . .

*Erik:* Fantasy?

*Lucy:* Yeah. Fantasy, and beautiful, and civilize . . . ation. Civilized. [EH: hmm.] Modern. [EH: Civilized, huh?] Yeah.

*Jake:*   And I heard people, uh, talking about Phú Mỹ Hưng like it's a dream of a lifetime. Something like that. [EH: really?] Yeah.

*Tom:*   I have an aunt who, um, lives in District One, somewhere near . . . in Điện Biên Phủ Street. And then, you know, in the summer, she, sometimes she'll go here and rent an apartment in Skygarden.

*Erik:*   Just for the summer?

*Tom:*   Just for . . . yeah, a few days in the summer. And she said that, you know, Phú Mỹ Hưng is like Singapore. [Erik: uh, huh.] You know, Phú Mỹ Hưng is just like a Singapore. It's so convenient for resting and staying and, you know, and getting some entertainments here.

Lucy, Tom, and Jake, who were then in the ninth grade, echoed sentiments that I had heard repeatedly from people of all ages throughout my fieldwork. "Phú Mỹ Hưng is like Singapore," people commonly told me: it is "a fantasy," "expensive," "luxurious," a "dream." When I told one of my own undergraduate students at Yale, who grew up in Ho Chi Minh City, that I was conducting a research project in Phú Mỹ Hưng, she laughed: "Well, if you can do research there, then I'd like to do a project in Beverly Hills!" In addition to all these things, Phú Mỹ Hưng is also, people repeatedly told me, "beautiful," "modern," and "civilized."

Many of these terms in fact blend seamlessly into each other, spilling forth from people's lips in a stream when they try to articulate what they think about Phú Mỹ Hưng. Later, in this same conversation, I asked Lucy what she meant by the term she had stumbled on: "civilize . . . ation. Civilized." I was not surprised to hear her use the term, because I had heard it used repeatedly during my research whenever people sought to describe the New Urban Zone. I also understood why she waffled between the verb, noun, and adjective forms of the word—she was translating as she spoke, trying to find the English equivalent for the Sino-Vietnamese word *văn minh,* a term that can, depending on context, mean civility, civilization, or civilized. But what, I asked her, did the word really *mean* to her? What kinds of images and associations did it conjure up when she used it to describe Phú Mỹ Hưng? Responding to my question, she explained that Phú Mỹ Hưng could be called "civilized" because it is "new" and "modern." Listening in, Jake and Tom agreed, and then added that people in Phú Mỹ Hưng are objectively more civilized than people in other parts of the city, because of "the way they act in public."

The purpose of this chapter is to linger on these kinds of descriptions about Phú Mỹ Hưng, and to think critically about what kinds of associations and meanings are wrapped up into the idea of living in a new urban zone in contemporary Ho Chi Minh City. I focus especially on the contextual and everyday uses of the ideas of civility, being civilized, and building a new kind of urban civilization. Other scholars have explored the historical meanings of the term *văn minh,* which entered popular Vietnamese usage in the early years of the twentieth century.[1] But rather than attempt to trace the origins of the term, my purpose here is to look ethnographically at how this language of civility is used to describe the contemporary city: to show how it springs forth from a nexus of fantasy and aspiration, but also how these fantasies are linked to dreams about social order—the wish people have to imagine new ways that they and their fellow citizens might "act in public." In doing so, I give special attention to how people I came to know closely in Phú Mỹ Hưng articulate the idea of civility as a way of imagining possibilities for new forms of social interaction. Like most anthropologists, I have personal and professional misgivings about terms like *civility, civilized,* and *civilization,* but my purpose here is to suspend my doubts for a period in order to take what people have to say about these concepts seriously, to try to contextualize them and understand them as part of the aspirational desires people so clearly articulated in their conversations with me.

## A CIVILIZED AND HUMANISTIC COMMUNITY

Phú Mỹ Hưng, according to the official English translation of its slogan, is a "civilization-city—human-oriented community."[2] The slogan appears on the logo of the Phú Mỹ Hưng Corporation and is printed on banners and placards throughout the development. The concept is also invoked in official rules and regulations as well as other contexts, including but not limited to the company's website, its glossy monthly news magazine, the notices stapled to the bulletin boards near apartment mailboxes, various flyers the customer service department sends to residents, and the large signs, printed in both Vietnamese and English, that instruct people on the proper ways to comport themselves in any of Phú Mỹ Hưng's many manicured parks; for example: "Visitors are required to behave a cultural and civilized lifestyle at public places" (fig. 2.1).[3] If there is one thing that Phú Mỹ Hưng's developers celebrate most, it is their claim to foster the construction of *văn minh.*

### Hegemonic Civility

The term *văn minh* is derived from the Chinese *wenming,* which, like the Vietnamese expression, can also be fairly accurately translated, depending on context, as civilization, civility, or being civilized. Scholars of contemporary China have analyzed the way this concept, like other forms of self-discipline such as "population quality" or "harmony," buttresses new forms of hegemonic control.[4] Writing of the emergence of a "civility pact" in Chinese urban developments, for example, the anthropologist Li Zhang convincingly shows that civility can be understood as a new form of governmentality through which everyday citizens willingly learn to police themselves and their actions, thereby internalizing forms of social control formerly directed by the Chinese Communist Party.[5] In anthropology as a whole, it should be noted, terms like *civility* or *civilization* are generally subjected to harsh

FIGURE 2.1. Park signs outlining required civilized behavior, in English and Vietnamese. Phú Mỹ Hưng. Author's photo, January 2011.

criticism, associated as they all too often are with forms of colonial domination, postcolonial authority, and hegemonic class exclusion. Among anthropologists, all one needs is a whiff of the term *civility,* and surely the stench of hegemony is bound to follow.[6]

Scholars familiar with Vietnamese history and society have many good reasons to look critically at civilizing discourses, which have been connected to histories of domination and exploitation associated with a range of governing regimes. It is well known, for example, that a civilizing discourse was used to legitimize some of the most unsavory aspects of French colonialism, which famously justified itself as a *mission civilisatrice.* However, the language of civility also offered some anticolonial Vietnamese intellectuals a powerful response to French cultural chauvinism. For some, the idea of *văn minh* helped express a concept of indigenous Vietnamese civilization as an alternative to colonial rule, one that could be celebrated as part of the Vietnamese emergence onto the world stage of equal civilizations.[7] But even if the cultivation of *văn minh* had anticolonial connotations for some, there were also important reasons to be skeptical about who in Vietnam truly gained from the celebration of civility. The idea of civility tended to prioritize elite culture, which sometimes conflated material extravagance with civility. In the 1930s, the famed satirist Vũ Trọng Phụng was highly critical of the term. In a recent study, Peter Zinoman shows how many of Vũ Trọng Phụng's works pointedly mocked the ways in which "agents of materialism" often deployed terms like *văn minh* to "hypocritically mask the destructive cultural impact of their efforts."[8]

Vũ Trọng Phụng's critiques ultimately proved prescient. In the postcolonial context, the term *văn minh* tied into some of the most sobering moments in the history of Vietnam's authoritarian brand of top-down socialism, a history in which the Vietnamese Communist Party often used the concept of *văn minh* or closely related concepts of "culture" *(văn hóa)* to justify its own rigid and stultifying vision for building New Socialist Man.[9] The idea of *văn minh* has also been central to the ways ethnic Vietnamese majority peoples (Kinh), both communist and anticommunist, have long legitimized their often violent denigration of ethnic minorities living on the margins of the nation-state.[10] And today, when Vietnamese use the concept of *văn minh* to refer to other Vietnamese, it is commonly uttered by urbanites attempting to denigrate the peasantry or enforce spatial segregation and class-based forms of urban exclusion.[11] When the term *văn minh* is used as a way of asserting class distinction, the implication is typically quite clear: some people have it, and some people don't.

But what does *văn minh* mean to those Vietnamese who have chosen to make a life in Phú Mỹ Hưng? Is it just an empty slogan—a late-socialist update on a long history of empty civilizing slogans, with precolonial, colonial, and postcolonial high-socialist precedents? Are the young kids at the beginning of this chapter intentionally seeking to impose their will-to-power over less powerful others? Or does civility operate on other levels as well, perhaps even promising something to the people who choose to live in Phú Mỹ Hưng? Answering these questions is in fact a surprisingly complex task, because *văn minh* is itself a slippery, many-faced concept. *Văn minh* certainly does have the capacity to embolden and legitimize the most disingenuous forces of elitism and political control. Yet it also offers, in unexpected ways that scholars too often ignore, the potential to mount innovative forms of critical resistance to the social and political status quo. In this way, *văn minh* swings like a pendulum between asymptotic poles of power and resistance: while it can swing into the realm of dogma and ideology, it can also quickly swing back into the realm of socio-political critique. The same idioms used as tactics of domination can be recast in the language of resistance. Similarly, while in some cases the term might be taken quite seriously and uttered with very real sincerity, in other cases it may be uttered with a sense of irony, sarcasm, or duplicity. In this feedback loop, the nature and meaning of *văn minh* quickly becomes quite muddled. The concept that emerges is one riven through with multiple meanings, becoming what Homi Bhabha calls "sly civility."[12]

### Civility's Double-Edge

There is no better place to see the ambivalent and contradictory potential of *văn minh* than in master-planned communities like Phú Mỹ Hưng, where the lived expression of civility works at once to legitimize socio-economic exclusion and to give voice to people who see themselves as trying to change the socio-political status quo. To demonstrate this, I focus at length in this chapter on the example of three strong-minded and independent women who evoke civility to challenge patriarchal authority and to assert their social and political rights to fair treatment. Even if it is not always clear what these different women mean when they invoke the concept of civility, in all three cases they deploy the concept as a means to comment on the actions of others, and to express their hopes and aspirations for the way they wish others would act in relationship to each other. In other words, the term *văn minh* allows them to express their expectations of citizenship and collective behavior. This is significant in the Vietnamese context, because the quest for open political expression and the will to express idioms of formal citizenship are often met by severe state repression. Within this context, despite its often unsavory pretensions to elitism, the language of civility sometimes affords a way to speak critically about moral relationships, to make demands about social rights and responsibilities, and to engage in a critical discourse that in other political systems might be understood as a political discourse of citizenship. It allows one to talk politics without being political. But this is also where the muddle thickens: as people deploy civility to resist forces they deem oppressive, and as they deploy its language to make claims about how they wish to be treated by others, they themselves are also compelled to exert the oppressive force of civility on others. In the process civility potentially delivers inclusion to some while excluding others.

I suggest that it is here, in this muddle of contradictory meanings, where the problematic discourse of civility gains its staying power: ostensible civilizers do not always see themselves as engaging first and foremost in acts of exclusion or willful domination of others, but more often see themselves as good-hearted, forward-thinking people. In some cases, they even see themselves as radical reformers fighting for certain kinds of rights that they feel have long been denied to them and to others. In the process, most people rarely think of civility as a means to deny other people "rights to the city" or to actively exclude them from urban space. In many cases, they see civility as a mechanism for agitating *for* a sense of rights, which are construed as emerging out of a set of obligations and responsibilities to members of a collective. For this reason, if we wish to understand how civility manages to persist as a mechanism of exclusion, and why the idea of a "civilized" new urban zone holds such attraction for so many people, we must begin by understanding the ways it often appears to those who wield it as an idiom of inclusion and liberation. Civility gives as much as civility takes away.

In everyday usage, the concept of civility is most commonly framed in benevolent, aspirational terms, employing an idiom that Tania Li has called the "will to improve."[13] In her influential analysis of development programs over two centuries in Indonesia, Li demonstrates how processes of plunder and exclusion are often intimately tied into—and essentially masked by—programs ostensibly designed to improve society. As a result, what ought to be recognized as processes of capitalist extraction and political-economic inequality are often framed in terms of benevolent uplift, and the logic of improvement commonly conceals the deep inequities that hinder attempts to improve the lot of so many people. This line of analysis is clearly relevant to the case of Phú Mỹ Hưng. The very nature of the development itself promotes obvious forms of inequality and spatial segregation, but the everyday  language used among residents, planners, and developers is almost always framed as a language of improvement.[14] Some of this discourse is of course consciously manipulated by property developers to legitimize their profit-seeking intentions. But as Li carefully notes, improvement is not always born from malicious intent, and the political-economic inequities masked by the will to improve are often unintentional. People generally see their quests for improvement as projects intended to contribute to the greater good. For this reason, Li observes, it is sometimes necessary to "take seriously the proposition that the will to improve can be taken at its word."[15] In the rest of this chapter I follow this approach as I relate the stories of three women, whom I call Ngọc, Hà, and Hương. In so doing, I listen carefully to their ideas about civility, and take them at their word. They are not Communist Party officials; they are not property developers; and they are not extraordinarily wealthy. But they take the idea of civility and new forms of urban consciousness very seriously.

## NGỌC: FROM GENDER VIOLENCE TO STABILITY

Ngọc was thirty-seven years old when I met her in 2011. She owned a French-inspired garden-style café with a wide, covered terrace in Phú Mỹ Hưng. She was (and still is) an exceedingly busy woman, and we had to squeeze our discussions in between the business deals she was constantly arranging on her cell phone, as she sat, laptop open, at a table she always claimed in the corner of her café.[16] In addition to running her café, she worked as an export broker, connecting Vietnamese specialty-food producers and craft-good suppliers with foreign clients and then arranging the export of anything from seafood and spices to flower pots and rattan goods. In recent months she had arranged the sale of dried fish to Nigeria; frozen fish, clothes, and jewelry to Europe; and octopus and handbags to Japan. As she put it, it was possible to make a lot more money from a few phone calls than from several months running a cafe. But even though running the café was "tiring" and not so profitable, she insisted that it was important to her, because she saw it as her small contribution to the social life of Phú Mỹ Hưng. She said her café provided a civilized space where people could come for conversation and interaction. And to really understand why having a civilized place was so important, she said she would have to tell me her life story.

### Ngọc's Story

Ngọc's present-day successes masked a life of struggle. She was scarred—*literally*, by repeated incidents of domestic violence, and *emotionally* by a lifetime of deceptions and injustices. Ngọc was born in 1974 in her paternal grandfather's house on the edge of the city (in Hóc Môn District); her mother then moved the family to her maternal hometown in Đồng Tháp Mười Province in the Mekong Delta when Ngọc's father was sent to a reeducation camp shortly after the end of the war in 1975. Ngọc had many nostalgic memories of the countryside and jokingly called herself a country bumpkin *(nhà quê),* but she also said that life in the provinces was not easy. Eighteen months of reeducation had driven her father mad, and he vented his inner frustrations by regularly beating Ngọc and her mother. Her mother's mother, *bà ngoại,* was no saint either, and added to the family troubles by accumulating onerous gambling debts, which ate up the family resources. It made for a tough childhood, and Ngọc had almost no material comforts growing up. At one point in her story she paused and asked me to linger on a single image, which was still vivid in her mind after all these years: as a little girl she used to stand next to a food vendor near her mother's house and stare dreamily at a fuzzy colored keychain that always dangled from the vendor's display case. She remembered out loud how badly she had wanted to have something beautiful like that keychain. But such an extravagant luxury was well beyond her reach.

Her youth had been a life of denial. She loved to sing, for example, but her grandfather always scolded her when she sang out loud, telling her that singing was for "bad people." Eventually, when she was around eighteen, she defied her grandfather and went off to sing in a circus troupe, where she spent a year traveling throughout the Mekong Delta by boat, singing in backwater towns. She never did anything "bad" during those travels, but ultimately, she said, fate may have proved her grandfather right. Her move to Saigon, in 1994, when she was about twenty years old, set her off on a long tumultuous journey of gendered exploitation out of which she was only now emerging.

Her life in Saigon all started with her "auntie," who suddenly showed up one day at her grandmother's home bearing a beautiful dress. "A gift! For me!" she said, recalling her excitement, and using the English word *auntie* to describe her mother's sister who had brought her the wonderful surprise. As she began to tell this story, however, I noticed that she began to nervously rub her hands across the raised ridges of a series of scars on her arm. Ngọc noticed me trying (but failing) to avoid looking at the scars and looked me directly in the eyes, drawing me into her story: "It was my *auntie*," she said in a serious voice, still rubbing the scars. Then, switching back to Vietnamese, she told me how her auntie gave her the dress and then took her to Saigon, where she had promised to take her to a restaurant to work as a waitress.

When they got to the restaurant in Saigon, Ngọc noticed that the restaurant didn't have a kitchen, and there was no dining room. But by then her aunt had already whispered a few words to the owner, dropped her off, and driven away. "What kind of restaurant is this?" she recalled asking herself. The restaurant did not in fact serve food, but instead offered *"bia ôm"* (hugging beer). At this curious restaurant, she and the other girls were expected to join male customers in small individual rooms, where they were told to sell as much beer as they could. If they wanted to earn any money for themselves, they would need to solicit tips by letting the men fondle them.[17] Her aunt had earlier promised her that the restaurant owners would teach her how to work as "a waitress," but Ngọc did not stick around for the lessons.[18] She managed to run away, living for a time in a church until she found a job at a fried chicken restaurant on Pasteur Street in District Three.

According to Ngọc, the Vietnamese sometimes say that the worst fate for a woman is to be born beautiful.[19] Ngọc suffered from this fate, and her boss at the restaurant turned out to be a lecherous womanizer, who constantly subjected her to unwanted sexual advances. By then she had a boyfriend, but she said he was a "weak" man—just a boy, really—and did nothing to stand up for her in the face of her boss. So she left the job, ditched the boyfriend, and decided to put her beauty to work by taking up a job as a Dunhill cigarette girl, dressing in tight miniskirts while toting a box of cigarettes to sell to drunk men across a wide circuit of the city's many bars and sidewalk drinking places *(quán nhậu)*. She endured ogling and unwanted touches, but made a stable salary of US$130 per month. Her work there soon landed her a higher-paying job working for a well-known foreign beverage distributor—doing similar work, wearing similar clothes, but making more money. She quickly caught the eye of the company's Scandinavian regional manager, who ensured that she got promoted to progressively higher paying positions, and always made sure that she was invited to special events. He also made sure that she noticed the special way he looked at her. They soon got married.

Her Scandinavian husband was well respected in the business community and earned a generous salary. They lived an expensive lifestyle in a fine villa in the elite foreign enclave of An Phú, an upscale riverfront district across the Saigon Bridge from downtown. But for all his initial charms, her new husband was also a philandering drunk with a violent streak—he physically injured her on multiple occasions. She wanted to leave him, but he was the father of Ngọc's only daughter and he threatened to take the child back to Europe and cut Ngọc off from all financial support. He had connections and expensive lawyers, and she had nothing but her stubbornness. Reaching this point in her story, Ngọc suddenly paused. She smiled a wry smile, cocked her head, and looked me straight in the eyes. Then she said that bad fortune sometimes slips into good: one of her husband's bursts of violence had been so excessive that their maid started screaming and called the police. It turned out that he was the source of all the scars on her arm. The newspapers even ended up reporting on the case, it had been so bad. When the world eventually saw his bad side, Ngọc said, she was finally able to reach a settlement that gave her custody of her daughter and some property to start a new life.[20]

Bad fortune, when bad enough, sometimes slips into good. This was how Ngọc got the money to start her café. She sold the upscale apartment she had received as a form of hush money in conjunction with the divorce. And now she lives in Phú Mỹ Hưng, in the Skygarden apartments, not far from her café. Things had since stabilized, and she had married again, this time to an Englishman. She wouldn't say his age but only said, "He is very old" (over sixty) and that he liked to stay at home and watch television all day. His favorite thing to do was to draw a bath, turn on music, and relax. He wasn't even interested in going out for meals but bought prepared foods to eat at home. He was not particularly exciting, and they rarely did anything together, but she said she liked it this way. She had already had enough excitement in her life.

Then—as if out of nowhere—Ngọc "concluded" this long and rather devastating story with a simple assertion: "That was my life before. Phú Mỹ Hưng is more civilized [văn minh]. Creating civility [văn minh] is the biggest issue facing Vietnam today. There is so much mention of civility here [in this country] because there is such an extreme lack of it."

### Ngọc's Attitudes about Civility in Phú Mỹ Hưng

What is the connection between Ngọc's statement about civility in Phú Mỹ Hưng and the life history she shared—punctuated by reeducation camps, family gambling debts, the shock of nearly being sold into sex work by a family member, and recurrent bouts of domestic violence? I asked her to explain what she meant: "What *is văn minh?*" At first Ngọc stumbled, saying that *văn minh* was connected to "having money" and "living in a sophisticated manner." But then she paused, shook her head, and tracked her words backwards, correcting herself by saying that many wealthy people were in fact not very civilized. The wealthy but morally bankrupt men in her story were obvious cases in point, but she added further examples, talking of people who drive fancy cars but still throw trash out the window and mentioning wealthy men who spend cash freely but still spit on the ground in restaurants. *No,* she explained, civility was in fact not about having money, but was a way of carrying oneself, a mode of comportment. For all the critiques of how civility is a form of power that commonly serves the interests of the powerful, Ngọc's assertion raised an important point about the critical potential it has to subvert such hierarchies even as it reproduces them. In mobilizing the power of civility as a normative frame for critiquing the conduct of others, Ngọc had in fact discovered a language of righteous indignation that presented a powerful critique of the gendered status quo.

Recapturing the terms of civility gave Ngọc an observable confidence. Her story until this point had been a tale of despair, and her voice had been heavy with gravitas. But her tone shifted when she began to mock the lack of civility she had witnessed throughout her life in Vietnam. She now adopted an energetic tone of satire, laughing out loud as she began to describe the litany of obscene male behaviors she had come to witness in her time running the café. Turning civility into a weapon of critique, she described rich Vietnamese businessmen who would show up in their shiny chauffeured cars, holding their heads higher than the rest of the population, elevated in their own minds as icons of civility but reduced to crass buffoonery by all who observed them.[21] Were they truly civilized? No. In fact, they expressed the opposite of civility. There was one man, for example, who often came to the café. He was clearly very wealthy, and he flaunted his money. But he acted, she said, like an ape. He would lay his overweight body on the couches in the restaurant, flicking cigarette ashes and even spitting on the floor. Although he would pay very large sums for expensive orders every time he came in, Ngọc recounted one occasion when she asked her waiter, a very poor student from the Mekong Delta, what he thought of this man: "Do you respect him?" "No," replied the waiter. "Would you want to be like him?" "No." Civility, she concluded, could not be found in one's wallet but was a matter of "consciousness" (ý thức).

Ngọc spoke of these uncivilized rich men with a calm matter-of-fact detachment, letting her observations speak for themselves, but she also allowed a sly grin to break her deadpan expression. Mixing objective observation with satire, her tone and her stories of uncivilized pretensions to civility recalled the wry wit of Lê Minh Khuê, the celebrated Vietnamese short-story writer who had herself mocked the false civility of the newly rich in similar ways. In a short story called "Scenes from an Alley," Lê Minh Khuê shatters the illusion of false civility proffered by a newly risen elite man who was promoted to a managerial position but nevertheless remained quite vulgar:

> Once he had established his career, he dropped his peasant's name in favor of something more refined. Now he called himself Toàn. He had a secretary and whenever they rode in a car together, he would get out first and open the door for her. He entertained his customers with Western whiskey. But even though he'd attained a high position and a great deal of wealth, he was uncultured. After work he would order the chauffeur to drive straight to a club. He was crazy about massage and he liked to hold the tender thighs of the young women sitting on his lap in the dark and dreamy atmosphere. All of his colleagues liked that as well. With a woman on either leg, the men would wrap their arms around the women's waists, open their mouths

and wait to be fed like babies. This was an unusual form of enjoyment that men in our country loved.[22]

The operative word in Lê Minh Khuê's critique is *uncultured,* just as the operative concept in Ngọc's critique is the lack of civility. Both Ngọc and Lê Minh Khuê challenge the capacity of such men to call themselves civilized. But in presenting the critique, this language of civility is also founded on a disparaging, dismissive characterization of others. Critiquing false civility means equating it with "uncultured" behavior, which itself normalizes the assumption that certain forms of behavior are necessarily inferior to the urbane behavior of certain groups.

In their critique of men who lack civility, neither Ngọc nor Lê Minh Khuê ever rejected civility itself as an ideal. Instead, they demanded more of it, and they insisted that there might in fact be a real civility that could be found in spaces beyond the charlatan versions they deride, a civility that runs deeper than mere appearances. After recounting her difficult life story, for example, Ngọc insisted that the problem in Vietnam was the *lack* of civility, and she went on to describe Phú Mỹ Hưng as a potential safeguard against the kinds of gendered violence and impunity she equated with uncivilized behavior. Far from rejecting the concept, she insisted that Phú Mỹ Hưng was indeed a civilized space and for that reason truly had potential for her as a space in which to build an alternative moral order, where an emphasis on disciplined comportment and behavior could improve a woman's lot—in fact, it might hold the aggressive hypermasculinity of Vietnamese male authority figures in check and even make them accountable for their actions.

Ngọc saw a political role for civility as well. As she continued explaining what she meant by the term, she did not focus on male buffoonery alone, but spoke even more pointedly about the way civility could be mobilized to critique the often arbitrary actions of the police and city authorities. Civility was not just a form of social comportment but was linked in her descriptions to rule-oriented behavior, which, in theory, should offer everyday residents a righteous recourse to the rule of law. To illustrate this, she listed a barrage of examples about the uncivilized actions of various actors she had confronted in the course of running her café—from local police who demanded kickbacks in exchange for allowing her to put tables on the sidewalk to a landlord who had failed to live up to the terms of a contract he had signed with her. In these discussions, she consistently referred to the need for the rule of law and highlighted specifically how her problems were being exacerbated by the local district *(phường)* authorities who regularly ignored the law. In contrast to these uncivilized actors, she insisted that she was always treated with consistency and respect by the civilized professionals at the Phú Mỹ Hưng Corporation.[23]

To illustrate what she meant by the lack of civility among the Vietnamese police, she showed me a long series of text messages she had exchanged with a local police officer about his demands for bribes. The text messages showed him demanding money in order to allow her to continue setting up tables on the sidewalk in front of her café, and showed how she had been forced to "loan" him ten million đồng (approximately $US500). She also described how she had been forced to pay the local district $US100 a month under the table, but how the officials she had bribed became greedier and greedier and tried to accuse her of not having a license when she threatened to stop paying. When she did in fact stop paying them, they confiscated her tables and chairs. None of this kind of behavior ever happened during her interactions with the Phú Mỹ Hưng Corporation, but she said it was commonplace with the Vietnamese police and officials from the ward and city district. She insisted that the Vietnamese system of urban governance, unlike the Phú Mỹ Hưng Corporation, followed "the law of the jungle," and she even added that interacting with Vietnamese officials made it "hard for her to be a human." They made her feel like she was "an animal." As she said this, she looked at her own housecat, sleeping on the sill, and quickly added that the officials actually made her feel "worse than an animal." No one would ever treat a cat the way Vietnamese officials treated her.

Ngọc's critique and subsequent emphasis on the importance of civility is significant for its condemnation of officials employed by a state that claims to promote civility. But she makes this critique without rejecting the concept of civility itself; indeed, she expressly uses the terms of civility to mount her critique of urban administration. Her critique is not so much a challenge to the concept of civility as it is a skeptical reconsideration of who can honestly claim to embody it. The police, for example, may claim to be defending "order" *(trật tự),* which is itself a component of civility, but in fact they live by the "law of the jungle," the uncivilized realm of animals and raw nature.[24] And all of this brought us back to her café: she told me that she had come to Phú Mỹ Hưng for its tranquility and saw her café as making a small contribution to the emerging cultural consciousness that would define the district, a space for people to meet and engage in civilized conversation. Her efforts to make the café succeed in spite of all the uncivilized behavior of city officials, furthermore, served as evidence that civility required dedication and conviction. While it is true that civility in Vietnam is many ways entangled with the history of the *mission civilisatrice,* in this case Ngọc was engaging in a small-scale civilizing mission of her own. She was on a mission to civilize what she considered to be Vietnam's unruly and lecherous men, and to shame its corrupt cops and incompetent urban authorities into following the rule of law.

## HÀ: A SINGLE DIVORCED WOMAN

Ngọc was not the only woman I met who felt empowered by the kind of civility promised by Phú Mỹ Hưng. Another woman, Hà, who was thirty-five years old when I met her in 2012, gave a simple reason for moving to Phú Mỹ Hưng: she was divorced and was from Hanoi. Where else, she asked rhetorically, could she feel safe living alone in Ho Chi Minh City? After leaving a self-serving, narcissistic, unfaithful husband from a wealthy and self-righteous Hanoi family, she decided to move as far away as possible and start a new life in the south. She explained that she absolutely loved her studio apartment in the Skygarden complex because she felt secure there. It fostered in her a newfound sense of independence, far from the oppressive social structure she had fled from in Hanoi. At the same time, her new apartment complex felt more predictable and safe than neighborhoods she knew in the rest of Ho Chi Minh City, where she sometimes felt like an outsider constantly being scrutinized by the locals.

Hà was employed in a stable, well-paying job downtown as an agent for a foreign airline. She was able to purchase her studio apartment in Skygarden with a ten-year loan with affordable payments. (The apartment cost about $US90,000 in 2009.) She was delighted by the place. The one-room apartment was decorated in a modern style, with a stylish kitchen she designed herself and hand-painted walls created by a hip young artist, whom she hired to make the room evoke a scene from the south of France—it was vaguely Provençal, with yellow trim accented by a lavender flower motif. She had even purchased Provence-style glassware and tablecloths, evoking a kind of European sophistication, which she had cultivated through her work at the airline and by hanging out with her network of foreign acquaintances. The interior space was relatively small, and the bedroom flowed into the kitchen, separated only by the smartly set dining table. But her floor-to-ceiling sliding windows opened onto a large shared patio, where she sometimes held dinner parties with her friends. It was ideal, she said—small enough to keep life simple, but never cramped, and big enough to host guests when she felt inclined.

The only drawback to Phú Mỹ Hưng, Hà said, was the lack of things to do and the dangerous commute downtown. While it is only seven kilometers door-to-door from home to office, the road into town is hot and dusty in the dry season and muddy in the wet, and the traffic is erratic. The commute made her feel uneasy—the route passed through a crowded working-class district, and she often felt like she could be killed on the road at any moment. She did not have the means to "raise and care for" (nuôi) a car,[25] and she certainly could not afford a driver and didn't want to waste her money on daily taxi rides. Despite these difficulties, she had devised an ingenious solution. She rented a monthly parking space for her motorbike in District One and rode the comfortable, air-conditioned Phú Mỹ Hưng shuttle in and out of downtown each day. She only had to walk one block from the downtown shuttle stop to retrieve her motorbike, and then she could ride a few breezy blocks through the orderly downtown streets to work, where her office building had a subterranean parking garage. This gave her freedom and mobility when she was downtown, without forcing her to risk her life on the longer stretches through unruly periurban neighborhoods or suffer the discomfort of the daily commute. She had a favorite yoga class downtown, and she could zip there straight from work, go out with friends afterward, before returning her motorbike to the garage and taking the shuttle back home. It worked great!

In this way, Hà had overcome the fact that Phú Mỹ Hưng was a bit boring for a single woman (the yoga studios there are subpar, she noted in particular, and the restaurants are both overpriced and bland) but was still able to enjoy the peace and security she felt in her apartment. Even so, Hà's commute seemed quite complicated, and I wondered if she wasn't missing some of the joys of life in the city center. So I asked her why she didn't just find a place closer to downtown. She told me that she had tried living downtown but always found it alienating and unsafe. Although Vietnam was now unified and the division between north and south was supposedly relegated to the past, she confided that many northern transplants like her still felt like they might be cheated by Saigon locals—sometimes perhaps, because of lingering historical resentments, but more often due to the simple fact that they were not locals. They felt like easy marks for scams. But more importantly, she truly felt that the lifestyle in Phú Mỹ Hưng was more suitable to a single woman. She could come and go at any hour of the day, even late at night, and feel safe, and not have to endure the moralizing gossip or harassment so commonly endured by single women living in alleyways in the city. Life in the old Saigon alleyways, while fun and always interesting, was "complicated" *(phức tạp).* For example, she insisted that she was not a promiscuous woman, but she also said that she did not want to have to even think about what people would say if she had male guests visit her home. As evidence of that very point, she pointed out the fact that I was there, interviewing her in her apartment. In Phú Mỹ Hưng it was totally normal for a male to visit a female in her home; there was nothing to be suspicious about. But in other parts of the city, people would "talk."

Summing up the differences between Phú Mỹ Hưng and the rest of the city, Hà explained, rather bluntly, that the people in Phú Mỹ Hưng possessed a "higher consciousness" *(ý thức cao hơn).* On another occasion, while discussing life in Phú Mỹ Hưng at a local sushi restaurant, she mentioned a similar theme, saying that Phú Mỹ Hưng was more *"văn minh."* "Why is that?" I asked. She replied that it was quite simple, really. The people who choose to live in Phú Mỹ Hưng have a higher education level than others and are for that reason clearly more civilized.

In Hà's discussion of Phú Mỹ Hưng, the pendulum of civility swings back and forth. On the one hand, civility provides a progressive space of autonomy and releases her from the shackles of patriarchy, giving her a sense of freedom as a single woman. It offers a safe place for a divorced woman to craft her own lifestyle, on her own terms. On the other hand, the very space of liberation she described is founded on a discourse of exclusion in which she elevates herself into a hierarchal position of superiority, denigrating those outside her safe world as uneducated or having a "lower consciousness." She has achieved a form of inclusion that she could not find anywhere else in the city, but this inclusion rests on deep powers of exclusion.[26] In this case, gender inclusion comes at the expense of class exclusion. Civility gives and civility takes away.

## HƯƠNG: A MARRIED MOTHER OF TWO

These themes of security, safety, and consciousness were also important to Hương, who was forty-six years old when I met her in 2012 and who lived with her husband and two teenage sons in a three-bedroom apartment, also in the Skygarden complex. She also happens to be the mother of Tom, the boy at the beginning of this chapter who said his aunt thought Phú Mỹ Hưng is like Singapore. Hương's perspectives are especially illuminating, because she had a complex and multifaceted way of thinking about the concept of *văn minh*. On some levels, she dismissed the term as little more than an advertising slogan, but on different levels she insisted that life in Phú Mỹ Hưng truly represented what she called an "ideological revolution" that contributed to the production of new kinds of consciousness, which actually enacted what she considered to be an authentic experience of civility. Like Ngọc and Hà, in order to fully explain what so impressed her about Phú Mỹ Hưng, Hương had to tell me her story.

Born in Saigon in 1966, Hương's childhood roughly coincided with the tail end of the Vietnam War. She came of age during the postwar subsidy period *(thời bao cấp)* and the failed attempts to institute collective agriculture in the southern parts of the country. During the postwar period, food had been scarce and people constantly worried about the unpredictability of government policies. The city was a mess: infrastructure was failing, everyone flaunted zoning rules; it was poor, dirty, crowded, hot, and chaotic. To make matters worse, the urban political system was rife with corruption—underpaid and morally suspect police and urban officials at all levels did not work to protect and serve but instead sought bribes and kickbacks. Thus, when Hương first visited Phú Mỹ Hưng she said that she was immediately struck by the modern amenities and by the clear and straightforward interactions she had with sales staff and company officials. For these reasons, the New Urban Zone stood out in her mind as a dramatic example of social change—it inspired confidence and trust. But if change held out promises, she also worried about the hidden costs. How, she wondered, would it be possible to reconcile apartment living with traditional Vietnamese conceptions of home? For Hương, as for most of the people she knew, having a home meant building something directly on one's own plot of land. If you lived in an apartment, she remembered wondering, where was your land? Confronting this new mode of living and all of the uncertainties it implied, Hương and her husband took a very long time to decide to move into Phú Mỹ Hưng.

Their search for a home began back in 2001, when she and her husband had finally saved enough money to move out on their own. Until then, they had lived with her husband's parents in District Eight while working to save up a nest egg.[27] When they had accumulated 165 taels *(cây)* of gold (approx. $US64,285),[28] they started traveling around the city looking at properties. Hương said that she and her husband immediately thought the Phú Mỹ Hưng model apartments were like a "dream" *(giấc mơ)* because they were so clean and modern, just like they imagined life in a foreign country might be. The apartment prices were within their reach, but Hương and her husband were both excited and afraid of this new form of living. They faced a very difficult choice, which she described in great detail:

*Hương:* It was a huge dream. [ . . . ] the first time we had seen Phú Mỹ Hưng was in 2001. And so there we were, standing before a huge decision: return to District One or go to Phú Mỹ Hưng? And I can tell you this, professor,[29] we still had the psychology and thinking of the old generation *[cái tâm lý và cái tư tưởng của thế hệ cũ]*, which meant that what was important for us was having a home that was built directly on top of the land so that we could build up, and if we had more money, we could build higher.

*Erik:* Hmm.

*Hương:* In Phú Mỹ Hưng they offered only *"Apartments"* [she used the English word here] or land, but the houses built on land in areas like Mỹ Kim [a villa section in Phú Mỹ Hưng] were beyond our reach—500 taels [of gold]—beyond our reach. But homes in [some parts of] District One were around 165 taels, which was within our reach. So then, with our 165 taels we were faced with the choice: buy a home built on a plot of land or buy an apartment? Now I'm sorry, professor, but of course we chose the house built on a plot of land.

*Erik:* Hmm.

*Hương:* We did not have enough self-confidence to demolish that way of thinking *[phá vỡ cái tư tưởng đó]* in order to buy an *"Apartment."* So at that time my husband and I would go back and forth every day to look at Phú Mỹ Hưng. We saw everything, and were shown all the aspects, but when we had to choose between the two, we knew that we had to choose District One. And then we promised ourselves that ten years later we would try to get to Phú Mỹ Hưng.

So it was. In 2001 they bought a house in District One, in an alleyway off of Trần Hưng Đạo Street, for 165 taels of gold. She added: "Buying an apartment is ideologically revolutionary *[tư tưởng cách mạng]*! It's a new idea. A change to the new *[đổi mới]*." But at that time they felt that they were not quite ready for a revolution, choosing instead to stay with what Hương called the "older" way of living.

In the recording of this interview, Hương's choice of language is noticeably dramatic. She describes this new potential living space as deeply infused with meaning and social significance: the idea of living in an *Apartment* evoked larger conceptions about society, politics, and consciousness. Hương was not a cadre—and was in fact quite critical of government policy and anything that smacked of "communism"—but she nevertheless spoke of a kind of revolution in consciousness, using language that converged in many ways with government discourses. Indeed, in making this connection, she specifically used the word for revolution, *cách mạng*. Furthermore, the specific term she used to emphasize change, *đổi mới*, is of course famously associated with the very sort of reforms that had changed the country's political orientation over the previous three decades. Recalling themes discussed in the previous chapter about how Phú Mỹ Hưng at times came to symbolize the clearing of a wasteland and a vanguard political movement, Hương's comments emphasized the notion that Phú Mỹ Hưng represented a symbolic break with an older way of thinking. This idea was common not only among cadres and developers, but also among everyday residents.[30]

In 2009, Hương's son Tom got accepted into the Lawrence S. Ting School (discussed in chapter 1). This school styled itself as a kind of revolutionary "fence breaker" in the field of education, with its new kind of curriculum and modern teaching methods. Although it followed "foreign methods" and sought to meet international standards, classes were still taught in Vietnamese, and students still engaged in the study of Vietnamese history and culture. Tom was a very promising student, but Hương and her husband worried that he lost valuable study time riding the bus back and forth to school each day. So they decided that it was a good time to realize the promise they had made themselves of someday moving to Phú Mỹ Hưng. Tom would be able to walk to school if they lived there, and they also believed the quiet environment would be good for his studies.

By this time, Hương had been working for a few years for CB Richard Ellis, an international real estate firm, and she had become more and more familiar with the merits of apartment living. She was, as she explained, developing the kind of consciousness she would need to break free from the "old ways," by which people felt compelled to live in homes that touched the surface of the earth. Furthermore, she and her husband had devised a plan that would make a move work out well financially. Because they had paid for their District One property in a lump sum, they had no mortgage; they could rent that house out and use the income to pay off the loan they needed to take out for an apartment in Phú Mỹ Hưng.[31] In 2009, therefore, they moved to Phú Mỹ Hưng and had been living there ever since.

Hương had initially been afraid that apartment living would be something of a cultural shock. One of her primary concerns was whether her family would be able to control the geomantic properties of their living space. Skygarden apartments were in such demand that they had to be sold by lottery, and she worried that there would be no way to consult a master of *phong thủy* (feng shui) or that she'd have no way to choose a home facing in an auspicious direction suited to her family members' own personal attributes. But as she told the story, Hương began laughing out loud, insisting that her fears had all been unfounded. She pointed out, for example, that she ultimately ended up with a house on the eighth floor, which symbolized prosperity; furthermore, the apartment actually faced in a better orientation than their previous house had. After moving into the apartment, they were also able to employ a *phong thủy* master with little difficulty. At one point, I asked her how she and her husband chose where to put their ancestral altars. She replied:

*Hương:* We let the *phong thủy* master decide.

   *Erik:* Oh really?

*Hương:* Yes. We believed in him so much. He decided where to put the altar, where to put the study desks for the two kids, the desk for my husband, where the living room should be.

*[ . . . ]*

   *Erik:* Where do you find those people?

*Hương:* I work in real estate, so I know a lot of people.

*[ . . . ]*

*Hương:* They consider *phong thủy* a science; they study it and then practice it. And by word of mouth, one person tells another. They practice very well. You see, if you practice *phong thủy* for your house, you have peace in life. Or if you care about advancing your career or any other things, then you need *phong thủy*. That's what they say.

   *Erik:* Right.

*Hương:* Each person has his own goal in life. For me, my goal is for my family to be happy, the kids to study well. I told this to the *phong thủy* master and asked him to help me achieve that goal.

Her fears of culture shock proved exaggerated. It turned out that there were quite straightforward technical solutions for reconciling apartment living with traditional Vietnamese culture. With the aid of a *phong thủy* master, spirits could be controlled, ancestors could find their proper place in the home, and spiritual practices could be accommodated to a modern lifestyle.

Ultimately, the "ideological revolution" Hương had expected was not a cultural one. She had no real difficulty adjusting to apartment living. Instead, she explained, the real revolution took place in the realm of administration, in social comportment, and even in the sense people had about rights and responsibilities when living in an apartment. While she admitted that she was a bit saddened by the fact that few people knew their neighbors in the apartment buildings (whereas everyone knew everyone in residential alleyways downtown), she repeatedly emphasized that life in Phú Mỹ Hưng was liberating because she almost never had to interact with the city government. It was this sense of living in a world somewhat insulated from the Vietnamese political system that proved to be one of the most welcome features of life in the New Urban Zone. All of the interactions she might have previously had with Vietnamese ward or district-level offices were now largely handled directly by the Phú Mỹ Hưng Corporation. It was here, she said, where the concept of "civility" became real to her, when it was realized in actual behavior, and in the mode of managing urban life that was founded on a sense of responsibility and the disciplined conduct of conduct.

### Civility as Empty Slogan and as Lived Reality

According to Hương, the concept of *văn minh* is both vacuous and real at the same time. On the one hand, as someone involved in the real estate business herself, she said quite directly that she thought the use of the term was nothing more than a marketing slogan. For that reason, she didn't think about it much and considered it to be just an "abstract" idea. She did not, she said, spend her days walking around wondering, "What is *văn minh?*" But at the same time, when I asked her specifically what she thought about the Phú Mỹ Hưng Corporation's use of *văn minh* as a slogan, she insisted that she felt that Phú Mỹ Hưng in many ways "expressed" *(thể hiện)* a true sense of civility. Just as Ngọc had explained the difference between a false and a real civility, Hương insisted that one should ignore formal pronouncements about civility and instead pay attention to the ways in which people acted. In doing so, she said, it was possible to see that Phú Mỹ Hưng was in fact more civilized than other parts of the city—not because the corporation said so in its advertisements, but because people's actions and consciousness demonstrated it in everyday life. When I asked her again what *văn minh* meant to her, she offered a thoughtful answer:

*Hương:*  I do not care much about that [referring to *văn minh*]. I care about whether it is clean, safe, and has a lot of green trees. If a place satisfies all that, I think that it is already civilized. I think so because in District One [downtown Ho Chi Minh City] it is very dirty; there is litter everywhere. Here, people are mindful of the environment, and Phú Mỹ Hưng itself takes the matter of cleanliness and safety very seriously. I think all of that combined make this place civilized.

What is interesting here is that she first says that she "does not care" about *văn minh* but then almost immediately offers up examples of things that she feels "make this place civilized." Turning toward concrete examples—which she consistently favored over abstract terminology—she then began to reflect on the way people drive in traffic as evidence of civilized behavior and consciousness:

*Hương:* In addition to that I think people here drive slowly. They don't drive too fast. They respect the traffic lights. Outside of Phú Mỹ Hưng, traffic lights are only effective when there are police officers standing by them. Without the police the lights are always green. [ . . . ] It doesn't matter what colors the lights are, they all mean green! [Laughing] Here, I observe, people respect the traffic lights, people do stop at red lights. Even on the street to Đinh Thiện Lý [Lawrence S. Ting] school, professor . . . What is the name of the street, dear?

While discussing traffic behavior as a sign of civility, she asked her son, who had just joined us, to help her remember the name of the street. Hương's son said that the street was called Nguyễn Hữu Cảnh street (it is actually Nguyễn Đức Cảnh street), and Hương continued:

*Hương:* From the beginning of Nguyễn Hữu Cảnh Street to Nguyễn Văn Linh Street, to Lawrence S. Ting School, there are intersections with traffic lights. From my observation, every time the light turns red, people stop, even when there is no traffic on the street. They can run red lights without getting caught, but they don't do that.

*Erik:* What do *you* think? [Turning to ask Hương's son]

*Hương's son:* They *do* run red lights.

*Hương's other son:* Sometimes when people are in a hurry, they have to run red lights.

After debating about whether or not people in Phú Mỹ Hưng actually did or did not run red lights, Hương conceded that drivers in the New Urban Zone were not perfect. But still, they were better than people in other districts:

*Hương:* So what I see here [in Phú Mỹ Hưng] is that running red lights does happen, but it doesn't happen frequently. In the city center and other places, if people can run a red light without getting caught, then they will. They will run a red light without any reason, even when not in a hurry. However, Phú Mỹ Hưng is not totally disciplined. I'm very annoyed with the way people park their cars here, professor.

The conversation continued in this manner, and it became clear that Hương associated "civility" with orderliness and rule-oriented behavior. To express this, she referred to concrete examples of cleanliness, the act of following traffic laws, parking one's car properly, and maintaining a sense of order.[32] As she continued, she noted that the idea of civility was most certainly a marketing slogan, but also that there was something about Phú Mỹ Hưng that encouraged people, at least generally speaking, and of course with some exceptions, to follow rules more than they did in other parts of the city. She continued:

*Hương:* Here, Phú Mỹ Hưng's marketing theme is about a "civilized" urban area; it attracts people who want to live here or to invest in this area. So I think that is an attractive slogan in marketing. There are investors who can make good on that promise, and there are investors who can't. I think the investors of Phú Mỹ Hưng have been trying hard, and they are able to make people here proud of being residents of Phú Mỹ Hưng. Like I said before, I don't have an exact definition of "civilized," because I don't care much about that word. To me, that word sounds a bit too distant, too polite.

*Erik:* Too distant?

*Hương:* I don't really care [about abstract terms]. I care about more specific things: whether it is clean, safe, and whether the air is pure; whether there are enough windows, whether there is enough natural light; whether it is safe and security demands are met instantly. I just make a call and the customer service people come immediately. Those things are what I need to care about. I don't need to go the extra mile to define what "civilized" is, how much is enough, how much is not enough. For example, I told you earlier that people here drive slowly and pay attention to traffic lights, but they park awkwardly and I don't like it. If everyone paid attention to park his car correctly, I think it would look more disciplined and that would be better. And I see very little litter here. I do see litter sometimes, but it gets cleaned up immediately. So I think those little things add up to show that this place is civilized. However, when I get angry here, I sometimes say bad words. In District One, I hear swear words a lot on the street, but I don't hear any here. Here, if people want to swear, they do it inside. On the street [here in Phú Mỹ Hưng] I don't hear any bad words, and I feel comfortable. In District One, just take one step outside and you'll hear swear words.

In this discussion, it's clear that Hương identifies civility with self-discipline, orderliness, law-abiding behavior, and good manners, but she also resists the idea of reducing civility to a slogan. She does not care what civility "means" but is instead primarily interested in action—how people behave—and insists that real civility depends on action. She then turns to her son and asks: "Do you think it is civilized here?"

*Hương's son:*  Here? It is somewhat better than District One. The way people behave, the way people act here, is somewhat different from that in District One. For the definition of "civilized," you should see the civic education textbook.

*Erik:*  I've met many people who said they wanted to live here because it was more civilized than other places. When I finally asked them how they understood the word *civilized,* they couldn't answer. That's very perplexing.

*Hương:*  Yes, I agree with you, professor. I think about it this way. Look at the people in ethnic minority groups. When we look at them, we might think we're more civilized than them. Because we live in an urban area, when we go to the countryside and see the farmers, we think that we're one level above them, that we're more civilized than them, that we know the world more than they do. However, they're not uncivilized. For example, when we eat we use different kinds of soap to clean [our hands before the meal], and we use different kinds of lotion for our skin, so we think we're more civilized than them. However in fact we are being exploited by marketing. [Laughing] In fact, the norms for interaction among people are different in different places, and we have to respect them. If you go to the agricultural area and walk in the fields, you can't wear high heels because you'll trip and fall, professor.

*Erik:*  Right.

*Hương:*  Right? What shoes should we wear? Wearing high heels does not make us "civilized." No. The essential thing is how you behave so that there is mutual respect in the community and so that you get along well with people. That's much more important. Now, talking about the light of civilization, I find that image very funny. We were first monkeys, right? After the Bronze Age we gradually managed to stand straight, very gradually. [ . . . ] But do you know what the final image of that is? Humans sit and type on computers so much they have hunched backs! [Laughing]

Throughout this conversation, Hương maintained a cynical critique of the abstract idea of civilization or civility. She even challenged the notion that there was a linear progress from uncivilized to civilized, and instead expressed a clear sense of cultural relativism. What really mattered in her account was not the meaning of abstract pronouncements, but the interpretation of actual behaviors within the context of lived life. And in the realm of behavior, she said, Phú Mỹ Hưng was indeed civilized, even if she had no interest in the idea of civility in the abstract.

As we were finishing our conversation, Hương's husband walked in the door, dressed in tennis clothes and wet with perspiration from what must have been a hard-fought match. The kids introduced me to him as "the American who can speak Vietnamese—a professor." In response he asked me, as Vietnamese men commonly do when they meet me for the first time, if I liked to "*nhậu*" (go drinking and eating with male buddies, a common male pastime). His voice was a bit unsure, and he asked the question as if by reflex, though with a certain sense of longing. I admitted that I sometimes do enjoy having a few drinks. "Do you often go to *nhậu*?" I asked. "No," he said, "there is no place to *nhậu* around here. I just play tennis and watch TV." In contrast to the downtown districts of the city, where the male-dominated drinking dens—like the places where Ngọc once sold Dunhill cigarettes—proliferate on nearly every street, the gendered spaces of the New Urban Zone were different indeed: civility was clean and orderly; people stopped at traffic lights; and the boys were disciplined.

## CONCLUSION: CIVILITY AS POLITICAL CRITIQUE AND MODE OF EXCLUSION

In his classic argument about the dialectical relationship between space and social consciousness, the Marxist sociologist Henri Lefebvre argued that a "social transformation, to be truly revolutionary in character, must manifest a creative capacity in its effects on daily life, on language and on space."[33] In other words, he insisted, in part, that there can be no enduring social revolution without a corresponding revolution in the organization of space. The residents I met in Phú Mỹ Hưng would largely agree with this claim. In a similar spirit, they described the New Urban Zone as more than a collection of modern buildings, broad avenues, and green parks and instead insisted that the new spatial relations produced by the development are intimately entwined with new forms of social consciousness, new modes of interpersonal interaction, and new kinds of subjectivity. It is a civilized space because people within it act civilized, and people act civilized because it is a civilized space. When Hương described apartment living as "ideologically revolutionary," for example, she expressed a common belief about the significance of these new forms of spatial organization to social organization and consciousness. But there is, of course, a big difference between the conception of revolutionary ways of living expressed by the people in Phú Mỹ Hưng and the socialist vision coursing through the work of Lefebvre. Lefebvre wanted to see the emergence of a truly socialist space, and he longed to see the development of cities that could foster the enduring consciousness necessary to achieve socialist egalitarianism. In contrast, like many Vietnamese who lived through the country's difficult postwar experiments with actually existing socialism, the residents of this "civilization city" see their revolution as a move away from, rather than toward, socialism.

Nevertheless, even as they celebrate the emergence of privatized, corporate forms of urban planning that generally rebuff the socialist project, the residents of Phú Mỹ Hưng have not rejected all of the utopian hopes of their predecessors. Like Vietnamese reformers and revolutionaries throughout the twentieth century, both communist and anticommunist, the residents of this New Urban Zone place a good deal of faith in the civilizing potential of *văn minh*. In all of the examples presented in this chapter, people assert that life in the New Urban Zone will encourage a sense of disciplined and orderly action, which will make their hope for civility become real. And they too, in their own way, believe that civility is connected to a vision of a just and moral society.

What might we make of this new spatial order founded on overt expressions of civility? On the one hand, it is clear that the discipline and order associated with civility can be used to legitimize inequality by enforcing hierarchy and exclusion—insisting that some people are more civilized than others. In this way, civility can be a euphemism for putting people "in their place" and reifying forms of class differentiation. The Phú Mỹ Hưng development is a clear example of what Li Zhang calls the "spatialization of class" emerging in late-socialist Asian cities.[34] On the other hand, the stories in this chapter clearly illustrate the ways in which civility challenges long-entrenched power dynamics within Vietnamese society, posing critical questions about the political and social status quo. In their stories, Ngọc, Hà, and Hương all describe ways in which a focus on civility has transformed the gender dynamics and other social aspects of the worlds in which they live. For Ngọc and Hà, the civilized space of Phú Mỹ Hưng offered an alternative to dominant gender dynamics in Vietnamese society that had subordinated them to unsavory husbands. Life in the New Urban Zone allowed them to construct safe, inclusive spaces for themselves. For Hương, furthermore, the space offered a space to raise her young boys in an environment where they could focus on their education and where her husband would not be drawn to drinking dens and other distractions, but would instead be domesticated by the new mode of apartment living. There is nothing particularly new or particularly Vietnamese about these ambivalent political implications, for human beings have long used the language of civility as a way of imposing discipline, both on a society's rulers and on the ruled. Almost half a millennium before my conversations with the residents of Phú Mỹ Hưng, in 1532, on the other side of the globe, Erasmus of Rotterdam wrote a treatise, *On Civility in Boys,* in which he sought to outline "the whole range of conduct, the chief situations of social and convivial life" as a means of discipline.[35] Like Erasmus so many centuries before them, Ngọc, Hà, and Hương also mobilize a form of civility that will aid them in "the instruction of boys."[36] But in their case, their words are intended not to cultivate aristocracy but rather to control the behavior of men who not only have grown too big for their britches but also inflict violence on women, abuse their positions of authority, and corrupt the public good. Ngọc, Hà, and Hương deploy civility to "discipline the boys" and in the process insist on a sort of orderly comportment that enhances their own "right to the city."

But the right to the city in this vision is not all-inclusive. The civility described in this chapter is of course a bourgeois civility, founded on exclusion and class distinction, enforced by the spatial dynamics of increasingly unequal Vietnamese cities. Concepts that promise to deliver rights to some people exclude others from those same rights. For this reason, the belief in civility described here deserves skeptical treatment as well. For such a critique, one might well turn to the famous Vietnamese satire of civility penned in the 1930s by Vũ Trọng Phụng, whose biting sarcasm mercilessly lampooned the hollow civility displayed by Vietnamese elites during the waning years of the colonial period. In one scene from his most famous novel, *Dumb Luck,* Vũ Trọng Phụng described a self-important yet dim-witted fool named Mr. Civilization (Ông Văn Minh) as he gave a speech at the opening of a tennis complex before members of the Vietnamese elite: "Mr. Civilization rattled on for almost an hour," praising the "progressive vision" of the tennis court owner, while "the journalist who advocated progressive reforms for society at large and conservative practices for his own family scribbled down the great man's valuable ideas." Vũ Trọng Phụng then pokes fun at the charade with his typical brand of sarcasm: "In short, the speech possessed all the necessary attributes of a formal oratorical address by a great man of letters or an important politician: embellishment, fabrication, exaggeration, fantasy, and duplicity—all dressed up in the dishonest language of literature. The crowd applauded enthusiastically."[37] Vũ Trọng Phụng's entire novel, and indeed much of his work, lampoons the emptiness of *văn minh,* a term that had gained popularity among Vietnamese elites in the colonial era as both an assertion of national progress and a mode of asserting class status. Because *văn minh* was so intimately tied into elitism and exclusion, he mocked the pretension that it could express the potential for Vietnamese to reclaim a sense of civic life. For Vũ Trọng Phụng, this language of civility was empty rhetoric, worthy only of biting satire and condescension. Mr. Văn Minh's name was not in fact a political statement: "In fact, it signified nothing at all."[38]

Returning to twenty-first-century Phú Mỹ Hưng, aided by the wisdom of Vũ Trọng Phụng, it is tempting to leave the analysis of civility at that: to call the bluff of elite sentiments coming forth from a place like Phú Mỹ Hưng and to challenge the rhetorical self-satisfaction of those who utter the language of civility. But while it would be easy to stand back and satirize the language of a new urban zone founded on unapologetic pretensions of civility, and to mock the enthusiastic response of the gullible "crowd" to the rhetoric, such a perspective captures only part of the story, and it fails to explain the persistent allure that civilizing discourses have had in Vietnamese society. Today, nearly eighty years after Vũ Trọng Phụng penned his lines, very similar speeches are regularly being given in Vietnam, and very similar caricatures could easily be painted of some of the new rich, including many who live in Phú Mỹ Hưng, many of whom seem to embody similar contradictions and who often seem unable to distinguish between vulgar materialism and civility. Surely, such individuals are worthy of critique. But if this language of *văn minh* has lasted so long, then it is also worth pausing and asking what about it has held such consistent appeal.

If it is only empty rhetoric, why is the language of civility still around? Part of the appeal, I suggest, is that many people continue to believe that the idea of civility is not *only* empty rhetoric. Many of the residents in Vietnamese new urban zones have risen from adversity to secure themselves a place in the rising middle class, and maintain a sincere belief in the transformative possibility of *văn minh*. Most of these residents exhibit a sincere "will to improve." In order to understand the complexity and ambivalence inherent in the concept of civility in contemporary Vietnam, we must also account for the experiences of those everyday Phú Mỹ Hưng residents who deploy civility as a way to challenge the socio-political status quo, even while living in an urban development that has come to symbolize new forms of spatial exclusion. They may live lives riven with contradictions, and they may be ambivalent about the meaning of civility, but people like Ngọc, Hà, and Hương are not fools.

Calls for civility begin by evoking moral bonds of reciprocal obligation. But they can also blur into more explicit calls for *civitas,* a social order based on the rule of law, on carefully delineated rights and responsibilities, and on disciplined self-conduct and treatment of others. Throughout Phú Mỹ Hưng I regularly met residents who insisted that the orderly, predictable lifestyles being fostered in the New Urban Zone might also stand as a model of and a model for a modern brand of political order. Like Ngọc, who contrasted what she described as the civilized, rule-oriented management practices of the Phú Mỹ Hưng Corporation to the animalistic law of the jungle she experienced with Vietnamese government officials, and like Hương, who focused on behaviors rather than slogans, many of the Phú Mỹ Hưng residents I came to know consistently emphasized that the new kind of consciousness emerging in Phú Mỹ Hưng symbolized new possibilities for urban governance, and even offered a model for realizing an emergent sense of citizenship and rights.

This connection between civility, consciousness, and political possibility—the subject of the next chapter—became especially clear to me during early morning walks I took through Phú Mỹ Hưng's manicured parks with (mostly male) elderly retirees, former lawyers, officials, business leaders, and intellectuals. In the dawn light, the streets of Phú Mỹ Hưng were calm and clean, and one could walk unimpeded through its broad boulevards. There was open space, and my companions commonly turned to political discussions as they walked and talked their way along tidy, master-planned roads. These morning exercisers would start the morning by exercising their bodies, but the walking would get to their heads. By the end of each morning they were stretching their minds, engaging in conversation, and exercising a new form of consciousness.

3

# Exercising Consciousness

*Self and Society in a Privatizing Space of Exclusion*

*There is no face in which the political does not appear.*
—YAEL NAVARO-YASHIN, *FACES OF THE STATE: SECULARISM AND
PUBLIC LIFE IN TURKEY*

MORNING EXERCISES

Doctor Cao, a visibly old but still energetic retired doctor in his early eighties, strode across Phú Mỹ Hưng's Starlight Bridge (fig. 3.1) with long, exaggerated steps. It was just after 5:30 in the morning, and his every movement expressed the vigorous will of a man fighting to remain independent and strong in the face of old age. Every ten paces or so he would stop, arch his body backwards, swing his arms out as wide as they could go, and then lunge forward to touch his toes. He was dressed in loose pajamas. His trim white hair gleamed in the morning sun, while the new office and apartment towers rising behind him to the southeast formed silhouettes against an orange sky.

Off to the north and west, the soft glow cast by the rising sun crept across the red tile rooftops of the district's private villas and duplexes, glinting here and there off the windows of apartment towers. The curving façades of the concrete, glass, and metal buildings of the Crescent shopping district curled around the man-made Crescent Lake, spreading broad shadows across a traffic-free promenade, where scores of other exercisers—mostly men in groups of two or four, occasionally a husband-and-wife pair—were walking, playing badminton, kicking shuttlecocks, jogging, or riding bicycles. A group of five elderly women engaged in the slow, graceful movements of Tai Chi: their session would last only as long as the morning shade still covered the plaza by the fountain in front of the Crescent Mall, Ho Chi Minh City's largest and most modern shopping center. Vietnamese people almost never exercise under direct sun; as a result, Phú Mỹ Hưng's broad roads, cooled by the many shadows cast by its new apartment blocks and shopping districts, were a popular place for morning exercise. There were foreigners here too—a few scattered Koreans, Japanese, North Americans, and Europeans—but the different groups tended to stick with their own kind.

On this morning, like every morning (except the month he spent recovering from a long dizzy spell caused by his high blood pressure), Doctor Cao crossed the bridge and headed to its base, where a small circle of his friends—all men, all retirees—were engaged in various forms of dynamic stretching. For some of them, the style of their movements—lunges, twists, arm circles, and bends—gave them away as people from another place and another era. Their vaguely Soviet-style ballistic stretches and vigorous calisthenics were infused with the same Vietnamese-style motions most famously associated with the morning exercisers who gather around Hanoi's Hoàn Kiếm Lake, but who can also be seen at dawn in parks and public spaces everywhere across the country. Several of the men were bending backward in contortions over street furniture, while others massaged their backs and bottoms against the smooth granite surfaces of the phallus-shaped barrier stones that kept motor traffic off the bridge.

Approaching his friends, Doctor Cao called out to them, one at a time, in a loud and healthy call-and-response:

*Dr. Cao's Call:*   *Bác Lâm có khỏe không?* (Are you healthy, uncle Lâm?)

   *Response:*   [Replying as loudly as possible] *Khỏe!* (Yes, healthy!)

      *Call:*   *Bác Định có khỏe không?* (Are you healthy, uncle Định?)

   *Response:*   *Khỏe!* (Healthy!)

Doctor Cao told me why they called out like this every morning: to remind themselves that they were still alive. The louder they yelled the question and the louder they called in response, the more they knew they had once again cheated death, one morning at a time.

Doctor Cao lived behind the locked doors of an apartment building overseen by a private security guard. He sometimes walked alone—but never for very long.

## PRIVATIZED PUBLIC SPACE AND THE NEW "CONSCIOUSNESS" (Ý THỨC)

Linger for a moment, if you will, on the image of Doctor Cao's lone figure striding through the dawn toward his group of friends. It is the image of a man walking out from his private home each morning into a space consciously designed for public use but located in the middle of a master-planned development that is commonly understood as an exclusive space for the new rich. It may seem insignificant, but the image gives visual form to an otherwise intangible social process: the coming together of private persons in a public space.[1] This space, more precisely, is a *privately owned public space,* built by a profit-seeking Taiwanese-Vietnamese joint venture in a society whose government has, since the late 1980s, officially

FIGURE 3.1. The Starlight Bridge (Cầu Ánh Sao). Phú Mỹ Hưng. Author's photo, May 2012.

committed itself to constructing what it calls "a market economy with a socialist orientation." Simple daily behaviors like this may seem banal, but if you speak to the people engaging in them—people like Dr. Cao—they will tell you that the kinds of spaces where these actions are taking place, along with the new modes of interpersonal relations these actions are fostering, are an integral part of a quiet social revolution taking place in the New Urban Zone. It is, to be sure, a bourgeois revolution of the well-to-do, but in a one-party state still governed by the Communist Party of Vietnam, many Phú Mỹ Hưng residents genuinely see themselves as living on the vanguard edge of a larger historical shift that carries political and social significance for the nation.

Dr. Cao himself was originally from Quảng Ngãi Province along Vietnam's central coast, and he still spoke in the distinctive regional accent where short "a" sounds (like cat and bat) came out as "uh" sounds (like cut and but). During the war, he had been a doctor and field medic for the National Liberation Front (often referred to as Việt Cộng, or Vietnamese Communists) in that hotly contested region; after 1975 he made a life in Saigon, working in state-run hospitals around the city as a general practitioner. He never made a fortune as a doctor, but he was well respected, and his son had built from his reputation to start a small but successful business importing and selling "medicines" from Western countries (which, judging from the boxes stacked in their living room, were mainly vitamins and herbal supplements). Whenever I spoke to Dr. Cao, I was struck by the apparent lack of contradiction he saw between his youthful enthusiasm for the socialist revolution, to which he had dedicated his life, and his present-day enthusiasm for life in this master-planned new urban development. To my eyes, Phú Mỹ Hưng appeared to be a clear renunciation of socialism—an unambiguously capitalist model of urban development driven by real estate imperatives made possible by new relations of private property. But to Dr. Cao the means were less important than the ends. It didn't matter to him whether the project depended on market mechanisms to succeed. What really mattered was the way the development realized many of the ambitions that the revolution itself once promised to deliver: a highly planned, efficient society, where things were orderly and people had a sense of consciousness about their relationship to others within society. His morning exercises were an expression of this too: he knew he was responsible for caring for himself, and for having the discipline to wake up each day and stride forth into the world. In exchange for his own discipline, he could also expect that he would meet other people dedicated to self-improvement, and that when they came together each morning they would push each other and give each other reason to live. He also knew that the people around him would respect his space, that they could come together in civil social interaction, supporting each other but at the same time depending on each other's respect.

Dr. Cao was not alone in thinking this way. The notion that a meaningful public sphere depended on a renewed sense of the individual self, or that intensified privatization could actually buttress rather than undermine social life, was a common way of understanding the novel forms of sociality emerging in Phú Mỹ Hưng. Residents often told me that the lifestyle being built there depended on and produced new relationships between individual private spaces and public places of encounter. While many of these residents had lived through one social revolution, they commonly described Phú Mỹ Hưng's unique mode of living as revolutionary too, part of a larger social process that was reformulating the relationship between, and understandings of, self and society. Like any good revolution, the people I came to know in Phú Mỹ Hưng also saw themselves as producing new forms of consciousness.

### Consciousness

The Vietnamese term for consciousness is *ý thức* (pronounced, roughly, with sharp rising tones on both syllables, as "ee took"). This compound term, which combines the word for "thought" or "idea" (*ý*) with the word for "waking up" (*thức*), also carries the connotation of "awareness" and implies a certain level of education. The term, therefore, suggests an educated consciousness, born of discipline and awareness. In this way, *ý thức* is not unlike the concept of civility (*văn minh*) discussed in chapter 2. And like civility, people who live in Phú Mỹ Hưng commonly claim that they have more *ý thức* than other Vietnamese people.

While this notion of being more conscious and aware than others is of course rather self-aggrandizing, it is important to view such statements in context. When Phú Mỹ Hưng residents said they had *ý thức,* what they sought to express was the idea that living in the New Urban Zone had helped to foster in them a heightened awareness of the social world in which they were living. They often told me, for example, that living in a clean, orderly place helped them develop a robust understanding of the relationship between rights and responsibilities. They also told me that life in Phú Mỹ Hưng promoted this conscious awareness because it made it possible for them to think beyond their base individual desires, and thus to craft themselves as responsible citizens within a social community committed to the building of a better society. In this way, the notion that they possessed a superior consciousness was in fact simultaneously self-aggrandizing and self-effacing. When they invoked the idea of consciousness, they asserted that their acute and refined sense of self-awareness actually enhanced their sense of social consciousness and their awareness of others. Just as European Calvinists could assert that knowing oneself was key to knowing and thereby submitting oneself to God, the self-disciplined residents of Phú Mỹ Hưng insisted that knowing oneself was key to developing a sense of society. In their explanations, the inward turn of privatization actually intensified forms of social consciousness, even as privatization enacted barriers and exclusions that set these same socially conscious people off from many aspects of the very society they claimed to be increasingly conscious of.

Consciousness and action are interconnected. Once he arrives in the public space of the private development where he lives, Dr. Cao meets his friends for exercise, which soon morphs into conversation, and his private, individual self becomes integrated into a new kind of collective, what might be called a "privatized public." By dint of living in Phú Mỹ Hưng, the members of this exclusive collective have all set themselves off spatially and economically from the laboring masses of the city, but if you listen to their conversations you will also notice that they often seem to be thinking about the significance their new way of life has for "the Vietnamese people" *(người Việt).* While they are an exclusive group, and while their private homes have been turned spatially inward, they regularly debate the state of the nation, and their minds and conversations often turn to broadly political topics. The convivial morning antics Dr. Cao shares with his friends are just the beginning of this process. As the mornings turn to day, their exercise circles set the stage for sustained interactions that transcend mere bodily exercise: the relationships they have forged with one another form part of a new kind of social life emerging in the highly privatized world of the New Urban Zone. Clear and straightforward class exclusion also creates the conditions for new understandings about collective belonging and novel forms of consciousness that residents link to their own hopes for the future of Vietnamese society.

The resulting social interactions express the intersection of two seemingly contradictory forces: on the one hand, Phú Mỹ Hưng emerges as a space of intensified privatization; on the other hand, residents claim that living there has imbued them with an intensified consciousness of collective social aspiration. Residents regularly assert that privatization actually produced more rather than less civic awareness; that their enhanced attention to the self actually inspired them to focus on the group; that the rise of privately built corporate-designed housing actually produced new public spaces; that social atomization actually evolved in tandem with new forms of awareness about society—and so on. Describing similar processes in Kunming, China, Li Zhang calls this a "double movement" whereby homeowners living in master-planned developments simultaneously value privacy and join together as new collectivities in order to protect that privacy.[2] In China, Zhang adds, this leads to a paradox. On the one hand, "the appeal of the new middle classes" stems from their "projected openness and inclusiveness," at the very same time that "the social distinction the middle classes enjoy is often produced through exclusionary practices in everyday life."[3] In Indonesia, Lizzie Van Leeuwen made similar observations during the waning years of the Suharto era, when the proliferation of gated communities and hyperindividualistic consumerism in Jakarta emerged in tandem with the widespread development of ideas about rights and civil society.[4]

This same double movement is evident in the case of Phú Mỹ Hưng—where residents constantly talk about their elevated sense of social consciousness while strolling through urban spaces that are founded on obvious forms of urban exclusion. The residents I met in Phú Mỹ Hưng sincerely imagined themselves as a significant political force, promising to deliver social justice and political change to the country, despite the fact that their actions and lifestyles were clearly linked to rising inequities in society. The apparent contradictions produced by these opposing tendencies is one of the reasons why scholarly observers consistently disagree about the political significance of the Asian middle class: some see them as a vibrant force of political change, while others see them as so entrenched in systems of privilege that they cannot be expected to challenge the status quo.[5] My ethnographic research shows that both of these perspectives are correct in their own way. The privatized lifestyles of residents in Phú Mỹ Hưng simultaneously reinforce the forces of inequality in Vietnamese society and enable those very same residents to imagine themselves as part of a social movement dedicated to ideals of justice, founded on an ethic of rights and responsibilities.

## Class Exclusion and the Conscience Collective

Doctor Cao and his friends belong to a class of people commonly described, though typically with very little precision, as "elites," "the new rich," or the "rising middle class."[6] The place where they live tends to be depicted as a space of class exclusion filled with self-interested individuals primarily concerned with satisfying their personal pleasures and protecting their property interests.[7] There is of course good reason for observers to focus on the exclusionary aspects of the district. One of the first buildings one sees when arriving in the New Urban Zone via Nguyễn Văn Linh Boulevard is the showroom for the "Porsche Centre Saigon," built right next to a golf course and located just across the boulevard from the Crescent Mall, which is itself festooned with advertisements for expensive consumer products. Prices on the restaurant menus in this district are often at least twice those in other districts, sometimes rivaling the prices one might see in Europe, North America, or Singapore. Many of the people who live in the area either drive or are driven in their own cars; they dress well in designer clothing, wear fine watches, have all the newest electronic gadgets, get massages, visit hair salons, travel abroad, send their children to private schools, and live in private homes, some of which are quite large and almost all of which are cleaned by housekeepers or even live-in domestic helpers. Even some of the simple pleasures people enjoy in the district are founded on exclusion. For example, the main reason the streets of Phú Mỹ Hưng are such pleasant places for early-morning exercises is that they are comparatively empty of people. Only a select portion of the city's population can afford to live in Phú Mỹ Hưng, which means that population density there is up to ten times lower than in other districts of the city.

A writer looking to produce ironic caricatures of the new rich in a society still ruled by a Communist Party could certainly find some evocative characters to write about here.[8] One of the most amusing images I have in my notebooks of daily life in Phú Mỹ Hưng is a description of a man who often drove at exceedingly slow speeds around the district in a yellow Lamborghini, frequently moving slower than I could walk. He was obviously looking to flaunt his wealth, but it is doubtful that his car—one of the world's fastest automobiles—ever made it out of second gear. Driving fast, however, was not the point; the slower he went, the easier it was for people to see that he was a rich man. There is also a man (who might in fact be the same man, but I could never confirm it), infamous throughout Vietnam and known to live in Phú Mỹ Hưng, who is so rich that he built a villa just to house his luxury car collection—mostly Lamborghinis and Bentleys. He goes by the name Cường Đô La ("Dollar's Cường"). If one wished to find a modern-day character to play the role of Karl Marx's "Mr. Moneybags," known in some translations of *Capital* as "the money owner," Mr. Đô La would be a prime candidate. Even the name for Phú Mỹ Hưng—rich, beautiful, prosperity—shamelessly evokes status and privilege.

But the name real estate developers have given their development says very little about the people who actually live there, and not everyone in Phú Mỹ Hưng drives a Porsche or Lamborghini. In fact, minivans and SUVs are by far the car of choice. Most of the residents I knew tended to deemphasize rather than display their wealth in everyday encounters in the district's public spaces. On those occasions when they did flaunt their wealth, they largely did so in specific places where they could control their performances and in other districts of the city.[9] To be sure, Phú Mỹ Hưng residents are not poor, but to lump all of them under the uninformative label of "the new rich" is to miss a great deal about the lifestyles many of them aspire to.[10]

During this project, my research team and I carefully noted interactions and conversations with 187 people in Phú Mỹ Hưng, including both residents and service workers. Among the residents we met, there were, as we expected, several who could be classified as members of the "elite," including former members of the Communist Party who had held important positions (among them former members of the Ho Chi Minh City administration, one former head of the state bank of Vietnam, and one former vice-chair of the People's Committee) as well as wealthy business owners who ran everything from furniture factories to investment and trading companies. But the Phú Mỹ Hưng residents we interviewed and came to know well also included a wide range of well-educated but modestly paid academics, midlevel engineers, entry-level lawyers, office workers, struggling real estate agents, shop owners, restaurant owners, and teachers. Numerous residents owned property elsewhere in Ho Chi Minh City and even Hanoi but rented those places out so they could use the income to either rent or purchase a residence in Phú Mỹ Hưng. I also met several groups of people who would not have been able to afford living in Phú Mỹ Hưng on their own but who managed to live there by pooling their resources together to share a small apartment as roommates. In one case, six women (for a short period, eight) shared a one-bedroom apartment; in another case, four women shared a single room. To make such crowded accommodations work, these young professionals staggered their work and sleeping shifts to regulate how many bodies would be crowded into the apartment at the same time. In yet another case, the owner of a hair salon secretly (and illegally) slept each night on his barber chairs in order to make ends meet. Furthermore, most of the café owners in the district allowed their wait-staff to sleep overnight on the premises (also illegally). Even some of the more upwardly mobile types, who might be classified in a scholarly account as members of the "rising middle classes," often shared small one- or two-bedroom apartments with their parents, many of whom who had come to the city from other cities and provinces to help with the burden of childcare as their highly educated sons and daughters struggled to balance dual-career households. I knew lawyers whose in-laws slept on roll-out mats in the kitchen, engineers who slept three to a bed. And of course, among the wealthier families, the live-in housekeepers, nannies, and Filipina English teachers were all residents in their own right too, contributing to the diversity of the district.

These caveats aside, it is true that the morning exercisers I discuss in this chapter, especially the gray-haired retirees like Dr. Cao, were indeed relatively well off, and all of them had enough spending money and leisure time to linger for long breakfasts after their exercises were done. Some of them had made their fortunes through contacts with the party elite, but others, like Dr. Cao, told me that they were able to live in Phú Mỹ Hưng only because their children had purchased a home there. One friend told me—reminded me almost every day, in fact, in a voice that was both proud and self-deprecating—that he was "living off his son" (ăn theo con) who ran an import-export company. Another retiree had a running account at a local restaurant, which his daughter, herself married to a Malaysian import-exporter, paid for him at the end of each month so he could feel free to invite his friends to breakfast without concern for the bill.

Although their children were well-to-do, and while they all had enough spending money for daily breakfasts and visits to cafés, these elderly retirees were far from ostentatious, and none of them acted like the caricatures so commonly developed to represent the new rich. They would generally circulate Crescent Lake in pajamas and sandals, or at best, in shorts, tennis shirts, and sneakers, and they tended to dress in simple clothes throughout the day. Furthermore, even the wealthiest residents I met, those living in the most exclusive villas, often expressed what for many Western readers seem like rather modest ambitions for their families: they wanted a house with a small yard, with enough space for an outdoor grill and some decorative plants; a safe environment for their children; opportunities for a quality education; a bit of peace and quiet; and occasional opportunities to travel. While many residents had significant incomes and tended to spend lavishly on meals and drink when entertaining business associates in downtown restaurants, their actions in Phú Mỹ Hưng were much more subdued. For the most part, the notion that Phú Mỹ Hưng residents are especially self-interested, narcissistic, or antisocial, or that all of the men living in these areas spend all their money on karaoke and sex workers, deserves more subtle analysis than the kind commonly offered in discussions of Asia's new rich.[11]

While it is true that some of the villas in the development are worth over a million dollars, and while the average property values of the duplexes and stand-alone apartments in Phú Mỹ Hưng may be beyond the reach of the poorest working-class residents, most apartments in the development are not in fact significantly more expensive than comparable properties in many other parts of the city. Indeed, housing is actually more affordable in parts of Phú Mỹ Hưng than in some of the city's central districts. Apartments in Phú Mỹ Hưng's oldest building, Hưng Vượng, for example, sold for as little as US$62,261 in 2012, and cost US$31,034 when they first went on sale in 2000; three-bedroom walk-ups in the development's Mỹ An apartment building sold for US$134,100 in 2012 but only cost US$41,379 in 2000. Similar residences in parts of Districts One, Three, and Five would be several times as expensive. Residents in these places felt like they had gotten some of the best deals in the entire city. But most importantly, for nearly all the residents I came to know during seven months living and researching life in Phú Mỹ Hưng, the primary attraction of living there focused on things like waking up in the morning to fresh dawn air, going for walks with friends, feeling safe, living in a community where people shared a mutual respect for one another, and, most notably, being able to find space for conversation. Far from imagining themselves as turning away from society, or seeking to flaunt wealth, most of the residents of Phú Mỹ Hưng genuinely and sincerely saw themselves as part of a world of intense social engagement, filled with friends and family committed to building a new form of community.

If this idea of "building community" in a planned urban development known as a space of class exclusion sounds like a contradiction, residents did not see it that way at all. Dr. Cao, his friends, and people like them were all deeply committed to the idea that privatization would help solve some of Vietnam's most intractable problems—from urban governance to infrastructure development. Although the privatization of public space has been justly subjected to vigorous critique by Western scholars, worried that it subordinates the public control of public spaces to corporate interests, the residents I interviewed in Phú Mỹ Hưng did not subscribe to such a view.[12] In fact, they saw privatization as a solution to many of the city's (and for that matter, the nation's) problems because they believed that it fostered an intensified attention to the self, which would in turn enhance the power of the collective.

Most of the older residents I met on these morning walks around Crescent Lake had lived through the waning years of French colonialism, and all of them had experienced the better part of a long and tumultuous socialist revolution, a world-historic war with the United States, difficult experiments with collectivization, close relations with the Soviet bloc, economic embargos, political reform, war with Cambodia, and border conflicts and enduring tensions with China. In the face of all this experience, for better or for worse, they truly believed that the vision of public life emerging in Phú Mỹ Hưng held much more promise for the future of Vietnam than most of the visions that had existed in the past. For them, it didn't matter whether the development was "privatized"; what mattered was that it helped foster a renewed sense of public life and community. In unexpected ways, the privatized space of the New Urban Zone offered them a place of social consciousness and community awareness. It is also a space where rights consciousness is in fact quite pronounced, even as the space inadvertently denies the rights of others.

### New Forms of Sociality

One of the standard critiques of master-planned developments is that they are devoid of sociality and that the strict demarcation they enact between public and private leads to a form of atomization, or that privatization is lonely and alienating. Doctor Cao and his wife, for example, lived alone in a private apartment in a four-story block built above a parking garage. Like all the homes in Phú Mỹ Hưng, their home was quiet. Compared to the multigenerational housing arrangements of the traditional Vietnamese household, one might even call it lonely. Indeed, many of my Vietnamese friends and colleagues living in parts of the city outside of Phú Mỹ Hưng said they would never consider living in such a place. They said it seemed *"buồn,"* an evocative Vietnamese word most often translated as "sad" but that also conveys feelings of loneliness and isolation.[13] On a superficial level, Doctor Cao's apartment might have been called *buồn*—it certainly stood in stark contrast to the bustling, noisy energy of the typical Vietnamese home in an urban alleyway, where private life spills out into public space, where the distinction between public and private is blurred, and where people from different social classes commonly live next to one another.[14] Compared to that form of sociality, doctor Cao's home seemed turned inward, isolated. When I asked him who his neighbors were, he didn't know: he said the people across the hall were "probably Korean," but he wasn't even sure of that, "maybe Japanese." His children, all professionals with busy lives, lived elsewhere. They often came to visit, his wife said, but it seemed from her voice and from the look in her eyes that this was never often enough. The entrance to the building was carefully watched by a security guard.

Dr. Cao's private home, like all the homes in Phú Mỹ Hưng, is a classic example of an urban residential form that the anthropologist Teresa Caldeira, building from research in São Paulo, Brazil has dubbed the fortified enclave: "They are private property for collective use; they are physically isolated, either by walls or empty spaces or other design devices; they are turned inward and not to the street; and they are controlled by armed guards and security systems that enforce rules of inclusion and exclusion."[15] Like the enclaves Caldeira described in São Paulo, the arrangement of the dwellings in Phú Mỹ Hưng is founded on powerful and often obvious forms of spatial and class exclusion. The district is filled with limited-access residential properties of all conceivable sort: high-rise apartment buildings with watchmen and key-card access; individual villas with tall iron gates and intercom systems; and an exclusive community of multimillion-dollar villas enclosed by a thick wall and protected by guards manning a booth and controlling access through a barrier gate. There are security cameras everywhere, and a privatized security force dressed in the Phú Mỹ Hưng uniform constantly circulates the district on motorbikes and in pickup trucks. Discourses of urban fear sometimes lead people to talk about others in disparaging tones and seek ways to protect themselves from the incursions of others. An early publication produced for residents by the Phú Mỹ Hưng Consumer Service Center, for example, instructed residents that they should watch their backs whenever they returned home, look around before taking their keys out to open the door, and always be vigilant. These kinds of warnings have been documented in studies of master-planned developments the world over.[16]

But despite this inward turn, securitization, and discourse of fear, Dr. Cao and the residents of Phú Mỹ Hưng did not describe themselves as isolated. They were not *buồn*. While some of them admitted that at one time they worried that living in a master-planned development might be *buồn,* they all quickly found the zone to be a vibrant and convivial space. And today, none of the residents I knew ever remained trapped behind the closed doors of their homes. They mostly spend their days gathering together and making friends, engaging in conversation and debate. Just as Dr. Cao emerges from his private and secure home each morning to engage with his group of friends, so too do other Phú Mỹ Hưng residents, who forge a new kind of public consciousness and new social relationships out of such spaces of intensified privatization. The morning exercises and the spaces where they take place within Phú Mỹ Hưng offer a visually rich social and spatial model for understanding these new relationships. Each individual comes to the public space to meet and engage with others, but they come as discrete individuals, emerging out of their own private space. They come to these meetings bearing intensified visions of selfhood and subjectivity, imagining themselves as rights- and responsibility-bearing individual subjects; but in the process of coming together they also produce, and are in many ways drawn into, engagement in a new form of collective sociality, as if compelled by a kind of unspoken force.

## EXERCISING CONSCIOUSNESS WITH UNCLE VIỆT AND FRIENDS

On one of our early-morning walks, Dr. Cao introduced me to Uncle Việt, a friend he had made in the exercise circle at the base of the Starlight Bridge. Uncle Việt didn't really enjoy exercising, but he still showed up every morning on a rusty old mountain bike with a loose seat, which fell too low on its stem and twisted side to side when he rode it. His house—a four-story shop-house in a row of many other shop-houses—was only a few short blocks away, yet he always rode out to the bridge on his bike, not for the exercise it offered but to avoid walking. Every morning, after doing a few perfunctory toe touches and stretches with the group, Uncle Việt put his real energy into wrangling members of the group to head off for breakfast at the local noodle-soup shop, a family-run place called Phở Bà Cố (Great-Grandma's Phở). In Vietnam, it is considered especially *buồn* to eat alone, and recruiting a group for soup was the real reason Uncle Việt came out each morning for exercise. My field notes from one of the first mornings eating breakfast with Uncle Việt give a sense of his boisterous style:

> We have just finished our morning bowl of soup at Phở Bà Cố and Uncle V really wants a cigarette. He says he knows he shouldn't have one. (He says the same thing

every morning). He had only been released from the hospital a few weeks earlier, where he had been rushed by ambulance after collapsing from a bout of blood pressure. It wasn't quite a stroke, but his doctor says he should consider it a warning. But his doctor is not here right now, and V has been biting his lips and nibbling on his fingertips ever since we sat down. And now that the soup is done, he has a nice cup of thick hot highly sweetened coffee sitting before him. He is fidgeting, fixed on getting his fix.

All of a sudden, V leaps to his feet, waving his hands toward the street. He leans out over the rail surrounding the restaurant patio and shouts across the street to a woman riding slowly by on a sagging, heavy motorbike. She is covered head to toe in loose garments to block the sun, riding low under the weight of all the snacks and beverages she has lashed to the motorbike. She slows down, nodding toward V to signal that she is on her way. The bike wobbles through a u-turn, before she lumbers up the curb, and then coasts right up to the restaurant. V asks for cigarettes and she opens one of the many plastic bags hanging from her handlebars, letting him rifle through a jumble of packs until he pulls out his brand. They are skinny Korean cigarettes. He says, turning back to us at the table, that the skinny cigarettes aren't as bad for you as the fat Vietnamese ones.

Uncle Việt was a ball of energy, a joke master, a fast talker, and an all-around *bon vivant* with an exceedingly curious mind. In 2012, when we first met, he was seventy-six years old; originally from the northern port city of Hải Phòng, he was now retired after a decades-long career running a state-owned factory in one of Saigon's oldest industrial areas. With a job like that, I knew without asking that he was a long-standing member of the Vietnamese Communist Party, but he preferred not to talk about that—in fact, like many people of his generation, he seemed disappointed by the party and what it had become. Still, he remained committed to the social ideals and love of country that had once enamored him with socialism, and now, though retired, he diligently occupied himself as the unpaid director of a state-sanctioned but largely independent and self-sustaining consumer protection organization. He was committed to the vision of developing consumer rights in Vietnam because he saw it as a kind of public good through which citizens could maintain a collective voice in the face of often unchecked corporate impunity. By protecting the rights of individuals, he once told me, one could protect the rights of all. For Uncle Việt, the proprietary rights of individuals and the strength of the collective were not opposites but synergistic complements to each other.

This notion of the intertwining of individual proprietary rights and collective responsibility serves as a model both of and for the way that various relationships between private individuals and larger groups play out in the space of the new urban zone. After private individuals like Doctor Cao and Uncle Việt came together in the morning exercise circles, they would then congregate at noodle soup and breakfast shops, in cafés, and in other spaces, where they were in turn joined by other friends. Far from being atomized and locked away in their private homes, they all emerged from their private spaces to socialize and linger over drawn-out breakfasts and conversations. After their exercises were done, and once they gathered together, their conversations over breakfast and coffee turned into joking circles (or, as I sometimes like to imagine them, small jazz bands), in which each participant would share a story or a joke, followed by commentary and individual interjections, which were then followed by a different person's commentary or joke. To pursue the jazz metaphor, each "musician" in the "band" of discourse would go through a round of trading eights, improvising in successive turns with their own vocal instrument—scatting and jamming, one might say, through the topics of the day.

The topics of conversation were open, and would move across the spectrum of all possible discussion, effortlessly careening from the personal to the political and back again. A typical conversation, for example, might begin with everyday discussions of family and health (should Uncle Việt really smoke those skinny cigarettes?), then meander into speculation about rising and falling real estate values (the economy in 2011–12 was tanking due to a bursting housing bubble), pause to debate the quality of the soup on the table (it was without fail deemed the best in Phú Mỹ Hưng), followed by consideration of the restaurants in Phú Mỹ Hưng more generally (disappointing and mostly overpriced) and the relative merits of northern versus southern styles of Vietnamese cookery (of course, this group, all of whom hailed from the north, considered northern food best), and settle into an assessment of what was good about northern Vietnam and why they all chose to live in Saigon rather than Hanoi (the north was more "cultured," it was the "cradle of Vietnamese civilization," but Saigon's weather was better and southern society was more "open"). But what was most interesting was the way these conversations would always, every day without exception, circle around to politics and the news. Although public discourse about the news and the government in Vietnam is heavily censored, in the privacy of small face-to-face groups like this there was no censorship when it came to discussing the many perceived failures of the Vietnamese government. There were, however, polite social conventions: any critique of the government was always framed in terms that expressed love of country; the only real taboo, it seemed, was not being nationalistic enough—not loving Vietnam.

And so, in this way, the morning exercises in Phú Mỹ Hưng would morph into conversation, and individuals joined a collective identity as parts of a larger social whole. Talk about themselves and their own personal concerns would lead to talk about society. Then, inevitably, before taking leave of each other each morning, the group would make plans to meet again, later in the day, when they would visit one another's homes or go out for afternoon coffee, and talk some more. In between these morning and afternoon sessions, in addition to all the errands of their private lives, they would read newspapers or go online and scour the internet. They would read blogs, surf past government-imposed internet firewalls using

VPNs, and gather intellectual fodder for the discussions that would pick up again later in the day. This was the structure of daily life for the people I met around the lake: meet for exercise; gather for morning conversation over breakfast and coffee; disperse; read the news; get together again for afternoon conversation; exchange information. This structure repeated itself every day.

At the end of breakfast, as the coffee wound down and he fought back but then gave into the urge to furtively smoke a few skinny Korean cigarettes, Uncle Việt would often invite us to stop by his house after lunch. He lived only a few blocks from Great-Grandma's Phở, and on most days at least two or three guests would stop by for tea and further conversation. Uncle Việt lived with his wife and their grown-up, recently divorced son, who was a busy professional with a successful import business. But their son worked long hours on the other side of town, and Uncle Việt's wife, though always welcoming, often stuck to the back of the house or slipped away on errands of her own. (She still enjoyed visiting the "wet market" at chợ Tân Mỹ, in Tân Phú Ward, a working-class area located just beyond Phú Mỹ Hưng's official boundaries.) The groups that would come to visit were always male, highly educated, either retired or near retirement, and Uncle Việt received them in the living room, which was clearly designed for long conversations and for drinking tea (and, when his wife was out of the house, for furtively smoking too many of those skinny Korean cigarettes). His guests would sit around a broad coffee table surrounded by couches and easy chairs, all facing inward. Newspapers and magazines were piled everywhere on the coffee table and on side tables.

When guests arrived at his house, Uncle Việt would direct them to sit down on the couches in the living room. Then he would disappear into the kitchen to make tea, and his guests would make small talk, picking up the random newspapers scattered across the coffee table, flipping through the pages, sometimes pausing to read an article, sometimes simply looking for something of interest. Slowly, picking out whatever headlines caught the eye, they would launch into conversation, riffing off the news of the day, scatting to the beat of the daily headlines: "What do you think about the ASEAN meeting?"; "Do you think the National Assembly is really interested in hearing the people's criticism?"

No one really trusted the state-run media. The headlines only served as prompts for intellectual debate, and the content of every news article was subjected to scrutiny and critical evaluation.[17] For example, a headline might allude to tensions with China, or touch on issues related to the "Eastern Sea" (also known as the South China Sea). But the conversation itself could veer in a very different direction, focusing, say, on the inability or unwillingness (which one of these it was could itself be a subject of debate) of the Vietnamese Communist Party leadership to develop a strong position defending Vietnam's sovereignty. As they talked, the conversations would move between topics, and a political tone would gradually rise forth from everyday banter. The conversations rapidly shifted and meandered along switchbacks and detours, but all these discursive roads would lead to political destinations: one moment debating whether the collapse of the Communist Party of Vietnam was imminent, and the next wondering whether the public debates in the National Assembly were staged performances or real signs of political transparency.

In the privatized world of Phú Mỹ Hưng, first in small groups at restaurants and cafés and then later behind closed doors in people's homes, such conversations were happening everywhere. Uncle Việt's group consisted mostly of northerners, all highly educated, most of them with long histories of involvement with the Communist Party. But I had similar conversations with people who had been on the other side during the Vietnam War, including small circles of Vietnamese-American or Vietnamese-Australian retirees who had settled in Phú Mỹ Hưng, and Saigon locals who had moved there to escape the crush of downtown. While these small groups tended to form along regional lines—southerners with southerners and northerners with northerners—they were not purposefully exclusive, and there was usually some crossover, especially when people shared business or work connections or other common interests, like playing badminton, golf, soccer, or tennis together, or other pursuits, like collecting porcelain or discussing music and poetry. On several occasions, I was invited to socialize and meet with small groups of people who had all studied together in the former Soviet Union—some would get together to reminisce about their days studying engineering in Ukraine, while others would bond over their shared time in Minsk. What makes these groups significant, and what they all shared, was the way they were, on the one hand, private and exclusive—largely limited to face-to-face circles of three to five people—and, on the other hand, engaged in similar patterns of interaction. Within these groups, which formed from clusters of individuals who met each other in public spaces within the private development, a sense of community and conversation was emerging, and talk of the self would gently morph into political talk about the state of the country as a whole. Individuals flowed into these small groups out of their private homes, first by meeting in public spaces, then by coalescing; the groups would then convene and gather for a while, before breaking back apart into their individual elements and retreating into individual spheres, before reconvening once again. Between their meetings, back in their private realms, everyone would go online, sending emails and text messages across the globe and reading blogs and online news aggregators, many of which were compiled by overseas Vietnamese intellectuals—sites like Talawas, BBC tiếng Việt, VietStudies, and more.[18]

This was where consciousness (*ý thức*) emerged—in the individual's movement between private space and the small group, with the group in turn becoming a mediating space between the individual and an imagined concept of the larger national social body. What started out for many as a morning walk in the park subsequently morphed over the course of the day into a space to stretch one's mind and exercise a burgeoning sense of collective consciousness.

DISCIPLINE, SELF-AWARENESS, AND THE
COLLECTIVE GOOD

It is tempting to dismiss this kind of consciousness as "false consciousness," or, less dismissively but perhaps more cynically, to denounce it as a form of self-legitimization deployed by a group of wealthy elites who see themselves as the intellectual vanguard of society while failing to address their own privilege. Certainly, the notion that some of the most privatized property-holding elites in this supposedly socialist society imagined themselves as carriers of the collective ideals of the nation seems deeply contradictory. But for almost all the residents I knew, the relationship between self and society they claimed to see emerging in Phú Mỹ Hưng was a topic of significant reflection, and in fact animated many of the conversations we had together. Whenever people learned that I was a scholar studying social life in Vietnam's new urban zones, for example, they quickly said how important it was to study places like Phú Mỹ Hưng. This community, they emphasized, was a model for building a new vision of society, a place where self-discipline and social consciousness were intimately connected.

One morning while Doctor Cao and I were stretching at the Starlight Bridge, we bumped into Uncle Nam, a retired lawyer whom I had met on several other morning walks and whom I had come to recognize as someone both critical of and partly connected to Vietnam's political leadership.[19] His connections were twofold: he had benefited from some of the educational opportunities reserved for the elites within the socialist system—he had studied for many years in an Eastern European country—and his wife came from a family of Vietnamese diplomats. His training as a lawyer, however, compelled him to criticize the very kinds of relations that made him connected. He said he was strongly committed to defending the rule of law, which he, like many other Vietnamese lawyers I met during my research, felt was seriously compromised in the country. He supported many of the professed ideals of the Vietnamese state (such as the commitment to civility and the stated ideals of social justice) but had numerous practical observations about the country's failure to live up to those ideals. Although he had personally benefited from the system, and he by no means preferred the materialism of capitalism—a point he stressed—he worried that socialism as it actually existed had led many Vietnamese to lose their sense of self-responsibility and self-awareness.

Nearly all of Uncle Nam's criticisms came back to a simple principle, which he found a way to mention whenever we met: freedom requires discipline. The only way to truly guarantee the rule of law and a just society, he said, is to develop a synergistic relationship between individual rights and responsibilities,

defended by legal rules that transcend individual self-interest. This, he continued, was a lesson that needed to be learned by people at all levels of society. It
was clearly necessary at high levels of government, where individual avarice and
rampant corruption often trumped respect for legal process. But it also needed
to extend to the everyday actions of the common man. If ordinary Vietnamese wished to achieve a just society that would realize and protect their rights,
he insisted that they also needed to look inward, at themselves, and cultivate
self-discipline. This emphasis on self-discipline, he emphasized, was the missing part of the equation so often overlooked in discussions about the problem of
establishing a sense of citizenship rights in Vietnam. Rights, he averred, could
never be achieved if people felt no responsibility to the larger social collective of
which they were a member.[20]

When we met him that morning, Uncle Nam was carrying a string of 108
wooden Buddhist prayer beads. He invited me to join him on his walk, and we
continued around the lake. As we walked, he clicked through his prayer beads
in time with our steps. He told me that the real reason he chose to live in Phú
Mỹ Hưng had little to do with material comfort. Rather, he had moved there because he believed the New Urban Zone modeled the very kinds of relationships
he wished to see extended to the Vietnamese political system, and to Vietnamese
society at large. To illustrate this, he asked me to consider the landscape through
which we walked. The reason it was so comfortable to walk here in the morning, he explained, was that people had self-discipline. Phú Mỹ Hưng was a rule-
oriented place, and its success depended on the fact that people agreed to follow
the regulations. This could be seen, he said, just by looking at the layout of the
buildings. By adhering to the principles of the master plan, the project developers
had actually modeled the sense of self-discipline that people needed to inculcate
in their behaviors. In this way, Uncle Nam insisted, the built landscape itself could
be read as a daily reminder of the benefits available if people respected the principles of order and restraint. He pointed out that the developers could have easily
squeezed more buildings into the development in order to maximize the number
of units they could put up for sale; but instead, they restricted themselves, following the master plan in order to preserve open space. It was this willingness to
adhere to regulations, he said, that marked Phú Mỹ Hưng as different from other
developments. And in the end, he added, this was what made the development
so profitable. By resisting the temptation to maximize profit in the short term,
the developers had created what turned out to be the most lucrative development
in the entire country. Self-restraint, in this case, benefited the collective without
undermining the accrual of benefits to the individual.

I often heard comments like this when people tried to explain what they ap-
preciated most about Phú Mỹ Hưng. The three women I introduced in chapter 2
all emphasized, in their own different ways, the comfort and safety they felt in Phú

Mỹ Hưng, which they said resulted from rule-oriented behavior—the imposed discipline that put Vietnamese men in their place. Throughout my research, people highlighted the orderliness and discipline of Phú Mỹ Hưng, contrasting that to the rest of the city, which they derided as unplanned, haphazard, or plagued by "spontaneous urbanization" *(đô thị hóa tự phát).*[21] These kinds of statements also mirrored people's effusive praise when speaking of Phú Mỹ Hưng's late Taiwanese developer, Lawrence Ting, who was lauded for his "long-term vision" and self-sacrifice (see chapter 1). Even the fact that Mr. Ting had died by suicide—the ultimate self-sacrifice—reinforced how he was remembered: not as a profit-seeking businessman, but as a civilizing hero who ultimately gave his life for the sake of the urban civilization he held so dear.

As we walked, Uncle Nam, still clicking through his prayer beads, repeated that same story of Lawrence Ting. Then he paused and made an unexpected connection: he explained that Buddhism, too, was a way of finding self-discipline, which in turned produced a kind of enlightened consciousness. In his own personal studies of Buddhism, he had learned that self-discipline need not lead to self-oppression, but was instead part of the pathway leading to mental release and freedom. The most pressing problems in Vietnam, he asserted, could be solved by teaching people that self-aggrandizement ultimately undermines the collective good, and in turn harms the true liberation of the self. Thus, being conscious of others and cultivating a sense of awareness through practices of self-discipline could create the possibility for true and enduring self-realization.

The landscape we walked through offered further examples. Uncle Nam pointed to the streets, noting that they were clean and free of trash. Everyone benefited from these clean and wide open streets, he said, but keeping them that way depended on discipline. Walking these streets, he continued, allowed people to feel free and unencumbered, but this sense of freedom depended on strict regulation that could only be achieved by people who regulated themselves, who had the proper form of consciousness. This was no small matter, he added; it was not just a question of trash on the street, but could serve as a model for society and politics more broadly. The political system in Vietnam would all be fixed, he explained, if people had a sense of responsibility. All of Uncle Nam's examples—about the streets, about the way Phú Mỹ Hưng was built up (and not built up), about Lawrence Ting's vision, about Buddhist self-discipline—added up to a series of parables about the proper relationship between self and society and about the mutual constitution of rights and responsibilities. Our stroll through the clean streets of Phú Mỹ Hưng and tales of the benefits of master-planning had all of a sudden become a political commentary on how to deliver rights to the Vietnamese people. Walking through the landscape and talking about the need for discipline and self-responsibility, he told me that he was exercising his rights. The lawyer had turned the landscape into an argument for the rule of law.

Throughout my research in Phú Mỹ Hưng, seemingly banal conversations on life in the New Urban Zone often ended up conveying political messages. These conversations then led to invitations for further conversations. Just like Uncle Việt, Uncle Nam also regularly invited people to his home for long-drawn-out discussions. Sunday gatherings were especially important. After meeting for breakfast at a local café, his friends would arrive at his home on the seventh floor of a luxury apartment building,[22] where they would all sit cross-legged or lie around in a circle on a straw mat spread across the living room floor, surrounded by stacks of books (in Vietnamese and English) and piles of newspapers and magazines. While Uncle Nam and his wife made everyone espressos on an imported machine, the guests would rummage through the scattered newspapers looking for something to read, searching for phrases to start conversations. These Sunday meetings had the air of an intellectual salon, with discussion of politics and philosophical topics. One guest, who was in the construction industry, made a point of telling me that construction was tied into nation-building. Another guest, who was involved in foreign affairs and had spent three years in Hawaii, told me how his experience there primed him to live in Phú Mỹ Hưng, where the rule-oriented behavior of the residents most approximated what he saw as the consciousness underlying American democratic public life. And Uncle Nam, the lead philosopher in our conversations, explained that he was very interested in "freedom" and ideas of "the self" (*cái tôi*). He was the most talkative and spoke like a professor, so I asked him if he planned to write a book. He said yes, the book would be called *Self-Management: The Road to Happiness.*

We then listened to music while sipping our espresso and tasting a fine whisky ("One must drink it slowly," he said, "don't gulp it down," adding that few Vietnamese had developed the sense of discipline required to savor a fine spirit), as Uncle Nam described his travels with his wife to Buddhist lands for mindfulness retreats. He repeated his points about the connection between rule of law and self-discipline, and then he told me that looking at Phú Mỹ Hưng was a perfect way to understand the emergence of the rule of law in Vietnam. At that very moment, in fact, he was active in a legal fight for the rights of Phú Mỹ Hưng property owners, who were engaged in a dispute with the city and the Phú Mỹ Hưng Corporation about who should pay heavy land-use right fees. The fight over land use fees was in his mind connected to an emerging sense of collective and community, all based on a concept of individual rights.[23]

## POLITICS OF THE EVERYDAY

Early-morning exercise became an excuse for conversation; from this would follow invitations to private homes or small face-to-face discussions over coffee, which themselves became moments and spaces to further discuss the rule of law and the problems of the Vietnamese state. Bill Hayton, a BBC journalist known for his astute observations of Vietnamese political life, notes that "there are many constraints upon public expressions of anger in Vietnam. . . . People chat, people grumble, but people, generally, don't challenge the rule of the Communist Party in the street."[24] Indeed, although there are some exceptions, when it comes to open political speech, the most overt criticisms of the public sphere in contemporary Vietnam are not to be found expressed "in the street," but are more typically found in the traffic of social media and private conversations among friends. Thus, in contrast to common assumptions made about political discourse, which are based on theories derived largely from the experience of Western democracies, or are informed by images of mass popular uprisings in the world's public squares, the most active forms of political discourse in Vietnam are not to be found in physical kinds of public space. To get to the political requires winding one's way through the personal and the banal. If, as Yael Navaro-Yashin has noted of Turkey, there "is no face in which the political does not appear,"[25] in Vietnam the insight must be taken a step further. The most critical face of politics always emerges unexpectedly, springing forth in daily banter and spontaneous conversation. While formal, overt, and publicly visible political faces are often concealed by masks of rhetoric or dissimulation, the most vibrant spaces of Vietnamese political discourse are found in everyday discussions, in the kinds of visits to homes I have been describing or in the thousands of coffee shops that exist in every corner of the city.

As people move out from privatized spaces to spaces where they can engage a broader consciousness, political thought is not just a topic of discussion *within* everyday conversation; it is guided by the very *form* of the groups themselves—by the coming together of private persons in small nodes, who together add up to "the public." In these spaces, banal everyday concerns and joking relationships often morph into political commentary, following subtle, unpredictable shifts that connect inward reflection with collective consciousness. These small, face-to-face groups coalesce when individuals came together in privatized public spaces.

### Poems, Jokes, Double Entendres, and Political Critique

To see how a conversation among friends can flow from the personal and banal to the political, let's follow a meandering conversation I had with Uncle Việt and three of his friends at Gloria Jeans Coffee, an upscale café located at the base of the Grandview apartment complex in Phú Mỹ Hưng (fig. 3.2). On a surface level, these four friends had simply gathered together for small talk, conversation, and luxury snacks in an expensive, highly gentrified café. But the substance and style of the conversation expressed their private individualism as well as their conception of society. While their group was an exclusive group composed of private individuals, they had come together to articulate what it meant to be members of a much larger imagined community, the Vietnamese nation.

FIGURE 3.2. A typical café in Phú Mỹ Hưng, located at the mixed-use base of the Grandview Apartment Building. Author's photo, May 2011.

As we sat in a circle around a table, the conversation actually began by focusing on me, the foreign scholar among them, and how important they all felt it was for me to develop a deep understanding of Vietnamese culture if I wanted to understand anything about life in Phú Mỹ Hưng. They each took their turn, peppering me with advice. They told me that my study of Phú Mỹ Hưng could never really be only about Phú Mỹ Hưng, but really had to be about the future of Vietnam. Phú Mỹ Hưng, they insisted, was more than pretty buildings; it was an expression of what they hoped Vietnam could become—an orderly, planned, and rational society governed by rules (if not laws) that people—both citizens and the state—actually followed. But to get to what that meant, they said, one had to dig beneath the surface. If I wanted to understand social life in Phú Mỹ Hưng, I had to learn how to read between the lines, because Vietnam was a place where surface meaning always obscured deeper meaning. Uncle Việt further insisted that it was not possible to understand something like "urbanization" in Vietnam, for example, without understanding the depth of Vietnamese history, literature, and poetry, or without engaging with the subtleties of language. His friend, Uncle Quốc, continued in this vein, and then added that I needed to live up to *their* expectations, not simply satisfy my superiors at my university by completing a superficial research project. (I heartily agreed!)

Uncle Lòng then jumped in and told me that they wanted to help me understand the "real" Vietnam. To do this, they all agreed that I needed to learn a few things. The most important lesson was to recognize how the Vietnamese language was always shot through with multiple meanings, and how even the most banal statements could be fraught with symbolism and double entendres. To illustrate this, Uncle Quốc started with a well-known example, the poetry of Hồ Xuân Hương. "Have you heard the one about the jackfruit?" he asked, before reciting it from memory.[26]

*Uncle Quốc:* Here's a poem by the female poet Hồ Xuân Hương that speaks about women; it speaks of vulgar things using delicate words; it also speaks of delicate things that turn out to be quite vulgar.

> Thân em như quả mít trên cành.
> Da nó xù xì múi nó dày.
> Quân tử có thương thì đóng nõ.
> Xin đừng mân mó nhựa ra tay.

> I'm a jackfruit on the branch.
> Its skin is rough, its flesh thick.
> As lovestruck men poke and prick
> Sap will make their fingers stick

That's Hồ Xuân Hương!

*Erik:* Can you explain it?

*Uncle Quốc:* Explain it? In all truth, well, it speaks, it speaks about . . . sorry but it speaks about the sexual organs of a woman as if they were a fragrant jackfruit on the branch. Its skin appears rough but the flesh is thick and luscious. [nervous laughter]

*Uncle Lòng:* [more nervous laughter]

*Uncle Quốc:* And the part about "the gentleman who loves" *[quân tử có thương]*, well, um, sorry, but it says that he "bangs it," which is, like we sometimes say today, like "pile driving" *[đóng cọc]*, or what we sometimes call "brick laying" *[đóng gạch]* [all slang terms for sexual intercourse]. Do you get it yet? And the part about the sap making their fingers stick. Well, you know if you poke "it" with your fingers the "sap" will of course come out. If you poke a "jackfruit," its "sap" will get on your fingers. Completely brilliant, isn't it?

*Erik:* Impressive.

*Uncle Quốc:* There you go. Write that one down![27]

Uncle Quốc was on a roll. He went on to repeat several other poems, including a humorous tongue-twister that played on the use of homonyms with double meanings: *"Vợ cả vợ hai, cả hai vợ đều là vợ cả."* This couplet might be translated, roughly, in the following way, playing on the many meanings of the English word *one:* "Wife one, wife two, each one is one's wife."²⁸

The point they wished to make with these examples was to emphasize both the importance of "wordplay" *(chơi chữ)* in Vietnamese and the ways in which Vietnamese people commonly make use of multiple meanings. Furthermore, the gendered dimensions of their examples had the effect of reinforcing our little circle as a space of male bonding. Reciting vulgar poems and dirty ditties was, to borrow a concept from Michael Herzfeld, a literal expression of the "poetics of manhood."²⁹ Continuing his lessons, Uncle Quốc almost broke into schoolboy giggles as he offered me another example, also sexualized:

"Vợ mình là cơm nguội nhà ta nhưng vẫn là phở tái của thằng cha láng giếng."

In our own home my wife tastes like cold rice, but to the old man next door she's noodle soup with sliced rare beef.

"Do you get it?" they all chimed in, laughing. "Yes," I replied, "I get it." Slapping the table with joy, they continued, snickering and holding back laughs as they explained the obvious meaning:

*Uncle Quốc:*  Cold rice at our house: you've eaten that rice so many times that it's boring.

*Uncle Lòng:*  You eat it all the time, so it's boring! [laughing]

*Uncle Quốc:*  But to the old man next door, it's still like noodle soup with sliced rare beef *(phở tái)!* Still number one! [laughing]

At this point I was wondering (as I'm sure you might be wondering) where all this was going. But then the conversation suddenly shifted. If funny poems, with their multiple meanings, offered a polite way to talk dirty about sex, love, and infidelity, they also offered ways to talk about the sensitive subject of politics. Uncle Quốc made the shift with a six-eight verse:

*Uncle Quốc:*  Another poem speaks about officials who don't know how to lead:

> Cùng trong một chuyến đò ngang
> Người thì đi đến kẻ đang đi về
> Lái đò lái mãi thành mê
> Qua sống đếch nhớ mình về hay sang.
>
> On a boat crossing the river
> People are going, others returning
> Steering the boat, endless steering, into confusion
> He can't tell if he is coming or going.

Do you get it?

*Erik:* Not quite. [I actually did, but wanted to hear his explanation.]

*Uncle Quốc:* They are all together on a boat together. Let us explain it to you.

*Uncle Lòng:* Go ahead and explain it, brother.

*Uncle Quốc:* They are all together on a boat. On this boat there are people coming and going, coming and going. But the boat driver, well he just
goes back and forth, going and returning. And then in the end he
loses his senses, and he himself doesn't even know if he is coming
or going anymore. A number of today's leaders are just like that. Do
you understand, professor?

The table had been laughing through all these poems, tongue-twisters, and word-
plays. But the point was serious: they insisted that this was how one needed to understand Vietnam. It had to be like reading a poem, where everything had multiple
meanings: one must never take the external story at face value. You had to be educated to understand Vietnamese society as a whole. Furthermore—and this was
the main point of the entire conversation, like so many of their conversations—the
leaders of Vietnam's political system had lost their direction.

They then told me that the rational, orderly, rule-oriented life of Phú Mỹ Hưng,
by contrast, promised to help Vietnam find its direction. If a story or a poem could
be read in many ways, the same was true when looking at the people of Phú Mỹ
Hưng. On the surface, one might see it as a place for rich people to retreat behind their gates—a space of intense privatization and self-interest. But the cultivation of self-interest could not be misunderstood as something confined to the self
alone. Even this gathering around the table was more than a fun meeting—it was
a moment in which four educated men from an older generation were passing on
collective wisdom about the meaning of Vietnamese culture and politics. They
demonstrated their refinement by reciting poetry, and in the process of trying to
teach me how to make sense of their words by reading between the lines, they were
reproducing a particular way of understanding their relationship to the national
consciousness through language and innuendo.

As they continued explaining the significance of Phú Mỹ Hưng and what it
meant to be Vietnamese, the focus shifted to the cultivation of the responsible self
as an essential component of the collective, and how developing a responsible collective would in turn contribute to a better world for the self. To explain this, they
reminded me of the importance of the concept of *ý thức* (consciousness) and of
Phú Mỹ Hưng as a key place where such a form of consciousness could be cultivated. This was a difficult topic, they explained, because many assumed that people
in Phú Mỹ Hưng were "just rich people." As a result, some people mistakenly assumed that "consciousness" was connected to wealth, that it was nothing more than
having an abundance of refined material possessions. As they saw it, however, *ý
thức* was a product of education, which was itself achieved through self-discipline.

And educated and self-disciplined people, on average, tended to have higher incomes. This was why it was possible to misunderstand the relationship between wealth, consciousness, and civility. (At this point they used the terms *civility* and *consciousness* interchangeably.) But one could not mistake cause for effect: what really mattered was the fact that people with higher *ý thức* have a higher level of education. The fact that educated people tend to be wealthier was secondary—wealth was a side benefit of *ý thức,* but not the cause.

This conversation illustrates, in one setting, the multiple levels at play in the production of consciousness in a private development like Phú Mỹ Hưng. These multiple levels all operate simultaneously. Consciousness emerges through the coming together of individuals in a group, through the way a conversation takes place, and through the content of that talk itself, which offers reflexive commentary that stands outside of and looks back onto the very sense of consciousness emerging within that group. In this banal conversation, there is action and everyday behavior (a group of men hanging out at a fancy coffee shop), which produces a certain kind of consciousness (formed from the coming together of private individuals into a group), which both encourages and is in turn reinforced by verbal play (which reinforces group solidarity and also conveys meaning and commentary of its own). And finally, there is also a secondary level of analytic reflection about the meaning of the consciousness represented by that action, in which the members of the group reflect on their own status as carriers of a special kind of consciousness with political significance for the nation as a whole. This example also shows, again in a single sitting, how a simple conversation over coffee can meander from telling jokes that play on the subtleties of the Vietnamese language, to making political jabs at the government, all before circling back to assertions about the superior qualities of the people who live in the exclusive realm of the master-planned community. These kinds of exchanges took place over and over with the people I knew in Phú Mỹ Hưng

These sorts of exchanges also illustrate the central tension in Phú Mỹ Hưng. People there see themselves as the carriers of a new consciousness, which they believe holds potential for liberating the country from the shackles of its own misguided historical and present-day ideologies. But in asserting this sense of their own elevated consciousness, they are also legitimizing their privileged position within society. As a result, they both challenge and reproduce the structures of power and inequality that run through contemporary Vietnamese society. The result is a political landscape that is both revolutionary and conservative at once.

## CONCLUSION: EXERCISING CONSCIOUSNESS

In the anthropological scholarship on master-planned urban developments around the world, the standard story holds that they are sterile and empty, devoid of sociality—lonely places without history. In the "modernist city" of Brasilia, for example, James Holston described "a profound sense of social isolation" that led residents to describe life in the city as a kind of trauma that emerged out of the "interiorization of social life." Residents in Brasilia even had a name for this condition, purposely made to sound like a disease: they called it *brasilite,* which Holston translates as Brasilia-itis.[30] In China, a woman in one of Kunming's new exclusive housing developments echoed this sense of alienating hyper-individuation with a simple but telling confession to the anthropologist Li Zhang: "I do not even know my neighbors."[31] According to Zhang, whose ethnography echoes the findings of many other scholars, many of China's "New Towns" are sites of "atomization" or even "serial individualism." Scholars have noted similar trends in cities across China, as well as in social contexts as distinct as Delhi, Jakarta, Manila, São Paulo, and, of course, the suburbs of the United States.[32] In Ho Chi Minh City, many people living in the more established districts of the city would agree with these critical assessments. It was not uncommon for city residents to say that living in an apartment could be compared to living in "a box," or even, as I heard on several occasions, to living behind the closed doors of a refrigerator: suffocating, cold, isolating. These stories of atomization and of being closed off from the world speak to important points about the transformations of social life that come with new forms of urban development. As scholars working in such places have shown, master-planned developments are objectively different from the urban worlds they purport to replace with their "new" modes of living.

But privatization and atomization are only part of the story. As Zhang perceptively noted in her study of Kunming, the inward turn and the sense of increased individuation are intimately entangled with new and unexpected kinds of outward connection and political consciousness. Zhang usefully describes this as a "double movement," a process whereby privatized subjectivities develop in concert with emerging forms of civic consciousness. As social theorists have long understood, it turns out that privatization and public consciousness coproduce each other in often unexpected ways. At first glance, this may seem a contradiction, because in common language, "the individual" and "the collective" are often construed as opposites. More than a century ago, however, Emile Durkheim noted the connection between the rise of individualism associated with the division of labor and new kinds of social solidarity.[33] Marcel Mauss, Durkheim's nephew, also demonstrated that "the notion of the person, the notion of self," is itself tied to specific social and historical conditions.[34] The self, in short, rather than being the opposite of the social, is a social concept through and through. Similarly, as conceptions of "the self" become transformed, consciousness of society also changes.

In a place like Phú Mỹ Hưng, increased atomization changes how social solidarity operates. But that does not necessarily mean that the new kinds of individuals living in such a society have no consciousness of society. In fact, a host of scholars have noted that the rise of twentieth-century nationalism—itself a sign of intensified "social solidarity"—emerged in tandem with the formation of new kinds of "liberal" subjectivities. In the history of Vietnamese radicalism, for example, many of the most fervent anticolonialists were themselves products of an increasingly individualistic bourgeois society; but they went on to develop new conceptions of a robust public sphere.[35] In a more broadly theoretical sense, this is all quite well understood: Jürgen Habermas famously argued that core aspects of a democratic public sphere depended on the emergence of private personhood.[36] It is thus no deep contradiction when residents of Phú Mỹ Hưng see themselves as the bearers of a new social consciousness, even despite the development's promotion of class exclusion.

But there are also good reasons to be skeptical about any assertion that the new consciousness in Phú Mỹ Hưng will lead to a "democratic public sphere." Even if we recognize that groups and individuals are not opposites, this does not deny the fact that these new urban zones are built on relations of exclusion and privatization. According to Michael Waibel, a scholar of Vietnamese urban environments, "Vietnam is moving away from being one of the most egalitarian towards becoming one of the most unequal societies in the world." He then adds that the "development of the new urban areas appears to have aggravated housing inequality, for example. The latter developments, at least, are in sharp contrast to the still existing egalitarian ideology of the Communist Party of Vietnam."[37] Social life in these places is part of a process, always in motion, in which relations of privacy cannot be disentangled from emergent understandings of the public. But what that means for politics cannot be extrapolated from the sense of consciousness that is emerging in Phú Mỹ Hưng.

There is, however, a productive tension between privacy and ideas of community, and all of the elements of this tension play out in the new urban zone, where the well-to-do willingly repress their individual desires and subject themselves to self-discipline in order to foster a sense of collective consciousness, all while vigorously defending their right to private property and politely ignoring the fact that this inclusive sense of civilized community is itself founded on a much larger process of urban exclusion. In the process of walking, talking, and interacting with other people on their own terms, and in the process of developing an inward form of individual discipline, the morning exercisers are cultivating a distinct sense of individuality as well as collective social engagement. These morning walkers were not just "out for a walk" but were also meeting each other for engaged conversation, which contributed to a new awareness of social relations with others in their social context. This is what they meant when they spoke of consciousness, of *ý thức*. But as we will see in the second half of this book, this consciousness is also founded on a form of blindness: blindness to the struggles of the great numbers of city residents whose lives are reduced to rubble in the process of building the civilizing visions of other new urban zones. Across the Saigon River, in a place called Thủ Thiêm, the eviction of 14,600 households is the direct by-product of a vision of the future explicitly modeled on Phú Mỹ Hưng.

PART II

# Rubble

4

————

# Thủ Thiêm Futures Past

## A Short History of Seeing without Seeing

*We will restrict ourselves to the perspective we possess from the onetime future of past generations or, more pithily, from a former future.*
—REINHART KOSELLECK, *FUTURES PAST*

*On my desk is a beautiful picture of how Saigon might look someday. I keep my fingers crossed that it will happen.*
—GUY WRIGHT, "SAIGON OF TOMORROW"

### BEHIND THE BILLBOARDS: THỦ THIÊM WARD, DISTRICT 2, HO CHI MINH CITY

For as long as Saigon has been a city, its cosmopolitan urban core has ended abruptly at its eastern edge, where riverboat wakes and tidal currents splash against the reinforced banks of the Saigon River. For most of the twentieth century, reaching the edge of the city was easy: one only needed to walk the end of the city's famous tree-lined shopping and entertainment street known today as Đồng Khởi (Uprising) Street, previously known as Tự Do (Freedom) Street during the American War, and before that as Rue Catinat. The street there forms a T-junction with the river, and after crossing the busy riverfront boulevard that curves around the old historic core of the city, one reaches bến Bạch Đằng, the waterfront and wharf that has served as a picturesque boundary to the city ever since the colonial period.[1] It was possible to linger here at the river's edge and gaze at the other side, beyond the edge of the city, looking at a place called Thủ Thiêm.

Saigon residents, at least those who see themselves as real "city people," *dân thành phố,* have long described the world across the river in Thủ Thiêm as beyond the pale; until a redistricting program in 1997 changed many of the city's district boundaries, it was an "outer-city district," a space ranked low on the urban status hierarchy.[2] As late as the completion of the Thủ Thiêm Tunnel, which linked the area with downtown on November 20, 2011, city residents described Thủ Thiêm as, at best, a sliver of seemingly untouched countryside housing the marginalized poor just a quick ferry ride across from the city, and at worst, an unhygienic den of bandits, thieves, and other undesirables.[3] One of my closest informants, a long-time Thủ Thiêm resident who lived there until his family was evicted from their home in 2011, often described the negative impressions Saigon residents used to have of the area by repeating a popular ditty: "Eat in District Five; Play in District One; Sleep in District Three; and . . . *Brawl* in District Four and Thủ Thiêm."[4] Other Thủ Thiêm residents lamented how people living on the Saigon side of the river stereotyped them as illegal squatters, unemployed good-for-nothings, beggars, gamblers, drug addicts, or prostitutes. Like residents of cities around the world, Saigon residents often rank the districts of their city in a hierarchy of stereotypes. Thủ Thiêm, the proverbial "other side of the river," had long occupied the bottom ranks.[5]

This supposedly underdeveloped, rough-and-tumble world across the river was for many years shrouded in billboards and illuminated neon advertisements. When viewed from downtown, these billboards worked like screens to mask what lay beyond. They also seemed to act like vanity mirrors, reflecting Saigon's hopes and aspirations back onto itself. Standing there at the edge of the city, or sitting on one of the many park benches facing the river, city residents could gaze over at Thủ Thiêm without actually looking at it, dreaming of the products advertised on the billboards and projecting their own desires onto a space they commonly imagined as empty, undeveloped, or in need of improvement. Gazing across the river was more about imagining a city-yet-to-come than about looking at Thủ Thiêm for what it really was (fig. 4.1). As a result, when city officials renewed dormant plans to build the Thủ Thiêm New Urban Zone in the 1980s and 1990s, it was possible for planners and developers to imagine, and for many Saigon residents to sincerely believe, that they were truly turning nothing into something.

Regardless of the ways the area tends to be depicted, however, the historical evidence is clear: until the demolition and land clearance began there in the 2000s, Thủ Thiêm was not empty. It had not been empty for a long time. Indeed, it had been populated for as long as Saigon itself. Evidence of people living there appears regularly in the historical records. And once the project to build the Thủ Thiêm New Urban Zone officially began, at least 14,600 "dossiers" were registered in the compensation books, each dossier representing a household, sometimes including more than one generation, for a total of nearly 60,000 people. But the story of the people whose lives make up the files in those dossiers has long been told in a rather curious manner—as the story of other people looking at them while erasing their existence, staring directly at their homes without seeing them there, dreaming of what their neighborhoods might someday become while ignoring them for what they are and have always been in their own right. Thủ Thiêm, in other words, has

FIGURE 4.1. Thủ Thiêm, looking east from Saigon's bến Bạch Đằng waterfront. The Thủ Thiêm ferry terminal is in the center of the image, directly underneath the faded Fujifilm sign and the sign that reads "Contact CIAT." The CARIC ship repair buildings, built in the late nineteenth century, are located toward the right side of the image, underneath the Vietnam tourism and LG advertisements. Author's photo, July 2000.

long been the object of sustained attention, but this attention has almost always been distorted by the optics through which it has been viewed. And this attention has more often than not worked to Thủ Thiêm's disadvantage—either rendering it invisible or denigrating the people who live there, leading to projects that bring the area into view primarily in order to change it.

### Obscured by Maps and Legends

City maps provide the best visual evidence for this curious relationship between visibility, invisibility, and the will to know about a place in order to radically transform it. From as far back as the French period, the explanatory legends on tourist maps of Saigon have almost always been placed directly over Thủ Thiêm. This practice continued on Vietnamese-made tourist maps well into the first decade of the twenty-first century. Despite the fact that Thủ Thiêm is located close to the historic core of Saigon–Ho Chi Minh City, the placement of these map legends demonstrates precisely the district's reputation as an empty zone, unworthy of notice in its own right. On these maps, Thủ Thiêm is not so much invisible as occluded by other interests, obscured by value judgments its observers make about what counts as urban space or places worth visiting. In a map called "Ville de Saigon" from a book about Cochinchina printed on the occasion of the International Colonial Exposition of 1931 in Paris, Thủ Thiêm is located underneath the legend

FIGURE 4.2. A French map of Saigon, published in Saigon as part of a commemorative volume on Cochinchina for the 1931 International Colonial Exposition in Paris. Thủ Thiêm is located underneath the legend.

SOURCE: Exposition Coloniale Internationale, Paris (1931). *La Cochinchine*. Saigon, P. Gastaldy, Éditeur, 28–29.

(fig. 4.2). In a map from the American period, in 1964, it is located underneath the compass rose (fig. 4.3). In a Vietnamese-made map from 1990, during a time when city officials were beginning to actively recruit foreign investors, Thủ Thiêm is completely obscured by advertisements (fig. 4.4). And in a tourist map from 2005, it is once again located beneath the map legend (fig. 4.5).

The conceptual disregard for Thủ Thiêm seen in tourist maps does not mean, however, that the space was actually invisible to mapmakers. As I will show in this chapter, in other maps and representations produced throughout the nineteenth and twentieth centuries, especially those produced by geographers and explorers or for reconnaissance purposes, there is clear knowledge that people were living in Thủ Thiêm. Many such maps include small cartographic details—such as road outlines, village names, or building shapes—that plainly indicate that the mapmakers indeed knew Thủ Thiêm was inhabited. While building styles in Thủ Thiêm may have been quite different than in the city center on the other side of the river, the mapmakers' use of small dots to indicate individual houses, as well as lines and hatch marks indicating inhabited spaces, all regularly organized around a riverfront road, is typically quite clear on these maps. In other maps, especially those made by architects and planners throughout the twentieth century and up until today, Thủ Thiêm becomes the opposite of empty: every inch is carefully planned and filled in with imaginative dreams of futuristic urban utopias. But in the process of laying out these visions of the future, the existing space of Thủ Thiêm becomes covered up by the planner's agenda.[6] These future visions universally imagine a new Thủ Thiêm that has been built on a blank slate, devoid of preexisting human occupation, despite all evidence to the contrary.

Although Thủ Thiêm is often described through representational practices or in colloquial speech by Saigon residents, planners, and government officials as a dangerous, empty, or wasted space, it is plainly incorrect to say that Saigon residents, planners, or government officials ever believed it was in fact empty in any real sense.[7] Since at least the Nguyễn dynasty, the area has been registered in the dynastic, colonial, or state records of all the regimes that have controlled it.[8] Furthermore, all the standard technologies of governance—including records of the Village Councils (as they were called in previous eras) or People's Committees (in the current government), cadastral surveys, surveillance records, taxation rolls, land titles, maps—have consistently included Thủ Thiêm in their records. A market was established there in 1751, and since the middle of the nineteenth century Thủ Thiêm has been the site of an active Catholic church as well as a convent associated with the Congregation of the Lovers of the Holy Cross.[9] Furthermore, although the records are scattered and sometimes contradictory, it is clear that even before the nineteenth century the land there was dotted with pagodas, temples, shrines, and community halls. Since the middle of the twentieth century, the space has been even more populated, and there have been public schools, a leper colony,

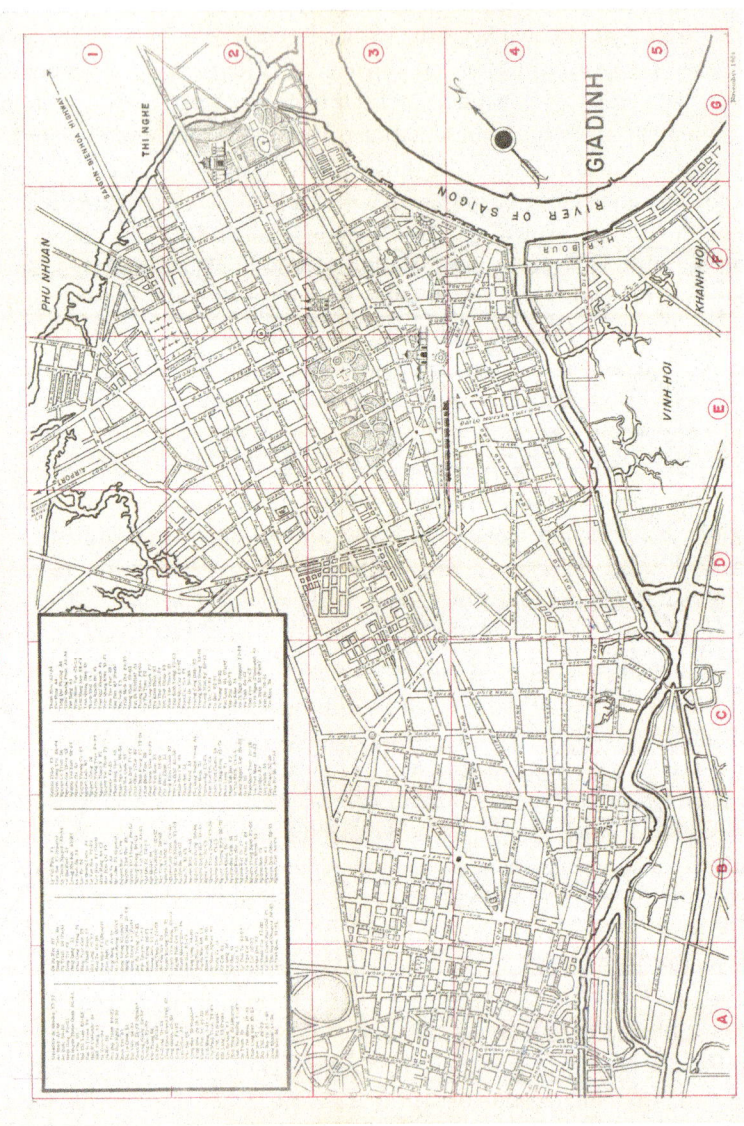

FIGURE 4.3. Map of Saigon, November 1964. Thủ Thiêm is located underneath the compass rose.
SOURCE: MAP1209010IB, Vietnam Archive Map Collection, The Vietnam Center and Archive, Texas Tech University.

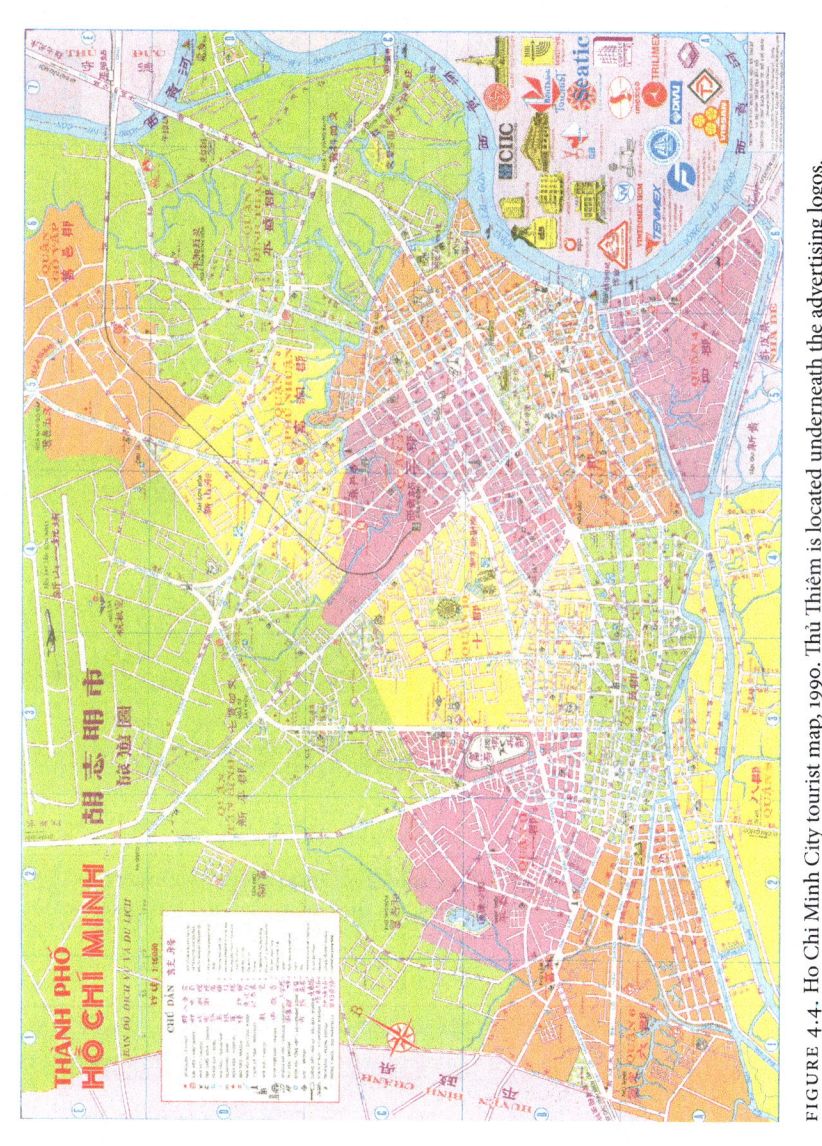

FIGURE 4.4. Ho Chi Minh City tourist map, 1990. Thủ Thiêm is located underneath the advertising logos.

SOURCE: MAP1209020S, Vietnam Archive Map Collection, The Vietnam Center and Archive, Texas Tech University. Produced by Trung tâm ứng dụng khoa học kỹ thuật và Bộ môn trắc địa bản đồ Trường Đại học Bách khoa TP. Hồ Chí Minh; Editor: Trần Tân Lộc. Cartographer: Lê Tiến Thuận.

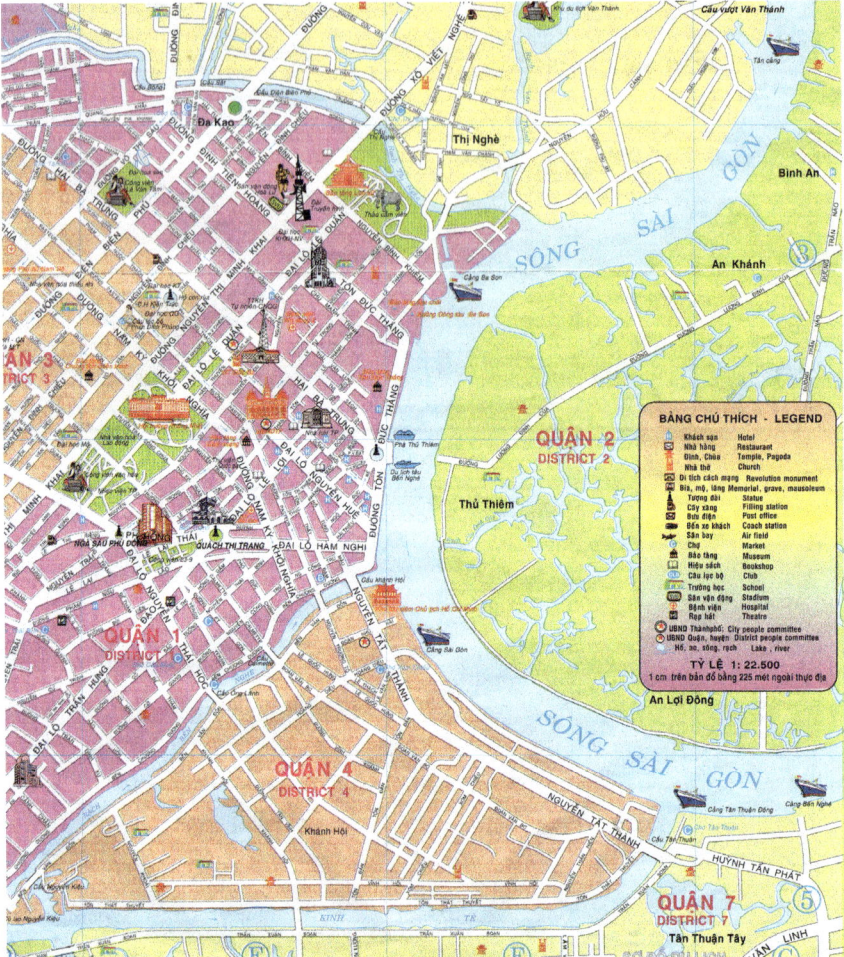

FIGURE 4.5. Ho Chi Minh City tourist map, ca. 2005. Thủ Thiêm is located beneath the legend. Author's collection. Produced by Nhà Xuất bản Giao thông Vận tải. Cartographers: Đặng Quang Thịnh and Thái Văn Thuận.

and scores of other highly visible institutions, including a large ship repair business, a seafood freezing plant, and no small number of People's Committee offices associated with official governance.

What all this means is that Thủ Thiêm is not and was never described as empty because it was not known that people lived there; rather, it has been and is described this way *in spite of* extensive knowledge about its inhabitants. It might even be asserted—admittedly with some (but I think not too much) hyperbole—that over the course of the twentieth century and through the first decades of the twenty-first, official knowledge about Thủ Thiêm and discourses of its emptiness have been mutually reinforcing: as official knowledge about Thủ Thiêm has grown, the more it has been described as empty. In telling this curious story about seeing without seeing, my goal is not to provide a proper chronological history of Thủ Thiêm; instead, my aim, in an anthropological spirit, is to explore a series of "futures past," all of which show how it has been possible for people in different moments of history to stare at Thủ Thiêm without seeing it. Along the way, in the process of highlighting the various modes of seeing and representing Thủ Thiêm over the years, it will also be possible to catch some fleeting glimpses of this often misrepresented world behind the billboards.

## SEEING THỦ THIÊM WITHOUT SEEING IT

Commonly described in Vietnamese as a peninsula *(bán đảo)*, Thủ Thiêm is more precisely an oxbow, formed at a dramatic horseshoe-shaped bend in the Saigon River across from the heart of Ho Chi Minh City. An extensive network of natural waterways and tributary streams crisscrosses the land here, creating what was for most of its history only partially solid ground, suitable to small-scale agricultural pursuits, temporary housing, and linear settlements built—like many of the settlements in the Mekong Delta region further to the south and west—along river and canal banks and atop raised roadways that double as earthwork embankments. Subject to the rise and fall of tidal currents, and marked by geological challenges that hinder building, the largely swampy land in this space has long thwarted attempts to establish extensive fixed forms of development. Studies conducted in the 1970s determined that any permanent urban development would require adding an average of 1.5 meters of infill across the area.[10] But its position across the river from the city center also means that Thủ Thiêm has almost always been occupied, certainly since 1698, the date commonly cited as the founding of Saigon as a Vietnamese city, and probably longer.[11] The most vivid descriptions we have of the area begin in the nineteenth century and give a sense of life across the river from Saigon, which was then a growing regional entrepôt and a space of bustling commerce protected by Nguyễn dynasty military fortifications. It is worth lingering on some of those descriptions.

### Historical Views of Thủ Thiêm

On October 7, 1819, John White, a lieutenant in the United States Navy sailing on the brig *Franklin*, reached the city of Saigon, which was "hidden from view, by a row of miserable huts, extending along the borders of the river, on which was moored a vast number of the craft of the country."[12] White's vessel moored "on the opposite bank" from Saigon—likely the site of Thủ Thiêm.[13] His descriptions of a visit ashore provide a sense of life in the area at that time, well before French colonial urban planning transformed the city of Saigon:

> An intimate view of the few huts on the bank, within fifty yards of the place where we lay at anchor, did not materially raise our opinion of their domestic economy, or general habits. [ . . . ]
>
> The appearance of several boats, of light and airy construction, each, in many cases, managed by a single woman, in picturesque costume, was novel and pleasing; while great numbers of the native vessels, of different sizes, plying in various directions upon the stream, gave a busy and lively interest to the scene.
>
> Just below us, on both sides of the river, were the ruins of ancient fortifications, with their glacis overgrown with shrubbery, and their moats filled with reeds, shooting their taper leaves above the "green mantle of the standing pool."[14]

The two fortifications White described were remnants of the Tây Sơn wars, leftover ruins from the time when Nguyễn Phúc Ánh, who became the Gia Long emperor in 1802, set up military posts (đồn) on either side of the river to protect Saigon, which was then part of the phủ (prefecture) of Gia Định. The two posts faced each other across the river: one at Thảo Câu (on the Saigon side of the river), the other at Giác Ngư (đồn Cá Trê) in Thủ Thiêm.[15] Nguyễn Ánh had also constructed a floating bridge connecting the two posts to facilitate traffic between them. A well-known map first produced by Trần Văn Học during Gia Long's reign, published for the first time in 1816, three years before White's visit, not only shows these two forts, but also indicates that there was a village or settlement of some sort in Thủ Thiêm (fig. 4.6).[16]

Although it is difficult to say from these scattered descriptions just what life in Thủ Thiêm was like or how the space looked in any detail, the people in this area were clearly connected to the world beyond the immediate region. White's group, for example, was greeted by a Tagalog man named Pasqual, who was originally from Luzon but who had lived in Cochinchina for the previous twenty years, and was married to the daughter of a mandarin from "Don-nai" (now written as Đồng Nai). The sailors were invited to visit his house, which was also located across the river from Saigon, on what appears to have been the Thủ Thiêm side: "On this side the river banks had been washed away from the edge of the channel, about fifty or sixty feet, leaving a space of very soft mud, between low-water mark and dry land; over this mud flat were erected, at short distances apart, causeways, or stages, constructed of crutched trunks of trees, driven into the earth, supporting rafters of rough timber, on which were laid platforms of hewn plank, to facilitate the intercourse between the river and the shore." Despite the mud, the ground was arranged in a way that made habitation possible. Yet the houses were relatively impermanent in nature: "[Pasqual's] house was situated in the centre of the enclosure, which was nearly square, containing less than half an acre, and planted with

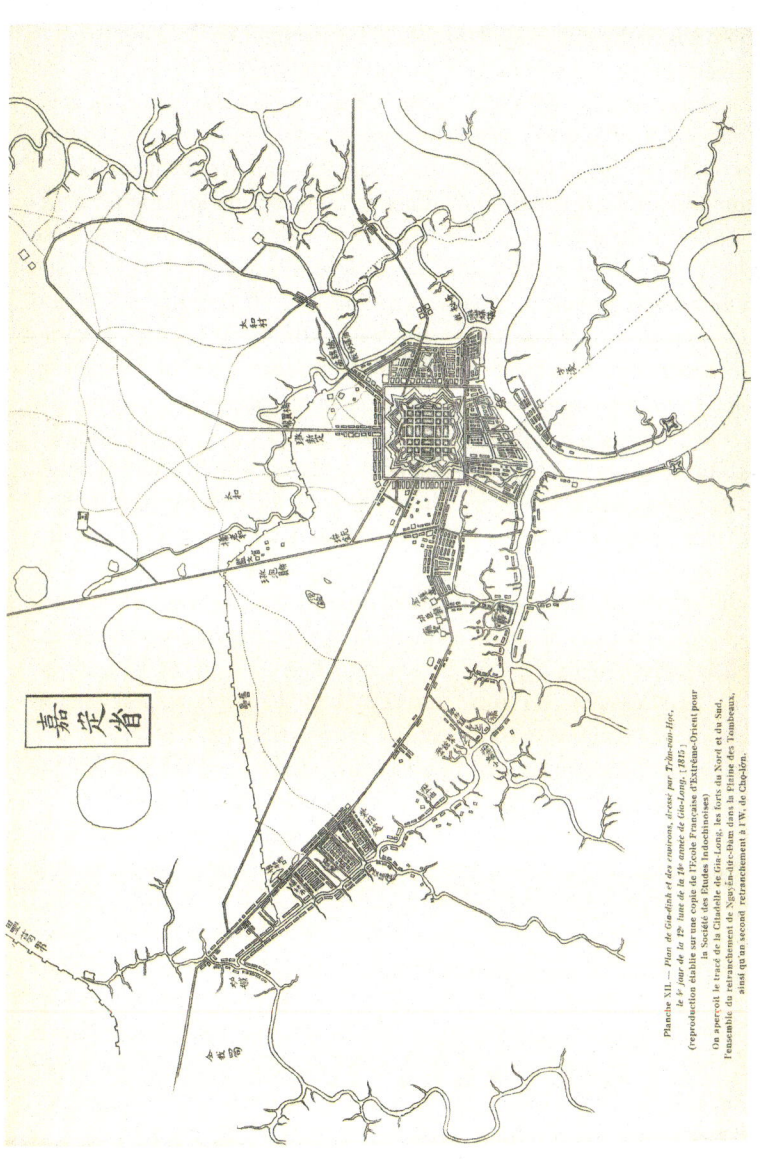

Planche XII. — *Plan de Gia-dinh et des environs, dressé par Trần-van-Học,
le 4ᵉ jour de la 12ᵉ lune de la 14ᵉ année de Gia-Long, (1815).*
(reproduction établie sur une copie de l'École Française d'Extrême-Orient pour
la Société des Études Indochinoises)

On aperçoit le tracé de la Citadelle de Gia-Long, les forts du Nord et du Sud,
l'ensemble du retranchement de Nguyễn-đế-Bạm dans la Plaine des Tombeaux,
ainsi qu'un second retranchement à l'W. de Cho-lớn.

FIGURE 4.6. Detail from reproduction of the "Tran Van Hoc map of 1815." This well-known map, first drawn by Trấn Văn Học in 1815 and later reproduced in the *Bulletin de la Société des études indochinoises*, depicts the presence of permanent development and even indicates the presence of a road, directly facing the more heavily built up city center.

SOURCE: Malleret, L. (1935). "Eléments d'une monographie des anciennes fortifications et citadelles de Saïgon." *Bulletin de la Société des études indochinoises, Saïgon.* Plate XII, following p. 108.

areka nut-trees. A few straggling plants were scattered about without any regard to order or regularity. Some loose stones were laid from the gateway to the house, over which we contrived, with some difficulty, to pass dryshod, the circumjacent grounds being completely inundated by the heavy rains which had recently fallen." The house stood above the soft ground on stilts: "The habitation was about twenty-five by thirty feet square, and was raised two and a half feet from the earth. It was of one story, composed of rough frame-work covered with boards, and its roof, which consisted of a thatching of palm-leaves, projected about ten feet outside the walls, and descended so low as to render it necessary to stoop in passing under it."[17]

White, who says in his text that he had come to Indochina looking for a rumored *El Dorado,* was clearly disappointed by Saigon and its surroundings. While he described life *on the river* as "pleasing" or "busy and lively," he denigrated the life *on shore* as impermanent, inundated, eroding, muddy, lacking order, and unfixed. White presents these qualities as unpleasing to his eyes, which were no doubt accustomed to the urban forms of New England, from where he had set sail. Despite being a seafarer himself, he lacked the conceptual ability to recognize life along the river as a form of cosmopolitan habitation of its own. He was looking for buildings and sturdy structures built on solid land, and thus fixated on the remains of the old fort, or the house of his Tagalog host, both of which left him dissatisfied.

Despite White's terrestrial bias, his descriptions still portray a world of bustling activity, humming with commerce. The river was teeming with small boats, which came alongside the *Franklin* laden with tropical fruits and teas. There were fishermen observing their adventures. And rowboats manned by nine rowers constantly plied a heavily trafficked river route, traveling back and forth from Cape St. James (now known as Vũng Tàu) to Saigon at regular intervals. "To these objects, we may add immense rafts of timber, bamboos, and new canoes, from various parts of the country, constantly arriving at the metropolis."[18] The people lived largely on the water, and the "population is dense near the river, but scattered farther remote from it."[19]

The scene White described differed from the burgeoning urbanism of nineteenth-century Boston or New York, but despite his disparaging tone, it is clear that areas across the river from Saigon were settled in a manner fairly typical of Southeast Asian riverside settlements, and in a manner well adjusted to the watery landscape of the region (fig. 4.7). Indeed, the kind of water-based commerce White described was typical not only of the time, but remains so even today throughout the Mekong Delta and other places in Southeast Asia.[20] It may have looked impermanent to White's eyes, but this form of settlement was appropriate to the region and largely integrated into the local political system, as evidenced by its inclusion in Nguyễn dynasty cadastral records.[21] It was neither empty nor invisible.

White's descriptions of life on the river anticipate the modes in which these kinds of riverine habitats have been described throughout the history of colonial and postcolonial urban development. In what sounds like an impossible contradiction,

RIVE DROITE DE LA RIVIÈRE DE SAIGON, DU COTÉ DU PARC A CHARBON.
d'après un croquis de M. A. SAINTYVES

FIGURE 4.7. The right bank of the Saigon River, looking toward Saigon from Thủ Thiêm.
SOURCE: Bouchot, J. (1927). *Documents pour servir à l'histoire de Saigon, 1858 à 1865*. Saigon, Editions Albert Portail.

but is in fact a normalized mode of representing unfixed forms of habitation, he manages to see them as both disappointingly empty and teeming with life. Indeed, throughout the twentieth and into the twenty-first century, impermanent settlements along Vietnam's waterways have regularly been depicted using similar kinds of disparaging language.[22] In different eras, despite radically different political ideologies, these kinds of developments have rarely, if ever, been recognized as a specific form of urbanism, one that develops in relationship to the transport and geo-climatic features of the region. Instead, they are denigrated as at best "temporary housing" or "stilt houses"—known as *maisons sur pilotis* in French, or *nhà sàn* in Vietnamese—and at worst as "slums," *trou à rats* or *nhà ổ chuột*.[23]

But if read differently, suspending moral judgment while paying close attention to the use of space, White's descriptions serve as a useful source for understanding the lived environment of Thủ Thiêm in an alternative sense, as a spatial form of habitation that developed in ways well suited to the nature of the place. Fixed and permanent development was in fact not absent; it was simply organized in different ways, concentrated in linear filaments of land that follow the river and other waterways, enabling maximum use of the transport networks. Homes were clustered in these spaces, creating a linear form of urbanism set against a backdrop of less developed land, which was reserved for agriculture, fishing, and gathering activities. The stiff fronds of water coconut palms growing in this land, for example, have long been used as a plentiful, sturdy, inexpensive, and renewable resource for roofing material; and the snakes, frogs, birds, river crabs, and turtles teeming in the waterways, canals, and wet-rice fields have long been popular local delicacies and sources of supplemental income. Indeed, long after White's time and throughout the twentieth century, the land in the interior of the Thủ Thiêm peninsula was never empty, but was owned and stewarded by people who used it to support their livelihoods, developing it incrementally and organically. Only after urban involution in more concentrated built-up areas reached its limits would the residents further build up the earth, expanding the livable area of solid land little by little away from the densely populated banks of the river. It is indeed possible to see in this slow and methodical form of development a distinctly sustainable model for urban growth, or even a form of garden city development, where urban life and appropriate land use are integrated with built space in ways that suit the unique geo-climatic characteristics of the region—and where urban growth comes through small additions made by everyday residents rather than in grand bursts of top-down planning.

An apocryphal legend for the origins of the name for Thủ Thiêm plays on this notion of incremental habitation, suggesting how people and natural processes slowly expanded the habitable high ground of an otherwise low-lying land. Thủ Thiêm is a place of alluvial silt, and the playful story of how it got its name says that "every day the land grows just a bit higher" (*mỗi ngày một cao thêm*). The Sino-Vietnamese word for land is *thổ*, and the Vietnamese word for more is *thêm*, and so, the folk etymology asserts, a place that each day acquired "more land" became known as Thổ Thêm, which the locals pronounced as Thủ Thiêm.[24] The additive form of development noted in this legend in many ways accurately describes the urbanization that took place there. Indeed, this pattern was seen not just in Thủ Thiêm but throughout Saigon, where, over time, as the city has grown, its swamps have been filled and its canals paved and turned into streets.[25]

The focus on settling and clustering near the river impacted Saigon's development as well. Several passages in a description of Saigon written in 1885 by Pétrus Ký note how congested *both* sides of the Saigon River were around the turn of the nineteenth century. For example: "The shorelines of Saigon were shrouded with houses on stilts. At the end of Catinat street, at the current ferry wharf of Thủ-thiêm, there was the Thủy-các (the pavilion for King of Water), the lương-tạ, the royal bathrooms constructed on the floating bamboo rafts." And: "What was there opposite Saigon, on the opposite bank? During Gia-long's time, it was the Xóm-tàu-ô (hamlet of the black junks); this place was assigned as the dwellings of Chinese pirates whose small sea junks were painted black."[26]

These descriptions underscore that Thủ Thiêm was not, and never has been, empty, and that it emerged in tandem with Saigon, its form of residential development tied to river commerce and the clustered linear-settlement morphologies common in Vietnam's south. But they also reveal the way in which "the opposite bank" developed a reputation as a place of darkness, home to quintessential "others" like Chinese pirates. Over the years, however, impacted by the terrestrial bias of colonial urban plans, the land use patterns on the Saigon side of the river became standardized into a system of grids and the land was increasingly built up. During this time, the two areas have increasingly diverged in their modes of development. But the absence of extensive permanent building did not mean that the land was not being used in Thủ Thiêm. It was simply being used differently.[27]

### The Thủ Thiêm Church and Other Fixed Institutions

Not all the buildings in Thủ Thiêm were temporary; indeed, several important structures were built on solid ground. The most significant of these, and the best documented, are the Thủ Thiêm church and the adjacent convent of the Congregation of the Lovers of the Holy Cross (Dòng Mến Thánh giá, or Amantes de la Croix de Jésus-Christ). In 2009, the Thủ Thiêm church published a commemorative volume documenting the 150th anniversary of the Catholic community that would eventually become the parish (giáo xứ) of Thủ Thiêm. According to evidence uncovered by the parish priests, a Catholic community has existed in Thủ Thiêm since at least the middle of the nineteenth century. In 1840, a female Congregation of the Lovers of the Holy Cross was established there, and in 1859 a full Catholic congregation was established under the direction of Father Gabriel Nguyễn Khắc Thành, who served the congregation until 1869. In 1865, Father Gabriel Thành built the first wooden church in Thủ Thiêm. Later, in 1875, Father M. Montmayeur built a parish house for the sisters of the Lovers of the Holy Cross, as well as two religious schools, one for boys and one for girls, before turning his efforts to rebuilding the main church, which he inaugurated in 1885. On May 25, 1921, the Thủ Thiêm congregation was formally declared a parish by Bishop Victor Carolus Quinton of the regional apostolic vicariate.[28] Throughout the twentieth century, further building projects followed: in 1930, a bell tower was constructed to hold the church's five bronze bells, which had been cast in France between 1889 and 1892. In 1956, the church was rebuilt—its third incarnation—under the leadership of Father Phaolô Huỳnh Ngọc Tiên. This church, in the midcentury style shared by hundreds of other churches built in South Vietnam after the 1954 Catholic migrations from the North, still stands in Thủ Thiêm.[29] The parish has remained active ever since, and even after most of the local residents were evicted from surrounding neighborhoods, parishioners returned each week to fill the pews in packed Sunday services (fig. 4.8).[30]

As late as 2016, both the church and the convent of the Lovers of the Holy Cross were as active as ever, and a dedicated community of parishioners maintained the church grounds. Even after almost every other permanent structure in the entire Thủ Thiêm project zone had been reduced to rubble, the Thủ Thiêm church and convent remained standing. The impeccable grounds of the convent, with its

FIGURE 4.8. Sunday Mass at the Thủ Thiêm church. Author's photo, March 2014.

manicured flowerbeds, carefully tended bonsai trees, spiritual grottos to Maria and revered saints, and historic buildings with freshly painted walls were carefully kept up, evincing the enduring will of the members of this religious institution to resist eviction. It was also clear that the church was mobilizing its history, as well as its connections to the Roman Catholic Church, as a means to stand its ground and resist eviction. When asked if they would ever accept persistent demands to leave the premises, however, the priests of the church and the sisters in the convent always demurred, carefully avoiding any confrontational words.[31] "We will see," they would say. But they also remained vigorously at work, leading parish activities, holding monthly feasts, teaching Sunday school classes, and raising vegetables and fish in the convent's large immaculate gardens and ponds (fig. 4.9).[32] And they would point out that the church had been there for more than one hundred and fifty years.

The church was not the only permanent structure defining the built environment in Thủ Thiêm. A survey conducted by a team of Vietnamese researchers well before the start of demolition catalogued at least twenty-nine religious structures in the three wards lying within the area slated for the Thủ Thiêm project.[33] In An Khánh Ward, there was an important community hall, Đình An Khánh; five pagodas (chùa), Chùa Thiền Tịnh, Chùa Đông Hưng, Chùa Liên Trì, Chùa Hội Đức,

FIGURE 4.9. The inner courtyard of the Thủ Thiêm Congregation of the Lovers of the Holy Cross, looking west across the Saigon River toward Ho Chi Minh City. The building on the right was built in 1933, mimicking the style of a rectory constructed in 1875 under the guidance of Father Montmayeur Louis Philippe (Minh). The chapel in the center of the image is not to be confused with the Thủ Thiêm church, located in the center of its own courtyard next door, immediately to the north. Author's photo, March 2014.

and Chùa Linh Sơn; three local place-based temples *(miễu)*, Miễu Cây Dương, Miễu Cây Trôm, and Miễu Cây Da; a small monastic Buddhist shrine, Tịnh thất Phước Quang, and a small Cao Đài temple, Ngọc điện Huỳnh Hà. In Thủ Thiêm Ward, in addition to the convent and the church described above, there were two spirit temples, Đền Quan Bơ and Đền Cô Bơ; a pagoda, Chùa Giác Chơn; two local temples, Miễu Ông Địa and Giai Qưới Miễu; and another small Cao Đài temple, Thánh thất Thủ Thiêm. In An Lợi Đông Ward, there was another community hall, Đình An Lợi Đông; three important Buddhist structures, Chùa Đông Thạnh, Tịnh xá Ngọc Thanh, and Tịnh xá Như Lai; five local temples, Miễu An Lợi Vạn, Miễu Bà Thủy Long, Miễu Ngũ hành Bảng Đỏ, Miễu Ngũ hành Ông Én, and Miễu Chiến sỹ; and a small Catholic chapel, Nhà nguyện Thánh Tâm.[34]

While most of these institutions are less carefully documented than is the Thủ Thiêm Catholic church, several of them are also quite old, indeed older than the church itself. According to one source, Đình An Khánh was established between 1679 and 1725, although this is difficult to verify; in terms of physical evidence, the oldest surviving vestiges of religious artifacts used by ferrymen in the area date only from the year 1858, and there is an undated silk scroll said to have been presented to the *đình* during the reign of Tự Đức (1847–83).[35] According to local recollection, another *đình*, in An Lợi Đông, was founded in 1849, but historical evidence combined with oral histories of local residents indicates a more likely date of 1909.[36] The Ông Én local temple, formerly known as the Cây Bàng Temple, is said to have been established in 1888 in a spot facing the Saigon River, but it was moved to its current location, further into the peninsula, in 1960.[37] Many of the other religious institutions were built over the course of the twentieth century, with many emerging in the 1920s and 1930s and others in the 1950s and 1960s. When asked, the residents in the area rarely knew precise dates, but only said the institutions had been there "lâu lắm rồi"—*a long time already*—or "mấy đời," *several generations*. Right up until the demolitions began, and even after they were ongoing, the institutions were popular: crowded during festivals, filled with the sounds of *hát bội* at the annual *đình* festivals, of secretive *lên đồng* séances at various temples, of Buddhist and Cao Đài incantations, and other human noises of the sort that do not come from empty places.

The built environment in Thủ Thiêm was not confined to religious structures. Houses and businesses abounded. Thủ Thiêm's position on the banks of the Saigon River made it a prime location for ship repairs, and in 1887 a large shipping repair warehouse was built under the name of CARIC (Les Chantiers et Ateliers Réunis d'Indochine).[38] The company's main office was on the Saigon side, along the riverfront road near the intersection with Rue Catinat, but their production facilities remained in Thủ Thiêm until they were demolished in late 2010. Throughout the twentieth century, large numbers of Thủ Thiêm residents were employed in the shipping repair business, and many of the older homes in Thủ Thiêm retained nineteenth- and early-twentieth-century colonial architectural flourishes (until they were demolished in 2010–11).[39] Residents of some of the more elegant of these homes recall their grandparents being employed as managers in these French industrial operations, as minor functionaries in the colonial administration, or at banks on the Saigon side of the river. As further evidence of Thủ Thiêm's role at the center of the shipping industry, enormous wooden posts driven deep into the banks of the river for mooring boats were still visible as late as 2012. These posts were formally recorded in the port records and were numbered, 1 to 17.[40] The historian Nguyễn Đình Đầu even asserts that, contrary to legend, Hồ Chí Minh (known at the time as Nguyễn Tất Thành) boarded his boat to leave for Europe not from the famous Nhà Rồng "dragon house" wharf (now a Ho Chi Minh museum), but rather in Thủ Thiêm.[41]

Far from a wasteland, Thủ Thiêm was in fact a prime location, just a ferry ride across from Saigon. As noted above, when demolition and eviction began, more than 14,600 households had to be removed, each with its own home.

## THỦ THIÊM FUTURES PAST

Just as Saigon grew and became integrated into a world system made possible by its location on the river, so too did Thủ Thiêm. Thủ Thiêm's perceived emptiness should be understood not in literal terms, but as a symbolic quality that emerges socially, as a function of its proximity to the city. When coupled with the ambitions of planners, this very proximity has made Thủ Thiêm both the object of great speculative attention and a seemingly contradictory, but in fact co-constituted, discourse of erasure. Indeed, it has been the attention paid to Thủ Thiêm that has rendered and continues to render it empty. To understand how it is possible to stare at a place full of people and call it empty, it is useful to look at the work of different planners over the course of many generations and many political regimes. The act of seeing without seeing is not just a recent phenomenon, but marks the work of French colonial planners, Vietnamese nationalist and American Cold War nation-builders, postwar Vietnamese utopian socialists, and contemporary postreform-era Vietnamese market-oriented socialists.[42]

Even before the advent of formal French colonial rule, a stark differentiation existed between the Saigon side of the river, with its straight, orderly roads radiating outward from the late-eighteenth-century Vauban-style citadel, and the Thủ Thiêm side, which lacks any sense of geometrical order. This is clear in a well-known early map drawn by military surveyor Théodore Le Brun in 1795 (fig. 4.10). In this map, the Saigon side of the river appears inhabited, marked with grid lines, while Thủ Thiêm, apart from the depiction of the military forts described in White's memoirs, is rendered as an empty landscape. But it is important to recognize that Le Brun's map views the landscape through a specific optic: he was, after all, working on order of the king of France as one of "his majesty's engineers." In terms of the kinds of human settlements shown, his map only depicts the citadel and formally demarcated roads. It details not the vernacular landscape but the regular, planned, and ordered landscape of an engineer's image of the ideal city, and is also most likely the first map to place the compass icon or legend on top of Thủ Thiêm. The map attempts to impose a sense of spatial order on Saigon, but in doing so it literally renders the inhabited space of Thủ Thiêm as an empty wasteland.

This conceptual occlusion of Thủ Thiêm can be seen in other maps as well. In 1862, a member of the French engineer corps, Colonel Coffyn, designed what is widely cited as the first formal urban plan of Saigon, "a city for 500,000 souls." The plan included formal development grids in Thủ Thiêm but shows little else existing in the area (fig. 4.11). Later, in 1928, Ernest Hébrard's descriptions of a "project d'extension" for Saigon included a grid of roads and city blocks in Thủ Thiêm (fig. 4.12).[43] During the late 1950s, Ngô Đình Diệm's government entertained serious plans for turning the district into a new administrative and entrepreneurial center (figs. 4.13–14). Project planners at that time exclaimed with confidence that

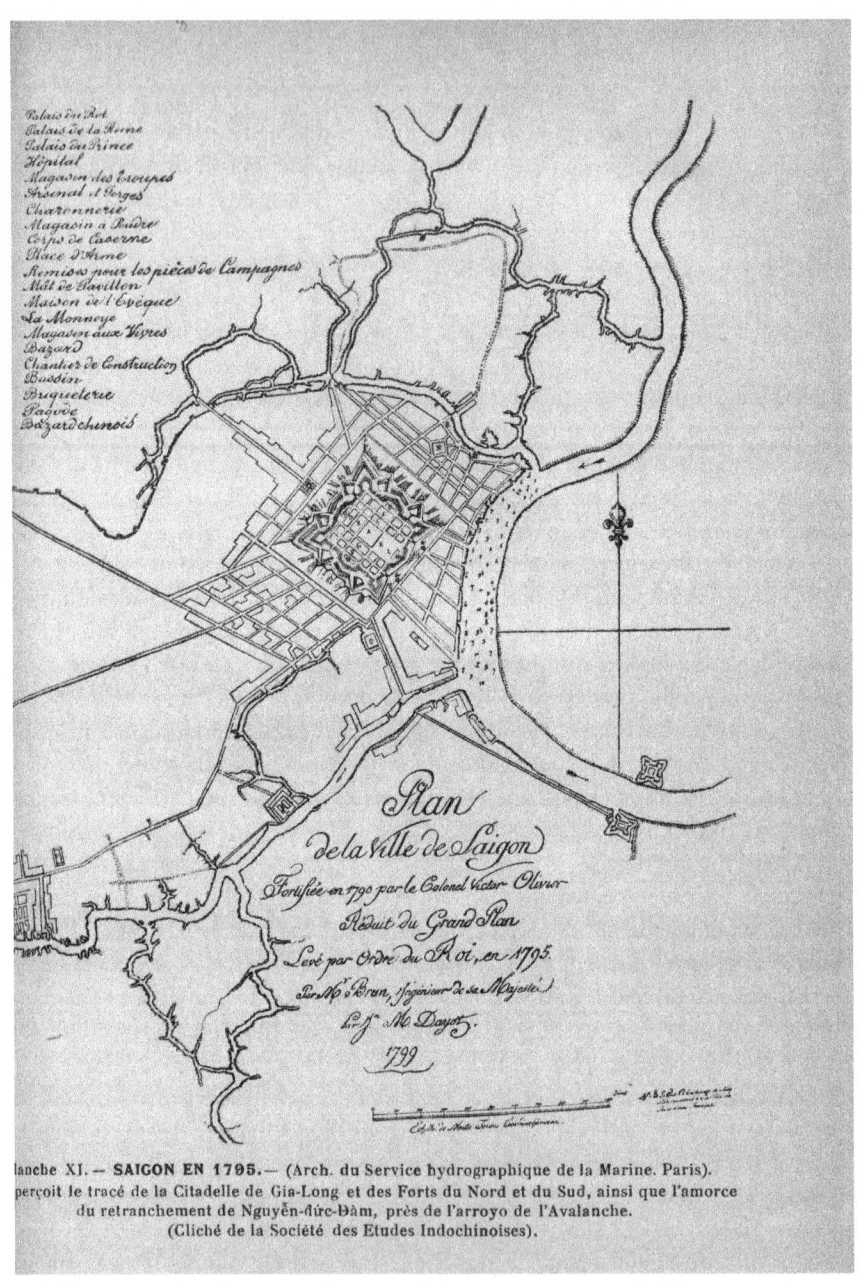

Palais du Roi
Palais de la Reine
Palais du Prince
Hôpital
Magasin des Troupes
Arsenal et Forges
Charonnerie
Magasin à Poudre
Corps de Caserne
Place d'Arme
Remises pour les pièces de Campagne
Mât de Pavillon
Maison de l'Evêque
La Monnoye
Magasin aux Vivres
Bazard
Chantier de Construction
Bassin
Briqueterie
Pagode
Bazard chinois

Plan
de la ville de Saïgon
Fortifiée en 1790 par le Colonel Victor Olivier
Réduit du Grand Plan
Levé par Ordre du Roi, en 1795.
Par Mr. Brun, Ingénieur de sa Majesté.
C.f.r. Mr. Dayot.
1799

Planche XI. — **SAIGON EN 1795.** — (Arch. du Service hydrographique de la Marine. Paris).
perçoit le tracé de la Citadelle de Gia-Long et des Forts du Nord et du Sud, ainsi que l'amorce
du retranchement de Nguyễn-đức-Đàm, près de l'arroyo de l'Avalanche.
(Cliché de la Société des Etudes Indochinoises).

FIGURE 4.10. Le Brun map of Saigon in 1795.
SOURCE: Malleret, L. (1935). "Eléments d'une monographie des anciennes fortifications et citadelles de Saïgon." *Bulletin de la Société des études indochinoises, Saïgon.* Plate XI, following p. 108.

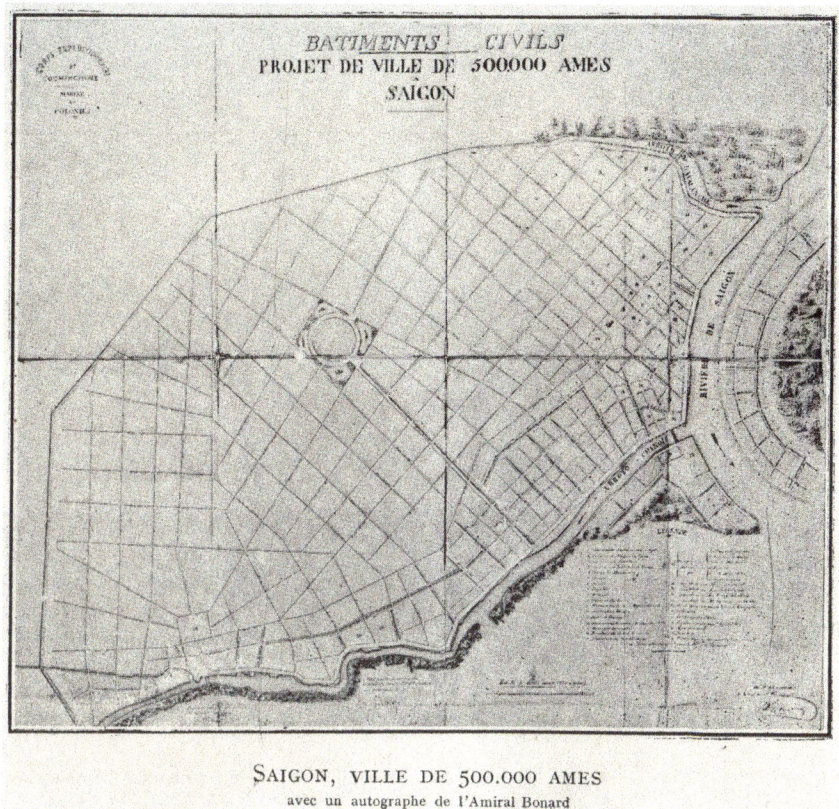

FIGURE 4.11. Project for a City of 500,000 Souls in Saigon by Colonel Coffyn, 1862. Note the planned development of Thủ Thiêm in the righthand (eastern) side of the map, across the Saigon River.

SOURCE: Bouchot, J. (1927). *Documents pour servir à l'histoire de Saigon, 1858 à 1865*. Saigon, Editions Albert Portail.

"the building of Thủ-Thiêm is no longer a distant aspiration."[44] But ultimately, engineering and hydraulic challenges associated with the watery land there proved insurmountable, and utopian plans faded away.[45] In all of these plans, one theme is consistent: visions of the future erase any sense of a preexisting human landscape.

These visions for the future of Thủ Thiêm continued forcefully into and beyond the period of the American advisory and military presence in Vietnam. From the middle of the twentieth century onward, the notion that Thủ Thiêm would have value only if it were wholly transformed emerged with great force, backed first by the "can do" spirit of midcentury modernism and later by the rationalism of economistic expertise. The most striking, and most fully elaborated, examples of this can be seen in two plans developed for Thủ Thiêm, first by the world-renowned

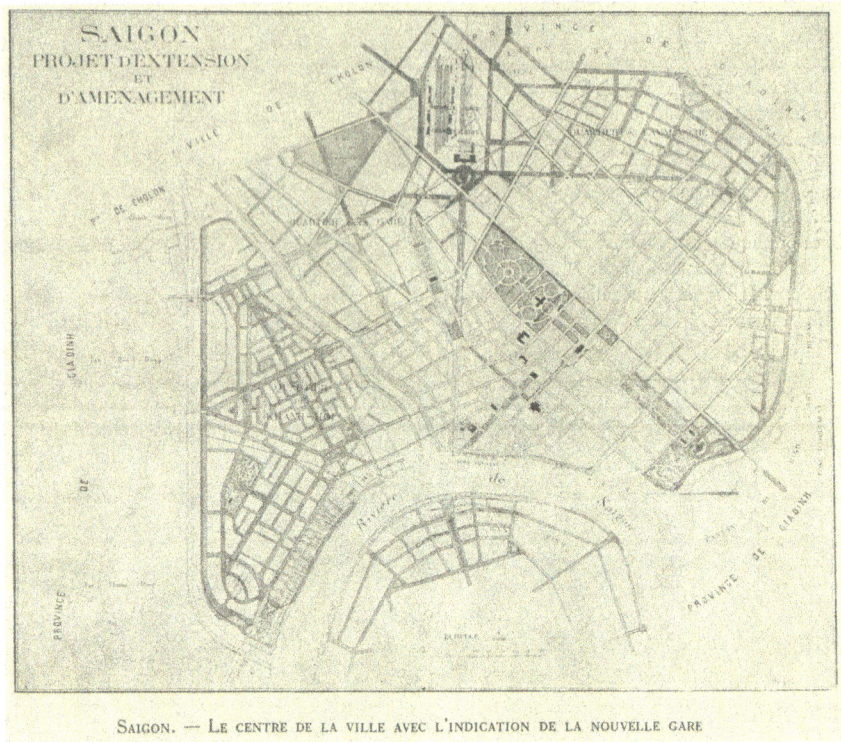

SAIGON. — LE CENTRE DE LA VILLE AVEC L'INDICATION DE LA NOUVELLE GARE

FIGURE 4.12. Hébrard's plan for extension and development of Saigon. Note that the map scale is placed over part of Thủ Thiêm, which is depicted as empty, while the portion of Thủ Thiêm immediately facing Saigon and following the river is marked out for anticipated development. SOURCE: Hébrard, Ernest. "L'urbanisme en Indochine." *L'architecture* 41, no. 2 (1928): 28.

modernist urban planner Constantinos Doxiadis in 1965, and seven years later by the San Francisco Bay Area planning firm of Wurster, Bernardi & Emmons. These plans, like all that had come before, envisioned a radical transformation of the Thủ Thiêm area, this time based on rational, modern planning principles. With their utopian designs, their hubris, and their bold promises for the future, these plans also anticipate the logic of the projects planned for Thủ Thiêm by the postwar Vietnamese government.

### Ideal Dynapolis: The Doxiadis Plan of 1965

On November 20, 1964, the Government of the Republic of Vietnam (a.k.a. South Vietnam), with financing from the United States Operations Mission to Vietnam, formally contracted Doxiadis Associates International Co. Ltd., of Athens, Greece, to prepare a "five-year action program of housing and a long-range outline

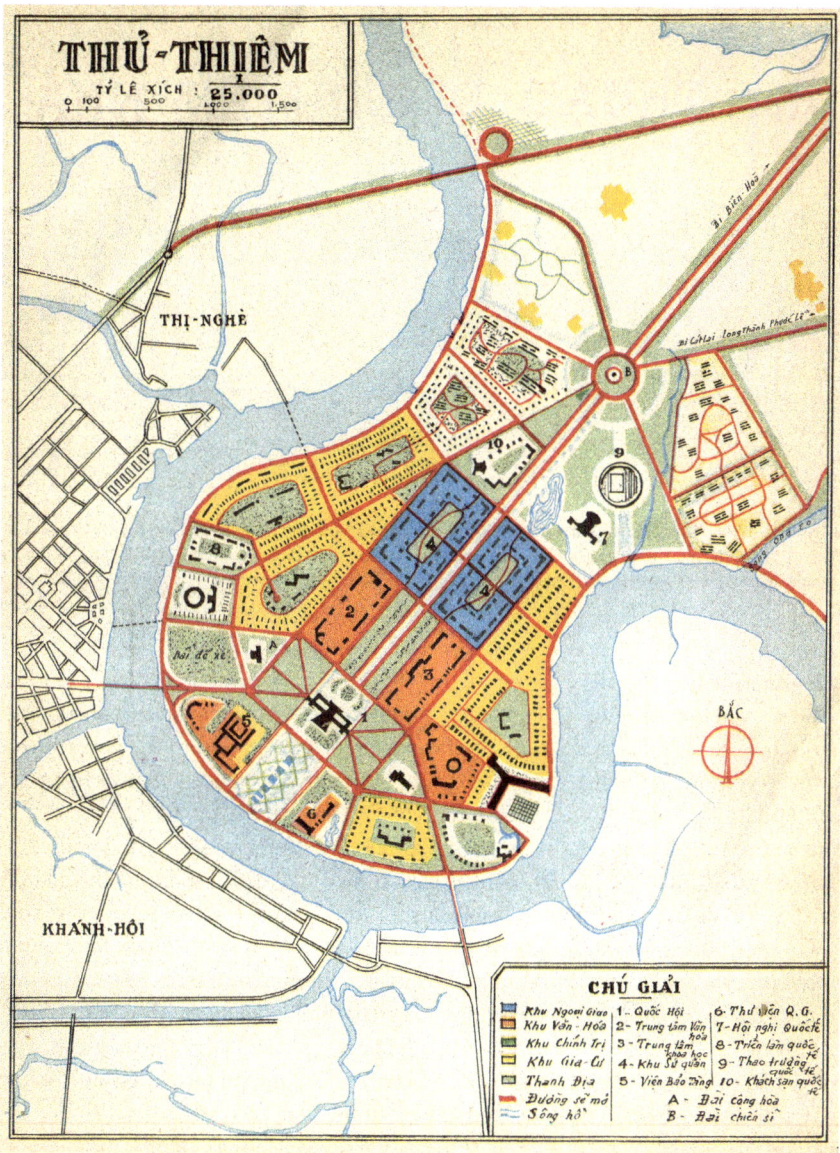

FIGURE 4.13. Thủ Thiêm plans during the Ngô Đình Diệm period, ca. 1957.

SOURCE: Xây dựng mới. "Thủ-Thiêm, Thành phố tương lai" [Thủ Thiêm, City of the future]. *Xây dựng mới: Nguyệt san văn hóa, mỹ thuật, kỹ thuật* [New building: A cultural, artistic, and technical monthly], 1957, 18–19.

FIGURE 4.14. Thủ Thiêm plans during the Ngô Đình Diệm period, ca. 1958.
SOURCE: Xây dựng mới. "Khu Thủ-Thiêm, Một thành phố tương lai" [Thủ Thiêm area, a city of the future]." *Xây dựng mới: Nguyệt san văn hóa, mỹ thuật, kỹ thuật* [New building: A cultural, artistic, and technical monthly], 1958, 10–11.

program for the overall development of the Saigon Metropolitan Area."[46] In just a little over two months—by January 26, 1965—a team of Doxiadis consultants, architects, and planners researched, developed, and presented to the government a three-volume, 518-page, map-filled plan, which they promoted as a "systematic method of approach to the development of the Saigon Metropolitan Area."[47] Volume 1 presented a long-term program for the development of housing and community facilities of Saigon-Cholon, as well as an outline plan to guide the growth of the city. Volume 2 presented proposals for new forms of urban administration, different housing types, and varied land uses, as well as suggestions for how to maximize the use of local building materials and "human resources." And volume 3 outlined a "pilot project" of urban development, with a focus on Thủ Thiêm.[48]

Work on the plan, which included investigating the history and current state of urban development in Saigon and preparing a comprehensive vision for the city's future development, "was carried out in Saigon and Athens . . . under the personal leadership of Dr. C. A. Doxiadis."[49] Constantinos Doxiadis, an architect most famous for creating the master plan of Islamabad in 1960, and a prolific architectural theorist who developed the concept of "ekistics" (the science of human settlement), was an urbanist of grand ambitions, cast in the same modernist mold as Le Corbusier.[50] He was a philosopher of human improvement and a draftsman of urban utopias, and his plan for Saigon might be called, borrowing a phrase from James Scott, a "textbook case" of high-modernist architecture.[51] In the Doxiadis

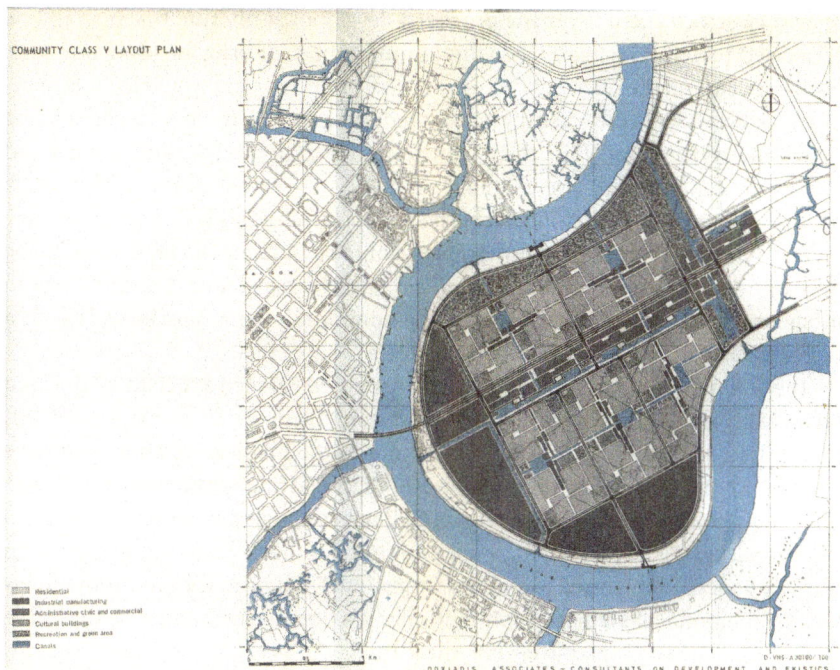

FIGURE 4.15. 1965 Doxiadis Plan for Thủ Thiêm.
SOURCE: Doxiadis Associates. "Saigon Metropolitan Area: Volume 3, Pilot Project." Athens, Greece: Prepared for the Government of the Republic of Vietnam, Ministry of Public Works, Directorate General of Reconstruction and City Planning, 1965, 9. © Constantinos and Emma Doxiadis Foundation, reproduced with permission of Constantinos A. Doxiadis Archives.

plan for Saigon, "the city of the present—the city undergoing an undesirable un-planned growth" would be entirely reconceived as a fully rationalized city designed to maximize human potential. In the futuristic language of ekistics, tinged with neologisms fashioned from ancient Greek, the Doxiadis planners claimed that the city they proposed would become an "ideal Dynapolis."[52] It was a proposal for a dy-namic city, designed to grow.[53] And the center of the plan was Thủ Thiêm (fig. 4.15).

The "pilot project" outlined for Thủ Thiêm—which like almost everything else in the Doxiadis plan for Saigon as a whole was never realized—involved an ex-perimental new urban development of one thousand houses (of an eventual ten to fifteen thousand) "suitable for Vietnamese environmental conditions."[54] After field trips, site inspection, air reconnaissance, and "analysis of land reclamation techniques and costs," Doxiadis decided that Thủ Thiêm was "the best alternative without question . . . [:] large enough; immediately available; very close to the cen-ter of employment, shopping, etc.; *undeveloped and will not require the relocation of existing settlements . . .* ["⁵⁵](#) The proposed development in Thủ Thiêm would be connected to central Saigon by a "minimum number of bridges" (only one such bridge appears on the plan, but two others were projected) and would include man-made canals and lakes for transportation, replacing the extensive naturally existing canals and waterways. While this might seem like unnecessary effort—why build man-made canals if there were already natural ones?—it was deemed worthwhile because the massive earth movement the project required would provide a source of land-fill for construction. Furthermore, completely reorganizing the landscape into a grid would allow Doxiadis to create one of his signature contributions to urbanism: "a systematic development of a community on a human scale with a hierarchical order of centers of public facilities to serve them."[56]

The hierarchy of communities Doxiadis proposed entailed a socially engineered series of rectangles nested within rectangles, ranging upward in scale from "Class I" to "Class V" (fig. 4.16). The Class I community, the smallest rectangle, would be the most "homogenous" in social composition, consisting of approximately ten to fifteen families (depicted as discrete, individual rectangles arranged along a rectilinear alleyway). The families grouped together at this level would be similar in class and social status, and would thus constitute "the primary unit in the interlocking hierarchical system of communities, making up the human sector."[57] The system would then progressively link these smaller Class I units together as it grew in scale (not unlike a segmentary model of social organization, which functional anthropologists have long identified as systems for maintaining social and political solidarity across space.)[58] Like segments in a larger form of social solidarity, Class II communities would be formed by binding several Class I communities together through shared playgrounds and local shops. Class III communities would unify several Class II communities around primary schools, shopping areas, and a church, as well as a garden or small square to "provide a focal point or public forum."[59] Class IV communities, which the plan called "the basic component of the urban structure," would form replicable units, large enough to be self-sustaining but small enough "for a man on foot to remain its master"; they would be able to "accommodate diverse social groups, both in income and cultural levels," and would be united by secondary schools and civic and commercial centers.[60] And finally, at the highest level of the urban hierarchy, Class V communities would combine four or five Class IV communities, united around a "community theatre, community health center and other specialized functions."[61]

Once joined together, all of these nested communities were designed to engineer a sense of urban solidarity that could theoretically extend across the entire urban landscape: "The basic elements of the design of a community, which achieves a human scale, should be a system of interlocking human communities, each creating optimum conditions for social communication, human growth and organization."[62] Seen in retrospect, this system of nested classes vaguely recalls a

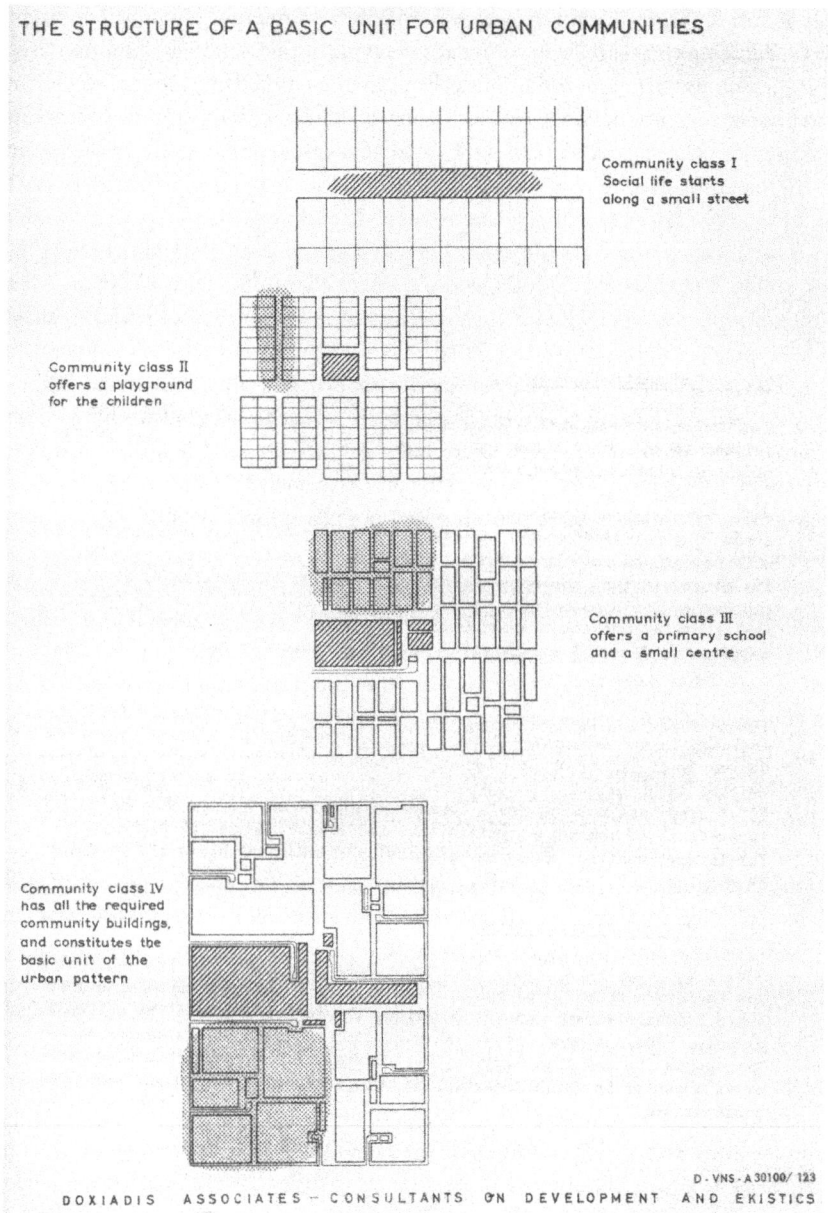

THE STRUCTURE OF A BASIC UNIT FOR URBAN COMMUNITIES

Community class I
Social life starts
along a small street

Community class II
offers a playground
for the children

Community class III
offers a primary school
and a small centre

Community class IV
has all the required
community buildings,
and constitutes the
basic unit of the
urban pattern

D - VNS - A 30100/ 123

DOXIADIS    ASSOCIATES – CONSULTANTS  ON  DEVELOPMENT  AND  EKISTICS

FIGURE 4.16. Doxiadis plan for developing a structure of hierarchically nested urban communities, classes I through IV.

SOURCE: Doxiadis Associates. "Saigon Metropolitan Area: Volume 3, Pilot Project." Athens, Greece: Prepared for the Government of the Republic of Vietnam, Ministry of Public Works, Directorate General of Reconstruction and City Planning, 1965, 283. © Constantinos and Emma Doxiadis Foundation, reproduced with permission of Constantinos A. Doxiadis Archives.

whole series of social technologies common at that time in Vietnam, all dedicated to establishing social solidarity. It recalls the logic of the National Liberation Front (NLF), with its various autonomous cells ultimately united at a higher level for the purpose of revolutionary activity, or the nested hierarchies of a military structure.

The design reflected the ethos of the age, a midcentury modernist commitment to engineering new forms of social solidarity. In a period when Vietnamese and foreign advisors of all persuasions were expending great energy and financial resources concocting ways of preserving allegiance in a time of political unrest, it takes little imagination to understand the allure behind the Doxiadis plan. At the time the report was delivered to the government in January 1965, the U.S. bachelor officer quarters at the Brink Hotel had only recently been bombed in downtown Saigon, on December 24, 1964. It was less than a year after the Gulf of Tonkin incident and only about two months before the first U.S. combat troops formally entered the country. Ngô Đình Diệm had been assassinated less than two years earlier, and the South Vietnamese leadership was itself in a state of constant upheaval. The promise of an urban plan that could engineer social solidarity must have been appealing indeed.

These grand plans for engineering cohesiveness through urban design also promised a way to reimagine the peripheries of the city, which, in addition to being seen as potential spaces for rational urban development, were feared as spaces of subversion,[63] where alternative forces—like the Bình Xuyên, Cao Đài, Hòa Hảo, and of course the Communist agents of the NLF known as "Việt Cộng"—might hold sway. In my interviews with Thủ Thiêm residents, I often heard that the area at that time had a reputation for harboring insurgents, and histories of Thủ Thiêm often reference the role it played in the revolution. Many of the longtime residents we interviewed also mentioned their own involvement with revolutionary activities, and sometimes displayed commendation certificates from the postwar government on their walls, honoring their resistance against the forces of the Republic of Vietnam.

Whether the intent was willful or unintentional is hard to know, but in the process of developing this vision for Thủ Thiêm, the Doxiadis plan occluded the elements of urbanism and human settlement that already existed there. The planning maps that fill the three volumes of the Doxiadis plan for Saigon are striking for their emphasis of formally shaped landscapes that tend to overshadow the vernacular lived landscape of Thủ Thiêm, making it appear at first glance as if it were nothing but a blank, uninhabited space. But this emptiness is an illusion, a form of selective blindness. In fact, it is clear from photographs of the period that Thủ Thiêm was not empty; instead, habitation followed a different pattern, one that was in tune with the natural environment: urban filaments follow the curve of the river, and all the land behind residential housing is subdivided into a patchwork of fields, which are marked by clear berms indicating ownership and property boundaries (fig. 4.17). Furthermore, evidence from within the Doxiadis

FIGURE 4.17. View of Thủ Thiêm (right), ca. 1960s. From the David Butler Collection, Rauner Special Collections Library, Dartmouth College. Courtesy of Dartmouth College Library.

This image also appears in Butler, D. 1985. *The Fall of Saigon: Scenes from the Sudden End of a Long War*. New York, Simon & Schuster. Plate 2, between pp. 41 and 45.

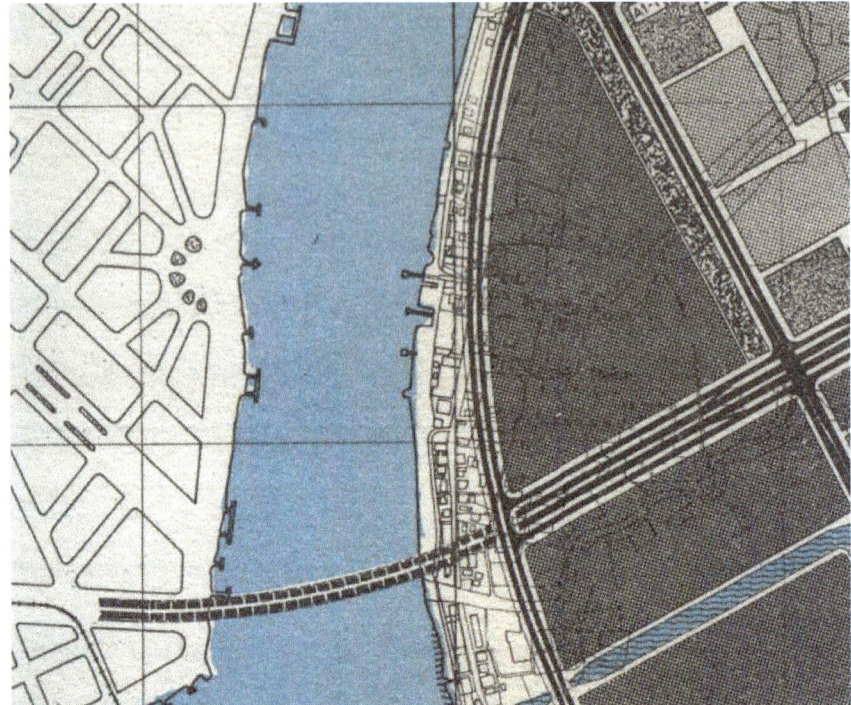

FIGURE 4.18. Detail of 1965 Doxiadis Plan for Thủ Thiêm. The jetties visible in the center of the image, on the righthand side (east bank) of the Saigon River, indicate the location of Thủ Thiêm ferry port. The rectangular and square line drawings along the bank of that side of the river extend underneath the dark shading of the planned Thủ Thiêm pilot project. These lines indicate that Doxiadis planners were clearly aware of extensive settlement in Thủ Thiêm, despite the illusion the plan itself gives of the area being empty.

SOURCE: Doxiadis Associates. "Saigon Metropolitan Area: Volume 3, Pilot Project." Athens, Greece: Prepared for the Government of the Republic of Vietnam, Ministry of Public Works, Directorate General of Reconstruction and City Planning, 1965, 9. © Constantinos and Emma Doxiadis Foundation, reproduced with permission of Constantinos A. Doxiadis Archives.

plan itself suggests that the planners were indeed aware that Thủ Thiêm was not empty, in spite of the claims to the contrary implied by the project. If one looks carefully at the Doxiadis plan for the Thủ Thiêm pilot project, for example, one can see that it has been superimposed on a detailed base map that indicates, in faded lines, the preexisting natural and built landscape of Thủ Thiêm (fig. 4.18). Outlines of buildings, roads, jetties, and other forms of construction belie any claim that Thủ Thiêm was empty.

Thus, the Doxiadis map contradicts claims elsewhere in the plan that Thủ Thiêm was "undeveloped and will not require the relocation of existing settlements." In the text, too, great attention is paid to the problem of Saigon's dense development, which is referred to, at various points, as "haphazard," "unplanned," "inadequate," "insufficient," or "bad quality" and which is said to be marked by "poor construction," "congestion," "obsolescence," or "deficit." For a city whose peripheries are depicted as undeveloped and empty, it is surprising that some of the most serious of the thirty-three "problems" Doxiadis identified as hindering urban development in Saigon relate to its extraordinary density. For example:

> 284. *Problem 8: Land overcrowding.* The combination of population pressures for housing, lack of land and low purchasing power, has resulted in over-utilization and overcrowding of existing land, housing and facilities in Saigon.
> 285. The intensive use of the land has produced high population densities per land area [ . . . ]
> 286. Saigon's density figures are even more alarming in the light of the fact that Saigon is practically a one-storey city.
> 287. *Problem 9: Squatters' colonies.* Nearly every piece of available land has been put to use. River and canal banks, swampy areas, garbage dumps, etc., are now the sites of squatter settlements. Densities are suffocating; there is an almost total lack of even the most rudimentary type of neighborhood pattern and community facilities. Construction is poor. Materials used are bamboo, thatch and whatever scraps of wood, cardboard and sheet metal, that can be found.[64]

Assertions that "nearly every piece of available land has been put to use" sit uneasily with their claims that places like Thủ Thiêm were empty. On the one hand, the Doxiadis plan states that the lands in Thủ Thiêm were empty and undeveloped, but on the other hand, it also proposed a program of "land expropriation," thus acknowledging that the land was already owned by Thủ Thiêm residents. This problematic way of justifying land expropriation by describing inhabited lands as empty and in need of development is a matter that would become one of the defining and most controversial features of urban development in Saigon, and later Ho Chi Minh City. As I will show in chapters 5 and 6, "land acquisition" has bedeviled Vietnam's postwar socialist government, both during the period of high socialism and also during the postreform period of expanding engagement with capital-intensive real estate development. While this problem is commonly attributed to the authoritarian impulses of Vietnam's single-party state, or simplistically blamed on "communism," the Doxiadis plan shows that land expropriation was an idea with roots going back long before the socialist victory in Vietnam. The following language from the 1965 plan could easily be mistaken for text from the pages of a twenty-first-century Vietnamese newspaper account, government report, or academic study:

> 323. *Problem 32: Land expropriation.* Execution of existing housing plans has been severely limited by the inability to assemble sufficiently large areas of land for

development. Vacant land within the Prefecture of Saigon has been exhausted to such an extent that no new housing is contemplated on land not at present under public ownership. Proposals for urban renewal activities are dismissed summarily because of the difficulty and cost of land acquisition.

324. The methods pertaining to the expropriation of land are archaic, costly and time consuming.[65]

As a result of these problems, the Doxiadis plan insists that "legal tools" would need to be devised in order to speed up land expropriation in proposed development areas like the one in Thủ Thiêm so as to minimize the effects of land speculation, which "will certainly be attempted as soon as the preliminary plans are made public." To avoid such land speculation, the plan insisted:

187. The goals of land expropriation procedure are not only to acquire land and property at realistic prices but also to carry out the procedures in a short period of time and to minimize ill-will from the owners of expropriated property.

188. Methods of speeding up the procedure of land expropriation include the blanket expropriation of many properties at the same time and the provision of special judicial bodies for the specific purpose of settling cases in dispute.[66]

References to "owners of expropriated property" and "cases in dispute" indicate that Doxiadis planners were well aware that places like Thủ Thiêm were not empty spaces, even if their plans for the pilot project implied otherwise. Thus, rather than being "illegible" or invisible to project planners, it is more accurate to say that the people living in Thủ Thiêm either were actively overlooked or, when they could not be ignored, were being set up to have their land expropriated. Put differently, it could be said that the Doxiadis planners were actually looking at multiple Thủ Thiêms: a real one full of people, one imagined as empty, and an ideal one they wished to will into existence. The one they wished to will into existence depended on imagining the real one as empty. Perhaps with enough imagination, the ideal could triumph over the real and the people would simply disappear. If not, as the plan explained, their land could always be expropriated.

Although the Doxiadis plan was integrated into the 1968 Saigon master plan, which was then published by the Directorate of Reconstruction and Urban Planning, it was ultimately never realized.[67] During interviews conducted between 2010 and 2014, I asked city planners and members of the Thủ Thiêm Investment and Construction Authority why the plan was never implemented. They blamed the failure simply on "the war," a plausible enough explanation but one impossible to verify. Other architects with knowledge of the earlier plans sometimes blamed the inherent problems of the Thủ Thiêm site, citing its soft soils and potential for flooding, as well as "the war." Older Thủ Thiêm residents, many of whom had been vaguely aware of the plan but none of whom knew anything specific about its details, explained matter-of-factly that it was common for Vietnamese government

FIGURE 4.19. Wurster Plan of 1972.
SOURCE: Wurster, Bernardi & Emmons, Inc. "Thu Thiem Peninsula Development Plan: Agency for International Development Contract Aid/Vn-101." Saigon, Wurster, Bernardi & Emmonds, Inc., 1972. Fold-out map.

planners to come up with plans on paper that were never carried out.[68] Yet while the Doxiadis plan never did go forward, the dream for wholly redesigning and building Thủ Thiêm never disappeared.

### "Saigon of Tomorrow": The Wurster Plan of 1972

In 1973, Guy Wright, a columnist for the *San Francisco Examiner,* wrote: "On my desk is a beautiful picture of how Saigon might look someday. I keep my fingers crossed that it will happen."[69] The picture to which Wright referred was a colorful map taken from a new, fully reconceived master plan for Thủ Thiêm (fig. 4.19), part of a lavishly illustrated 78-page document filled with extensive proposals and color-ful maps paid for by the U.S. Agency for International Development and produced by the San Francisco–based architectural firm Wurster, Bernardi & Emmons.[70]

In a way, the Wurster plan picked up from the abandoned Doxiadis plan for Thủ Thiêm, covering essentially the same geographic area and containing similar proposals. The Wurster plan even borrows data from the earlier plan, citing its population projections and using similar language when explaining why the loca-tion is desirable. The following passage, for example, echoes sentiments from 1965:

> This study demonstrates that the peninsula, even with its present limited access, has an advantageous time-distance relationship to downtown Saigon. Moreover, the peninsula compares very favorably to other potential development sites within the Saigon Metropolitan Area. These other sites are generally either to the south and west of the City, where major growth is unlikely to occur for many years. As access to the peninsula improves in the future, peninsula land values will rise far above these other areas. In fact, once bridges are in operation, no other location will match the peninsula's development potential.[71]

If the Wurster plan shared much of the same enthusiasm for Thủ Thiêm as the Doxiadis plan, it also differed in several important respects. While the previous plan focused on wholly transforming the space in order to construct utopian forms of cohesive social organization, the Wurster plan favored pragmatic engagement with preexisting social and natural variables. In other words, the Wurster plan, rather than relying on the force of urban design alone, recognized the need to adapt. For example, a major downfall of the Doxiadis project, it explained, was that "it proposed filling the natural waterways and superimposing a costly, geometri-cally-designed system of canals over the whole peninsula."[72] Moreover, whereas the Doxiadis plan was rapidly conceived, planned and presented to the govern-ment in just over two months, Wurster favored a gradualist approach: "Beginning in 1971, a year-long, detailed study was made of the peninsula, and a new develop-ment plan was prepared. Unlike the earlier plans, the primary purpose of the new plan is to encourage development of the peninsula in slow, feasible stages over a period of 20 to 30 years. The new plan emphasizes a combination of private initia-tive and public investment. It is a plan that is within the range of the economic and institutional resources of Vietnam."[73] This pragmatic approach, with its emphasis on self-sustaining, economically viable urbanization suited to the "resources of Vietnam," is dramatically different in spirit from the earlier proposal.

This approach may reflect, at least in part, the change in American attitudes following the unexpected duration and challenges of U.S. involvement in Vietnam. Since 1969 and the beginning of its gradual military withdrawal from the country, the United States had supported a policy of "Vietnamization," encouraging the Vietnamese to become increasingly responsible for waging the war as well as for their own nation-building. While the United States continued to provide enormous assistance to South Vietnam, the focus now was on expert-driven development planning rather than quick solutions. Accordingly, the Wurster plan, rather than attempting to remake society, sought to view it as an existing force to be understood and adapted to, using the tools of social science, especially economic analysis. For example, in Wurster's final accounting report for billable hours spent on the project, 745 went to preparation, 3,157 to planning, 4,636 to the pilot project and the report, and 5,401 to "research." Furthermore, whereas the principals and project directors claimed 2,730 billable hours, "specialists" accounted for a full 4,241.[74]

This reliance on specialist expertise is evident in the report's focus on land use, soil quality, financing, and administration, as opposed to aesthetic design per se. It develops extensive recommendations for a maximum population density of 300 persons per hectare, specifies the kinds of soils to be used for infill (recommending silty sand dredged from the Đồng Nai River rather than the muddy soil of Thủ Thiêm), and insists on making maximum use of existing roads and waterways. Furthermore, it develops economic models for the projected increase in land values following development of the area, thereby suggesting the project's ability to pay for itself. Yet this form of systematic, planned development depended on marketing land, which in turn required creation of a Land Development Agency: "Land will be obtained by negotiation where possible and by expropriation where necessary," the Wurster plan outlined. "After the land has been prepared for urban use, the Agency will market it through a combination of sales and rentals. In some cases the Agency will provide infrastructure serving a wider area, but will recover such costs from local authorities and private landowners whose property is increased in value by the installation."[75]

In this analysis, once again, the Wurster planners saw Thủ Thiêm as both empty and populated at once. The whole purpose for developing the space was based on the notion that it was undeveloped and relatively empty. But as the above passage shows, as the planners prepared to develop this space, they could not ignore the fact that it was populated by people with whom they would have to negotiate, or failing that, from whom they would have to expropriate the land. In the final instance, despite their different approaches, both Wurster and Doxiadis shared the same mode of seeing without seeing. For them, the people of Thủ Thiêm were problems to be dealt with, rather than proof that what they were dealing with was a populated space.

Despite the intensive research into the actual conditions of Thủ Thiêm, the planners continued on the assumption that the land was empty and underutilized—even though that same research "revealed that approximately 30 percent of the peninsula is currently owned by the Catholic Church and the Leper's Association. These large landholdings, their location, and the nature of their current use offer unique development opportunities. Large-scale land sales and trades to developer or direct development by the present owners are possible. The primary advantage to the prospective developer is that this land does not require the major consolidation of many small landholdings which will be necessary in other parts of the peninsula."[76] If Thủ Thiêm were indeed empty, why would it be necessary to consolidate "many small landholdings"? Simply put, because it was not actually empty. In addition to the 30 percent of land owned by the Church and the Leper's Association, Wurster's own research showed that "approximately 50 percent of the peninsula is owned by members of the District 9 Landowners Association.[77] This group was informally organized several years ago to act on behalf of the owners and to promote development of the peninsula. At that time the landowners offered to give the Government 50 percent of their land in return for government funding and construction of roads and utilities, or, as an alternative, to repay the Government for these improvements over a ten-year period."[78]

## FINGERS CROSSED

Guy Wright, the San Francisco journalist waiting with fingers crossed for the beautiful project to be realized in Thủ Thiêm, captured an age-old mode of looking at Thủ Thiêm: one that recognized the space as well populated and yet, without any sense of contradiction, saw it also as underutilized, even empty. Saigon, Wright wrote, "must expand or explode." But there was hope:

> Fortunately, cradled in a loop of the Saigon River just across from the downtown section is a large undeveloped area that begs to become the centerpiece of the Saigon of tomorrow.
>
> This 2500-acre godsend is called the Thu Thiem Peninsula. Not many Americans in Saigon ever went there because there was no real reason. Along the river bank are some small boat works and a Catholic church whose bell still rings the Angelus, and then the land gives way to rice paddy and not much else.
>
> [ ... ]
>
> The beauty of the Thu Thiem plan is that it isn't outskirt development. Because of the peculiar way the river bends, the peninsula is a thumb punching into the middle of the city. You walk down to the foot of fashionable Tu Do Street, look across the river and there it is.
>
> The main reason it hasn't been developed before is because the land is too low and wet. But we have the technology to overcome that. The plan is to bring in fill and raise the level 1.5 meters. We use the same technique to build airfields in the Mekong Delta.[79]

In these passages, Wright manages to do what Saigon residents, planners, and developers have long done when looking at Thủ Thiêm: to see it as empty while describing it as the future hope for a city plagued by overcrowding.

Wright's fingers must have remained crossed right up until his death in 2006. By that time, the most recent vision of the project was just getting under way. In the interim, the United States had withdrawn completely from Vietnam. For some, Saigon had fallen in 1975, while for others it had been liberated. Agricultural collectivization had forcefully come and ungraciously gone. New constitutions had been promulgated in 1980, 1992, and 2013. Market reforms had been introduced, and *Đổi Mới,* the oft-celebrated "change to the new," had become an old cliché. The Vietnamese Law on Land, revised in 1992, 2003, and 2013, increasingly allowed land use rights permits to be used as a proxy for land transfers; this enabled a real estate market to develop, which for many years pushed land prices to unimaginable heights. This was unfortunately later followed by a painful collapse, right as the houses in Thủ Thiêm were being demolished and the city was saddled with loan debt. The city had gone from postwar scarcity to burgeoning commerce, and while the poor were no longer malnourished, the rich were getting richer. The result was great income disparity, hoarding, and forms of real estate speculation and capital accumulation that have in many cases depended on the dispossession of precarious residents from their land.

After all this change, a great deal was different, not least the fact that the postwar plans for Thủ Thiêm were led by Vietnamese actors. But despite the differences, many of the dreams they held for the space on the other side of the river from Saigon looked curiously the same. Both through its past and into the present day, Thủ Thiêm futures have been built on a long history of seeing without seeing. The most recent version of these plans, described in the next chapter, has led to the wholesale demolition of the landscape in Thủ Thiêm. With the aid of bulldozers and eviction teams, an imagined emptiness has become real.

# Building a Civilized, Modern, and Sentimental City

## BILLBOARDS OF THE FUTURE

For a brief few years, between 2009 and 2012, the advertising billboards that had for so many years blocked the view of Thủ Thiêm from the other side of the river came down. Despite the impression commonly given by maps and plans for the city, the space behind the billboards was in fact not an empty wasteland but a bustling network of neighborhoods, graced by one of the city's oldest Catholic churches and the immaculately maintained convent for the Congregation of the Lovers of the Holy Cross (Dòng Mến Thánh giá). Across three city wards there were numerous temples, community halls, lineage halls, pagodas, and schools, three People's Committee offices, thousands of houses, and a waterfront road, animated by a steady stream of motorbike traffic.

For more than a century, the Thủ Thiêm ferry carried crowds of residents back and forth across the Saigon River, constantly repeating the five-minute journey between District One and the ferry station in Thủ Thiêm's An Khánh Ward (fig. 5.1).[1] Upon arrival, passengers would proceed in one of three directions: left into a dense neighborhood of houses; right along Cây Bàng Road, following the bend of the river past the church, the convent, and a long line of riverfront houses and several temples; or straight ahead along busy Lương Định Của Street, lined with working-class shops, restaurants, and houses that ran all the way from the ferry landing to the other side of District Two (fig. 5.2).

Just after midnight on January 1, 2012, however, the ferry officially ceased service, marking the beginning of the end of a certain way of life in Thủ Thiêm. Over the course of the preceding two years, the pace of demolition—carried out house by individual house—had picked up dramatically. Formal pronouncements issued

FIGURE 5.1. The Thủ Thiêm Ferry. Author's photo, September 2010.

by the District Two authorities in 2010 indicated that they were intent on moving the Thủ Thiêm New Urban Zone project swiftly forward. The intensified focus on land clearance was proof.[2] At that point, those residents who had not yet agreed to leave their homes began to receive notices announcing that they would be subject to "forced land reclamation" *(cưỡng chế thu hồi đất)*, and the pressure only intensified. Some groups of residents staged protests in front of government buildings in downtown Saigon, and daring reports on blogs and citizen journalism websites criticized the eviction proceedings, denouncing them as "land grabs" and challenging the legal basis of the project.[3] But the majority of residents either capitulated or quietly waited, making individual deals with the authorities as they tried to negotiate their own best outcome. Meanwhile, rows of barges, heavily laden with sand dredged from the Đồng Nai River, lined up along the Thủ Thiêm riverbank. Long tubes snaked out from the barges, pumping a slurry mix of sand and river water to fill in rivulets, raise the earth, and level out a uniform surface (fig. 5.3). By the summer of 2013, most of the houses in Thủ Thiêm had been flattened for the sake of land "clearance" *(giải tỏa),* what is sometimes called "land parcel liberation" *(giải phóng mặt bằng)* or "land reclamation" *(thu hồi đất)*. Stripped of euphemism, these words all meant the same thing to residents: eviction.[4]

The majority of residents were compelled to quietly sign the paperwork, accept the terms of compensation, and move out. By May 2014, in an interview with the official newspaper of the Ho Chi Minh City Communist Party, *Sài Gòn Giải Phóng*

FIGURE 5.2. Thủ Thiêm before demolition. Author's photo, 2010.

FIGURE 5.3. Flattening the landscape in Thủ Thiêm. Author's photo, November 2010.

FIGURE 5.4. Thủ Thiêm after demolition. Author's photo, 2012.

(Saigon Liberation), Trang Bảo Sơn, vice director of the Thủ Thiêm Investment and Construction Authority (ICA), said: "At this point, it is possible to say that the work of compensation and assistance for individuals and organizations affected by the project has basically been completed."[5] By the time of this pronouncement, the bulk of the demolitions and evictions had been carried out and the only significant structures still visible from the other side of the river in District One were the Catholic church and the convent housing the sisters of the Lovers of the Holy Cross (fig. 5.4). Two local community halls (đình) remained as well, in An Lợi Đông and An Khánh wards, but they were largely hidden from view by blankets of green overgrowth that had taken over the empty spaces where homes once stood. Deeper in the belly of Thủ Thiêm, along Lương Định Của Street, the Liên Trì Buddhist pagoda still stood, its leadership fiercely resisting displacement. In the meantime wild bushes, water coconut palms, and elephant grass grew tall over the rubble of crushed homes. Benign neglect joined bulldozers as a force of eviction. In April 2013, a large fire raged through an abandoned field of dry grass.[6] In the summer of 2014, cows roamed the edges of Thủ Thiêm, grazing on the grasses that grew wild on the sites of former homes.[7] By 2015, roads were being laid upon flattened land and foundations poured for the first sections of the new urban zone.

In 2014, after the ground was largely cleared, the city erected eight new billboards, replacing the commercial advertisements that had disappeared three years earlier. Four of the new billboards featured stylized pictures of saluting laborers, soldiers, intellectuals, scientists, and common people, all painted in the bold primary colors common to propaganda posters. One of these showed a group of sailors saluting from the shores of one of Vietnam's contested islands in the Spratlys and Paracels, defending the country's sovereignty against Chinese encroachments. In others, the slogans spoke in pronouncements. One sign read:

INCREASE AWARENESS OF THE RESPONSIBILITY
OF THE POLITICAL SYSTEM
IN THE IMPLEMENTATION OF THE STRENGTH
OF THE GREAT NATIONAL UNITY
MAKE THE GOAL "RICH PEOPLE, STRONG, DEMOCRATIC,
FAIR, AND CIVILIZED COUNTRY"
A POINT OF AGREEMENT AND UNITY,
TO GATHER THE DIFFERENT STRATA OF THE PEOPLE
TO BUILD AND PROTECT THE CITY AND THE COUNTRY[8]

Another read:

PEOPLE OF THE CITY JOIN HANDS TO BUILD
A CIVILIZED, MODERN, AND SENTIMENTAL HO CHI MINH CITY[9]

Next to the slogans, the remaining four billboards displayed a series of giant phone numbers—contact numbers for advertising space. By 2015, the advertising space had been occupied by four large ads for Heineken beer (fig. 5.5).

## THE PROMISES AND COSTS OF THE PLAN

As the land was cleared to make way for the new urban zone, Thủ Thiêm became a landscape of stark juxtapositions. On the one hand, there was massive displacement and the crushed rubble of 14,600 individual households; on the other, nationalistic propaganda, advertising billboards, and a series of utopian promises. The rubble and destruction plainly showed that thousands of Vietnamese households had been asked, with no small amount of force, to make enormous sacrifices to fulfill the goals on the billboards. There was no hiding the drama. For close to a decade, even Vietnamese newspapers, which are often simplistically understood as being fully controlled by the Party State, had been reporting on the struggles faced by residents of Thủ Thiêm.[10] While never overtly critical of the Thủ Thiêm project, reporters and editors sometimes managed to push the boundaries of acceptable discourse by writing in an investigative reporting style called *phóng sự;* never editorializing, but instead reporting on the lived experiences of residents, some of these works of reportage described the losses residents were enduring and the resulting anger, as well as contentious meetings between residents and project

FIGURE 5.5. New billboards in Thủ Thiêm, partially obscuring the Thủ Thiêm church and the Congregation of the Lovers of the Holy Cross. The East-West Highway, lined by administrative offices and passing through a toll plaza, can be seen running diagonally across the center of the image. In the background, the southern bend of the Saigon River is lined by export processing zones and port facilities. Author's photo, March 2014.

authorities. Residents did not mask their discontent. When I spoke with them, they told of being pressured *(ép)* by authorities to accept compensation they did not find satisfactory, and I recorded story after story of disputes over land measurements, paperwork, and classification.[11] Web pages and blogs posted pictures and videos of people being forcefully evicted, along with critical denunciations of the way people were being treated. Residents were exasperated *(bức xúc)* and steaming mad. They filed petitions, raised their voices, stood up, and even staged a few short protests in the city.

### Anger and Aspiration, Sacrifice and Desire

Yet despite the real hardships, and despite the serious disagreements residents had with the authorities about the way they were being treated, they directed almost all their anger at what might be called "quantifiable" issues. Most specifically, they were "not yet satisfied" *(chưa thỏa đáng)* with the level of compensation and the number of square meters they were told they had the right to claim. I will have more to say about the way this focus on compensation emerged in the following chapter, but one point must be made clear: despite common accusations of corruption leveled against city, district, and project authorities, interviews with residents revealed that most people both in Thủ Thiêm and across Ho Chi Minh City did not oppose the core ideas of the project, but in fact considered the proposed Thủ Thiêm New Urban Zone to be a worthy, even beautiful, undertaking.[12] By resisting eviction, they were not critiquing the idea of building "a civilized, modern, and sentimental Ho Chi Minh City"; rather, they were primarily angry about their treatment in the process. In interview after interview, even residents who strongly objected to what they deemed unsatisfactory restitution insisted that they were willing to make a sacrifice for what they considered to be the good of the city and the nation—as long as they were properly compensated.

When discussing the project, residents often specifically used the term *hy sinh* (sacrifice) to describe their displacement—the same term used to refer to those who died in Vietnam's many wars of the twentieth century. *Hy sinh* implies a sense of nationalist solidarity, a willingness to subordinate one's own interests to those of a larger collective. It also stakes a moral claim, setting up a relationship of debt and reciprocal obligation. Like the families of war martyrs, or "heroic mothers," use of this term implies that households called to make a sacrifice deserve to be honored and respected.[13] Even residents who had not supported the Communist revolution during the war, or who for other reasons harbored deep suspicions about the current Vietnamese government, used the term. Evicted households were not interested in making their sacrifice in vain, and the sacrifice they said they were willing to make was not intended as an unreturned gift to the state and its agents. In speaking of a willingness to sacrifice, they were not expressing blind faith in the government; they were aligning themselves with more transcendent communities of belonging: their sacrifice was for the city, for Vietnam, for the future.[14]

Indeed, even as they expressed a willingness to make a sacrifice, displaced residents often unambiguously voiced their suspicions of the government *(nhà nước)* and state agents, whom they often referred to as "those men" *(mấy ông)*. Sometimes, they even referred to the government by using the diminutive form of "it" *(nó)*. But their suspicions and complaints did not mean that they opposed the ideal of urban development the government was promoting. In fact, by framing their actions in terms of sacrifice, they showed their willingness to work to achieve many of the same ideals spelled out on the billboards and in formal government pronouncements. Using an idiom that scholars working in rural China have categorized as a language of "rightful resistance," the residents of Thủ Thiêm commonly made a point of telling us that they supported the goal, exhorted by the billboard, of a responsible, democratic, fair, and civilized political system.[15] Proud of Vietnam and believing deeply in the idea of national unity, they were, they said, willing to join hands with others to construct a modern, civilized city. And they most certainly had no objection to building a city made up of "rich people"—as long as they were included among them. What they wanted, in fact, was for reality to match the promises.

Listening to the stories residents told us, which were filled with both praise for the ideals of the development project and anger at being taken advantage of, I realized that any complete account of the Thủ Thiêm project required understanding how people could be angry over being evicted while simultaneously supporting forms of "modern" urban development that demand eviction in the first place. It is quite easy to grasp why people would be unhappy about being displaced from their homes. It is more difficult to explain why residents rarely directed their anger at the "idea" of the plan itself—how they could support the plan even as they resisted their own eviction. To get at this apparent contradiction, we must take the utopianism of the urban plan seriously, situating it within the historical context of postwar Vietnam. What does the plan for the Thủ Thiêm New Urban Zone promise to deliver to people of the city?

## THE SASAKI AND DESO PLANS: COMMERCE AS A PUBLIC CENTER OF NATIONAL PRIDE

In 2003, the Thủ Thiêm Investment and Construction Authority held an international design competition to select a master plan for the Thủ Thiêm New Urban Zone. Seventy-eight submissions from 23 countries were received. The clear winner, an ICA vice director told me, was Sasaki Associates, a design and planning firm based in Watertown, Massachusetts. The Sasaki entry, which is described in detail on the company's website, is a sophisticated, thoughtful plan that attends to local infrastructure needs as well as ecology. Here is Sasaki's own description:

> Sasaki's master plan focuses on development of Thu Thiem as a sustainable, dynamic, mixed-use central business district. The plan is based on a framework of transportation, land use, and public spaces that integrates the existing ecological conditions of the lower Saigon River and responds to the climate of southern Vietnam. The plan for Thu Thiem strengthens the city's extraordinary bond with the river and is a model for long-term sustainable growth in Ho Chi Minh City.
>
> Sasaki's plan for Thu Thiem also focuses on connections to the riverfront, linkages to the historic city center, and a compact, flexible urban form. The plan promotes density, integrated public transit (water- and land-based), and appropriate street and building orientation that encourages cross-ventilation and passive cooling. The plan incorporates the natural delta landscape and river fluctuations into the urban fabric and preserves native vegetation. A key ecological strategy is maintaining Thu Thiem as an "open system"—one that accommodates tidal regimes and high-water events through natural and man-made canals, lakes, and mangrove areas. All residential areas are in close proximity to the water and to the public spaces created through this strategy.[16]

As urban master plans go, Sasaki's is well conceived and generally well designed. It is decidedly modern, but in contrast to the "modernist" plans proposed by Doxiadis in 1965 and Wurster in 1972 (see chapter 4) this plan emphasizes sensitivity to local environmental, historical, and ecological contexts. The project is even featured as a model case-study in an academic volume called *The EcoEdge: Urgent Design Challenges in Building Sustainable Cities,* written for international planners who hope to use design to solve ecological problems in the developing world.[17] The Thủ Thiêm ICA vice director told me that they chose the Sasaki plan because it promised to improve the city's infrastructure and offered a striking skyline, modern amenities, and plenty of open space. In addition to seeking to meet the needs of a world-class financial, commercial, and residential city, it featured recreational space and was designed to harmonize with the environment, maximizing the effects of cooling winds, for example, and maintaining many of the area's natural waterways. On the whole, it accomplished everything the Vietnamese planners wanted it to.

The ICA advertised the plan widely. Posters depicting the plan were erected on public billboards all over Thủ Thiêm (fig. 5.6), articles describing it appeared in newspapers, a video animation was posted on YouTube, and in-depth information was provided on the ICA's website. In the 148 interviews we conducted with displaced residents of Thủ Thiêm, in further interviews with planners working on the project, and in my conversations with residents of Ho Chi Minh City generally, the general aesthetic content of the Sasaki plan never evoked complaints. People from all walks of life praised its modern, unified feel. While some experts debated its feasibility, questioning certain technical details (such as how high the ground would need to be raised to prevent flooding) or doubting the government's ability to carry the project out, no one objected to the plan's core idea: to develop a modern face for the city. What criticism we did hear about the plan was not about whether it was appropriate, but whether the Vietnamese state had the capacity to implement it as planned, and who ultimately would benefit from it.

For the residents being evicted, the primary source of conflict was not the appropriateness of the plan or its aesthetic value, but how it would be implemented and the unequal distribution of sacrifices required. In order to implement the Sasaki design, the developers have always been clear that they would need to completely "raze [the area] to nothing" (*giải tỏa trắng*) and rebuild its soft soils into developable land, forming a blank slate for the project. As the previous chapter showed, this approach was not new. Displacing residents had been the strategy of all plans made for Thủ Thiêm throughout the twentieth century—by French colonial planners, Vietnamese anti-Communists, and American modernization theorists alike. Like proposals made under previous governments, the plan specified from the very beginning that people would have to be moved and their land appropriated. In approving the Sasaki plan, therefore, the Thủ Thiêm ICA and

FIGURE 5.6. The master plan designed by Sasaki Associates for the Thủ Thiêm New Urban Zone is displayed outside the People's Committee office of a ward located within the boundaries of the proposed project. The panel to the left lists telephone "hotlines" for reporting illegal activities by officials involved in the relocation and compensation process. The text on the panel to the right reads: "Cadres and Party members shall raise their sense of responsibility, fully and tirelessly serving the people." Author's photo, An Lợi Đông, District 2, July 2009.

the city government, with backing at the national level, committed to completely demolishing and then reconstructing 737 hectares of land.[18] Of these, 657 hectares would be used for building the project itself, and 80 hectares would be used to construct resettlement housing estates or provide land for displaced residents to build new homes.

As the project was further refined, the Thủ Thiêm developers emphasized not only harmony with nature; they also sought to harmonize *(hài hòa)* private corporate development with public infrastructure needs.[19] In 2008, for example, the Thủ Thiêm ICA held an international design competition soliciting plans for a central public square that would someday form the centerpiece of the new district. Here, the watchword was *beauty.* The contest announcement in the newspaper *Sài Gòn Giải Phóng* (later reposted on the Thủ Thiêm authority's website) read: "Searching for a beautiful face for Ho Chi Minh City's central area."[20]

DeSo Architectes, a Paris-based architectural firm founded in 2005 by François Defrain and Olivier Souquet, won the competition. Their design centers on a linear park laid down between rows of modern high-rises, with commercial services at the base of the buildings and with a landscaped waterway coursing through the middle. Commenting on the DeSo plan, the ICA website notes: "The interior docks and the platform above the basins have been articulated with programs and linked to the commercial facades of the Thu Thiem District." In this way, the void formed between the facades of private commercial buildings becomes a site for the square itself. Between these buildings, the description continues, "a large valley resituates a climatic environment defined by the dominant East-West winds and creates the conditions of a microclimate capable of reducing the ambient temperature. The ensemble of architectural and landscape propositions constitute a rich and open base."[21] It is a cool and salubrious valley, destined for the public but carved out of exclusive private commercial space.

In this way, the architectural model chosen by the Thủ Thiêm planners, working together with Sasaki and supplemented by DeSo, celebrates an anticipated synergy between the private interests of capitalist corporations, who are depicted as occupying the built space of the design, and the needs of the public, which fills the void between buildings. In other words, the architectural form expresses precisely the precepts of a "market economy with a socialist orientation" that currently drive Vietnamese policies of economic reform. In an early version of the design, the DeSo website boldly declared that "the project develops vast public spaces chained to commercial spaces, and to man-made lacustral [i.e., lake-oriented] landscapes."[22] The architectural renderings in the original design were heavily decorated with corporate logos of major international consumer brands—Sony, Samsung, Calvin Klein, Chanel, Coach, Rolex, Gucci, Dior, Puma, Nike, and others. But the space between these corporate symbols also lays out a grand esplanade that is specifically designed to foster public interaction. The public space, in this rendering, is thus forged in direct dialogue with privately owned space, which is marked with the most obvious code of modern proprietary ownership available: the brand name. Readers will recall this same logic from the language used to celebrate the Phú Mỹ Hưng New Urban Zone (chapters 1–3).

These descriptions of the original DeSo plan might strike critical urbanists trained in a European and North American Marxist tradition as a crass attempt to subordinate public space to decidedly private corporate interests, and hence relinquish the democratic potential of the urban fabric.[23] In an email to me, however, one of DeSo's principal designers explained that the commercial advertisements were subsequently removed from the design. It is also clear that the small design firm is dedicated to constructing a project that attends to local geography, identity, and sustainability while also satisfying its client's demand for a modern urban center.[24] Furthermore, for most of the people I spoke with during my research in Vietnam, the plan was not seen as undermining democratic space but actually promises to deliver public space to the city in a grandiose form that residents and planners alike have long hoped for. Indeed, one of the most common criticisms Vietnamese city-dwellers have of urban development in their country concerns the way public spaces are often overrun by what they deride as "auto-urbanization" *(đô thị hóa tự phát),* also translated as "spontaneous urbanization."[25] Thủ Thiêm residents I spoke with, even when they decried the problems associated with their own evictions, repeatedly told me that they wished to see the project implemented in a "synchronous" or "unified" *(đồng bộ)* manner by a single organization, rather than a piecemeal approach in which competing interests, all getting their way, ultimately undermined the unity of the plan.[26] Indeed, they hoped that a major foreign development organization would take control of the project. This, people explained, would cut out all the intermediaries who had to get their cut, and who were, in their opinion, the true source of corruption. People were relatively unconcerned whether the investors were "corporate" or not. What they cared about was that the groups that would implement the plan had the capacity to carry it out as planned.

Despite the focus on corporate advertisement, the DeSo plan makes a conscious attempt to enact the so-called figure-ground convention of Western "democratic" urban architecture.[27] In this scenario, rows of privately owned commercial buildings frame a public space of civic intercourse, a kind of exterior room. In the DeSo plan, despite the prominence given to commercial space, the public is not construed as the antithesis of the private; rather, it finds itself in the space between, co-constituted by the commercial sphere. For a Vietnamese observer, the presence of the corporate logos or commercial shopping districts, furthermore, signals the extent to which Vietnamese planners have begun to support market-based solutions as an antidote to what is perceived as years of state inefficiency. DeSo's rendering thus asserts without embarrassment that commercialized space can foster robust public engagement. Although none of the people we interviewed in Thủ Thiêm ever philosophized about the "figure-ground" convention of democratic urban space per se, they regularly commented on the spaces formed by the channels between private buildings, which they saw as nice places that they would enjoy visiting and that might actually improve the public waterfront along the Saigon River.

While critical urbanists, myself included, might read the imposition of corporate presence into public space as a threat to the public sphere, Vietnamese architects, planners, and government officials, for their part, never expressed concerns about the commercialism in the DeSo plan, and instead praised the design. In an article timed for the period around the annual September national day celebrations, *Tuổi Trẻ* newspaper lauded the design, saying it reminds one of that most symbolic of all Vietnamese public spaces, Ba Đình Square, where Ho Chi Minh read Vietnam's Declaration of Independence on September 2, 1945, and where his embalmed body now resides in a Soviet-designed mausoleum. No apparent irony is intended in comparing the symbolic heart of the socialist revolution, where the Vietnamese formally renounced French colonial rule, with a proposed new node connecting Vietnam to capitalist global finance—designed, it just so happens, by French architects. In the article, Khương Văn Mười, then chairman of the Ho Chi Minh City Architects Association, ignored such historical ironies and expressed unreserved enthusiasm for the new project, citing the importance of public space in fostering civic life: "A large city very much needs an empty space, with low density in order to 'breathe.' A large city also needs a space that is big enough for organizing public activities, a space where important urban activities can take place, for the city, for the region. A public square *[quảng trường]* is the primary place to satisfy that thing."[28] To emphasize his point, the architect asked his readers to recall the disorder of 1998, when celebration of the three hundredth anniversary of the founding of Saigon was impeded by the lack of a public space; on that occasion people gathered haphazardly on their motorbikes in the middle of major downtown boulevards, causing gridlock and confusion.[29] The DeSo plan promised to rectify this problem and bring order back by delivering a public space to the city. For planners and average residents alike, the open spaces depicted in the Thủ Thiêm plan really do look like beautiful, orderly, clean, accessible public spaces, even if they are carved out of corporate-financed private spaces.

## THE PLAN FOR THỦ THIÊM AND
## THE POSTWAR CONTEXT

To understand the allure of the Thủ Thiêm project in general, however, requires more than reading the images on the proposed plans. It is also necessary to situate the idea of the new urban zone within the historical context of postwar Vietnam. "Big plans" like this one are made possible only by tapping into the mystery of capital hidden in property value, and thus symbolize the modern Vietnamese socialist state's embrace of the market economy. For many people, such projects stand as symbols of a significant, and largely celebrated, socio-political transformation. These designs, in short, do not simply express a modern aesthetic; they evoke the very ethos of "Đổi Mới" (renovation), including the notion that the Vietnamese government can achieve its developmental goals by embracing capitalist forces like the real estate market, foreign investment, and so on. Furthermore, while state-planned development, free markets, corporate investment, and other such forces might be justifiably criticized as "neoliberal" by academic scholars, they are commonly considered "progressive" or "forward thinking" within the Vietnamese context, where the most prevalent translation of the term *neoliberal* is "new freedom" *(tân tự do)*. Over the past several decades, attempts to introduce market mechanisms, scale back the role of state-owned enterprises, and expand property markets have been given positive labels like "fence breaking" *(phá rào)*, and histories of these processes generally depict the actors involved as brave, forward-thinking reformists who boldly sought to break through the conservative policies of a self-aggrandizing party.[30]

Recall, for example, the billboards that went up in Thủ Thiêm after the bulk of evictions had been completed in 2014. Four of the eight new billboards carried political slogans, and the other four carried advertisements for Heineken beer. This juxtaposition of socialist propaganda and global capitalism almost perfectly illustrates the official Vietnamese policy agenda that has come to be known as the "market economy with a socialist orientation" *(kinh tế thị trường định hướng xã hội chủ nghĩa)*. In this formulation, the market economy, embodied by the advertising billboards on the right, are mobilized to pay for the utopian visions of the party and city planners, announced by the billboards on the left. Few contemporary Vietnamese who lived through the extraordinary deprivation of the postwar period are prepared to critique the role of market capitalism, and most observers read the presence of ads by international corporations as a positive sign of global integration. While the alliance between free-market capitalism and a top-down single-party state drives this process, most Vietnamese consider it preferable to the privations they experienced under the command economy.

### Critical Perspectives on the Plan

As an outside observer, I find it easy to question the rhetoric of propaganda billboards and to be skeptical of the "unholy alliance" between socialism and capitalism. The stark juxtaposition of the billboards and the landscape of destruction demands critical analysis. In Vietnam, as in other postsocialist contexts, it is well known that the relationship between bureaucratic socialism and capitalist forms of accumulation have facilitated a host of unscrupulous real estate practices, many of which use insider knowledge and party connections to lay claim to property.[31] These practices recall the "primitive accumulation" of early capitalism everywhere, which Marx described as "nothing else than the historical process of divorcing the producer from the means of production"; it was, moreover, a violent, forceful history, "written in the annals of mankind in letters of fire and blood."[32] Such practices have been connected by more recent scholarship to global land grabs and exclusionary practices that have come to define urban development in much of contemporary Asia, especially in newly privatizing "transitional" economies with nascent land commodification.[33] In this logic, as scholars have shown, the best time to grab land is at the beginning of the privatization process, when land first becomes available for private ownership and when those who have connections, capital, or a combination of both can accumulate it while dispossessing less fortunate others. In addition to these critiques, scholars working across Asia and elsewhere have shown the pitfalls associated with corporate-driven urban developments, or "urban integrated megaprojects," which are often so corrupted by profit motivations that "the bottom line" trumps broader issues of social concern.[34]

In certain ways, these essentially political-economic critiques mirror the views of Thủ Thiêm residents themselves, who question the unjust distribution of the spoils of urbanization—who was getting the money and the land, and how much. But their complaints differ in a very important way: there is no reference to the Marxist analysis of capitalism or neoliberalism that commonly drives urban theory in places like North America, Europe, South Asia, or Latin America. Instead the objections that residents level tend to be directed against "the government," "communism," or "corruption," in ways that often blend together. In my conversations with them, residents regularly accused state officials of "stealing the people's land" *(cướp đất của dân)* and voiced suspicions that local officials were gleaning profits from the project. While their evidence mostly rested on rumor and guesswork, residents often mentioned the price differential between their rate of compensation and the amount foreign investors were reportedly paying for that same land. But while such differentials are the very basis of capitalist real estate transactions, I never once, in all of my interviews with residents, heard anyone condemn capitalism or property regimes. Nor did they complain about the foreign investors seeking profit. Instead, they focused their critique on the fact that they were not seeing those profits because the cadres were hoarding them for themselves.

There was, of course, much reason to be critical about these things, and residents frequently mentioned documented cases of corruption that had made the news. One was the "Vũ Huy Hoàng case," in which a land owner with party connections realized that his land had been flipped by local authorities, who then resold it at a great profit to a foreign investor. That case became something of an emblem of the problem people felt they were facing. Many residents also expressed convoluted suspicions (rarely with much concrete evidence) about then–Prime Minister Nguyễn Tấn Dũng, who was widely understood by most citizens to be a self-interested profiteer. It was often implied that he, his daughter, and his Vietnamese-American son-in-law were personally benefiting from the project, although exactly how was never made clear. None of this criticism, however, was constructed as a challenge to the commodification of land or capitalism; rather, what was at issue was the ways in which Communist Party officials had unfairly used their position to insert themselves into the process and profit at other people's expense.

Concern about corruption was not based on rumor alone, however, for there were many documented cases of malfeasance. For example, in 2010 Huỳnh Ngọc Sĩ, vice director of the city's Department of Transportation and former head of the East-West Highway Project Management Unit (PMU) responsible for building a major highway running right through Thủ Thiem, was sentenced to jail along with his deputy Lê Quả for receiving US$262,000 from Japanese executives in exchange for granting their firm a construction contract. This sum was only the tip of the iceberg. A Japanese court eventually convicted the Japanese executives for offering Mr. Sĩ US$2.3 million in bribes between 2002 and 2006 to help them gain the contract for the project.[35] Since Mr. Sĩ was only accused by Vietnamese authorities of receiving US$262,000, it was quite understandable that residents wondered where the rest of the money had gone. The absence of answers to such questions led to further rumors of still more corruption that would never be revealed. Indeed, the lack of concrete evidence itself became a kind of evidence for how deeply nontransparent the project was. But every piece of evidence that did exist would be used to spin increasingly conspiratorial—but never implausible—tales about the general corruption of government and Communist Party officials. On one occasion, a resident handed me a stack of documents intended to demonstrate the corruption that afflicted Thủ Thiêm. The documents in fact referred to a host of other scandals of the period, such as claims that country officials were selling land in the Vietnamese highlands to Chinese bauxite mining interests. While these did not implicate anyone in Thủ Thiêm, the implication was that government officials in general could not be trusted—that if these things were happening *there,* they were surely also happening in Thủ Thiêm.

Nevertheless, the very real concerns, suspicions, and condemnations people had about corrupt practices in real estate development or project administration were not conflated with the core ideals behind urban development as a whole. Indeed, what is fascinating in all of these critiques is the degree to which the blame was placed on "communism" or the Vietnamese leadership, while the structural dimensions of privatization, capitalist accumulation, and land commodification were never invoked at all. Dispossessed Vietnamese are quick to use terms like "land grab," yet unlike critics of similar processes taking place in cities around the globe, they almost never place the blame on foreign investors or market mechanisms, nor do they insist on wholesale critiques of master-planned new urban zones. There is, furthermore, almost no popular critique of "neoliberalism" in the country. Even residents undergoing eviction largely support privatization as a general process. They celebrate the emergence of real estate markets and land titling and genuinely wish to see *more* modern development. They just don't want to be left out of the opportunities being delivered by modern development. The bulk of their ire, then, is directed at state officials, corruption, and unjust compensation. In our interviews, we repeatedly heard people explain that they generally approved of urban development, even if they scorned the corrupt people charged with running it. Despite great discontentment, the story of Thủ Thiêm cannot be reduced to a simple story of resistance alone, for there was much about the project that residents found appealing.

*The Connection between "Renovation" and New Urban Zones*

On January 16, 1993, then–Deputy Prime Minister Phan Văn Khải signed a master plan for all of Ho Chi Minh City, stating that "it is necessary to truly build Ho Chi Minh City into the civilized city of the working people," in a way that would express the "national character," the "character of the people," as well as a "modern character and a character that gets results" *(tính hiện đại và tính hiệu quả).*[36] This curious-sounding final phrase, with its emphasis on results or effectiveness *(hiệu quả),* reflected what at the time was a bold new economistic focus on efficiency led by Prime Minister Võ Văn Kiệt, a longtime party stalwart but also a former economist and one of the so-called architects of Đổi Mới, who is widely credited with early attempts to bring foreign business to Ho Chi Minh City. (Readers may also recall from the introduction that an important section of the East-West Highway leading to the Thủ Thiêm tunnel was named after this well-loved leader, and that he was instrumental in creating the conditions necessary for the Phú Mỹ Hưng project, which was conceived around the same time that interest in Thủ Thiêm was rekindled by the postwar government.) Kiệt, who is remembered as a "friend of the people" and a forward-thinking "reformist," earnestly wished to transform Vietnamese urban development policy by increasingly engaging foreign developers, who in his estimation could promote rational, orderly, and fiscally profitable large-scale projects. Of all the Vietnamese political leaders to have held positions of power since 1975, Prime Minister Kiệt is also one of the very few who has escaped popular criticism. Almost universally, people agree that he had the country's interests in mind when he pushed hard to introduce reforms.[37]

The concept of the "new urban zone" *(khu đô thị mới)* offered one important model for the kind of rational and efficient development that Prime Minister Kiệt sought to introduce. Although Kiệt is particularly well remembered for his influence in Ho Chi Minh City, the interest in new urban zones was not confined to the southern parts of the country, but reflected a wider national-policy orientation. The 1992 master plan for Hanoi also promoted new urban zones. As the planning scholar Danielle Labbé points out, this focus on large-scale projects "went hand in hand with new discourses and regulations that delegitimized the small-scale, privately initiated, and largely informal activities responsible for much of the periurban transformation since the early years of the reforms."[38] Master-planned but also friendly to investors, new urban zones offered a compelling model that simultaneously resonated with Vietnam's long history of socialist planned housing and with new conceptions of real estate development spurred by market mechanisms. Moreover, the language of rationality and efficiency associated with these big projects echoed the technocratic language promoted by Vietnamese reformers sympathetic to Võ Văn Kiệt's line of thinking. It was in this context that city planners, in consultation with the prime minister's office, decided that the area across the Saigon River from the city's historic core would be the focus of efforts to build a "modern new urban zone, the commercial, financial, and services center."[39] In addition to authorizing the project, Deputy Prime Minister Khải's decision authorized planners and city officials to begin the search for foreign capital to help finance the ambitious proposals detailed in the plan.[40]

At the time, this call to search for foreign capital was nearly unprecedented. It was also intimately tied into important legal changes in Vietnam's policy on land, which were being instituted at the same time. Vietnam's new Law on Land, passed in 1992 and enacted in 1993, formally granted the right to transfer, exchange, inherit, rent, and mortgage land; it also established a system of "land-use right certificates" (LURC), which allowed for the transfer of those land use rights.[41] These changes created the conditions necessary for a real estate market to emerge.[42] At the same time, Thủ Thiêm, with its location across the river from the city core, was attractive to Vietnamese planners, who wanted to relieve population pressure downtown, and to foreign investors, who saw Vietnam as a new "frontier" for investment. Given the common discursive construction of Thủ Thiêm as an under- or undeveloped wasteland, this space across the Saigon River perfectly fit the image of Vietnam as a place of untapped opportunity for investors. Vietnamese officials and foreign investors slowly began to devise what appeared to all parties involved as mutually beneficial relationships: if the investors had the money to pay for infrastructure, the city could provide them with the necessary land use rights.[43] Given the very real need for infrastructure improvement in the city, this kind of plan had much to offer city officials.[44] And the political willingness to look for pragmatic solutions that pushed the limits of the stridently anticapitalist political status quo was for most people a sign of hope for the future.

Ho Chi Minh City officials soon began publishing descriptions of the planned Thủ Thiêm development in English-language brochures. A 1995 brochure published by the "Saigon Construction Department," for example, detailed a proposal for a "New Thu Thiem Center" of about 1,000 hectares "designed around a semi-circular fan-shaped plan," which they hoped would be completed by 2010 (fig. 5.7).[45] In addition, they proposed building a "world fair" (which in the imperfect English common to the period most likely referred to an international convention center), occupying about 80–100 hectares; "a center for cultural activities, entertainment and tourism"; financial, service, and commercial areas; cultural and sports areas; a natural ecological area "preserved in its primitive state"; and high-end residential districts. Infrastructure would be improved, and "perfect and modern public welfare works" were to be installed in residential districts designed "to serve all residents." Ample park land and "vegetation" would complement a main square, which would be constructed immediately opposite the Mê Linh traffic circle in District One, "with much ventilated space where the symbolic victory statue of HCM City can be erected."[46] The call for investors further noted that local

FIGURE 5.7. Investment brochure for Thủ Thiêm.
SOURCE: Saigon Construction Department. "Introduction of the Projects Planned for Investment in HCM City." *Saigon Investment and Construction* 3, no. 95 (March 1995): 7–12. Folder 2, Box 3, Walter Wylie Collection, The Vietnam Center and Archive, Texas Tech University.

residents were forbidden from improving their existing houses.[47] In this way, the same discursive tropes portraying the area as "empty" in the decades prior (see chapter 4) were again used to construct Thủ Thiêm as an unparalleled opportunity for the city and for developers.[48] Furthermore, planners insisted that the development would benefit city residents; it would "make the vegetation area considerably greater, and create a pure and clean environment for the future city."[49] Thủ Thiêm's imagined emptiness, long portrayed as a lack, became its primary asset for attracting land prospectors interested in "emerging markets."

Over the course of the mid to late 1990s, the basic elements of this plan were reaffirmed at both the national and city level, with occasional, generally minor modifications. In 1996, Prime Minister Kiệt personally approved the basic plan for the Thủ Thiêm New Urban Zone, this time revising the project dimensions to 930 hectares of development, of which 770 hectares would constitute the New Urban Zone itself. The remaining 160 hectares would be devoted to resettling what was then estimated to be around 45,000 people, who would have to be evicted for the project. The New Urban Zone itself, once completed, was projected to accommodate 200,000 residents and to include 92 hectares for financial and commercial services, 100 hectares for international exhibition and convention areas, 55 hectares for high-quality *(cao cấp)* housing, 100 hectares for a cultural center and tourism and leisure facilities, 95 hectares for a central park, and 18 hectares for an administrative area; in addition, 177 hectares would be devoted to traffic and circulation.

### Redistricting and Land-Based Infrastructure Development

At the time Võ Văn Kiệt approved this plan, the Thủ Thiêm project was just one part of a larger strategy to stimulate urban development. The following year, in January 1997, Kiệt also signed "Governmental Decision 03," which split and redistricted multiple rural "outer–city districts" *(huyện ngoại thành)* and established several new urban "inner-city districts" *(quận nội thành)* throughout the city. With this move, Thủ Thiêm, which had formerly been considered part of an expansive rural "outer-city district" called Thủ Đức, became part of newly formed inner-city District Two. This decision also established a new urban inner-city district in District Seven, the future site of Saigon South and Phú Mỹ Hưng, on land that had been carved out of Nhà Bè outer-city district.[50] Initially, Thủ Thiêm residents viewed this redistricting as a positive development, for it meant that they had been converted, essentially overnight, from "rural" landowners into "urban" residents of an inner-city district. Given the long history of negative stereotypes, invisibility, and general neglect that they had faced, many Thủ Thiêm residents saw this as acknowledgment that they were in fact "city people," *người thành phố,* and that they were situated in a favorable position to receive all the modern advantages of living in the city. In addition, they imagined that they could expect to benefit from the rise in property values that always comes with designation of land as urban. What they did not anticipate was how these same processes would soon contribute to the strong push to remove them from their land.

What might on the surface appear to have been nothing but a series of dry administrative decrees and shifting map boundaries in fact represented a fundamental restructuring of the approach to urban development in the city. The redistricting moves, for example, not only worked to implement some of the development intentions of the master plan, but also played an important role in transforming the real estate values of these new urban districts, a process that was central to the emerging strategy of "fiscal socialism," in which new financial instruments were used to support state plans for infrastructure development.[51] Reclassifying the boundaries of inner-city and outer-city districts drove up the perceived value of lands only recently brought into market processes thanks to the new land laws. In Vietnam, the official prices for lands designated as urban are dramatically higher than those designated as rural, which meant the value of land in an inner-city *quận* was almost always exponentially greater than it is in an outer-city *huyện*.[52] Because of these differentials, relatively undervalued "rural" or "outer-city" land could be reclassified and converted into extraordinarily valuable "urban" or "inner-city" land, all with the stroke of a government pen and the proper red stamp.

These practices, called "land conversion" in the academic literature, had several consequences, both positive and negative.[53] In the most positive sense, they opened up new fiscal possibilities for urban governments in the densely populated but cash-strapped country.[54] Instead of paying for infrastructure with money they did not have, the city and national governments could engage in what is called "land for infrastructure" transactions, a kind of financial innovation through which foreign developers promised to build infrastructure in exchange for which they would be granted valuable land-use rights in emergent real estate markets where land values were almost guaranteed to rise.[55] The more negative consequence of these land conversions (and a consequence that has infamously plagued Vietnamese urban development since the 1990s) is that they also promoted corruption and land speculation, particularly among officials with access to information about impending conversions before that information is made public.[56] In the process, local residents, primarily but not exclusively those living on the periurban margins of cities, became vulnerable to what were essentially insider trading schemes orchestrated by urban elites with access to both capital and restricted information about land policy and zoning. Excluded from knowledge of impending projects and policies that promised to stimulate rapid increases in land values, periurban households were regularly persuaded to sell land for what to them looked at first like a generous price, but which several years later turned out to be far less than the lands would quickly become worth.[57] Despite the often exploitative nature of these transactions, however, the subsequent impoverishment of displaced persons was often blamed on their so-called peasants' mentality, by which their difficulties were attributed to their inability to manage money or their purported tendency to squander large sums on karaoke, gambling, women, and booze.[58]

Despite the drawbacks, such innovations—often called "public-private partnerships" by their boosters, or derided as "neoliberalism" by their international critics—made it possible for Vietnamese to improve their cities' infrastructure and to plan in unprecedented ways for large-scale projects that promised to modernize them and theoretically make them more livable.[59] From a developer's or real estate investor's perspective, the "beauty" of these kinds of schemes was that they were largely made possible by processes that, from the outside perspective at least, appeared legal (after concealing the fact that they often depended on access to insider knowledge). The plans were themselves founded on the expectation that land values were supposed to rise, which in itself encouraged profiting from real estate. In stark contrast to the ideologies of high socialism, profiting from land in this emergent landscape was no longer seen as parasitic but formed a cornerstone to the fiscal logic of urban development. Real estate developers were increasingly celebrated as heroic individuals, literally building the city *(xây dựng thành phố)*. Furthermore, and quite importantly, it was not only elites and connected individuals who were cashing in on the rising values of land. Even lower-middle-class Vietnamese were engaging in small-time investing, and the potential for land to generate seemingly effortless income for people who had recently lived through several decades of postwar deprivation gave great hope to many. After the redistricting, District Two in general, and Thủ Thiêm in particular, was a very popular site for people at all levels to engage in land investment.[60] According to the Thủ Thiêm residents we interviewed, the problem with land conversion was not that it promoted the commodification of land and a dramatic rise in land values—that, in principle, was seen as a good thing, an opportunity to get rich. The problem was their feeling of being boxed out of that opportunity by government authorities who used these processes for self-aggrandizement.

Over the course of the 1990s and 2000s, furthermore, real estate and land-based capital accumulation were also associated with legal frameworks that, on the surface at least, appeared to most observers and most everyday Vietnamese as positive developments that were linked to the distribution of property rights. The fair and legal purchase of "undeveloped" agricultural land, for example, was founded on the process of land titling and the regularization of property rights, which was commonly associated with "market reforms" and expanding the rule of law. Such reforms were not just economic, but carried positive moral associations, because they were seen as heralding a gradual move away from the injustices people had come to associate with the period of high socialism. Against the context of their own historical experiences, furthermore, the ability to buy and sell land, for most Vietnamese and arguably even more so for Southern Vietnamese, was generally regarded as offering new and unprecedented opportunities. In addition to these factors, the new economic service industries that accompanied these changes also stimulated expanding credit, supported a growing financial sector, created new jobs for educated professionals, and fostered other emergent sources of non–labor intensive income. Having access to formal land titles seemed like progress when compared to the system of arbitrary central decision-making and "fuzzy property" that preceded it.[61] When viewed against their recent history with a system based on scarcity, most Vietnamese, especially those in the south, did not consider it exploitative to capitalize on real estate, but rather saw real estate as a path to economic prosperity. The evidence of the land markets' ability to improve life seemed to be present everywhere one looked, especially with the construction boom going on, glittering buildings going up everywhere in the city, and conspicuous consumer spending giving the city a sense of having turned an economic corner. While the precipitous decline in real estate values in 2008 tempered some of this enthusiasm about land as a guaranteed path to prosperity, for most of the period since the mid-1990s real estate investment in general has been seen as a positive result of economic reforms.[62]

Given this context of postwar redevelopment, by 1998, when Ho Chi Minh City's chief architect formally approved the 1/2000-scale master plan for Thủ Thiêm, support for urban development and the idea of building a modern city was widespread. A market in land use rights had increasingly come to work like a real estate market, and Thủ Thiêm had been formally redistricted as "inner-city land," which made the area a site of great development potential. Theoretically speaking, if done properly, the project could pay for itself.

## THE THỦ THIÊM INVESTMENT AND CONSTRUCTION AUTHORITY

For all these reasons, new urban zones appeared as symbols of progress. They were linked to the modernization and improvement of the city, which visually reflected Vietnam's economic renaissance. Unlocking land values to rebuild the city seemed almost like a magic solution that had suddenly been made available to the Vietnamese people once government leaders finally shed the ideological blinders of socialism. But one fundamental problem remained in this focus on progress and rising land values: maximizing Thủ Thiêm's potential to pay for itself would require controlling the process through which it generated value. For the plan to succeed in its goal of financing infrastructure, it required compensating residents at existing low land values (to keep total "land clearance" costs down) and leveraging the future on anticipated increases in land value. The difference between low compensation and high resale value, which the plan seemed to assume would apply without any protest, would then be used to pay off loans and generate profits for investors.

Once this process was set into motion, however, and once land speculators and everyday residents became aware of the project, it would be increasingly necessary to carefully steward the project by controlling and maintaining stable land compensation rates and also preventing new residents from moving to the land in order to stake claims. Vietnam's newly opened land market offered great potential, but if left to its own devices it also had the capacity to spiral out of control, due to land speculation and the proliferation of false land claims. Once unleashed, the property market had to be tamed. Yet markets, of course, are nothing less than the sum total of all the diverse economic activities of the people who make up a society. For this reason, taming a market means taming people; and taming people in the new era of transferrable land use rights and rising real estate values would require a whole new mechanism of governance.

As the project was increasingly formalized, the complexities of managing land, construction, design, investment, foreign capital, banking, resettlement, and the environment led to a complex framework that cut across multiple ministries, offices, and levels of government. According to Dennis Pieprz, a principal of Sasaki Associates and president of the company from 2004 to 2011, his design team had to work with over seventy local agencies associated with the Thủ Thiêm project.[63] Given all these interests, it was not just the people on the ground who needed to be tamed, but also the increasingly unwieldy government bureaucracy. Not only did multiple governmental offices have stakes in the project, but it is also well known that every independent government agency in Vietnam commonly requires its own paperwork (and associated bribes). Thus, it became necessary to streamline the investment procedures and develop what at the time was called a "one-stop shop" for development. To facilitate this process, On January 1, 2001, the People's Committee of Ho Chi Minh City issued a decision, signed by People's Committee Chairman Lê Thanh Hải, to establish the Thủ Thiêm Investment and Construction Authority (ICA), which would be given the mandate to conduct the investment and construction management of Thủ Thiêm New Urban Zone "as planned, regulated, and legislated."[64]

According to the official text of the decision, the Thủ Thiêm ICA would be under the direct authority of the Ho Chi Minh City People's Committee, but it would have "its own stamp," which meant it could make autonomous decisions related to the plan. It would also have its own bank accounts in the National Treasury and other banks. More specifically, the Thủ Thiêm ICA was tasked with the following: (1) creating the detailed master plan for the People's Committee and prime minister to approve; (2) attracting investment; (3) working with government agencies to organize and administer land, including land reclamation, resettlement, and compensation for moving people off their land; (4) keeping track of and administering investment projects; (5) administering and carrying out the construction projects according to the master plan; and (6) serving as a "single face" or a "one-stop shop" for the government in dealing with investors.[65] In short, the Thủ Thiêm ICA was established as a parastatal umbrella organization with great administrative and legal authority to make decisions and carry out the project. It was (and still is) charged with making the dream of the New Urban Zone into a reality.[66]

Thus, although the project was officially approved by the city architect's office in 1998, it was not until the Thủ Thiêm ICA was established in 2001 that it began to have the coherence necessary to bring it into fruition. Soon afterward, in 2002, the head of the Ho Chi Minh City People's Committee formally issued a decision that the city would "reclaim" 621 hectares of land in the Thủ Thiêm project area, which would be handed over to the Thủ Thiêm ICA, which was granted full authority to guide the process.[67] In its sixth session in June 2002, the 8th Ho Chi Minh City People's Council issued a resolution selecting the Thủ Thiêm New Urban Zone Construction Project as "the key work of Ho Chi Minh City in the beginning of the 21st century."[68] The details of the compensation process were laid out in a twenty-three-page decision by the Ho Chi Minh City People's Committee, which explains in seventeen multiclause articles all the cases in which people could and could not claim compensation, and all the levels and qualifications of that compensation, based on the kind of land paperwork they possessed, how long they had occupied the land, and the land's classification.[69] With the legal and administrative framework for the project set, the Thủ Thiêm ICA soon began implementing the land reclamation process.

It was precisely there, in the displacement and compensation process, where the core disagreements with residents emerged. The very mandate of the plan depended on the ICA compensating residents at low rates in order to generate the fiscal income required to make the plan a reality. But at the same time, it also required the ICA to negotiate the best prices for land from foreign investors. In other words, the basic structure depended on the ICA buying cheap from the residents and selling dear to investors, but without allowing residents to negotiate directly with investors themselves.[70] As the residents gradually came to understand the economics of the process, they realized that the entire logic of the Thủ Thiêm project depended on undervaluing their land, and that the project itself could not go forward unless they accepted the terms of compensation. Fully aware that the project itself would lead to rapidly rising land values, they also realized that holding out might enable them to negotiate for higher payments. And they were essentially correct in this assessment. Over the course of the project, the Thủ Thiêm ICA and the city, eager to speed up the process, had to revise the terms of compensation at least twice. From the initial base payment of 2,380,000 Vietnamese đồng (VND) per square meter of residential land offered in 2002, the compensation was raised to 6,380,000 VND in 2006, and three years later to 18,380,000 VND. While in many ways the Thủ Thiêm ICA can be said to have insisted on a kind of ruthless adherence to the plan, the very history of repeated concessions to resident demands for increased compensation shows that the residents were also quite competent in their negotiations.

But there was a further complication, one that ultimately undermined the gains residents were making through their foot-dragging and refusal to leave. As the Thủ Thiêm project advanced, the land surrounding the project's footprint became a prime site for real estate investment and land speculation. As a result, all of the land values surrounding the project also shot up in value, which made it harder for holdouts among the Thủ Thiêm residents to find suitable new housing, in spite of their increased compensation; this led them to demand even further compensation. Even as the residents fought for better deals, in other words, the real purchasing power of their compensation kept getting progressively lower. Taming the market, and the people who constituted it, turned out to be more difficult than expected as the fight over compensation became the central problem in Thủ Thiêm.

From a purely structural perspective, this controversy must be understood in light of a basic political-economic paradox. On the one hand, the new "rights" Vietnamese people had gained to transfer their land use rights unleashed the value of land for them. On the other hand, the new importance of land use rights as a transferrable thing of value also unleashed the pressure to strip people of what had all of a sudden become a valuable commodity. As the project unfolded, the very same concept of property value and land use rights that made it possible for Thủ Thiêm to hold such potential value also facilitated the formal and legal seizure of land from some of the very same people who had only recently gained those rights. These rights, and the knowledge of the economic value they promised, in short, only intensified residents' sense that they were not getting a fair return on the sacrifices they were being asked to make. What emerged was a structural condition that evaded easy solutions, going as it did to the heart of the basic economic logic of how land for infrastructure drives fiscal socialism.

In Thủ Thiêm, the idea of "buying cheap" and "selling dear" made it impossible to compensate displaced residents at values close to the anticipated future value of the land. Nevertheless, once the people facing eviction became aware of the high prices their land would command after they handed it over, their anger became difficult to control. From the perspective of project planners, the people quickly appeared as sources of disorder, disrupting what appeared to be a logical, fiscally innovative plan. The irony in this assessment, however, is that the project itself had always played on the promise that it would help lead the triumph of order over disorder through rational planning. But at root, the very economic logic of the plan itself had introduced many of the new forces of social disorder and contestation that came to define the Thủ Thiêm project. The residents were never opposed to urban development in principle. Their main gripe has always been that they are being asked to bear all the losses in a scheme organized around the logic of buying cheap and selling dear.

## CONVERGENCES AND DIVERGENCES

"It has turned into jungle," several former residents told me when describing Thủ Thiêm after the demolitions in 2012, 2013, and 2014. The evictees' demands for higher compensation had eventually been granted, whereupon they had moved from Thủ Thiêm. After their homes were demolished, goats wandered the streets, navigating potholes and rubble. Farmers from as far away as periurban Thủ Đức and District Nine would come to cut and gather the grasses, piling them like bulging haystacks onto three-wheeled motorcycles to carry off for their milk-cows back home.[71] Scavengers—mostly rural-urban migrants and displaced peasants from other newly urbanizing districts—began to come each day and dig through the dirt and rubble of a demolished shipyard originally built by the French. They were searching for a century's worth of metal scraps to be sold by the kilo. Sinewy men with their shirts off dug shoulder deep into black dirt like pit miners. Women of all ages raked through the soil, dressed like rice farmers in conical hats to fight the sun. Among one such group of women was a five-year-old girl, her pink outfit standing out against the black soil. She was turning the dirt with a stick while her mother loaded scraps of iron into an old fertilizer bag.[72] Only a few years earlier, the vibrant neighborhoods of Thủ Thiêm were wastelands in the discourse of planners only. But now, the very process of clearing the land *(giải tỏa)* had turned the area to waste for real.

Scenes of human struggle in the man-made wasteland were partly softened by ones of creativity and play. Urban pleasure-seekers from other city districts looking for open spaces flocked to the newly "liberated" lands. Long-distance runners and cyclists, decked out in performance gear and spandex, sped through the empty roads at dawn. Movie crews filmed fake rural scenes, wedding photographers posed happy couples in open fields, artists created modern art. Kite fliers took to the cleared lands, and the skies above Thủ Thiêm soon filled with paper phoenixes and dragons, rainbow tails streaming in the wind. Fishermen, students, and snack vendors crowded the Thủ Thiêm bridge.[73] At dusk, lovers came to the riverbanks and cuddled in a long string of anonymous silhouettes, sitting on the back seats of their motorbikes, watching the sun go down over the city, across the river. When the sun disappeared, the timid would go home, but the daring would linger on, doing what lovers only dare do in the darkness. People held picnics and drinking parties under the shade trees in the cemeteries behind the Catholic church. Instead of placing flowers, they decked the graves of the dead with empty cigarette boxes, crushed beer cans, and the occasional used condom. After midnight, daredevil youths raced their motorbikes. An American anthropologist conducted a study alongside Vietnamese colleagues. And journalists wrote stories about all these things.

Among all this, a few holdout households remained in Thủ Thiêm. Theirs were small houses, tucked deep inside the interior, off the main roads, hidden by tall grass and overgrown bushes. A few cafes were set up on top of the rubble, fashioned out of scavenged goods. The nuns at the convent continued their daily rounds, and crowds continued to come each week to busy Sunday masses at the church. The monks at the Liên Trì Pagoda announced that they would rather die than let their pagoda be razed. By the spring of 2014, officials announced that 14,336 out of 14,343 total eviction "dossiers" had been given their compensation.[74] Not all of the households represented by these files had fully vacated, but as living conditions became increasingly unbearable, even those who remained were planning to go, and even the holdouts were working out the final details of their compensation and relocation agreements. The holdouts said there was other business going on in the dark as well: heroin use, prostitution, and other vices known to favor the shadows. They, too, denounced the disorder condemned by state authorities, but much of the current disorder, they said, was a byproduct of the project itself. They blamed disorder on the state's own incompetence: disorder was a symptom of mismanagement, corruption, and a combination of dishonesty and poor planning.

Meanwhile, silty sand was being dredged from the waterways of the Đồng Nai River, floated to Thủ Thiêm on barges, then pumped through long tubes into the landscape, slowly filling in the rivulets and natural canals, increasing the tidal flooding in those places that people had not yet left, flattening and raising the rest of the surface into an elevated pancake, a clean slate upon which to build the Thủ Thiêm New Urban Zone. Big trucks and backhoes, their wheels caked with mud, moved loads of dirt. Mud on the main roads grew thick, turned to dust in the sun, and became a muddy bog again in the rain. The holdouts were living on borrowed time, but despite their impossible living conditions, they too played with time as best they could, waiting, playing cards, drinking coffee, hanging out, and holding parties and feasts in the rubble—lingering on as a tactic to press for more favorable compensation. With every passing day, the Thủ Thiêm ICA accumulated more interest on loans taken out to pay for the evictions and compensation claims.[75]

There had been domination and there had been resistance, but in the story of Thủ Thiêm the process of eviction, normally told as a battle of opposites, was complex and riven through with ambivalence. The New Urban Zone as a whole was linked to the larger national project of renovation, the brainchild of one of the few postwar Vietnamese leaders who can be said to have been genuinely loved by the people, Võ Văn Kiệt. Loud resistance to low levels of compensation was not itself a critique of the market-driven modernization invoked by Kiệt's dream, a dream that many of those being displaced shared, and still share. But then again, his dream was also being carried out by contemporary leaders whom few of the people trusted. The people, ostensibly the victims in all this, sometimes resisted the government and at other times seemed to share its dreams of building a "civilized" and modern city, through the magical value unleashed when land was turned into a commodity. But the people didn't want to be cheated, and the calculus of commodity value came to play a leading role in the language of resistance they came to use. In the meantime, those same people viewed with awe the often crushing forward march of demolition followed by construction, even as they cursed the losses on which that construction was being built.

· · ·

What strikes me now as I look back on all the displacement in Thủ Thiêm is the ambivalence that residents commonly expressed when they spoke about the project. It would be so much easier to tell a story of David and Goliath, or of oppressed victims standing up in unity against the forces of eviction. But the story of Thủ Thiêm was much more complicated. More than a story of good versus evil, it was the story of people of two minds. On the one hand, they believed in the larger ambitions of the project—the idea of building a civilized and modern city. On the other hand, they denounced the way they were treated for that project to become possible.

How could people marvel at the very project that had introduced so much misery into their lives? One image that sticks in my mind may begin to explain this contradiction.

On March 8, 2010, just when the pace of evictions was picking up, enthusiastic, mesmerized crowds gathered along the Saigon River to watch the installation of the central segment of the Thủ Thiêm Tunnel, billed as the longest underwater tunnel in Southeast Asia.[76] People watched from both banks, in District One and in Thủ Thiêm. The atmosphere was festive. This tunnel was a source of pride, and held great beauty and symbolic power. One might say it was a charismatic megastructure. As tugboats coaxed the section into position, Vietnamese flags waved in the air and the river provided a spectacular stage for the performance of state legitimacy. For the first time, with this tunnel, District One was linked to District Two as two parts of a whole, and the East-West Highway—part of which was to be formally named after Võ Văn Kiệt in July of that same year—was made whole.[77] The river itself never moved an inch. But it was, from this moment forward, no longer at the edge of the city. It now ran right through the city's new heart.

The people watching this spectacle from the Thủ Thiêm side of the river showed genuine admiration for this triumph of engineering. In a newspaper photo from that day, I can recognize some of the people I had come to know during my research, people who were being evicted from their homes. As they watched this scene unfold, their own homes were being torn to rubble, house by individual house. But in the face of it all, even the people being displaced told me they were proud of Vietnam's achievement, and they also said that moments like this were something to behold, something beautiful. Not long after the tunnel was installed, the Thủ Thiêm ferry service shut down. Not long after that, all the residents were gone.

# From the Rubble

*Tính đi!*
*Calculate this!*

—THỦ THIÊM RESIDENT DESCRIBING UNJUST
COMPENSATION, APRIL 2011

## QUIVERING WALLS

In March 2014, Mr. Tâm, a recently retired sixty-five-year-old electronics repair-man, plugged his digital camera into a television and played a video. The video, made on Tâm's pocket camera in August 2011, shows three men pulling with all their might on a thick rope. It was filmed in Thủ Thiêm, across the Saigon River from the old colonial boulevards and the new glass towers of District One. Everything in the video seems stretched to the limit—not just the rope, but the men too. Sweat accumulates in round stains on white shirts, graying with the dust of smashed concrete. The men brace their feet against a low cement curb (once the edge of an alleyway) and time their pulls in synchrony: one-*two*-THREE. Sway, jerk, pull in, lean back. They find a rhythm: crouching forward and then heaving backward, first with two small pulls, then arching all the way back like levers for a third. They pull until the rope seems ready to snap. When they reach their limit, the rope recoils, drawing them forward again. One of the men still wears his motorcycle helmet. They all wear plastic sandals. Crushed bricks are scattered everywhere (fig. 6.1).

The taut rope is attached to the quivering wall of an antique home. The roof is gone, but the house's distinctive archways and moldings, shaded veranda, and checkerboard tiles all provide evidence that it was an early- to mid-twentieth-century French colonial bungalow. In a previous era—until the mid-1900s at least—a home like this would have housed French-speaking Vietnamese merchants, minor functionaries of the colonial state, or managers in French enterprises. It might, for example, have been owned by a clerk employed at CARIC (Chantiers et Ateliers Réunis d'Indochine), the old French shipyard down the road where large numbers

FIGURE 6.1. The remains of Tâm's home, Thủ Thiêm, District 2, Ho Chi Minh City. Author's collection, August 2011.

of Thủ Thiêm residents used to work. But no: this house belonged to Tâm's father, an accountant who worked at a big bank across the river in District One. A cornerstone reads "1943," though Tâm says his father built the house in 1938. Whereas today's urban trendsetters might praise the house as an excellent example of "Indochine chic,"[1] no amount of chic will save it from demolition. The red clay roof tiles were sold by the kilo to interior designers in the city's more affluent districts. The windows and casings have since been sold to scrap merchants, leaving gaping holes in the walls. Even the bricks in these old homes are valuable. They, too, will be sold when the walls come down.

Mr. Tâm had lived in that old French-Vietnamese home his entire life, first as one of seven children, then with his own wife and children, and finally as empty-nest grandparents, until they were forced to demolish the house in 2011. He played the video in the living room of his new home, a skinny three-story house on the other side of District Two, tucked into a working-class alleyway far from the Saigon River, built recently on land as close to the old place as he could afford but in a completely different style. The new house, like all the houses in his new neighborhood, is a common type in Saigon; locals sometimes call these dwellings "city street houses" *(nhà phố)* or, more evocatively, "tube houses" *(nhà ống)* because their footprints are deep but narrow like tubes, maximizing the number that have direct access to the streets and alleyways along which they are built.[2] At 4 meters wide and 18 meters deep, Tâm's new house was set within a 5-by-22-meter plot of land. Like most tube houses, it had a tiny paved garden in front, just big enough to park a pair of motorbikes among the potted plants, behind a tall wall and a solid iron gate.

The new house was clean and modern, with stylish shelving, smart wall units, and new furniture made of glass, steel, lacquered wood, and clean vinyl. Hồng, Tâm's wife, said the white floor tiles came from Italy. The clean, well-lit living room was cooled by an array of new electric fans, and the interior was decorated everywhere with flowers: planted in pots, arrayed in vases, painted in paintings, printed on posters, and arranged in plastic bouquets along the walls. The walls were light and vibrant, painted in pure whites and primary colors. Tâm had salvaged about four square meters' worth of the tiles from the old house, but only used them to cover the floor in a storage room near the back. "I only saved a few and put them back here," he explained. "The old tiles don't really fit the new style." The new house was filled with new appliances, including the flat-screen television on which we viewed the video of the day his old house was torn down.

The video continues to play on the screen. The thick rope snakes through a broken window casing. Lashed back around the top of the wall, it offers a firm hold. With each pull of the rope, the wall sways forward a bit, then back again. The resistance of the wall sets the rhythm of the pulls, like a stiff inverted pendulum slowly beginning to rock. Each pull leads incrementally, almost imperceptibly, to an ever so slightly wider sway. As the swaying amplifies, the demolition workers start to rock and pull in step with the wall's own momentum, enlisting its resistance in the task of its own demolition.

## THE DEMOLITION OF THỦ THIÊM AND THE CREATION OF LAND VALUE AND RIGHTS

Tâm's old house, that bungalow with the quivering walls, was one of approximately 14,600 houses demolished in Thủ Thiêm over the course of a decade, mostly between the middle of 2010 and the end of 2011, but some as early as 2003 and some as late as 2014.[3] When it was still standing, Tâm's house was surrounded by lush tropical vegetation—star fruit, mango, and jackfruit trees—and pierced by the occasional trunk of a ficus tree growing into and out of its walls. It was the kind of house that evoked a sense of place embedded in a particular history, region, climate, and ecosystem—a classic Saigon bungalow. Although it evoked an older time, it had an unobstructed panoramic view of the Saigon skyline, with its rising monuments to modern economic development and future-oriented city building.

By the time Tâm and his family had been evicted and had moved into their new tube house several kilometers away, the land on which the old house once stood had been converted into an abstract calculus of value. Tâm noted matter-of-factly that he had received the same level of compensation, calculated in terms of square meters of land, as his neighbors, who, he said, had mostly unremarkable, even downright ugly, homes. This is what happens: when homes are torn down, land is assigned a value by abstract processes set by the market or the state rather than by emotional or aesthetic qualities. In the final instance, Tâm even participated in the process: he himself had arranged for the three men to pull the house down.

Watching the video of the demolition, Tâm spoke objectively, without revealing his emotions, as if narrating a documentary film: "The French bricks are thick and the mortar they used is strong. It took a long time to tear that wall down." One of his new neighbors, who had stopped by unannounced for a drink, sat down and watched the video with us. His reaction was more nostalgic than Tâm's: "It hurts the gut to watch this," he said. "Houses like that were strong. So many storms over the years. Strong winds, heavy downpours. Nothing ever happened to those houses." The wall in the video continued to sway with every pull.

Tâm's unsentimental response to the video did not mean he had no emotional attachment to the old home, where more than three generations of his family had spent at least part of their lives. After all, he had gone there with his camera to film the demolition, to preserve a record of the place. Neither he nor Hồng ever wanted to move away from that house in the first place. It was their home. But by the time it was demolished and their new house constructed, Tâm and Hồng had developed a new, fairly distant language for talking about the process—detached and clinical, often resigned. When they did speak about the old house, their language was infused with a detailed vocabulary that invoked land value and legal title, and securing just compensation based on a set of rights to property. Their new language gave them a way to talk about fairness and justice, and to assert their rights.

Still: in the process of gaining this language, they had lost their home.

### Values, Property Values, and Rights

The fact that human beings have emotional connections to their homes, and that they would prefer not to be evicted from them, should come as no great anthropological discovery. What is more difficult to understand, however, is the sometimes contradictory process that takes place when the assortment of qualitative values human beings attach to homes are forced to conjoin with a highly specific and reductive concept of "value," which tends to be defined quantitatively, most commonly in terms of money. This is a process grounded in political economy, buttressed by legality, linked to property markets, and legitimized by the rule of law. It is also informed by historical and cultural contexts—even though the process itself tends to obscure, or even forcibly deny, history and culture by assuming that thinking of property as a container of economic value is somehow inevitable. In this chapter, I reject the assumption that property has "natural" monetary worth, and instead focus on how the qualitative elements of people's attachment to the places they live become rearticulated in quantifiable terms. In so doing, I describe the demolition process in Thủ Thiêm as *transformative movement.* That is, demolition not only transforms physical space; it also restructures the very ways in which people imagine the meaning of land. One might say that the destruction of homes actually produces something new, even as it destroys.[4] As I will show, demolition produces an emergent notion of property value and of property rights, which in turn frames notions of justice and "rights" more generally.

Such notions of rights, and a corresponding sense of justice, come at a cost, however. For they are cobbled together from the rubble of an urban process that strips people of the very property these rights are meant to protect. In order to produce these new rights and values, large numbers of people are losing their homes. To become effective in their dealings with the state and other forces associated with the market economy, therefore, residents are forced to recalibrate their own language of affect and sentiment—of the poetic nature of space and place—in a way that allows them to speak in the language of economic value, of development and private property, that governs negotiations over eviction compensation. In the process, a largely unquantifiable language of home and place, nostalgia and sentiment, becomes subordinated to a more universalizing one of law and "rights," expressed increasingly in monetary terms. Rights do not fully displace the language of sentiment, but what emerges is a set of layered registers for speaking about and conceptualizing land and property. As people engage with the reality of their dispossession, they oscillate between these registers, struggling to reconcile the sentiment that informs their attachment to land with the commodified idioms of property value that both drive them from their land and give them a language of rights to contest the terms of their dispossession. In the process, residents begin, slowly and incrementally, to prioritize the language of rights, where property value—framed as a fair calculation of monetary value multiplied by square meters—comes to define the terms of justice.

It is impossible to quantify sentiment and nostalgia, but it is reasonable to assume that Vietnamese householders are just as sentimental about their homes as any other people in the world. In fact, most studies of traditional Vietnamese society emphasize the importance of patrilineal kinship, with Vietnamese personhood and identity being rooted in ancestral homes and places of origin. Indeed, the idea of what Vietnamese people call the *quê hương,* or the homeland, is so powerful that it might be called a "key symbol" in constructions of Vietnamese identity and nationalism.[5] Nevertheless, despite this cultural emphasis on the importance of a person's home in the construction of identity, when people's homes in Thủ Thiêm ended up in the path of the extraordinarily destructive modernization project known as the Thủ Thiêm New Urban Zone, a complex transformation took place that is much more subtle than a simple theory of loving and defending one's home could explain. While most residents certainly loved their homes, and while all of them had the capacity to articulate deep sentimental ties to their residences, when they described their negotiations with the authorities, the resistance they articulated against their displacement was ultimately not directed against the project itself; rather, it was almost always expressed in terms of inadequate compensation and how particular laws were being violated.

Because eviction required the demolition of their homes, residents understandably and quite bravely learned to stand up for their rights and demand justice. This language of rights gave many of them a strong voice, and engendered its own forms of affect—often expressed in a language of righteous indignation. They made it clear that they refused to be cheated. But in the very process of developing their voice of dissent, they became increasingly fixated on a particular, quantifiable sense of justice, itself founded on notions of proprietary value and private ownership. In the process, the idioms of their own resistance became transformed, and their voices became fragmented and atomized by the myriad conditions that made all of their cases unique and different, despite general similarities. This is not to say that the affective associations they had toward their homes played no role in the process of eviction and displacement. But instead of emphasizing their love of their homes and some kind of preexisting distaste for master-planned developments, residents became drawn over time into a *process* of engaging with and acquiescing to the terms of development in ways that actually transformed their qualitative values by engaging them deeply in the cold scrutiny of quantitative evaluation.[6] Sentiment and nostalgia have little currency in the discourse of universal justice and proprietary rights. Residents adjusted their language of resistance to reflect that.

Wittingly or not, they gradually subordinated the language of sentiment and nostalgia to the language of property rights, money, land value, and justice, all articulated in terms of individual ownership. The result of this transformation was a simple yet profound paradox: the idiom of their resistance increasingly grew to reflect, and in many ways to normalize and entrench, the degree to which property value has become the defining quality of land and the primary means for evaluating the degree of justice or injustice in urban development projects. Gradually, the idiom of land value came to frame the way residents voiced their resistance, but it was precisely this language that had set in motion the very process of eviction the residents themselves purported to resist. In the process of developing a language of justice and resistance based on property values, residents were drawn into the same language of proprietary rights that their resistance might have been directed against. Like the quivering wall in Tâm's old French bungalow, which was being coaxed down by workers Tâm himself had engaged, the language of their own resistance was enlisted in the process of their own eviction.

## TEACHER LONG'S STORY

The process through which qualitative *values* become reduced to quantitative economic *value* becomes particularly clear in conversations with evicted residents.
In many of the stories residents told about their evictions, they would toggle back
and forth between qualitative and quantitative assessments of the homes they were
losing. To illustrate this process, I will quote from a long recorded discussion we
had with an extremely articulate Thủ Thiêm resident, whom I will call Teacher
Long. Several evicted residents had insisted that we *absolutely needed* to interview
this man, who was a well-respected schoolteacher from a family with long roots
in Thủ Thiêm. Because Teacher Long was a *teacher,* they insisted, *he* would be able
to get the facts right; *he* knew the history of Thủ Thiêm and understood the legal
dynamics of the development project.

It turned out that Teacher Long had been forced by circumstances to move far away
from his home near the Saigon River to a hot and dusty neighborhood in a distant,
newly urbanizing sector of District Nine, and my colleague and I had to make several
trips and spend hours banging on doors to finally find him. But our search for him
was indeed worth the effort. He had a lot to say about Thủ Thiêm. The structure of his
long narrative also clearly illustrates the ways in which residents often shifted between
qualitative and quantitative modes of expressing the tragedy of their displacement.

Teacher Long's story hinges on an important shift that took place in the middle
of our long conversation. This shift illustrates what happens when discussions
about "sentiment" and qualitative descriptions of "place" morph into discussions
about property, land value, and rights. At the beginning of our conversation he
spoke largely in the language of sentiment, telling nostalgic stories of his family
as he described daily life in a place that has since been forever transformed. During that early portion of the conversation, his voice filled with wistful melancholy,
sometimes expressing great delight and sometimes verging on tears. Then, about
a third of the way into the recorded interview, which lasted for about an hour and
forty-five minutes, he shifted toward a language of justice and fair compensation,
filled with numbers and references to legal decrees. At that point, his voice quickened, his tone rose, and he became visibly angry at times. This shift from nostalgia
to righteous indignation is significant because it captures, in a single interview, a
shift that commonly occurred among Thủ Thiêm residents as they tried to articulate their predicament. It is also significant because, as with so many other Thủ
Thiêm residents, the fact that he was able to emphasize the incontrovertible legal
basis of his rights did not change the fact that he had been evicted from his home.

### Teacher Long Describes Thủ Thiêm

Teacher Long was just over sixty years old when we interviewed him in 2014. The
youngest of ten children, he began by telling a bit about his family, describing

stories he had heard passed down to him about life in Thủ Thiêm way back when his great-grandfather settled there, sometime in the nineteenth century. The facts he gave about the past were sometimes blurry, told in the loose style of a "once upon a time" story. But he was clearly telling the truth, at least as well as he understood it. As he began speaking, he focused not so much on specific details as on the broader sense of Thủ Thiêm as his ancestral land:

> I lived in Thủ Thiêm. I was part of the third generation of my family living in that piece of land, starting with my great-grandfather, then my paternal grandfather. Mine was the third generation. I'm sixty years old now. Yes, yes, sixty years old.
>
> The year eighteen hundred . . . around eighteen hundred and eighty something. Back then in my grandfather's day, there was my great-grandfather, who was named Nguyễn Văn XX, he was the village head *[đại hương cả]* for all of An Khánh village, which was part of old Gia Định.
>
> The village headman! He was seen as someone who had a great deal of farmland. My great-grandfather was one of the first people to clear the land *[khai phá]* in Thủ Thiêm.
>
> My great-grandfather was a village headman. There, so that is how it was! One of the first people to clear the land in Thủ Thiêm! Yes, it was so. He was one of those kinds of people. But one of the features of the Thủ Thiêm area was that it also had a lot of land named after foreign people—most of them were Khmer *[người Miên]*. The Khmers had their name on the land there, in that area. I'm not so good at remembering clearly the names of some of those people, but the land was a wasteland *[hoang vu]* of silt deposits *[phù sa]* . . . Movement was very difficult, because every time the tide flooded up, it spread out and covered thirty or forty percent of the entire Thủ Thiêm peninsula. Because of that, only those people who lived off of agriculture or hunting were able to live there. That! That was one of the unique qualities of how it was in Thủ Thiêm.

The details Teacher Long gave were not precise, but the central point was clear: his great-grandfather had been a wealthy patriarch, who had managed to acquire "several dozen *mẫu*" of land, which Teacher Long insisted had been reclaimed for agriculture out of uncultivated wastelands. A *mẫu* is a unit of land measurement, about 850 square meters larger than an acre,[7] and this was clearly a sizable amount of land.

Moving on to the next generation of his family, Teacher Long described how his grandfather made good use of all the land he inherited, emphasizing that he also happened to be a generous man, who often granted land to people moving up from the Mekong Delta, who in turn then built houses on the land and made a living off of agriculture. Long was describing his ancestors as important agents in the settling of Thủ Thiêm. The story he told followed a common trope in Vietnamese civilizing narratives about "clearing the wasteland" in the region surrounding Saigon as well as the Mekong Delta.[8] In this story, he described a kind of settler lifestyle, emphasizing the labors expended by people who had made the best out of a relatively difficult environment and who had cleared the land through their frontier spirit. Notably, when he discussed these earlier times, he always used the old name of the region, Nam Kỳ Lục Tỉnh (Six Southern Provinces), which even further linked his narrative to standard historical narratives about settling the south.[9]

This mode of storytelling continued as Teacher Long walked through the history of his family, generation by generation. During his father's generation, for example, there had still not been any fresh water in Thủ Thiêm. But in the bootstrap spirit of the area, Teacher Long describes how his father turned hardship into a business opportunity that also served his community:

> The water was acidic [nước phèn],[10] so people could only use it to bathe and wash and for household use. But in order to drink, it was necessary to have a way to get water from other places by means of small transport boats [chiếc ghe]. My father would provide water . . . with [his] three boats. The youngsters in the old times would row by hand—there were no motors. It wasn't until about 1970 when they finally had a "co-le motor" [Kohler engine]. But in the old days, they had to row by hand from Thủ Thiêm across [the Saigon River] to the docks by the Thị Nghè Bridge [adjacent to District One, at the mouth of the canal that runs behind the Saigon zoo]. Beyond the Thị Nghè Bridge, there was treated water. There, they would pump the water into the boats, and then row. They'd row back to Thủ Thiêm, and then call out, and people would carry the water off the boats, in those big drums, like the drums used to carry oil in the old days. They'd carry the water, bring it home, and leave it there. Because Thủ Thiêm is completely alluvial, so the water is acidic, really heavy in acidity, so that no one could use the water there at all. [ . . . ] [My father did that] from 1952 on . . . Thủ Thiêm didn't have fresh water until 1970.

Teacher Long then described the sentimental feelings he had for his old home in Thủ Thiêm, focusing on the ecological setting and the kind of people who lived in the area. The people there were special, a hardy lot: "Almost all the people in Thủ Thiêm were great swimmers, because they lived next to the Saigon River—near rivers and streams. They could swim from this side all the way across to the other side of the Saigon River, all the way to Bến Nhà Rồng [the current site of the Ho Chi Minh Museum, located at the mouth of the Bến Nghé Canal, formerly the Arroyo Chinois]. They were not afraid."

Later, he talked about all the kinds of fish people would catch in the area—cá lóc (northern snakehead, Channa argus), cá rô (climbing perch, Anabas testudineus), cá sặc (snakeskin gourami, Trichogaster pectoralis), cá lăng hải (Asian red-tail catfish, Hemibagrus nemurus), cá ngát (eeltail catfish, Euristhmus microceps), and cá trê (airbreathing catfish, Clariidae family). He mentioned the simple meals people ate, consisting of vegetables people grew themselves, and all of these fish— before the water was polluted by industry and heavy water traffic. He described how people only went to the market to buy things like salt, oil, and fish sauce, or manufactured products. When they did go to the market, they would only visit the working-class markets at chợ Xóm Chiếu across the river in District Four (and never in the fancy markets of District One). These kinds of stories depicted a distinct sense of place in Thủ Thiêm and described a hard-working, humble people. It was quite moving, the way Teacher Long used personal storytelling to depict a bygone era and to locate himself and his family within the longer history of Thủ Thiêm. Toward the end of this discussion of what might be called "Thủ Thiêm in the old days," he explained that he sometimes cried when passing by the area in Thủ Thiêm where his ancestral home once stood.

This sentimental, affect-laden mode of storytelling continued until it reached something of a crescendo, which then launched directly into a moral statement about how Thủ Thiêm residents were willing to make a sacrifice, not just for the city but for the nation:

> My father . . . built his house there in 1940. I'm from the third generation; my children are the fourth generation. Now that they have begun the evictions, I can honestly say that the compensation policy does not satisfy the people. The people have suffered great losses *[bị thiệt thòi]*. We are ready to make a sacrifice *[hy sinh]*, sacrifice the life we had in in our native place *[nơi chôn nhau cắt rốn]*;[11] we've abandoned our homeland *[quê hương]* and have gone off to different places, with great anguish. Every time I pass by the place, tears stream out. Why? Because that place is where I was born, where the first umbilical cord was cut and where my people are also buried. The place we call the native place[12] is for the Vietnamese people the most sacred thing, no one can even express it. And I must say that everyone has a homeland. We all know that "the homeland is the sweet cluster of star fruit" *[quê hương là chùm khế ngọt]*[13], and it is something sacred, so that when people make this sacrifice, they leave their land, they give up that piece of land so that they can build the Vietnamese nation. They are prepared to go, in order to build Ho Chi Minh City.
>
> However . . .

### Teacher Long's Language of Rights

Although he said that tears stream out when he passes his old home, Teacher Long did not, ultimately, wallow in those tears. Instead, at precisely this point in the interview—immediately following the moment when he says "however"—his language and the content of his discussion shifted dramatically. What appeared at first like a set-up for a tale of sorrow and desperation soon turned into an expression of righteous indignation—with an emphasis on the *rights* in righteousness—that linked his and his fellow residents' sacrifices to a larger national sacrifice. His moral claims, from this point on, were primarily expressed by detailing an extended litany of facts about land compensation, Vietnamese land laws, and even the Vietnamese Constitution, which allowed Teacher Long to articulate his feeling of having suffered a clear injustice. Nostalgia was one thing, but rights were something else entirely. From this point on, his narrative highlighted the tangible injustice that lay in the violation of his rights. And the degree to which they had been violated could be expressed in square meters of land multiplied by land value, expressed in money.

What is important to note here is the pronounced shift that Teacher Long makes from a focus on qualitative affective *values* to a focus on quantitative expressions of *value*. This does not mean that Teacher Long all of a sudden renounces his affective, sentimental ties to land. Clearly, he has strong emotional ties to his ancestral home. In fact, at the beginning of his discussion, Long was engaging in what might be called a mobilization of affect, using of an idiom of resistance that scholars have called "affective urbanism."[14] In this sense, Long's use of narrative was similar to strategies residents have used elsewhere in Vietnam. Building from ethnographic research on urban redevelopment in the Vietnamese city of Vinh, for example, Christina Schwenkel has shown how residents facing displacement from older socialist-era housing often recounted affect-laden stories about the labor they had put into building the city, to emphasize their moral claims to a right to housing. In their telling, even the bricks of their buildings recalled a heroic past.[15] Similarly, Annette Kim's content analysis of Vietnamese media reports shows how Vietnamese "talk back" and resist what they see as unfair compensation practices through the use of "narratives" of "greedy" officials.[16] These are not isolated cases, and scholars studying land disputes across Vietnam have shown how residents invoke these kinds of moral claims as they insist on achieving justice or fairness in a wide variety of contexts.[17] The tactic of deploying affect, sentiment, narrative, or moral claims can actually be effective in some cases, and some evidence even shows that Vietnamese judges regularly incorporate "reason and sentiment in applying the law."[18] Nevertheless, despite the potential power such ways of framing injustice afford, the contours of what counts as "justice," or even as reason and sentiment, are themselves conditioned by the ways in which land has become commodified in the contemporary market economy.

Qualitative moral claims do not reside in isolation from more quantitative economic claims; typically, they are interlayered. A person's history of sacrifice to the nation, a resident's status as a citizen, or the story of a household head's longtime occupation and stewardship of a plot of land may be used to invoke a moral imperative that one *should* be treated fairly. Nevertheless, what counts as fairness itself is just as often articulated in more quantitative terms. Benedict Kerkvliet, for example, shows that the very meaning of "justice and fairness," while often linked to people's moral worthiness, can be expressed in very pragmatic terms, such as wanting to be granted a stronger voice in the negotiation for adequate compensation. Kerkvliet explains the way many affected residents understand and respond to the situation thus:

> To determine an acceptable compensation, villagers typically want to negotiate with those who will get the land and object to government authorities imposing an amount. They suspect that authorities, after paying them a small amount, will later sell the land for considerably more and keep much of the difference or personally benefit in some other way. This, plus harsh, even violent actions by authorities prompts protesting villagers to rest part of their grievances on officials' undemocratic behavior. Rarely, however, do protesters publicly condemn the political system. On the contrary, they typically affirm their allegiance to the state and the Communist Party.[19]

Although the label "villagers" would not apply to most of the residents of Thủ Thiêm, who see themselves as recently urbanized city dwellers, the description Kerkvliet outlines here is similar to the approach and attitudes commonly expressed by Thủ Thiêm residents. They were thoroughly suspicious of the negotiation process, nearly always considered their compensation to be unfair, and largely framed their cries for justice in terms of receiving accurate measures of their land and compensation for that land at fair market values. Kerkvliet notes that many "villagers" in recent land disputes "invoke the market as a mechanism for determining fair compensation."[20] The same was true in Thủ Thiêm.

Market-based assessments of land values also play an important role in what John Gillespie has described as prevalent "legitimacy expectations" in Vietnamese land disputes—the ways disputing parties assess the contours of justice, or what they consider fair or right, by paying attention to "pragmatic," "normative," and "cognitive" notions of legitimacy. In other words, when disputants attempt to assess the legitimacy of a claim, they tend to think in terms of three things: a kind of cost-benefit (or pragmatic) analysis of who wins and who loses in a dispute; what seems normatively right or fair judged in terms of how things are generally expected to work in society; and ideological or spiritual convictions that shape attitudes about what is right when land is in dispute.[21] In normative terms, for example, residents who lost their land to a development project would assess the legitimacy of the process by "comparing the compensation they received with the compensation given to other land users."[22] That is, a case might be considered fair if they were not being cheated or given a bad deal, based on other people's experience with similar lands.

Teacher Long's narrative up to this point confirms this layering of qualitative and quantitative idioms in the assessment land disputes. But as he proceeds, quantitative judgments begin to subtly overshadow or displace the qualitative aspects of his story. He began the long discussion of his situation by mobilizing a set of moral claims about the labor his family contributed in the clearing of the land, which he linked to Vietnamese notions of conquering and civilizing the south—all of this recalling what Schwenkel termed affective urbanism, or Gillespie would call cognitive legitimacy. Nevertheless, when Teacher Long tried to express what he understood to be the most tangible injustice facing him, together with appropriate redress, he subordinated this affective narrative to a quantitative language of compensation, primarily framed by citations of legal texts and monetary expressions of land values.

Sentimental, qualitative claims serve as a set-up to his real critique, but get him only so far. After moving from tears to hard facts, Teacher Long's narrative focused less on the personal attributes of his family or his sense of place in Thủ Thiêm, and increasingly on the Vietnamese nation, its laws, edicts, and proclamations. The substance now shifted from an origin story to a tale of injustice, framed in the language of law and economic value. Picking up from where the passage above left off, he continued:

> However . . . according to the Land Law, well, article 50 from the 2003 Land Law stipulates that when the government compensates, that when I leave, "the new residence must be equal to or better than the old residence."[23] Ahh! . . . But in reality, that is just talk, and talk and action don't go together. And we have filed a suit [thừa kiện] all the way to Hanoi even, my entire file and land papers have been filed as a suit all the way to Hanoi even, but in the end I still lost.
>
> I went to the Court of First Instance [Sơ thẩm] in District Two and lost, went up to the Court of Appeals [Phúc thẩm] and also lost. That's because those two places are all paid off by the city and by District Two. Because of that, those courts won't hear the cases. But I have evidence that my land is residential land, I have paid taxes on it as residential land, and according to the Land Law, if it is residential land it must be compensated as residential land. But because I had planted some trees, then those guys [mấy ông] said it was agricultural land mixed in with it. That point doesn't make any sense, because it does not say anything . . . For example, I have the paperwork for my house [sổ hồng]. Just because I have planted two plum trees doesn't make it into agricultural land. What do you think?

This shift to talking about law and lawsuits took place at minute 32 of the interview. For the next hour and fifteen minutes, Teacher Long described Vietnamese land laws, invoked the Vietnamese Constitution, and engaged in a series of mathematical calculations. In the process, he spent extended moments multiplying lengths by widths to arrive at square meters, and then multiplying the total by various values commonly ascribed to land by various sources, such as official compensation rate documents, official land schedules determined by the state, price tabulations determined by the real estate market, and so on. He talked about taxes, juggled land prices from the past and the present, projected future land values, and commented on prices rumored to have been paid by foreign investors. And of course, as is done in all conversations about land in Vietnam, he converted these values between various monetary instruments—Vietnamese đồng, taels of gold, and U.S. dollars—all while speculating on the fluctuating exchange rates between them.[24] Here is a selection from this part of the interview, illustrating his focus on questions of money and meters:

> But for that compensation, I had to provide evidence that it was residential land, and at the same time, there was a limit to the maximum amount of land that could be compensated, which was 200 square meters, there's no way to get more, and even if I had 2,000 square meters, then I still could only get compensated for 200. And then everything beyond that I have to calculate completely as agricultural land. And that is one of the things that has made the people suffer the greatest losses. We are very pained, and, as I told you before, every time I go by there, tears stream from my eyes because my grandparents, my mother and father, four or five generations have lived on that piece of land, but now all of a sudden I have to go, that's my life. . . . Honestly, I bought this house and to get this place here I have had to move 17 kilometers away from there, from District Two all the way across to District Nine. And in this area where I've purchased [my new home], it's like around 80 square meters and costs around 1 billion 150 million. Building the house was another 250 million, which is to say that [in total] it cost about 1.4 billion just to get a house like this. Meanwhile, on the land I had down there I had two houses, and each was 200-something [square meters]. But when they offered to compensate in 2001, they only compensated 30 percent as residential land for the house located at [Thủ Thiêm, precise address redacted]. And the house at [Thủ Thiêm, address redacted] was facing the street, and was just under 200 square meters. But all in all, those men [mấy ông] only compensated about 45 square meters as residential land, and for the rest of the 150 square meters they calculated it as agricultural land. And I have no idea why. I don't know what to say, because I have said that it's my land, and can prove that almost 200 square meters is residential land, so why do they only compensate me for 45 square meters, which is about 1.5 billion [đồng], when the rest of the land is only calculated as agricultural land at 200,000 [đồng] per square meter? And then they say that because my father gave it to me after 2001, they will calculate it all as agricultural land.

Although Teacher Long briefly references being brought to tears and expresses his pain at losing the home of his ancestors, these qualitative attributes are soon buried under a torrent of facts and figures, and after this point, for the final two-thirds of the interview, he focused on legal claims and techniques for calculating land. By the end of the interview, Teacher Long's voice had quickened as he highlighted a wide assortment of injustices, mostly having to do with the level of compensation he was legally entitled to receive and how that compensation would enable him to rebuild the homes he was being forced to sacrifice. He focused on the amount of land that was attributed to him, how what he considered to be residential land was being classified as agricultural land, and the way land compensation rates were calculated by the state rather than by market prices. In the process of reframing the circumstances of his dispossession in these terms, Teacher Long developed very specific and quantifiable claims about the degree to which he had been subjected to injustice. What began as a classic case of "affective urbanism," framed in the poetics of place, ended up as a math problem.

## TÂM AND HỒNG'S STORY: ENUMERATING INJUSTICE

Teacher Long's story highlights a discursive shift that that I witnessed over and over again in Thủ Thiêm, whenever people talked about their eviction. Regardless of the affective ties they had to the land or their own personal reasons for wishing to stay in their homes, people inevitably moved away from a description of Thủ Thiêm in nostalgic, qualitative terms and toward a view of their own land there as property, expressed as size in square meters multiplied by market value. Such quantitative measures offered the primary idiom through which something called "rights" were said to have been violated by the process of eviction. This familiar pattern framed the story Mr. Tâm and his wife, Hồng, told us in 2010, about a year before the old French bungalow described at the beginning of this chapter came down. Let us return, then, to their bungalow, a year before the walls began to sway against the pulling ropes of the demolition crew.

My colleague and I interviewed Tâm and Hồng while sitting in the living room of that bungalow in September 2010, drinking beers Tâm poured over ice, seated in front of an intricately carved antique altar holding a very beautiful crucifix as well as photos of Tâm's parents and scenes from the life of his devout Catholic family. (The photos of his grandparents, unfortunately, were burned after the Vietnam War.) For the next hour and a half, in the first of many conversations we would share over the years, they too told of us life in Thủ Thiêm, before bringing us to the present-day circumstances of their eviction. As we spoke, Tâm and Hồng kept our glasses filled, regularly replacing the chunks of ice, all while explaining why they were (at that time) still holding out and refusing to leave their house, even as their neighbors were leaving one by one. When all was said and done, they explained, the real reason they refused to leave was that they were not yet satisfied with the terms of compensation they were being pressured to accept by the Thủ Thiêm authorities.

But to get to that point of the story, Tâm began, like Teacher Long and many other Thủ Thiêm residents, by telling the story of his ancestors. He started with his grandfather, who had moved to Thủ Thiêm from Quảng Ngãi Province in the early twentieth century to escape poverty. First, he cleared the land [khai hoang] out of nothing. Tâm said that Thủ Thiêm was only "swamp" back then, and Hồng added that it was just a cù lao, a kind of river island common to the Mekong Delta—"just the river and canals, ah, water coconuts, just dry grass and nothing else." Tâm's grandfather died at a relatively young age, soon after the birth of his son, Tâm's father, in 1915, and his grandmother then got remarried to a well-off local bachelor with no children, whose family had lived in the area "since the founding of the Thủ Thiêm church," some 150 years earlier.[25] As a result of this union, the family came into more than thirty *mẫu* of land, some of it in Thủ Thiêm and some of it in surrounding areas. This land, which was worked by tenant farmers, remained in the family until 1970, when it was appropriated and redistributed to landless peasants by President Nguyễn Văn Thiệu's Land to the Tiller program.[26] From this point onward, Tâm and Hồng's story covered nothing less than the progressive loss of their land, with each significant moment in late-twentieth-century Vietnamese history signaling a new form of land appropriation and loss. After the 1970 land redistribution, the family managed to retain six or seven *mẫu* within Thủ Thiêm. But after "liberation" in 1975, most of that land was confiscated as well. In the end they only had a bit more than 600 square meters of land in the area immediately surrounding the old family home, the French bungalow Tâm's father built in 1938, the house where we sat listening to their story, the place he would film being torn down less than a year later.

Six hundred square meters in contemporary Ho Chi Minh City is a significant amount of land. But the house and the land on which it sat belonged to all seven siblings in Tâm's family, and it would have to be divided among them. Over the years, three of Tâm's brothers had migrated abroad, and they generously gave up their claims to the house out of sympathy for those who had stayed behind in Vietnam. But there were still two sisters and another brother living in Vietnam, making a total of three nuclear families besides Tâm with claims to the land and the house. I asked Tâm if this had led to feuding. "No," he replied, "our family is strong." But many other families in the area were locked in bitter disputes, he said. This was true—many residents had told us as much in the course of our interviews (which was why I asked Tâm in the first place).

In this old house with its striking view across the river to growing Ho Chi Minh City, Tâm described how his father, a humble man with a sophisticated occupation, would ride a bicycle to work, taking the Thủ Thiêm ferry and then pedaling up fashionable Nguyễn Huệ Street to his important job at the bank. During that period, Tâm noted, it was possible for a man to raise seven children on a single income. His father had even sent Tâm and his brothers to French schools, starting with the École Taberd (now Trần Đại Nghĩa), and then off to boarding schools in Đà Lạt, Đà Nẵng, Nha Trang, and Huế. (His two sisters stayed at local schools.) Like Teacher Long, Tâm and Hồng told how people in Thủ Thiêm swam in the rivers and canals and caught local fish, which they ate in simple yet nourishing traditional meals. That all changed, however, with the war, the postwar experiments in socialism, and then later, the rising cost of living and the environmental pollution associated with the market economy.

The war ended in 1975, about a year before Tâm would have finished his training as an officer cadet for the Army of the Republic of Vietnam. After that, most of their family's land was nationalized, except for the house and some surrounding land around it. For a while, they continued to own some of the neighboring houses as well, but they were forced to share those houses with cadres relocated to Saigon from the north, and they would have had to keep paying taxes on the land if they wanted to keep them. That was about the same time that Tâm's brothers left Vietnam, renouncing their individual claims to the land. With everyone unemployed and in economic straits, the family gave up the parcels they weren't occupying. One of Tâm's brothers, who had been an aircraft engineer, taught him how to repair electronics, and Tâm eventually became known in the area as "the guy who fixes electronics." While the work never made him wealthy, it proved to be a generally stable occupation. With few new goods to buy in postwar Vietnam, people needed to keep fixing those electronic devices they had managed to hold on to, so he always had business. Later, as the market economy slowly opened up, Tâm supplemented the family income by taking care of the advertising billboard that had been erected in front of their house, receiving a small wage for refilling the gas in the generator that powered the billboard lights. In this way they lived through difficult times, and made do.

It was in 1998, Tâm said, that he first heard rumors that a project might be built in Thủ Thiêm. But there was little actual movement. Ever since he was a kid, he recalled, various pie-in-the-sky projects had been planned for Thủ Thiêm, even during the American period (see chapter 4). But none of them ever got off the ground, so Tâm remained skeptical. By 2001, however, he began to sense that something real was happening. Surveyors started showing up. Aircraft flew over taking aerial photographs. Cadres started visiting, measuring and drawing maps of everyone's plots of land. Around 2003, the first houses in the neighborhood started to be knocked down, and people moved out. There weren't many—mainly people with serious debts, or those who wanted to move for other reasons anyhow. His brother and two sisters, who all lived in houses next door to Tâm's, left a few years later:

Hồng: [Tâm's] older brother and two younger sisters have already demolished their houses and gone over to live in Saigon.

Erik: Oh. So they just recently knocked down their houses?

Tâm: The house right next door here. [Pointing out the door to the empty space where the neighbor's house once stood]

Hồng: The house right there, next door. [Pointing out the door to the rubble pile where the other neighbor's house once stood]

Erik: I see.

Tâm: They went first; they were the first to go.

Hồng: See, in the old days it was really crowded here. But now that they've all gone, it's just the old man here [referring to Tâm, playfully].

*Erik:* Ah.

*Tâm:* Pretty soon we're gonna go completely, too.

*Hồng:* If we had been satisfied with the compensation, then surely we'd have gone already too.

Hồng's final comment here seemed out of place, incongruous. After all this talk of family history, her straightforward focus on compensation appeared to come out of nowhere. It was difficult to believe that everything boiled down to a matter of financial compensation. But that is precisely what they told me.

Once they turned to the circumstances of their family, friends, and neighbors packing up their things and leaving, the story Tâm and Hồng told shifted dramatically. Until this point, they had spoken mostly about their ancestors and their family, expressing a sense of nostalgia and deep, sentimental ties to their home. From here on out, however, Tâm and Hồng focused primarily on compensation and why it was inadequate. They explained how difficult it was to find similar housing to purchase at the levels of compensation they were being offered. Tâm's sisters, who had already moved, exemplified that difficulty. The sisters had all agreed to move to Saigon because they had gotten married. But now they were living on land provided by their husbands' families, on plots less than forty square meters in size, and were relatively far away. They had hoped to use the compensation to supplement their purchasing power for new houses, but even with inputs from their husbands, the sisters were way off in District Eleven and Gò Vấp, on the other side of the city. Tâm's brother, who had moved to District Four, had also found it to be extremely difficult to find an affordable place to live.

What began as the story of an ancestral home transformed into a discussion of land values and monetary compensation, eventually fixating on the problem of finding new and equivalent housing within Saigon's raging real estate market. These financial considerations had led to Tâm and Hồng's initial decision to hold out. Less than a year after our interview, following further discussions with the compensation authorities, they finally reached an agreement. They bought the plot of land for their new house on the other side of District Two, and Tâm engaged a demolition crew to come tear the house down. The crew worked for free, in exchange for the rights to salvage scrap metal left in the house. If one did not do it oneself, one had to pay a fee to the Thủ Thiêm authority for the labor of tearing down the home. In the end, orchestrating the demolition of his own home made economic sense, and by this point the story of their old home, like the story of Thủ Thiêm in general, had become one of money and land values.

### The Mathematics of Justice

During the many months my research colleagues and I spent visiting and talking with Thủ Thiêm residents about their eviction, I came to recognize a pattern.

Nearly all of the stories we collected followed some version of the narrative arc seen in Tâm and Hồng's and Teacher Long's stories. Typically, after beginning with a description of the history of their residence in the area, these stories would shift to a detailed enumeration of the size and location of their plots of land, and these calculations would subsequently dominate the conversation. My research notes are filled with page after page of what look like computations—so many square meters multiplied by so many square meters, over and over again. These calculations represent the different understandings people held about the size of their plots of land, juxtaposed against the numbers the Thủ Thiêm compensation authorities had actually used to calculate how much they would receive for that land. The differences between the people's calculations and the sums offered by the authorities represented different interpretations of a wide range of criteria used to calculate land value, such as how much of the land was classified as residential, how much as agricultural, or whether it was even "land" at all, as opposed to being part of a river or a canal, which according to the authorities merited no compensation.

All of these calculations represented enormously different sums of money. Land classified as residential, for example, could potentially warrant compensation at a rate of more than 20 million đồng (about US$1,000) per square meter, whereas land classified as agricultural was only valued at 200,000 đồng (US$10) per square meter. With a square meter of land being worth a hundred times more if it was labeled residential versus agricultural, the stakes were high indeed. From the perspective of a resident who disagreed with how their land was measured or classified, the injustice was quite literally quantifiable.

Over time, as the process of eviction continued, it became clear that moral claims based on nostalgia, sentiment, "style," or other nonquantifiable criteria had little place in negotiations with authorities. While residents of course had their own personal reasons for not wanting to leave their homes, over time they referred less and less to these affective qualities and increasingly articulated their claims in quantifiable calculations of value, measured in total square meters multiplied by the assessed value of the land in question. This is not to say that the residents of Thủ Thiêm never had any sentimental attachment to land, or that their sentiment suddenly vanished when they started to think in terms of the value of their land. Rather, it shows how idioms of value and monetary compensation began to dictate the articulation of dissent *in spite of* such attachments, and how the idioms residents used to describe their relationship to their land changed over time. Only in this way could they argue for rights and justice. This mode of conceptualizing land in terms of its market value, however, was entangled within the very system of property speculation that had underscored the economy of land-for-infrastructure development that demanded their eviction. All of this is to say that while residents may have a wide range of sentimental reasons for loving Thủ Thiêm or their houses there, and in spite of all their particularized and sentimental attachment to the place, they ended up articulating their demands for justice primarily in terms of a simple calculus of value. In the rubble of displacement, such stories were everywhere.

## STORIES FROM THE RUBBLE CAFÉ

By late 2010 and into early 2011, during the height of our most intensive period of fieldwork and interviewing, the Thủ Thiêm authorities had "cleared," by their own estimation, nearly 85 percent of the residents from the planned site of the Thủ Thiêm New Urban Zone.[27] By that time, Teacher Long had decided to cut his losses and move to District Nine, the only place he could afford. Tâm and Hồng were still deciding what to do, one among more than two thousand households remaining in the midst of the rubble. Those who stayed went about their daily lives as best they could, surrounded by crushed bricks, bent rebar, broken tiles, and abandoned homes.[28] Each day, for approximately seven months, my research colleagues and I would visit the rubble fields of Thủ Thiêm and interview residents about the eviction process. We would begin our days just after dawn, sitting down in a place I came to call the "rubble café," a collection of plastic chairs and salvaged advertising banners that had been set up on the crushed remains of recently destroyed homes (fig. 6.2). Patrons of the rubble café openly discussed the circumstances of their displacement from Thủ Thiêm and introduced us to residents throughout the eviction zone. In this way, we interviewed 148 residents about their experiences with the project, including people who had already left and those who were still holding out for higher compensation.

In all of these interviews, three major themes emerged: First, compensation trumped everything. While some residents expressed deep affective attachment to their land, and others expressed distinct pleasure moving into more modern resettlement apartments, all made their ultimate decision to come or go, and declared themselves satisfied or dissatisfied with the process, based primarily on the terms of their compensation. Second, residents typically separated their anger about the low levels of compensation from their views of the project as a whole. Even people who were extraordinarily angry about the economic suffering they had been forced to bear described the project itself as beautiful and desirable. For they were not angry about the project itself but at the fact that they were not being fairly compensated.[29] Third, despite their shared fate of eviction, each household faced that fate through highly individualized circumstances, which were determined by the specific features of their own properties and their personal histories of occupation. Every case of displacement had to be worked out individually. It worked out well for some residents, less well for others.

The most common complaint interviewees had about the eviction and resettlement process had to do with inadequate compensation. One resident, whose family

FIGURE 6.2. The view from the "rubble café," Thủ Thiêm. Author's photo, September 2010.

lived in Thủ Thiêm for "seventy or eighty years," said the government should have provided more financial support, and expressed a common opinion, widely held among Thủ Thiêm residents, that the compensation process was largely undermined by official corruption—that those involved were profiting personally from the project. In this case, the resident claimed the profit was being gleaned from the interest that accrues from money that is deposited in the bank, when it was supposed to be given to the people.

> Those on the compensation committee profit, while the people are left on their own. Calculate this: the house was valued at 2 million đồng, but now it's at 16 million đồng. Sixteen million đồng in the bank. Think about how many square meters of land that could buy here. For instance, let's say we have five hectares; how many square meters is that? Now one square meter is only 16 million đồng, but the total, whatever that is, is deposited into the bank. Think about how much interest accumulates each year. The people lose, while *they* profit.

When we asked what happened to the interest, the resident became agitated and nearly yelled out a reply: "It doesn't go to the people. Sixteen is sixteen. Twelve is twelve. Yet they compensate slowly. Excuse me, but they party and play lavishly, and that money left in the bank for just one week or one month can generate a billion in cash."

"Calculate this!" *(Tính đi!)*. This key phrase jumps out in the above discussion. "Sixteen is sixteen. Twelve is twelve." For this resident, numbers are facts, and the calculations speak for themselves; they purport to reveal an obvious injustice in incontrovertible terms of fact. These facts, in turn, are used to justify accusations of corruption, for which the evidence is less clear but made to sound convincing by the force of the calculation.

In another example, a resident places less emphasis on willful official malfeasance, but still insists that the problems people are facing are inseparable from the problem of compensation. At the time of the interview, this woman—a mother, part of a nuclear family of four—had been living in a temporary residence for two years, waiting for better compensation from the government. She did not think that the people's concerns were being heard, even though they had had multiple meetings with the authorities. As she put it, the issue was not whether the project itself was a good idea, but boiled down quite simply to the problem of compensation. The interview was conducted by one my research colleagues, assisted by a local university student whose direct (but slightly insensitive) question prompted an equally direct response:

*Student Interviewer:* Do you like to live a modern lifestyle like one presented in this new urban zone project?

*Interviewee:* How can you ask this? Who doesn't like an improved life?

*Student Interviewer:*  But why does it seem like you are not happy at the mentioning of this project?

*Interviewee:*  I do like it, but I cannot accept the compensation policy.

*Student Interviewer:*  What is your opinion of Thủ Thiêm? What is it that you like and dislike about the construction of this new urban zone?

*Interviewee:*  I have heard about it for a long time. The eviction has begun. I think that they can do what they want but in a way that is in accordance with the people. Everybody likes a new urban zone, but nobody likes a new urban zone that causes poor folks to live on the streets.

Here again, the problem the resident had was not with the government's desire to modernize the city, but with inadequate compensation, and the suffering borne by those who were displaced. This point is further highlighted by other cases—decidedly more rare—in which the terms of compensation actually worked out favorably for the residents. In those cases, the tone residents took was often quite positive, but it still focused on compensation. The following resident, for example, had been living in a resettlement apartment building for two years. A retired sixty-year-old wedding photographer with four grown and married children, he seemed to be enjoying a relaxing life, taking pictures more as a hobby now and only working when he found a job interesting, on his own terms. His wife ran a coffee shop in the city, and they had become comfortable living in their new apartment in the Thạnh Mỹ Lợi resettlement area. He described how well the compensation and relocation policies had worked in his case:

> I am relatively satisfied with the government's compensation policy. The government compensated 16 million đồng per square meter. Recently, the policy had an error, so the government paid an additional 6 million đồng per square meter. Currently, the area of my house is 62 square meters. Furthermore, there are many other policies that provide assistance to the people, such as giving gifts to the children during the Mid-Autumn Festival; [during the festival] each household receives 500,000 đồng and healthcare. The one problem is that there are no stores, and so people struggle to sell and buy things.

In the course of conducting these interviews, it became clear that the terms of justice and fairness were defined almost wholly in terms of compensation. And while all the old houses in the entire Thủ Thiêm project area were gradually being reduced to rubble, the process was taking place one house at a time, the terms worked out case by case.

As each individual household came to their own set of negotiated terms, it was possible for some to find what they considered justice within the larger project. One resident explained quite directly that justice depended on each household coming to its own deal with the authorities. When we asked if she was ever jealous of the compensation neighbors received, she replied: "Oh, no, because every family has its own story, so how can I be jealous? I just hope that all the papers get processed smoothly. Those with fortune get to enjoy it. If one is fortunate, then one's compensation corresponds to the total area of one's house. If not, then the area is reduced, cut off here and there. I'm lucky that only two square meters were cut off mine." She further argued that it was actually understandable why some households were being compensated at low rates. She felt that many residents had been freeloading in the area for too long anyhow. Some of them, she pointed out, were squatters, encroaching on river land:

> The [areas of] other houses near the river were pitifully reduced because these families have been appropriating the space stretching out to the riverside. They're quite pitiful. Before, they used water from the river, which saved them money. Now, they have to primarily use public water, which makes it a little difficult for them. But this is good, too. The river is disgusting; it would be strange if they didn't fall ill using the river all the time like that. [One has to] endure the cost a bit in exchange for guaranteed good health. "Village affection, neighbor bonds." I'm really not jealous.

In these interviews, when eviction and displacement were articulated in terms of particular, unique households, any sense of collective interest became subordinated to the individual context. People, now atomized, discussed their situations not in terms determined by a sense of place, but in terms of how they would make out economically.

Despite the fact that so many people were being evicted, there was surprisingly little solidarity among those affected, and the process was largely reduced to procedural battles between individual residents and the authorities. One resident even went so far as to say that it was impossible to rely on others and that one had to look out for oneself. The resident then ended up denigrating other Thủ Thiêm residents:

> Not so many people are educated. In this district, many could not afford an education for their children, so whenever we have a debate/fight—like the one now—we aren't able to fight or have educated people to represent us. So people here don't really know where they would move out of here . . . we just know that around New Year's that they [local government officials] might ask us to move. Because they are not educated, they don't understand the procedure and just register to leave when others do. For those who stay like us, we are not sure we should fight [against the government] anymore. We don't have that much energy to continue for a lost cause.

Some residents who were able to negotiate acceptable deals with the Thủ Thiêm authorities said that they were better off after moving to resettlement housing. One woman who used to live in Thủ Thiêm, rowing her boat, shrimping, and doing odd jobs, spoke with us while sitting in her new home in the Thạnh Mỹ Lợi resettlement apartment, which had been provided by the government as compensation for eviction. In her case, she supported the compensation policies, which had given her a proper home compared to her old one in Thủ Thiêm: "There are many advantages because our house is spacious, and so I'm very happy. I feel less worried, more assured. Before, when we still lived in Thủ Thiêm, our house had wood flooring, which was very problematic when there was flooding. The house here is solid, stable, and clean. The air is clean. I feel much more comfortable here."

Another resident explained that, in the end, how one made out depended primarily on one's own preparation. Because her family had made an early commitment to the new land policy, she explained, they were able to take advantage of the eviction, coming out better in the end:

> In general, I'm telling you that my life was a struggle there [in Thủ Thiêm]. Life was hard without any job. My husband rode the cycle rickshaw because it was the only thing he could do, but then they banned it, so he couldn't find a means to do it. He only had this rickshaw job, so he stopped then. For me, I was selling groceries in front of our house and did whatever people paid me for.
>
> [ ... ]
>
> Yes. [I'd do] whatever people asked me to do, like, "Hey Sister Sáu, can you help me clean the house?" or "Today my family has some business to take care of, can you come help us?" I helped those people and later in the afternoon they paid me 10,000 [đồng] or 20,000 and food, too. I brought the food back for my kids. Those 10,000 or 20,000 would help pay for rice and groceries for the next day. In general everything was the same. Life was hard. Now, thank God, I have moved here. Now I am old, my kids are running a business, so I don't have to make a living anymore.

Every household interviewed had its own stories of compensation. But one thing overshadowed everything else: the calculative language of money. Sometimes the compensation was deemed appropriate, and people appeared calm and even grateful for the project. Other times this language would erupt into noisy shouts of anger, about being cheated, hoodwinked, fooled. They have "stolen the people's land," people would sometimes yell—*cướp đất của dân*. But when these money matters were settled, case by individual case, a strange silence took over, as people packed their belongings and left, individual house by individual house.

## COLLAPSE

A similar silence permeated the air in 2014 when I found myself at Tâm's tube house in the dense alleyway of his new neighborhood, staring at his flat-screen television, watching the video of the day his home was torn down three years earlier. The scene was too long for his pocket camera, so he had filmed it in three clips. At one point, while switching between the clips, Tâm took a moment to scan through all the other images he had saved on the camera. The camera was still plugged into the television, so it was as if he was giving a slide show of his household move. In addition to images of rubble and demolition, the bulk of the shots consisted of a mix of still pictures taken of the old house in Thủ Thiêm and the new one where we now sat on the other side of District Two. Tâm had also taken digital shots of some of his own older print photographs, mostly old black-and-white family photos, including one of a much younger Tâm in uniform, from his time at officer school under the old Saigon regime. As he scanned through the images, the resulting slideshow depicted a back-and-forth movement, through time and across space, between the old house in Thủ Thiêm and the construction and later occupation of the new one. At the old house, he had taken photos of the trees in the garden, of the ficus roots growing into the side of the house, of the roof tiles being removed, and there was a photo taken in the kitchen, after all the cookware and cabinets had been removed. "It was pretty dirty," Tâm said. At the new house, he had snapped pictures of the construction workers balancing on scaffolding, laying bricks. As Tâm scrolled through the photos on the camera, the order of the images conveyed the impression of a person moving house, making trips back and forth between the old and the new.

In one photo, Tâm pointed out the roots of a large star fruit tree being dug up from the old house. "It didn't survive," he said. Another photo, taken not long after, was of the yellow fruits of a new star fruit tree growing in a pot in front of the new house. He then pointed out to the garden, where the same star fruit tree sat in the same pot, again with yellow fruits. Now he flipped from a photo of wild plants growing over the veranda of the old house to one depicting decorative potted bamboo plants arranged in neat rows against a white wall in the small garden of the new home. In another photo, the household dog grinned from his old spot in the old home, with the distinctive colonial checkerboard tiles visible in the background; then we saw the same dog lounging on the white tile floor of the new house, next to another, much younger puppy. Fecund jungles of wide-leaf garden plants at the old house were juxtaposed against decorative potted plants, arranged in orderly pairs, at the new one. More photos from the old house: an old grandfather clock and a beautiful antique wooden ancestral altar. Then a series of pictures depicting Tâm's wife, Hồng, posing like a fashion model (sometimes in designer sunglasses with large round dark lenses) in every room of the new house: in front of the clean new kitchen cabinets, next to the flat-screen television in the living room, beside the designer bookcase, sitting on the vinyl sofa, and finally next to the curtains in the bedroom, looking out the window in that pensive way that fashion models do. In other photos, Tâm and his wife posed together as a couple, standing next to friends or in front of the fruit baskets and floral arrangements they had received as gifts when they moved into their new place. There were a few curious images mixed into Tâm's collection: one—actually a digital photograph of an image on a computer screen (fig. 6.3)—showed a bald eagle in the foreground,

FIGURE 6.3. Image saved on Tâm's camera. Author's collection, August 2011.

surrounded by a faint, slightly blurred, faded background depiction of the World Trade Center in New York City, black smoke billowing from its side. A glistening tear rolled down from the eagle's eye.

These photos were filled with affect. The before-and-after sequence in Tâm's camera evoked all the drama of the eviction, the move, and this couple's attempt to make a new life in a new neighborhood far from the place they had always called home. When we returned to watch the final two clips of the video, Tâm no longer had the capacity to speak, choosing near silence instead. As the video resumed, Tâm's wife brought out a bowl of fresh mango slices, laid out on ice. The walls of the old French bungalow were swaying wider now. We all grew quiet. With each pull, the end was visibly closer. The wall swayed forward and seemed to hang there for a moment, before swaying back again. Tâm whispered, "There, almost there." On the next sway, the three men pulled with all their might. The entire wall slowly started to bend forward. "Almost," Tâm said again, drawing out the syllables, biting quietly into the flesh of the mango. Then he paused, watching and waiting, before adding, right on cue, in a soft whisper, one last word, perfectly synchronized with the collapse of the wall: "Boom."

# Conclusion

# Civility and Dispossession

*And the Rights of Man turned out to be the rights of the rightless, of the populations hunted out of their homes and land . . .*
—JACQUES RANCIÈRE, "WHO IS THE SUBJECT OF THE RIGHTS OF MAN?"

*When we start considering this possibility, we come upon a contention which is so astonishing that we must dwell upon it. This contention holds that what we call our civilization is largely responsible for our misery, and that we should be much happier if we gave it up and returned to primitive conditions.*
—SIGMUND FREUD, *CIVILIZATION AND ITS DISCONTENTS*

## RIGHTS TALK ON THE RISE

In recent years, especially when it comes to conflicts over land, more and more people in Vietnam appear ready to make vocal demands for something called "rights." Between 2008 and 2011, according to government sources, people paid 1.57 million visits to official offices to register complaints and denunciations *(khiếu nại, tố cáo)*, and they submitted nearly 673,000 formal petitions *(đơn thư)*. Of those complaints, 70 percent were related to land. At the Ministry of Natural Resources and Environment, 98 percent of the petitions received each year were related to land issues.[1]

Most of these complaints focused on land clearance for development projects, especially low compensation and problems with resettlement. They also regularly denounced government officials, whom they accused of abusing their positions to engage in graft and corruption. According to the minister of Natural Resources and the Environment, Chu Phạm Ngọc Hiển, the core of the problem could be explained quite simply: cadres involved with land compensation "still have low levels of understanding regarding land laws."[2] Vietnam's prime minister at the time, Nguyễn Tấn Dũng, had his own take on the problem, reducing it to a cost-benefit calculus: "Naturally," he said, "it is necessary to reclaim land according to the master plan" because doing so supports economic and social development. "However," he added, "we must smooth things out [*làm hài hòa*, lit. "work harmoniously"] in order to avoid spawning further land complaints."[3] The government position on the problem of land complaints is clear: land reclamation is necessary for national development. However, if cadres could learn to more clearly understand the law, and if only the Vietnamese people and the government would try harder to work "smoothly" or "harmoniously" together, then everything would be all right.

Perhaps it is true that Vietnamese officials don't quite understand the country's land laws. There is certainly enough evidence to show that the laws are often flouted. But most Vietnamese citizens, for their part, understand the land laws quite well. They know, for example, that when they are asked to give up land for development projects, the law grants them the right to demand that their resettlement conditions be, in the words of the 2003 Land Law, "equal to or better than the place of former residence."[4] They also know the market value of their land, and are able to identify the difference between that amount and what the government tells them the land is worth. Indeed, the large number of petitions and complaints cited above, as well as recent research on Vietnamese land conflicts, indicates that citizens across the country are reading the law, discussing it, sharing their interpretations with each other, and strategizing about ways to defend their legally granted rights. In short, a rising sense of political consciousness appears to be overtaking the country.[5] Residents facing eviction and low compensation for their sacrificed land, or who are otherwise dissatisfied with the ways their land claims are handled, increasingly denounce the wrongs they have been forced to endure.[6] Achieving the smooth harmony invoked by Nguyễn Tấn Dũng is often the last thing on their minds: what they want is justice and a fair deal, all of which the written law formally entitles them to. Across the country, the loud agitation over property rights and land, a boisterous presence on the internet and a constant topic in private conversations among trusted friends, sometimes even spills into the streets.[7] This vibrant discourse is regularly punctuated by cries for "rights," "justice," or "fairness," and by demands that policy follow the "rule of law."[8]

In a political system known over the past several decades for its repression of dissent and general contempt for the law, and in a country where, because of this political landscape, citizens tend to avoid openly criticizing government policies, these are significant developments.[9] Indeed, when seeing people clamor for their rights in blogs or YouTube videos, it is sometimes possible to imagine the rise of "insurgent citizenship," a term coined by the anthropologist James Holston to describe the way marginalized Brazilians parlay property claims into demands for urban inclusion.[10] On the margins of Vietnamese cities, where land is especially contested, there is no question that people are acutely aware of something called rights and how the Vietnamese land law supposedly protects those rights.

These demands for justice and law, furthermore, seem to emanate from all levels of society. The rising middle classes living in new urban zones invoke the law to express concerns about their property values and rising land use fees, while more marginalized groups on the edges of cities or in rural communities use it to voice displeasure with the terms of their dispossession or low compensation. The kinds of grievances may be different, but they all deploy similar idioms of justice and make similar recourse to the letter of the law. One working-class family facing eviction in Thủ Thiêm, for example, could boldly claim that the actions of the development authorities were "completely illegal! deliberately against the law, purposeful and systematic," and then publicly demand redress.[11] At the same time, well-to-do residents living in the luxury housing development of Phú Mỹ Hưng could similarly invoke the law to justify their refusal to pay a set of unexpected land-use right fees. On a website devoted to their fee disputes, Phú Mỹ Hưng residents forcefully argued that actions of the city government and the local tax office were "illegal," based on collusion, or founded on "ghost decisions" *(quyết định "ma")* with no real legal basis.[12] These are two very different socioeconomic groups, but in both cases the invocation of rights before the law sounds very similar.

## RIGHTS GONE WRONG

But if rights talk is on the rise, the reality on the ground also shows that something is going seriously wrong with rights. The flashes of protest and the bold words of resistance coexist with sobering facts about the continued inequities people have been forced to endure in the face of Vietnam's urban development schemes. When one looks around Vietnamese cities, it is impossible not to notice that these calls for rights and justice are not slowing down the general tide of dispossession. At the same time that this rights consciousness gains momentum, and at the same time that belief in the rule of law seems everywhere on the rise, the country is seeing the wholesale displacement of unprecedented numbers of people. All across Vietnam, land reclamation has escalated rather than abated. One report, based on figures from the General Statistics Office, noted that 697,410 hectares of land were reclaimed nationwide between 1990 and 2003—153,979 hectares in the period 2001–3 alone. While many of those reclaimed hectares included large-scale infrastructure projects, such as highways and dams, the report also specified "that the area of land taken in the service of building projects was greater in three years (2001–2003) than in the ten previous years."[13] In other words, even as rights talk has increased, land has been expropriated for building projects like the new urban zones discussed in this book at ever higher rates, the brunt of this dispossession being felt especially in places of rapid economic development, including sites in and around Ho Chi Minh City, where 4,000 hectares of dense urban land were appropriated between 2001 and 2005.[14] In 2010, at precisely the moment when Thủ Thiêm residents most loudly began to assert their rights, newspaper accounts indicated that Ho Chi Minh City authorities expected to implement close to 500 major projects that would require the eviction and resettlement of nearly 83,000 house-holds.[15] In Vietnamese cities, especially on urban peripheries where formerly rural land is rapidly and often quite profitably converted to urban land, there is literally rubble everywhere—crushed homes, demolished lives, evicted families, abhorrent resettlement zones. As time goes on, and as rights discourse continues to rise in the face of so much human dispossession, something else is happening: there is a rising disconnect between talk *about* the law and the practical effects this dis-course has for redressing people's sense of injustice. The people's cries about rights and justice may well be getting louder, but the rumble of bulldozers and the sound of jackhammers are growing louder still.

Furthermore, while the language of rights may cross class boundaries, the ac-tual distribution of rights is much less equitable. As luxurious housing develop-ments and commercial districts designed for more affluent citizens relentlessly replace working-class neighborhoods, it has become clear that very few of the increasingly frequent protests waged over land in Vietnam have led to serious agi-tation for more inclusive urban development or democratic citizenship. Increased *talk* about rights and the rule of law does not seem to deliver *actual* rights or legal protection for large numbers of living, breathing human beings. As Mahmood Mamdani points out, in the contemporary world "rights talk" is, on its own, often meaningless; rather, the significance of rights can only be understood by how they play out in people's lived lives. Indeed, as Mamdani argues, "rights discourse can have a liberating effect at one moment and can facilitate domination at an-other. . . . There is no way to guarantee how a right will be applied in context."[16] In Vietnam, as the two cases in this book have shown, rights have come to look a lot like parcels of land: some people have more than others. This is not a coinci-dence, because the rise of rights talk in contemporary Vietnam has roughly paral-leled the expansion of liberal conceptions of private property, the implications of which I will describe below.

On paper, Vietnamese law increasingly seems to provide a basis from which to advocate for justice and rights. But in practice, people are not "equal before the law." For Vietnam scholars, this should come as no surprise. Observers of the country have long recognized that formal pronouncements rarely correspond to actual social reality. Mark Sidel, one of the foremost scholars of the Vietnamese legal system, has described the situation thus: "[The] modernization and renova-tion of Vietnam's economic law has resulted in a system that is more detailed, more legal, arguably more regulated and, today, used with considerably more effective-ness by those within Vietnam with great economic and political power and against those with less power."[17] In other words, if you have economic or political connec-tions, the law can work for you; without such connections, the law can actually be used against you. According to John Gillespie, another legal scholar with extensive experience in Vietnam, this situation results in part because the Vietnamese legal system lacks judicial independence: judges are not expected to uphold the law by carrying out their own fair and independent readings of legal codes, but rather to enforce the demands of the Party. In this context, the "formalization" of legal rules in recent years has actually made it more difficult for judges to develop solutions that satisfy communities.[18] Sometimes, as Laura Nader and Ugo Mattei have argued, the rule of law can even be illegal.[19]

The rise in the numbers of petitions described above can thus be read in two ways. On the one hand, the petitions show that people are demanding recourse from the legal system: they have discovered their rights. On the other hand, it shows that the system is doing very little for them and that those petitions are in many cases being thrown into a legal void. In the current legal environment, residents complaining about the procedures by which they have been evicted from their land might as well stuff their petitions in bottles and throw them out to sea, so unlikely are they to get fair consideration by impartial courts. Citizens are forced to seek justice using other idioms, like "talking back" through newspapers and blog posts or muttering under their breath about corruption.[20] These forms of resistance have no juridical power, however, and their proliferation illustrates two aspects of the same situation: people are clamoring to assert their rights, even as they recognize that their "rights" are not founded on written law, but on a spoils system that distributes those rights as a form of privilege.[21] In Vietnam's current legal environment, as in other societies both historical and contemporary, there is one fundamental open secret that everyone knows to be true and that continues to trump all else: on paper, people may be equal before the law, but in the real world some people have more rights than others.

## RIGHTS TALK AS TAUTOLOGY AND VOID

While the rising and extraordinarily brave emphasis placed on rights in Vietnam can be read as an inspiring example of bottom-up resistance to entrenched systems of power, it also requires a healthy dose of caution. It is worth reflecting, as Jacques Rancière has done in a different but analogous context, on the possibility that the concept of rights has itself become a distraction that potentially short-circuits more trenchant political debate about the unequal burden being shouldered by the dispossessed in the world's civilizing projects.[22] Reflecting on the idea of the "Rights of Man," Rancière considers a question first posed by Hannah Arendt in the aftermath of World War II. Why, he asks, channeling Arendt's critique of the post-Holocaust rights regime, has the idea of rights proliferated around the world at precisely the same moment that political and ethnic violence has driven so many people into abject misery and suffering? The parallel question in urbanizing Vietnam is clear: Why has the idea of rights proliferated so forcefully in land disputes at precisely the same time that so many people are being pushed off their land? The reason, Rancière argues, is that the language of rights implies a language of reconciliation and consensus, while the proliferating conditions of injustice in fact demand vigorous resistance and "dissensus." Invoking the power of rights as an overarching concept when people are increasingly stripped of meaningful rights in their lived lives sends us into complacent and self-satisfied—and essentially meaningless—traps of rhetoric that sound good on paper but have no substance. To invoke Mamdani, it is nothing but "rights talk." This is especially pernicious in the case of land disputes, given that land is not a limitless resource: one person's claim to rights over land necessarily means rejecting another person's claim to those same rights. In such a system, not everyone can claim the same rights, and any assertion to the contrary is nothing less than a fantasy.[23] To *speak* of universal rights is not the same as actually having them or ensuring that they are enjoyed equally by all.

On the one hand, Rancière notes, the idea of rights has been reduced to "the rights of those who have no rights, which amounts to nothing," what he calls "a void." By this, he means that we tend to invoke rights most loudly when considering the most disenfranchised, dispossessed, and disempowered people of our time. But such ritualized incantations do not deliver rights to those people, so much as make a moral claim that those people should have what they do not have. On the other hand, he also notes that we tend to celebrate the banal rights enjoyed by the most privileged, those who are never in danger of losing anything. This is also a form of meaningless rhetoric, because those rights being celebrated "are the rights of those who have rights, which amounts to a tautology."[24]

This oscillation between the rights of those who already have rights and the rights of those who have none—the ceaseless movement between tautology and void—elegantly captures the essence of what I have described in Thủ Thiêm and Phú Mỹ Hưng over the course of this book. In the rubble of Thủ Thiêm, the "right" that people have achieved in the process of resisting their own eviction is the market-based right to demand a certain level of compensation for their land. But in achieving that right, they have also been forced to acknowledge that they do not have the right to live on that land. When the Thủ Thiêm project began, it was a foregone conclusion that the residents would have to go. And in the end, after all their agitation and resistance, all their invocations of rights and the rule of law, they ended up with monetary compensation that, while technically higher than the impossibly low sums they were first offered, was actually worth less, in terms of its purchasing power, than what they would have retained if they had never fought for their rights in the first place. "At least I fought for my rights," I remember one man telling me as we sat in a distant relocation settlement, far from the home from which he had been evicted. He had lost everything, but "at least he fought for his rights"—the rights of those who have no rights.

In Phú Mỹ Hưng, by contrast, the well-to-do residents of this luxurious New Urban Zone have always been assured of their rights—as long as they remained confined to discussions of property, of course, and did not become mixed in with broader political ideas about democratization or multiparty rule.[25] Under those conditions, they spoke of building a civilized society populated by people with self-discipline and an elevated consciousness of others, where life was governed by transparent rules and regulations and relationships built on trust. In this urban development, which they commonly described as a revolutionary space of new subjectivity, they mobilized the law as well as public opinion to further defend their right to have the rights they always knew they had. The biggest threat they ever faced was the perceived injustice of being asked to pay higher land-use right fees than they would otherwise like to have paid.[26] With muffled voices in private conversations they often spoke of political topics, questioning the legitimacy of the Communist Party say, and saw themselves as part of a movement heralding a political discourse, but this political consciousness never spilled out into open public discourse. Their biggest public concern, aside from keeping their land use fees low, was all about "civility" *(văn minh)* and "consciousness" *(ý thức).* In other words, they were, generally speaking, all socially committed people with good intentions, seeking to build a society of consensus and polite conversation, where people managed their own behavior, where fees and urban services were predictable, and where residents conformed to the will of the group, resisting dissensus and disagreement in the process of developing a harmonious, peaceful, and orderly world.

## CIVILITY, PRIVATE PROPERTY, AND THE PROBLEM OF RIGHTS

It is not difficult to understand why the residents of Vietnamese cities might find the idea of a harmonious and peaceful world appealing. The nation is populated by people who have personally endured (or, if they are young, heard vivid stories of) a twentieth century defined by the injustices of colonialism and a seemingly non-stop series of hardships brought on by revolution, civil war, American imperialism, socialist central planning, border conflicts, economic embargoes, wrenching poverty, failing infrastructure, unmanaged rural-urban migration, as well as rapid, and largely unplanned, urbanization. Thus, when the government claims its intention to build a new kind of "urban civility" *(văn minh đô thị),* they are often both skeptical and hopeful at once. Most people know that "civility" or "civilization" is often a thinly veiled way to speak of social control. But many people also hold on to the hope that civility could offer desirable forms of self-discipline that might, just might, enable people to function together as a cohesive society.

The idea of urban civilization entails a tradeoff, not unlike the tradeoff Sigmund Freud presented in his rambling but at times inspiring *Civilization and Its Discontents*. In that volume, Freud essentially condenses a long tradition of Western liberal thought from Hobbes to Rousseau and asserts that "civilization" is based on the idea of "right," which can only be defended by the collective: "Human life in common is only made possible when a majority comes together which is stronger than any separate individual and which remains united against all separate individuals. The power of this community is then set up as 'right' in opposition to the power of the individual, which is condemned as 'brute force.' This replacement of the power of the individual by the power of a community constitutes the decisive step of civilization." He later asserts that the "first requisite of civilization, therefore, is that of justice—that is, the assurance that a law once made will not be broken in favor of an individual. [ . . . ] The final outcome should be a rule of law . . . "[27]

This is very much the same dilemma facing the new Saigon, where the story of building supposedly civilized new urban zones cuts to the very heart of people's hopes, desires, and fears about the changes taking place in their city. Many people hope that these changes will deliver justice and the rule of law, but others also insist that building these developments depends on subordinating the rights of individuals to the sometimes onerous demands of the collective. These new urban zones, like civilization itself, both promise to deliver rights and force people to relinquish them. Residents in Phú Mỹ Hưng commonly expressed this basic idea, saying they were genuinely excited that new urban zones might resolve so many of the issues they themselves thought about. They sincerely believed that the project had emerged out of a wasteland to provide a modern, civilized, new form of urban living that could serve as a model for the rest of society, which they hoped would be disciplined and orderly but also liberating. Residents of Thủ Thiêm were similarly enthusiastic about the idea of modernizing the city, but they also knew full well that such modernization was built on the backs of people like them, who were being displaced from their land. People in both places understood that building new urban zones was part of a larger commitment to building a city worth living in. But for many, this process of building a new urban civilization meant either dismantling the very city they thought they knew or rendering it inaccessible to them. As Freud noted, although civilization is idealized in societies around the world, it is also the source of great misery. Rights and law are built on sacrifice, and civilization always imposes limits on liberty.

The Vietnamese government is fully aware of the problems associated with building its vision of a modern, industrialized, and civilized urban society, and academics in the country have openly recognized those problems by framing them in terms of cost-benefit analysis. Even government-sponsored scholars have studied the livelihoods and struggles of people who have been forced to give up their land. In one such study, published by the Political Publishing House (by no means a subversive organization), a team of scholars highlighted the growing number of people who had to give up land for development projects and carefully detailed the ever-increasing number of hectares being converted each year from rural to urban uses. The authors were clear about the challenges these residents were facing, but they also made it clear that the sacrifices associated with urbanization had to be situated within the larger trajectory of Vietnamese development: "in sum, if industrialization, modernization and urbanization are necessary objectives for our country, then the act of reclaiming land in the service of industrialization, modernization, and urbanization is a topic of important significance. For that reason, in the process of industrialization, modernization, and urbanization, any country will have to change some amount of its land from agrarian land into industrial and urban land."[28]

This kind of cost-benefit analysis is common in contemporary Vietnam, where people of all walks of life readily acknowledge that modernization entails deep costs. The fact that it is a tautological claim—that urbanization will require converting rural land to urban, and that industrialization will require reclaiming land in in its own service—is beside the point. What matters is that the Vietnamese government is aware of the costs that come with building an urban civilization. However, because the goal of building an urban civilization has already been determined a "necessary" aim for the country, the government has decided that the people must be ready to bear those costs.

All this goes to show that the story of dispossession and the story of building urban civility are intimately entangled. The ethnographic evidence from the two new urban zones described in this book makes that clear. On the one hand, Vietnam is liberalizing property rights and increasingly developing the political and legal apparatus to acknowledge significant land use rights. On the other hand, massive numbers of people are being evicted from their homes, with unprecedented amounts of land being requisitioned and converted to new uses. The conclusion to be drawn from these two observations is simple, unambiguous, and stark: mass eviction and the emergence of property rights go hand in hand. Likewise, the production of civilized spaces of new urban living is founded on mass dispossession.

At the same time, as these intertwined processes of mass eviction and invocations of urban civility proceed in parallel, a new kind of person is emerging in Vietnam, what we might call a "rights-bearing subject." This is a person who goes up against inequity and denounces corruption, by mobilizing idioms of "rights," "justice," and "law." How do we reconcile the massive increase in dispossession with the thriving language of rights in the country? The answer, on one level, is quite simple, and can be linked to the way the generalizable notion of rights currently emerging in Vietnam is actually intertwined with and inseparable from property rights. The rights that so many people are agitating for are in fact little more than the right to maximize land values in a superheated real estate market, where fortunes and livelihoods can be made through land transactions. When the notion of rights becomes fully enmeshed with the ability to profit from land values, there is no escaping the fact that some people will gain from this market while others will lose. All forms of property rights are founded on exclusion to some degree, and when the right to the city is reduced to the right to profit from land, then some people will be excluded from those rights, even as they loudly demand to be included in the profitable game. The right to own very quickly devolves into the right to evict. The foundations of civilized modes of interaction are built on decidedly uncivil forces of dispossession.

People's consciousness of their rights, however, is forged in a dynamic relationship with proprietary ownership, and the forces of inclusion and exclusion entailed therein also impact the way people see themselves as rights-bearing subjects. Anthropologists have long understood the connection between property and personhood, and it is well known that a person's identity as a rights-bearing subject is always forged in relation to proprietary claims that impact others. As Eric Hirsch puts it, property "requires a boundary to be formed, a network of relations to be cut, and the claims of other persons to be severed." And maintaining these boundaries "requires the assertion of law as much as power" because "in all forms of property the boundary is often contested." These forms of contestation, furthermore, produce novel forms of sociality; as "people contest or accommodate these assertions of property, . . . there emerge new ways to be a person or collective of persons."[29] We are back, in a way, to Freud's assertion that the coming together of private persons in a collective group both depends on a notion of "right" and sets the condition for a particular relationship of law and justice. This process also produces new forms of consciousness that structure the way the conflict between the individual and the group plays out.

This is precisely what I have described taking place in contemporary Vietnam: the emergence of people whose very conception of self is tied to their sense of themselves as property-owning subjects, and whose understanding of "rights" is entangled with ideas of private property. After many years of socialism, when all property was nationalized, this is why so many Vietnamese people consider the return of private property—officially understood as the right to transfer "land use rights"—as a stepping stone on the pathway to increased freedom. But what is often ignored is the degree to which these relations—these rights—are themselves founded on powers of exclusion.[30] In a society marked by limited access to valuable land, when the very idea of rights is inseparable from relations of property, then those rights are necessarily subject to the same limits and conditions that pertain to property rights: they are, in a word, founded on exclusion, and the accumulation of rights by some depends on the dispossession of others.[31] The sociality that emerges in this return to private property relations is connected to emergent forms of consciousness, and people who live in privatized spaces like Phú Mỹ Hưng, or who are evicted from places like Thủ Thiêm, are simultaneously engaged with collective political issues, thereby becoming willing participants in the process of privatization that has spawned many of those issues in the first place. Their idea of rights may be founded on exclusion, but the idiom of rights thus produced also gives them the language to fight that exclusion.

A paradox emerges: while emergent sociality and rights consciousness in Phú Mỹ Hưng and Thủ Thiêm depend on privatization and the commoditization of land, and while they clearly depend on a certain elevation of the individual self, the very people who are involved in this process see themselves as deeply committed to the public sphere. Philosophers of liberty, rights, freedom, and civil society have long understood the connection between individual subjectivity and public ideals. For Rousseau, civic liberty was a proprietary form, dependent on exclusions that were defended by the state.[32] For Marx, private property only emerged from "original sin," a moment of violent "primitive accumulation," forming a foundation of injustice upon which later conceptions of liberal right were built.[33] Orlando Patterson has shown how Western conceptions of freedom depended on contexts of slavery and the systematic subordination of others.[34] For Jürgen Habermas, the emergence of a public sphere depended on the development of private property–owning individuals.[35] Critical scholars have long shown how all of these traditions are founded on exclusion, but the allure of rights, and the promise of civilized modes of social engagement that supposedly emerge from these foundational inequities, have remained appealing nonetheless.

All this talk of rights might be consigned to the heady world of philosophy and theory. But it has real-world consequences, which are dramatically illustrated in the stories told in this book. When we juxtapose the plight of displaced residents in a place like Thủ Thiêm against the lives of well-to-do residents in a place like Phú Mỹ Hưng, we see very different aspects of Vietnam's quest to build a new form of urban civility. Placing these stories side by side reveals that both places are informed by a vociferous championing of personal rights, much of which has been framed, if not wholly defined, by people's emergent conceptions of land use rights and the new forms of consciousness these engender. But examining these cases in concert also highlights stark inequities in the way rights mobilization, when framed in an idiom of land rights, actually works out for differently placed actors. In both cases, people often invoked the language of rights, and in both cases people actively mobilized around those rights. But the outcomes could not be more different: in Phú Mỹ Hưng, the result was to reinforce the rights of those who already have rights, whereas in Thủ Thiêm the rights for which so many people fought, and for which many continue to fight, are the rights of those who have no rights at all. The two cases represent contrasting aspects of an ongoing struggle for rights as Vietnam seeks to build a modern, industrialized, urban civilization. The struggle in both cases may share the same language of rights, but what those rights actually mean for people living in the midst of either luxury or rubble couldn't be more different. For some, those rights are little more than a tautology; for others, a void.

# ACKNOWLEDGMENTS

This book would not have been possible without the openness and good will of the people of Thủ Thiêm and Phú Mỹ Hưng. Both anthropological convention and the sensitive nature of research into urban development in Vietnam prevent me from naming the many people who brought me into their homes and shared intimate details of their lives. But it is their words and experiences that give life to this book, which is my small attempt to convey the challenges they face as they grapple with the historic changes transforming their city and country. The people who appear in these pages are much more than "informants." I am honored to call them friends and look forward to many more conversations and meals together. I cannot repay them for the stories they have shared with me, and I can most certainly never match the meals they have shared. So in thanks for all they have given me, I've decided to make this book available as an open access publication so that it will be available free of charge to readers everywhere, in Vietnam and around the world. I hope people will come to pay attention to their stories and develop an awareness of all the messiness that comes with urban development, which is, in today's Vietnam, almost always bound up with urban demolition.

Researching, writing, and publishing an academic book is costly. Making this book into an open access publication depended both on the forward-thinking vision of University of California Press and on the financial support of the Department of Anthropology, the Council on Southeast Asian Studies, the MacMillan Center for International and Areas Studies, and the Frederick W. Hilles Publication Fund at Yale University. The research itself was funded by National Science Foundation Award No. BCS- 1026754. I wish to thank Deborah Winslow and Jeffrey Mantz for stewarding me through the grant process and for involving me in the important work of NSF ever since. Yale has also supported this work in numerous other ways: a Non-Tenured Faculty Leave and Faculty Research Grant in 2010–11 allowed me to carry out the bulk of the fieldwork on which this book is based, and an Associate Professor Leave in 2014–15 allowed me to complete the manuscript. In addition, annual research funds from the Council on Southeast Asian Studies and the Department of Anthropology have allowed me to return to Vietnam regularly for follow-up research, and conference travel funding from the Office of the Provost has enabled me to present on this research every year since coming to Yale. I also benefited from mentorship funds from the Office of the Vice-Provost, which allowed me to work closely with and learn from Professor Michael Herzfeld, who has become an enthusiastic supporter of my work and a valuable source of inspiration and guidance ever since.

In the Department of Anthropology at Yale I have found supportive colleagues across the four subfields, and I am proud to be a member of a department that resists the temptation to divide and subdivide. In particular, Helen Siu and K. Sivaramakrishnan deserve special mention for supporting my work in urban anthropology, pushing me to think about InterAsia connections, involving me in their innovative projects, and supporting my attempts to expand interest in the study of Asian cities at Yale. Joe Errington and Bill Kelly have also been tireless advocates and mentors, and Paul Kockelman's arrival in our department has given me both inspiration and friendship. Most importantly, I would never have been able to bear the trials and tribulations of life as a "junior faculty" without sharing this experience with inspiring comrades like Jafari Allen, Brenda Bradley, Sean Brotherton, Oswaldo Chinchilla, Narges Erami, Karen Hébert, Bill Honeychurch, Louisa Lombard, Mike McGovern, Karen Nakamura, Doug Rogers, Sara Shneiderman, and Brian Wood. I remain deeply indebted to the selflessness and uplifting spirit of the late Barney Bate, whose life and legacy will never be forgotten.

The scholars associated with Yale's Council on Southeast Asian Studies have made this large research university feel like a family. Thank you to Dinny Aletheiani, Ruth Barnes, Carol Carpenter, Nayan Chanda, Amity Doolittle, Michael Dove, Joe Errington, Ben Kiernan, Richard Richie, Jim Scott, Indriyo Sukmono, and especially Quang Phu Van, who is not only the life and soul of the Yale Vietnam Studies Group but a true friend. I also extend sincere thanks to Kris Mooseker, without whom we might still be a family, but a much more destitute and dysfunctional one. I have also benefited from the extraordinary intellectual vigor of an amazing group of graduate students working with me on the study of Southeast Asian anthropology: Andrew Carruthers, Tram Luong, Emily Nguyen, Tri Phuong, Elliott Prasse-Freeman—and now, thanks to InterAsian connections, Alyssa Paredes and George Bayuga as well. Their insights and observations, along with those of countless other Yale graduate students, can be found coursing through every page of this book. I also wish to thank Emily Nguyen, Trevor Williams, Mitchell Tan, Titania

Nguyen, Levi Truong, Ben Garfinkel, and Daniel Vernick, all students in my course on postwar Vietnam, who read the entire manuscript and provided detailed comments and critiques. For the research itself, I lucked out hiring Christine Nguyen, who ended up being an outstanding project manager, helping to coordinate all the outstanding contributions of a hard-working group of Yale undergraduate research assistants: Andrew Chun, Eva Guadamillas, Khai-Hoan Huynh, Hanh Nguyen, Linh Nguyen, Mary Nguyen, Thao Nguyen, and Lien Tran.

In Vietnam I have long enjoyed the support and friendship of scholars in the Department of Anthropology at the University of Social Sciences and Humanities in Ho Chi Minh City. My friends there have helped me navigate the tensions of what some might construe to be a sensitive research topic. I have especially enjoyed collaborating with Phạm Thành Thôi, who is, in my opinion, one of Vietnam's most tireless and talented ethnographic fieldworkers, and with Phạm Thành Duy, whose combination of careful fieldwork with a broad grasp of social processes is equally outstanding. Although many of the interpretations in this book are based on my own eclectic analysis of the data, and while my errors can't be blamed on them, none of the work I have done would have been possible without them. I also benefited greatly from the assistance of Phạm Thị Thu Thủy and the intellectual support of Ngô Thị Phương Lan and Huỳnh Ngọc Thu. Tôn Nữ Quỳnh Trần, director of Center for Urban and Development Studies in Ho Chi Minh City, has been generous at all turns, and her work on Thủ Thiêm was indispensable for my own investigations. Huỳnh Thế Du has from the very beginning been a lively interlocutor about urban development in Ho Chi Minh City, and his Ph.D. thesis was a helpful guide to the convoluted world of urban politics in the city. Tiffany Chung has given me an insider's view into the world of Vietnamese art, and her respect for my work has been one of the greatest compliments I have ever had.

Over the years, I have benefited from inspiring conversations and collaborations with the small but intellectually vivacious group of Vietnam studies scholars working in anthropology and related fields. I owe special thanks to the constant engagement I have had with Maggie Bodemer, Olga Dror, Kirsten Endres, Jamie Gillen, Tim Karis, Christian Lentz, Ann Marie Leshkowich, Ken MacLean, Anh Thu Ngo, Christophe Robert, Christina Schwenkel, Merav Shohet, and Allen Tran, as well as urbanists like Mike Douglass, Annette Kim, Danielle Labbé, and others. Every step of my way into Vietnam scholarship has been guided by the work of Vietnam scholars like John Gillespie, Ben Kerkvliet, Hy Van Luong, Philip Taylor, and others. Furthermore, I have received valuable feedback and intellectual sustenance from members of the Connecticut Vietnam Studies Group: Mitch Aso, Bradley Davis, Lauren Meeker, Marguerite Nguyen, John Phan, Ivan Small, Michele Thompson, Nu-Anh Tran, and Wynn Wilcox. At one of our recent CVSG meetings, John Phan and Wynn Wilcox provided me with extremely useful historical sources for understanding ideas of "wasteland" in classical Nôm literature.

Eli Elinoff, who is not a Vietnam specialist, gave me essential feedback on the introduction and conclusion which saved me from embarrassment. And Li Zhang has not only inspired me with her own writing on urban development in China, but always given me strong and valuable encouragement.

The ideas in this book have also benefited from multiple opportunities to share my work with engaged audiences of scholars at universities around the world. I gave my first presentation on Thủ Thiêm at one of the many workshops Huê-Tam Ho Tai has invited me to at Harvard, and followed it up with a presentation at a workshop in Hanoi organized by Mike DeGregorio and Mike Douglass. At that conference, I became more connected with the work of critical planning scholars like John Friedmann, Danielle Labbé, and Michael Leaf, who have pushed me to see the important intersections my work has with theirs and also to recognize how much I have to learn about cities. Later, Johan Lindquist invited me to Stockholm University, where the faculty of anthropology gave me outstanding comments that still inspire me today. Collaborations with Johan and Joshua Barker, while not directly related to this book project, have refined my writing and sharpened my critical eye in numerous ways. My old friend Henrik Vigh invited me to share my work at the University of Copenhagen (although he was away when I finally came). I benefited from comments offered on that occasion by Oscar Salemink, Tine Gammeltoft, Ayo Wahlberg, Edyta Roszko, and the other brilliant scholars working in the outstanding anthropology department there. Tusind tak! Suzanne Brenner invited me to present on my work at UC San Diego, and Ann Marie Lesh-kowich invited me to the College of the Holy Cross. Collaborations with Ian Baird, Tony Day, and Jane Ferguson at a workshop David Biggs organized at UC River-side urged me to develop and refine my ideas regarding discourses of the waste-land in Southeast Asia. My ideas about civility benefited from a workshop at Rice University, where I learned a great deal from the incisive comments provided by Kimberly Hoang, Aynne Kokas, Jessica Lockrem, and Allison Truitt. I have since gone on to learn still more from Jessica as a member of her PhD thesis committee. These ideas were pushed further at the Indian Institute for Advanced Studies in Shimla, where I benefited from the comments of N. Jayaram and Vivian Bickford-Smith on a paper discussing notions of civility. Michael Montesano's interest in the paper led to a separate publication, the preparation of which helped me refine general ideas that have informed my larger thinking on the topic. I also learned a lot from a Monday colloquium presentation I gave at the Harvard Department of Anthropology, thanks to an invitation from Ajantha Subramanian.

My understanding of "rights gone wrong" that I introduce in the conclusion of this book began to take shape when Ralph Litzinger and friends invited me to a conference on global cities at Duke University. I was later productively taken to task on the argument at a presentation sponsored by Angie Heo, Tam Ngo, Peter van der Veer, and colleagues at the Max Planck Institute in Göttingen, Germany.

Lisa Björkman was especially kind in helping me refine some of the finer points of the argument, a task I continued in conversations with Dan Reichman and colleagues at the University of Rochester; Ian Baird and colleagues at the University of Wisconsin, Madison; Alejandra Leal, Nitzan Shoshan, and colleagues at UNAM and El Colegio de México; Asher Ghertner and comrades at Rutgers; Andrea Ballestero, Dominic Boyer, Cymene Howe, and colleagues at Rice; Duncan McCargo's Southeast Asian studies group at Columbia University's Weatherhead Institute, and the graduate student–run Ethnography and Social Theory colloquium series at Yale. I also benefited from presenting schematic discussions of the major themes organizing the book when Elizabeth Perry invited me to present on my work in Shanghai, when Ivan Small invited me to Connecticut State University, and when Nicholas Harkness invited me to present aspects of the work at Harvard. Thanks also to Emiko Stock and Alexander McGrath, who invited me to give a reading from a chapter at Cornell in the spring of 2014, when I was able to meet the fantastic group of Vietnam studies scholars there, including Alex-Thai Vo, Yen Vu, and Hoang Vu. Special thanks to Alex-Thai for help scanning an important image that appears in the book. For access to library collections, I thank Rich Richie at Yale, the archivists at Texas Tech and librarians at Columbia University's Avery Library, as well as the Rauner Special Collections library at Dartmouth, where Pat Cope went out of her way to help me locate and scan a certain image. At UC Press, Reed Malcolm was encouraging from the very beginning, and the editorial staff—Zuha Kahn and Rachel Berchten, and Paige MacKay at Luminos Open Access—made the production process smooth and efficient. Valuable comments on the manuscript from Michael Leaf and an anonymous reviewer helped improve the text immensely. The book has also been greatly improved by maps prepared by Bill Nelson, copy-editing by Anne Canright, and indexing by Roberta Engleman.

One of the biggest challenges of being a scholar is being forced to live far from the places we would otherwise call home. New Haven is a long way off from San Diego, the only place, if given the chance, I would genuinely call home. My only regret is being so far from my mother, Marie-Louise Lind Harms, who has done so much to make me the person I am today. I thank her for bearing the distance with understanding. I also thank Eugene Davis and Theo Bellow for being there. Scott Moir remains in my heart always, as do Terry Turner, Andrew Hill, Hal Scheffler, and Hal Conklin. As I write these acknowledgments, people are mourning the loss of a pop star named Prince, but these men were true kings.

The greatest challenge in writing a book, however, is the way it tears you away from your family. In my case, this has been particularly rough, because my family is so outlandishly perfect and wonderful. If it weren't for them, I might actually enjoy some of the time spent writing. But I loathe the moment when the taskmaster calls and I have to peel myself away from my kids to head back for another date with the keyboard. My daughters, Lena and Giulia, try to make it easier: they have told me they were proud to know I was writing a book. But in the end, I know they have not been *that* impressed because, as they remind me often, they've read books much longer than mine. Cora, who can't yet read, didn't seem to mind too much when I disappeared to the office for another round of writing, revision, and editing. Isabella did mind, I think, but she was nice enough to pretend otherwise. I dedicate this book to Isabella for making it all possible.

# NOTES

## INTRODUCTION: LUXURY AND RUBBLE

1. Gastón Gordillo, *Rubble: The Afterlife of Destruction* (Durham, NC: Duke University Press, 2014), 81.

2. Ibid.

3. Ibid., 269.

4. Ibid., 25.

5. The connection between an emergent land market and the process of "accumulation through dispossession" resonates with studies of neoliberal development across the developing world. See David Harvey, "Accumulation by Dispossession," in *The New Imperialism* (New York: Oxford University Press, 2005), 137–82.

6. The term *khu* in Vietnamese can be translated as either "zone" or "area." While some scholars commonly translate *khu đô thị mới* as "new urban area," I use the term *zone* in order to emphasize the role of "zoning" in the development of these spaces. They are, in many ways, residential and commercial equivalents of export processing zones. In the case of Phú Mỹ Hưng, furthermore, the development of the New Urban Zone was itself tied into a larger master plan that also included the development of the Tân Thuận Export Processing Zone. On the importance of zoning technologies, see Aihwa Ong, "Zoning Technologies in East Asia," in *Neoliberalism as Exception: Mutations in Citizenship and Sovereignty* (Durham, NC: Duke University Press, 2006), 97–118. For important studies of Vietnamese new urban zones, see Mike Douglass and Liling Huang, "Globalizing the City in Southeast Asia: Utopia on the Urban Edge—The Case of Phu My Hung, Saigon," *International Journal of Asia-Pacific Studies* 3, no. 2 (2007): 1–41; Danielle Labbé, "Understanding the Causes of Urban Fragmentation in Hanoi: The Case of New Urban Areas," *International Development Planning Review* 33, no. 3 (2011): 273–91; and Michael Leaf, "Vietnam's Urban Edge: The Administration of Urban Development in Hanoi," *TWPR* 21, no. 3 (1999): 297–315.

7. The literature on New Towns in Asia is extensive. Some of the most influential works include: Deborah Davis, "Urban Consumer Culture," *China Quarterly*, no. 183 (2005): 692–709; idem, "The New Rich in China: Future Rulers, Present Lives," *China Quarterly*, no. 196 (2008): 935–36; idem, "Who Gets the House? Renegotiating Property Rights in Post-Socialist Urban China," *Modern China* 36, no. 5 (2010): 463–92; Davis Fraser, "Inventing Oasis: Luxury Housing Advertisements in Reconfiguring Domestic Space in Shanghai," in *The Consumer Revolution in Urban China*, ed. Deborah Davis (Berkeley: University of California Press, 2000), 25–53; You-tien Hsing, *The Great Urban Transformation: Politics of Land and Property in China* (Oxford: Oxford University Press, 2010); Li Zhang, *In Search of Paradise: Middle-Class Living in a Chinese Metropolis* (Ithaca, NY: Cornell University Press, 2010); Gavin Shatkin, "The City and the Bottom Line: Urban Megaprojects and the Privatization of Planning in Southeast Asia," *Environment and Planning A* 40, no. 2 (2008): 383–401; Luigi Tomba, "Of Quality, Harmony, and Community: Civilization and the Middle Class in Urban China," *Positions* 17, no. 3 (2009): 591–616; idem, "Middle Classes in China: Force for Political Change or Guarantee of Stability?" *PORTAL: Journal of Multidisciplinary International Studies* 6, no. 2 (2009); Li Zhang and Aihwa Ong, *Privatizing China: Socialism from Afar* (Ithaca, NY: Cornell University Press, 2008).

8. For a useful study of the new forms of urban governance associated with the "privatization of planning," see esp. Shatkin, "City and the Bottom Line."

9. CBRE, "Thu Thiem: The PuDong of Saigon" (market report), CBRE Vietnam, Ho Chi Minh City, 2015.

10. Hải Nam and Trung Hiếu, "Căng thẳng đối thoại về dự án Thủ Thiêm" [Tense discussion about the Thủ Thiêm project], *Thanh Niên*, June 11, 2016, 3.

11. On the importance of seriously attending to the sense of aspiration and hope that guides urban life in developing cities, see AbdouMaliq Simone, *For the City Yet to Come: Changing African Life in Four Cities* (Durham, NC: Duke University Press, 2004).

12. For complex, essentially political, reasons, I am not able to name my Vietnamese research collaborators in this book. Asking too many questions about urban development in Ho Chi Minh City makes the city and national government nervous, and this nervousness commonly translates into political repression and scholarly censorship.

13. Of these interviews, 148 were conducted in Thủ Thiêm, and 187 in Phú Mỹ Hưng. While some of those interviews were brief, 122 of them were formal extended ethnographic interviews, all of which were recorded and later transcribed. The ethnographic examples and quotations from informants used as evidence in this book draw primarily from the more extended interviews, but the insights gained from all the interviews inform much of the theorization and understanding I have developed of the issues animating the lives of residents in both fieldsites.

14. Nguyễn Văn Kích, Phan Chánh Dưỡng, and Tôn Sĩ Kinh, *Nhà Bè Hồi sinh từ công nghiệp: Tập 2 Phú Mỹ Hưng—Đô thị Phát triển bền vững* [Nha Be revived by industry: Volume 2, Phu My Hung—A sustainable urban development] (Ho Chi Minh City: Nhà xuất bản Tổng hợp TP. Hồ Chí Minh, 2006), 43.

15. This theme of populations being marginalized by urban development projects while nonetheless expressing support for the aesthetic promises of those same developments has been described in recent cases in the Congo and India, as well as in my

own work in Ho Chi Minh City. See, e.g., Filip De Boeck, "Inhabiting Ocular Ground: Kinshasa's Future in the Light of Congo's Spectral Urban Politics," *Cultural Anthropology* 26, no. 2 (2011): 263–86; D. Asher Ghertner, "Rule by Aesthetics: World-Class City Making in Delhi," in *Worlding Cities: Asian Experiments and the Art of Being Global,* ed. Ananya Roy and Aihwa Ong (Malden, MA: Wiley-Blackwell, 2011), 279–306; Erik Harms, "Beauty as Control in the New Saigon: Eviction, New Urban Zones, and Atomized Dissent in a Southeast Asian City," *American Ethnologist* 39, no. 4 (2012): 735–50.

16.  On socialist legality and rule by law, see John Gillespie, "Changing Concepts of Socialist Law in Vietnam," in *Asian Socialism and Legal Change: The Dynamics of Vietnamese and Chinese Reform,* ed. John Gillespie and Pip Nicholson (Canberra: ANU Press, 2005), 45–75.

17.  For sophisticated ethnographic analyses of the emergence of rights claims among residents facing eviction in the city of Vinh, see Christina Schwenkel, "Civilizing the City: Socialist Ruins and Urban Renewal in Central Vietnam," *positions* 20, no. 2 (2012): 437–70; idem, "Post/Socialist Affect: Ruination and Reconstruction of the Nation in Urban Vietnam," *Cultural Anthropology* 28, no. 2 (2013): 252–77; idem, "Reclaiming Rights to the Socialist City: Bureaucratic Artefacts and the Affective Appeal of Petitions," *Southeast Asia Research* 23, no. 2 (2015): 205–25.

18.  Derek Hall, Philip Hirsch, and Tania Murray Li, *Powers of Exclusion: Land Dilemmas in Southeast Asia* (Singapore: NUS Press, 2011).

19.  Annette Miae Kim, *Sidewalk City: Remapping Public Space in Ho Chi Minh City* (Chicago: University of Chicago Press, 2015), 181.

20.  The phrase "thành phố mang tên Bác" literally means "the city that carries the name of the uncle." For an example of this term and of the ways infrastructure is commonly mobilized to legitimize the state's stewardship of urban development, see Tùng Nguyên and Trung Kiên, "Hình ảnh thành phố mang tên Bác sau 39 năm giải phóng" [Photos of the city that bears Uncle's name after 39 years of liberation], *Dân trí,* April 30, 2014. The article also explicitly highlights how the Phú Mỹ Bridge, along with the Thủ Thiêm Bridge, should be seen as part of a development process determined to "open the city to the east" (mở phố về Đông).

21.  For images of the social life on the bridge, see Kính Cận/Viễn Đông, "Hóng mát trên cầu Phú Mỹ" [Savoring the cool air on the Phú Mỹ Bridge], *Viễn Đông Daily,* Oct. 20, 2011, www.viendongdaily.com/hong-mat-tren-cau-phu-my-YvOJSyi4.html.

22.  Michel de Certeau, *The Practice of Everyday Life* (Berkeley: University of California Press, 1984), 91.

23.  Zhang, *In Search of Paradise.*

24.  Dennis Rodgers and Bruce O'Neill, "Infrastructural Violence: Introduction to the Special Issue," *Ethnography* 13, no. 4 (Dec. 1, 2012): 401–12.

25.  Hữu Nguyên, "Cố Thủ tướng Võ Văn Kiệt —'Kiến trúc sư' Đổi mới'" [Former Prime Minister Võ Văn Kiệt—"Architect of Đổi Mới"], *VnExpress,* Nov. 17, 2012.

26.  Thanks to Phạm Thành Duy for bringing the importance of the Friday Group to my attention and for highlighting the connection between members of this group and the early development of Phú Mỹ Hưng. For more on the role of these early negotiations, see Nguyễn Văn Kích, Phan Chánh Dưỡng, and Tôn Sĩ Kinh, *Nhà Bè Hồi sinh từ công nghiệp: Tập 2 Phú Mỹ Hưng.*

## 1. CIVILIZING THE WASTELANDS: A SHORT HISTORY OF URBAN DEVELOPMENT IN PHÚ MỸ HƯNG

1. See George W. Stocking, *Observers Observed: Essays on Ethnographic Fieldwork* (Madison: University of Wisconsin Press, 1984).

2. Phú Mỹ Hưng, *Vươn lên từ đầm lầy* [Rising from the swamps] (Ho Chi Minh City: Phú Mỹ Hưng Corp., 2005).

3. For a discussion of "key symbols" as well as "root metaphors" and "key scenarios," of which the wasteland story is a bit of all, see Sherry B. Ortner, "On Key Symbols," *American Anthropologist* 75, no. 5 (1973): 1341.

4. Lawrence S. Ting School Students, "Change of the Community with the Example of Phu My Hung: Submission to British Council Connecting Classroom Competition," Lawrence S. Ting School, Ho Chi Minh City, 2010, 1–2.

5. Ibid., 11–12.

6. Ibid., 17.

7. Phú Mỹ Hưng, *Vươn lên từ đầm lầy.*

8. David Dillon, "Honor Award Suburban Design," *Architectural Record,* May 1997, 86. The evidence given by the architectural review for why Vietnamese accept "big ideas," however, was decidedly ethnocentric: "in among the towers are canals, gardens, and pedestrian ways that reveal a sophisticated balancing of aggressive Western capitalism and Asian delicacy."

9. There is nothing particularly Vietnamese about this practice. American school kids are commonly assigned projects to learn about the history behind the names of schools like Lincoln, Washington, or Grant.

10. Phú Mỹ Hưng, *Vươn lên từ đầm lầy,* 7. I have also quoted this same passage in Erik Harms, "Knowing into Oblivion: Clearing Wastelands and Imagining Emptiness in Vietnamese New Urban Zones," *Singapore Journal of Tropical Geography* 35, no. 2 (2014): 319. Some of the arguments in this section were also presented, in modified form, in that article.

11. Trần Văn Giàu, *Địa chí văn hóa Thành phố Hồ Chí Minh* [Monograph on the Culture of Ho Chi Minh City] (Ho Chi Minh City: Nhà xuất bản Thành phố Hồ Chí Minh, 1987), 237.

12. On the concept of tale-types, see Alan Dundes, "The Motif-Index and the Tale Type Index: A Critique," *Journal of Folklore Research* 34, no. 3 (1997): 195–202.

13. Hùynh Phú Sang, "Presentation," in *From Saigon to Ho Chi Minh City: 300-Year History,* ed. Nguyễn Đình Đầu (Ho Chi Minh City: Land Service Science and Technics Publishing House., 1998), 6.

14. This was not only a "socialist" concept. For evidence of this wasteland narrative in the southern Republic of Vietnam under Ngô Đình Diệm, see Philip E. Catton, *Diem's Final Failure: Prelude to America's War in Vietnam* (Lawrence: University Press of Kansas, 2003), 57. Furthermore, according to the linguistic historian John D. Phan (email, Nov. 26, 2015), the language of "opening up the wasteland" has a very long history in both Chinese and Vietnamese texts about frontiers and agricultural expansion. In Chinese, discussion of the importance of "cultivating" or "opening up" (墾/*khẩn*) agricultural lands appear as early as the 8th–3rd century BCE in the *Guanzi,* a classical text from the Eastern Zhou. In Chinese classical training, the idea of opening up lands by cultivating them was considered essential

to the civilizing project, especially during imperial times. It is clear that the idea carried on into the twentieth century as well. The combination of *khẩn* (墾, meaning "reclaim" or "cultivate") with *hoang* (荒, meaning "wastes" or "wasteland") commonly seen in Vietnamese historical texts was also used by Mao Zedong. The historian Wynn Wilcox (email, Dec. 17, 2015) also notes that an approving reference to "reclaiming the wasteland" can be found in the text of a policy question posed to candidates at the Nguyễn dynasty's 1910 imperial palace exams.

15. David Biggs, *Quagmire: Nation-Building and Nature in the Mekong Delta* (Seattle: University of Washington Press, 2010).

16. Excavations by the French archaeologist Louis Malleret in the 1930s and 1940s had already shown that the site that became Saigon was a place of human settlement in the prehistoric period: Malyo-Polynesian peoples and highland groups like the Stieng, Chema, Koho, and other Mnong were all present to some degree in the area, and it is common knowledge that the city of Saigon was a Khmer settlement before the arrival of Vietnamese. Louis Malleret, "A la recherche de Prei Nokor, note sur l'emplacement présumé de l'ancien Saïgon khmer," *Bulletin de la Société des Etudes Indochinois, Saïgon,* 1942; Philippe Peycam, "Saigon, des origines à 1859," in *Saigon, 1698–1998: Architectures/Urbanisme,* ed. Lê Quang Ninh and Stéphane Dovert (Ho Chi Minh City: Nhà xuất bản Thành phố Ho Chi Minh, 1998).

17. Philip Taylor, in *The Khmer Lands of Vietnam: Environment, Cosmology, and Sovereignty* (Singapore: NUS Press, 2014), describes the largely overlooked history and livelihood of Khmer people in the larger region now politically (but not always culturally) incorporated into southern Vietnam. He also describes the Vietnamese wasteland narrative in the following way: "Visions of the region as chronically underpopulated, underutilized and wild proposed that the ecological potential of the region remained latent until released by the application of imported technology in the hands of visionary outsiders and dynamic newcomers possessing superior civilizational resources" (7). For a more historical analysis of Khmer-Vietnamese relations, see Shawn McHale, "Ethnicity, Violence, and Khmer-Vietnamese Relations: The Significance of the Lower Mekong Delta, 1757–1954," *Journal of Asian Studies* 72, no. 2 (2013): 367–90.

18. On being culturally rich while being derided by the state as impoverished in rural Vietnam, see Philip Taylor, "Poor Policies, Wealthy Peasants: Alternative Trajectories of Rural Development in Vietnam," *Journal of Vietnamese Studies* 2, no. 2 (2007): 3–56.

19. These kinds of invented historical traditions have become increasingly challenged by contemporary scholars. For critiques of the notion of a Vietnamese "March to the South," see Steve Graw, "Nam Tien and the Development of Vietnamese Regionalism" (thesis, Cornell University, 1995); Keith W. Taylor, "Surface Orientations in Vietnam: Beyond Histories of Nation and Region," *Journal of Asian Studies* 57, no. 4 (1998): 949–78. Despite the critiques, these notions of the march of progress continue in depictions of Vietnamese history, and I argue that they find clear parallels in contemporary descriptions of periurban development.

20. The "Eastern Sea" is the Vietnamese name for what the Chinese call the "South China Sea."

21. Phú Mỹ Hưng, *Vươn lên từ đầm lầy,* 9.

22. These statistics come from a copy of a speech given by an office of the Phú Mỹ Hưng Corporation to city leaders and members of the ministry of construction in 2007. Lidai Ming, "Một số phương pháp thực hiện trong việc xây dựng phát triển và quản lý khu trung tâm đô thị mới Nam Sài Gòn của công ty Phú Mỹ Hưng" [Some implementation methods for the work of building, developing, and managing the central Saigon South urban area of the Phú Mỹ Hưng Corporation], Phú Mỹ Hưng Corp., Ho Chi Minh City, 2007.

23. See chapter 5 for a discussion of this same redistricting regulation and its connection to real estate values in Thủ Thiêm.

24. Ủy ban Nhân dân Quận 7 Phòng Thống kê [District 7 People's Committee Statistics Office], *Niên giám Thống kê: 1997–2007* [Statistical yearbook: 1997–2007] (Ho Chi Minh City: Ủy ban Nhân dân Quận 7, 2006), 8.

25. Ibid., 9.

26. Cục Thống kê Thành phố Hồ Chí Minh [Ho Chi Minh City Statistical Office], *Niên giám Thống kê năm 2011* [Statistical yearbook 2011] (Ho Chi Minh City, 2011), 23; available online at www.pso.hochiminhcity.gov.vn.

27. See Phu My Hung Corp., "RESIDENT'S INFORMATION Customer Service Center Information," www.phumyhung.com.vn/eng/ttcudan_detail.php?id=3; idem, "Trung Tâm Phục Vụ Khách Hàng" [RESIDENT'S INFORMATION Customer Service Center Information] (Vietnamese version), www.phumyhung.com.vn/v2/gioi-thieu/trung-tam-phuc-vu-khach-hang.html.

28. On the concept of "auto-construction," developed to describe the self-made housing on the periurban margins of Brazilian cities, see James Holston, *Insurgent Citizenship: Disjunctions of Democracy and Modernity in Brazil* (Princeton, NJ: Princeton University Press, 2008). It is interesting to note that the Vietnamese term for the same process, *đô thị hóa tự phát,* while commonly translated as "spontaneous urbanization," could more accurately be translated as "auto-urbanization."

29. It may be reading too much into the story of this union to note that the union of male and female founders here resonates with many other Vietnamese origin stories.

30. On the symbolic and political-economic denigration of outer-city districts, see Erik Harms, *Saigon's Edge: On the Margins of Ho Chi Minh City* (Minneapolis: University of Minnesota Press, 2011); idem, "Material Symbolism of Saigon's Edge: The Political-Economic and Symbolic Transformation of Hồ Chí Minh City's Periurban Zones," *Pacific Affairs* 84, no. 3 (2011): 455–73. For an important discussion of how the devaluation of rural land is connected to the legacy of socialist collectivization, see Danielle Labbé, *Land Politics and Livelihoods on the Margins of Hanoi, 1920–2010* (Vancouver, BC: UBC Press, 2014), 71.

31. The Saigon Development Corporation is also known in Vietnamese as Công ty Cổ phần Phát triển Nam Sài Gòn.

32. IPC, "Mốc sự kiện" [Milestones], Công ty TNHH MTV Phát triển Công nghiệp Tân Thuận, www.ttipc.vn/moc-su-kien.

33. Nguyễn Đình Đầu, *Nghiên cứu địa ba Triều Nguyễn* [Cadastral registers study of the Nguyễn dynasty] (Ho Chi Minh City: Nhà xuất bản Thành phố Hồ Chí Minh, 1994), vol. on Gia Định, 251–52.

34. Nguyễn Văn Kích, Phan Chánh Dưỡng, and Tôn Sĩ Kinh, *Nhà Bè Hồi sinh từ công nghiệp: Tập 1 Khu Chế xuất Tân Thuận—Bước đột phá* [Nha Be revived by industry: Volume 1,

The Tan Thuan Export Processing Zone—the breakthrough step] (Ho Chi Minh City: Nhà xuất bản Tổng hợp TP. Hồ Chí Minh, 2006), 151.

35. This value was calculated as an estimate of the total productive value of the land over the life of a household. This was arrived at by taking the sum total of the average annual income from agricultural output expected on that land, multiplied by a thirty-year period. With the value of the agricultural output in Tân Thuận assessed at three million đồng per year per hectare, the compensation value of the land over this thirty-year period thus amounted to ninety million đồng per hectare. Adding a buffer, presumably for the inconvenience of displacement, the IPC offered residents a total of 110 to 130 million đồng per hectare, which works out to between 11,000 and 13,000 đồng per square meter of land. With the exchange rate at that time averaging about 11,162 dong per U.S. Dollar, the land was thus valued at just under one U.S. dollar per square meter, or about 10,000 US$ per hectare (ibid., 156).

36. Nguyễn Văn Kích, Phan Chánh Dưỡng, and Tôn Sĩ Kinh, *Nhà Bè Hồi sinh từ công nghiệp: Tập 2 Phú Mỹ Hưng*, 119.

37. Ibid., 204–5; bold and italics in original.

38. For an extended discussion of this connection between political aspiration and aesthetics in Phú Mỹ Hưng, see Erik Harms, "Modern Views, Unblocked: Looking into the Distance in Phu My Hung, a Vietnamese New Urban Zone," *Anthropological Quarterly* 89, no. 2 (2016): 369–98.

39. For thoughtful and influential critiques of Đổi Mới, see esp. M. Gainsborough, *Vietnam: Rethinking the State* (London: Zed Books, 2010); Hy Van Luong, "Wealth, Power, and Inequality: Global Market, the State, and Local Sociocultural Dynamics," in *Postwar Vietnam: Dynamics of a Transforming Society* (Lanham, MD: Rowman & Littlefield, 2003), 81–106; and Philip Taylor, "Social Inequality in a Socialist State," in *Social Inequality in Vietnam and the Challenges to Reform*, ed. Philip Taylor (Singapore: ISEAS, 2004), 1–40.

40. Katherine Verdery, *What Was Socialism, and What Comes Next?* (Princeton, NJ: Princeton University Press, 1996), 205.

41. Ibid., 213.

42. Gainsborough, *Vietnam: Rethinking the State*, 16.

43. Nguyễn, Phan, and Tôn, *Nhà Bè Hồi sinh từ công nghiệp: Tập 2 Phú Mỹ Hưng*, 7.

44. Ibid., 8.

45. For a concise discussion of the "Chinese exodus" following the nationalization of industry and commerce in 1978, see William J. Duiker, *Vietnam since the Fall of Saigon*, Monographs in International Studies, Southeast Asia Series, no. 56A, updated ed. (Athens: Ohio University Center for International Studies, 1989), 58–69.

46. Du The Huynh, "The Transformation of Ho Chi Minh City: Issues in Managing Growth" (PhD thesis, Harvard University, 2012), 118. On the notion of the regime fearing for its legitimacy at this time, and the implications for allowing new economic experiments, see Labbé, *Land Politics and Livelihoods*, 67–70.

47. Gainsborough, *Vietnam: Rethinking the State*, 27; Gerard Sasges and Scott Cheshier, "Competing Legacies: Rupture and Continuity in Vietnamese Political Economy," *South East Asia Research* 20, no. 1 (2012): 18.

48. Huynh, "Transformation of Ho Chi Minh City," 118.

49. Sasges and Cheshier, "Competing Legacies," 18–19.

50. Nguyễn Văn Kích, Phan Chánh Dưỡng, and Tôn Sĩ Kinh, *Nhà Bè Hồi sinh từ công nghiệp: Tập 1 Khu Chế xuất Tân Thuận*, 63.

51. Huynh, "Transformation of Ho Chi Minh City," 119.

52. Ibid.

53. Nguyễn Văn Kích, Phan Chánh Dưỡng, and Tôn Sĩ Kinh, *Nhà Bè Hồi sinh từ công nghiệp: Tập 1 Khu Chế xuất Tân Thuận*, 89.

54. Huynh, "Transformation of Ho Chi Minh City," 118; Nguyễn Văn Kích, Phan Chánh Dưỡng, and Tôn Sĩ Kinh, *Nhà Bè Hồi sinh từ công nghiệp: Tập 1 Khu Chế xuất Tân Thuận*, 95.

55. In one particularly telling anecdote, Nguyễn Văn Kích, who was one of Phan Chánh Dưỡng's colleagues, described how excited the Vietnamese would get when they received a business card from foreign business people bearing such high-sounding titles as "General Director" or "Chairman of the Board" for this or that company. Surely, they assumed, these were great business leaders. Yet after spending several days and plenty of resources taking these "directors" and "chairmen" around the city, wining and dining them, they noted that nothing seemed to result from their efforts. After a while, the Vietnamese side figured out that no leader from a foreign company of any real significance would bother wasting a whole week hunting around in Ho Chi Minh City for opportunities, and that the lower the position printed on a business card, the more likely that person was affiliated with a big company. A truly big boss would appear only after his underlings had done due diligence investigating the situation.

56. Phú Mỹ Hưng, *Xin nhận nơi này làm quê hương: Những hồi ức về cố chủ tịch hội đồng quản trị Lawrence S. Ting* [Let this place become my homeland: Recollections of the former chairman of the board Lawrence S. Ting] (Ho Chi Minh City: Phú Mỹ Hưng Corp., 2005), 17.

57. Nguyễn Văn Kích, Phan Chánh Dưỡng, and Tôn Sĩ Kinh, *Nhà Bè Hồi sinh từ công nghiệp: Tập 2 Phú Mỹ Hưng—Đô thị Phát triển bền vững*, 50.

58. Discussed in Huynh, "Transformation of Ho Chi Minh City."

59. For a Vietnamese history of some of the early "fence breakers," see Đặng Phong, *"Phá rào" trong kinh tế vào đêm trước Đổi mới* [Economic "fence breaking" on the eve of Đổi Mới] (Hanoi: Nhà xuất bản Trí thức, 2009).

60. For a list of milestones, see Phu My Hung Corp., "Introduction," www.phumyhung.com.vn/eng/introduce.php?id=1.

61. This very statement, as well as the comparison between Phú Mỹ Hưng and Thủ Thiêm, was almost exactly the same story recounted by others in multiple contexts during my fieldwork.

62. By the time of this interview, in 2011, the Thu Thiem Investment and Construction Authority hadn't even finished what they euphemistically termed "land clearance."

63. Hsiang Yi-Chang, "The Quiet Princes—Carving out a Kingdom in Vietnam," *China Post*, Nov. 1, 2010.

64. In the classic Vietnamese story of "clearing the wasteland," the plot often hinges on the selfless acts of a historic founding figure. In the standard storyline, these figures are then transformed into revered ancestors, and in traditional Vietnam they are sometimes even worshipped as tutelary deities in village communal halls *(đình)*. Lawrence S. Ting's memory

is constructed in a strikingly similar way, and the way he is remembered with hagiographic reverence might also be understood as part of this larger narrative structure that integrates the New Urban Zone into a story of civilizational progress.

65. Yi-Chang, "Quiet Princes."

66. Lan Anh Nguyen, "Battleground," *Forbes,* Sept. 19, 2008. "He was a military man, and honor was the most important thing to him. Some people went out of their way to discredit him, using various means that were not honest," said Arthur Ting, his younger son. "But there are people . . . who see Lawrence Ting's suicide as an act to save his family business and his legacy."

67. Ibid.

68. Lawrence S. Ting Memorial Fund, "About Us," www.lawrencestingfund.org//aboutus.

69. Students of the Lawrence S. Ting School, "Nhà trường: MỤC ĐÍCH THÀNH LẬP" [Purpose for establishing the school]," Lawrence S. Ting School, http://lsts.edu.vn/?opt=info&act=view&id=651211d43d9caa6e02c990b0a82652dca.

70. Phú Mỹ Hưng, *Xin nhận nơi này làm quê hương,* 8.

71. Ibid., 15.

72. Ibid., 18.

73. Ibid., 33–34.

74. Ibid., 41.

75. Ibid., 52.

76. Ibid., 71–71.

77. Ibid., 84.

78. Ibid., 141.

79. Ibid., 19.

80. Gavin Shatkin, "Planning Privatopolis: Representation and Contestation in the Development of Urban Integrated Mega-Projects," in *Worlding Cities: Asian Experiments and the Art of Being Global,* ed. Ananya Roy and Aihwa Ong (Malden, MA: Wiley-Blackwell, 2011), 79.

81. More than a decade ago, the anthropologist Philip Taylor described how the Đổi Mới storyline told in Vietnam commonly evokes a "rhetorical distancing from past practices" in which practices associated with the market economy are bathed in the light of modernity, while those associated with certain failed experiments in high-socialism are consigned to darkness. See Philip Taylor, *Fragments of the Present: Searching for Modernity in Vietnam's South* (Honolulu: University of Hawai'i Press, 2001), 65 and chap. 2 passim.

## 2. CIVILIZATION CITY

1. For a fascinating discussion of the polymorphous meanings of *văn minh* as it was introduced to Vietnam by the Reform Movement in the early 1900s, see Mark P. Bradley, "Becoming *Van Minh*: Civilizational Discourse and Visions of the Self in Twentieth-Century Vietnam," *Journal of World History* 15, no. 1 (2004): 65–83.

2. In Vietnamese the Phú Mỹ Hưng slogan reads, "Đô thị văn minh—Cộng đồng nhân văn." This might be more gracefully rendered in English as "A Civilized and Humanistic

Community." Regardless of the translation, the core message of the slogan is clear: Phú Mỹ Hưng is supposed to be a "civilized" *(văn minh)* urban development that has the capacity to inspire people to live together with a sense of community *(cộng đồng)* that will bring out the best humanistic *(nhân văn)* qualities.

3. For the full text of this sign, and further discussion of its implications, see Erik Harms, "Civility's Footprint: Ethnographic Conversations about Urban Civility and Sustainability in Ho Chi Minh City," *SOJOURN: Journal of Social Issues in Southeast Asia* 29, no. 2 (July 2014): 247.

4. For a critical study of the term *wenming* (civility) in China, see Ann Anagnost, *National Past-Times: Narrative, Representation and Power in Modern China* (Durham, NC: Duke University Press, 1997). For a critical study of how this term represents a new kind of subjectivity in Chinese urban developments, see Zhang, *In Search of Paradise*, 19, 125–27.

5. Zhang, *In Search of Paradise*, 19.

6. There is good reason to adopt this approach, of course. Academics in the United States are well aware, for example, of the way calls for "civility" in academic discourse can operate as thinly veiled attempts to suppress academic free speech. See Peter Schmidt, "Pleas for Civility Meet Cynicism," *Chronicle of Higher Education*, Sept. 10, 2014.

7. Bradley, "Becoming *Van Minh.*"

8. Peter Zinoman, *Vietnamese Colonial Republican: The Political Vision of Vu Trong Phung* (Berkeley: University of California Press, 2013), 152. Zinoman's discussion (116) of "the idiotic social reformer Mr. Civilization" in Vũ Trọng Phụng's satirical novel *Dumb Luck* is an especially useful window into how the rhetoric of civility might be critiqued as empty language.

9. On the connection between culture and the building of New Socialist Man in revolutionary Vietnam, see Shaun K. Malarney, *Culture, Ritual, and Revolution in Vietnam* (London: RoutledgeCurzon, 2002); and Kim N. B. Ninh, *A World Transformed: The Politics of Culture in Revolutionary Vietnam, 1945–1965* (Ann Arbor: University of Michigan Press, 2002).

10. For a concise and useful review of the socialist policies toward ethnic minorities, see Pamela McElwee, "Becoming Socialist or Becoming Kinh? Government Policies for Ethnic Minorities in the Socialist Republic of Viet Nam," in *Civilizing the Margins: Southeast Asian Government Policies for the Development of Minorities,* ed. Christopher Duncan (Ithaca, NY: Cornell University Press, 2004), 182–213. For a critical discussion of the treatment of highland ethnic minorities by the southern Republic of Vietnam, with especially useful descriptions of treatment by officials under Ngô Đình Diệm, see Gerald Cannon Hickey, *Free in the Forest: Ethnohistory of the Vietnamese Central Highlands, 1954–1976* (New Haven, CT: Yale University Press, 1982).

11. For an extended discussion of the use of *văn minh* as a term of disparagement, see Harms, *Saigon's Edge*, 193–220.

12. The notion of "sly civility" refers to a dialectical oscillation between the hegemonic and counterhegemonic, or colonial and anticolonial, implications of civility. See Homi K. Bhabha, "Sly Civility," *October* 34 (1985): 71–80.

13. Tania Murray Li, *The Will to Improve: Governmentality, Development, and the Practice of Politics* (Durham, NC: Duke University Press, 2007).

14. That is, after all, precisely how the story of "clearing the wasteland" described in the previous chapter was constructed.

15. Li, *Will to Improve*, 9. People often truly want to improve the world in which they live, and the concept of civility often emerges as an idiom through which they can articulate that desire.

16. The following story is based on more than a month of conversations, conducted almost daily between April 2011 and May 2011. For every hour we spent in one-on-one conversation, Ngọc would spend at least half of the time making and responding to phone calls. Sometimes we'd talk for an hour straight, and other times I'd wait an hour while she concluded a deal or shifted tables to meet with a client. Ethnography can be slow.

17. On the economy of sex work and the commodification of the body, see Kimberly Kay Hoang, "She's Not a Dirty Low Class Girl: Sex Work in Ho Chi Minh City," *Journal of Contemporary Ethnography* 40, no. 4 (2011): 367–96; idem, "Economies of Emotion, Familiarity, Fantasy, and Desire: Emotional Labor in Ho Chi Minh City's Sex Industry," *Sexualities* 13, no. 2 (2010): 255–72.

18. For a similar, and more detailed, story of female family members in the Mekong Delta guiding daughters into sex work, see Nicolas Lainez, "Commodified Sexuality and Mother-Daughter Power Dynamics in the Mekong Delta," *Journal of Vietnamese Studies* 7, no. 1 (2012): 149–80.

19. It is debatable whether the Vietnamese really have a philosophy about the cursed fate of a beautiful woman, but interpretations of the Vietnamese classic poem "The Tale of Kiều" do often turn on the fact that the tragic heroine was both talented and beautiful but subject to the cruel fate of living a life in prostitution.

20. Until then, Ngọc's husband had been demanding custody of her daughter, not because he wanted anything to do with the child but because he wanted to see Ngọc suffer and to punish her for daring to think of leaving him.

21. Ngọc's description of vulgar elites arriving by luxury automobile recalls a famous scene from Vũ Trọng Phụng's *Dumb Luck* when two of the central characters, Mr. and Mrs. Civilization (Ông Bà Văn Minh), arrive at the tennis courts in colonial Hanoi in "a sleek automobile" before acting in crass, ostentatious, and self-important ways that call attention to their distinct lack of civility. For the hilarious scene, see Vũ Trọng Phụng, *Dumb Luck*, 37.

22. Le Minh Khue, "Scenes from an Alley," in *Night, Again: Contemporary Fiction from Vietnam*, ed. Linh Dinh (New York: Seven Stories Press, 2006), 63–64.

23. I put the word for district *(phường)* in parentheses to indicate that Ngọc was referring to those authorities associated with the Vietnamese urban administrative structure, which she carefully distinguished from the administration of the New Urban Zone.

24. The opposition between human civility and animal nature, it just so happens, is also a symbolic theme in Lê Minh Khuê's story.

25. Interestingly, when Ho Chi Minh City residents describe car ownership, they use the term *nuôi* (lit., "to raise"), which is the same term that would be used to describe raising a child or farm animal. This indicates that caring for a car is a significant investment.

26. On the connection between inclusion and exclusion generally, see Hall, Hirsch, and Li, *Powers of Exclusion*, 4, 7–14. On this connection as it relates specifically to cities in Asia,

see Erik Harms, "Urban Space and Exclusion in Asia," *Annual Review of Anthropology* 45 (Oct. 2016).

27. Postnuptial patrilocality followed by neolocal residence was a common pattern of household formation for Saigon locals.

28. One tael (*cây*, or *lượng*) is 37.5 grams of 24-karat gold. In 2001, one tael was worth six million Vietnamese đồng, while one U.S. dollar was worth approximately 15,400 đồng, making 165 taels worth approximately US$64,285. These values are necessarily rough approximations, because gold prices and đồng-to-dollar exchange rates are constantly in flux. On the importance of gold in Ho Chi Minh City, see Allison Truitt, *Dreaming of Money in Ho Chi Minh City* (Seattle: University of Washington Press, 2013), 69–72.

29. Hương calls me "professor" or "teacher" *(thầy)* because her children originally introduced me to her as "the professor from America."

30. This sense that apartment living represented a dramatic departure from traditional Vietnamese forms of living is widespread. Newspapers and periodicals often run articles discussing the pros and cons of the shift to life in apartments. The vice director of the Ho Chi Minh City Architects Association once told me that the central dilemma facing Vietnam was how to develop an urban form of living that does not lose the Vietnamese "cultural essence" *(bản sắc văn hóa)*. He also gave me a magazine article on how city residents were reconciling apartment living with their traditional lifestyles. See Vĩnh Phương and Tùng Quang, "Sống ở chung cư: những điều được mất" [Living in an apartment building: Things gained and lost], *Kiến trúc & đời sống* [Architecture and living], 2010, 84.

31. This financial arrangement—using income from a downtown property to either rent or pay off a loan for a Phú Mỹ Hưng apartment—was a popular way in which long-term Ho Chi Minh City residents would experiment with living in Phú Mỹ Hưng. In this way, they were able to mitigate the deep fear they had of not owning actual "land," while also enjoying what they described as modern apartment living.

32. For more on the way traffic is used to express a notion of civility and political order, see Harms, "Civility's Footprint."

33. Henri Lefebvre, *The Production of Space* (1974; London: Blackwell, 1991), 54.

34. Zhang, *In Search of Paradise,* 107–36.

35. Norbert Elias, *The Civilizing Process* (1939; Malden, MA: Blackwell, 2000), 51.

36. Ibid., 48.

37. Vũ Trọng Phụng, *Dumb Luck,* 113.

38. Ibid., 40.

### 3. EXERCISING CONSCIOUSNESS: SELF AND SOCIETY IN A PRIVATIZING SPACE OF EXCLUSION

1. This sentence purposefully evokes Habermas's conception of the public sphere. According to Habermas, a "portion of the public sphere is constituted in every conversation in which private citizens come together to form a public." See Jürgen Habermas, "The Public Sphere," in *Jürgen Habermas on Society and Politics: A Reader,* ed. Steven Seidman (Boston: Beacon Press, 1989), 231. For critical perspectives on this concept, see Nick Crossley and John Michael Roberts, eds., *After Habermas: New Perspectives on the Public Sphere* (Oxford: Blackwell, 2004).

2. Zhang, *In Search of Paradise*, 10.

3. Ibid., 13.

4. Lizzy Van Leeuwen, *Lost in Mall: An Ethnography of Middle-Class Jakarta in the 1990s* (Leiden: KITLV Press, 2011), 157.

5. For a synthetic discussion regarding debates about the political role of the middle class in Asia, see ibid. For a powerful assertion that Vietnamese middle classes do not promise to foment political change, see Martin Gainsborough, "Political Change in Vietnam: In Search of the Middle-Class Challenge to the State," *Asian Survey* 42, no. 5 (Sept./Oct. 2002): 694–707; idem, *Vietnam*.

6. In this book, I have consciously chosen to avoid any attempt to define "the middle class." I do this largely because it would distract from the ethnography. Furthermore, this topic has already been expertly addressed by Van Nguyen-Marshall, Lisa B. Welch Drummond, and Danièle Bélanger, *The Reinvention of Distinction: Modernity and the Middle Class in Urban Vietnam* (Dordrecht, Neth.: Springer, 2012), 9. They emphasize a definition of social class grounded in identity performances and the habitus, rather than a quantitative assessment of relative wealth. I largely agree with their method of referring to "'social classes' as social groups sharing certain lifestyles, which, in turn, are related to certain types of social relations shaped by the symbolic power embedded in those lifestyles. [. . .] In this view, 'middle class' is a social group (including sub-groups) which adheres to a certain lifestyle (or set of lifestyles), or is encouraged to do so by market or state actors, in order to assert its social position in the respective class structures of colonial capitalism or socialist capitalism (post-1986)."

7. See, e.g., Douglass and Huang, "Globalizing the City in Southeast Asia"; Michael Waibel, "The Production of Urban Space in Vietnam's Metropolis in the Course of Transition: Internationalization, Polarization and Newly Emerging Lifestyles in Vietnamese Society," *Trialog* 89, no. 2 (2006): 43–48.

8. There is a small genre of journalistic writing popular in the Western news media devoted to ironic descriptions of the new rich in Asia. For examples referring to Vietnam, starting from the 1990s and persisting to this day, see Nicholas Cumming-Bruce, "Vietnam's Communists Rely on the New Rich," *Guardian*, Jan. 1, 1990; idem, "Vietnam Learns the Way of the Market; Nick Cumming-Bruce in Hanoi Finds a Brave New World Flawed by the Emerging Gap between the New Rich and the Poor," *Guardian*, July 17, 1993; idem, "Old Guard Secures the Way for Vietnam's New Rich," *Guardian*, July 17, 1996; John Gittings, "Other Worlds: Socialism Chases the Tainted Spoils of Capitalism," *Guardian*, Jan. 13, 1995; William Barnes, "Vietnam Eager to Learn Capitalism's Lessons," FT.com [*Financial Times* online], Nov. 20, 2006; Roger Cohen, "Status in the New Asia," *International New York Times*, May 13, 2014; and Sheridan Prasso, "Boomtown, Vietnam," *New York Times Travel Magazine*, Nov. 19 2006.

9. For an extended discussion of the way some Phú Mỹ Hưng residents manage what can and cannot be seen about their wealth, see Erik Harms, "The Boss: Conspicuous Invisibility in Ho Chi Minh City," *City & Society* 25, no. 2 (2013): 195–215. Similar attempts to manage what Ann Marie Leshkowich calls "the political economy of appearances" have been observed by ethnographers working among market traders in Ho Chi Minh City's Bến Thành market, as well as among the city's sex workers. See Kimberly Kay Hoang, *Dealing in*

*Desire: Asian Ascendancy, Western Decline, and the Hidden Currencies of Global Sex Work* (Oakland: University of California Press, 2015), 17; Ann Marie Leshkowich, *Essential Trade: Vietnamese Women in a Changing Marketplace* (Honolulu: University of Hawai'i Press, 2014), 21.

10. For a useful critique of studies of the "new rich in Asia," as well as a useful review of literature on the middle-class in Asia more broadly construed, see Van Leeuwen, *Lost in Mall*, 1–28. For a comprehensive discussion of this literature as it relates to the literature on the middle class in Ho Chi Minh City, see Catherine Earl, *Vietnam's New Middle Classes: Gender, Career, City* (Copenhagen: NIAS Press, 2014), 1–42. For an outstanding analysis of middle-classness as a performance and means of navigating political economic structures in Ho Chi Minh City, see Ann Marie Leshkowich, *Essential Trade: Vietnamese Women in a Changing Marketplace* (Honolulu: University of Hawai'i Press, 2014), 174–94.

11. This is not to say that wealth and ostentatious display does not exist. But it is only one part of the performance of class that one finds in Phú Mỹ Hưng.

12. In a useful critique of Phú Mỹ Hưng, Mike Douglass and Liling Huang borrow from the work of geographer Michael J. Dear to describe the role of the corporation as developing into a form of "shadow government," where the power of corporate governance sometimes overrides the authority of the state. They perceptively note the important ramifications this has for how we understand state sovereignty in these kinds of new urban zones. See Douglass and Huang, "Globalizing the City in Southeast Asia," 28–29.

13. A person sitting alone in a café, for example, or an empty city street, might be described as *buồn*. The lone man sitting at the counter in Edward Hopper's famous painting *Nighthawks* would definitely be *buồn*.

14. For an excellent study of Ho Chi Minh City's "alleyway culture," see Tôn Nữ Quỳnh Trân and Nguyễn Trọng Hòa, *Văn hóa hẻm phố Sài Gòn—Thành phố Hồ Chí Minh* [Alleyway culture in Saigon—Ho Chi Minh City] (Ho Chi Minh City: Nhà xuất bản Tổng hợp, 2007).

15. Teresa Caldeira, "Fortified Enclaves: The New Urban Segregation," in *Cities and Citizenship*, ed. James Holston (Durham, NC: Duke University Press, 1999), 119.

16. In the late 1990s, critical urbanists and anthropologists of North American cities produced important work on the proliferation of a sense of "urban fear." See, e.g., ibid.; Mike Davis, "Fortress Los Angeles: The Militarization of Urban Space," in *Variations on a Theme Park: The New American City and the End of Public Space*, ed. Michael Sorkin (New York: Hill & Wang, 1992); Setha Low, "Urban Fear: Building the Fortress City," *City & Society* 9, no. 1 (1997): 53–71. Subsequent research by anthropologists working in other global contexts showed similar discourses of fear in other societies, but also recognized different ways in which such fear was manifested. It is not always a fear of physical violence but sometimes a fear of "disorder" that permeates the language driving master-planned developments. See, e.g., Anne Waldrop, "Gating and Class Relations: The Case of a New Delhi 'Colony,'" *City & Society* 16, no. 2 (Dec. 2004): 93–116.

17. Similarly, Sasha Newell reports that men in Côte d'Ivoire commonly riff off of the titles of newspaper articles, often without reading the entire article. The phenomenon there is known as "titrologie," and "titrologues" are often derided as half-informed gossips. Among Vietnamese intellectuals, the practice is slightly different. They do commonly read

the entire article, but they also subject the content to critical skepticism, trying, as it were, to get beyond the headlines toward some semblance of truth. But in the quest for such truth, they, too, often embellish the news with speculation and gossip.

18. On one occasion, I first learned during one of these morning conversations that an academic article I had written about Vietnam's real estate fever had been posted to the overseas website VietStudies. "I saw your article on VietStudies," one of Uncle Việt's friends told me: "It was hard to understand!"

19. For a similar description of this encounter, and more detailed discussion of the way residents often sought to read political orientation in the built landscape, see Harms, "Modern Views, Unblocked."

20. For important discussions of the rise in an ethic of self-responsibility in Ho Chi Minh City, see Ann Marie Leshkowich, "Finances, Family, Fashion, Fitness, and . . . Freedom? The Changing Lives of Urban Middle-Class Vietnamese Women," in Nguyen-Marshall, Drummond, and Bélanger (eds.,) *Reinvention of Distinction,* chap. 6; idem, "Standardized Forms of Vietnamese Selfhood: An Ethnographic Genealogy of Documentation," *American Ethnologist* 41, no. 1 (2014): 143–62; and Christina Schwenkel and Ann Marie Leshkowich, "Guest Editors' Introduction: How Is Neoliberalism Good to Think Vietnam? How Is Vietnam Good to Think Neoliberalism?" *positions* 20, no. 2 (2012): 379–401.

21. See Harms, "Civility's Footprint," 233, 240.

22. I have changed the location slightly.

23. For a useful discussion of Phú Mỹ Hưng's controversy over land-use fees, see John Gillespie, "Public Land Disputes in Vietnam: A Multi-Actor Analysis of Five Case Studies with an East Asian Comparative" (Hanoi: Transformation and Change Management Consulting Co., Ltd., for the Asia Foundation, 2014). For a parallel discussion about how homeowners develop a sense of collective identity through their fights with developers over fees and other aspects of management, see Zhang, *In Search of Paradise,* 187–210.

24. Bill Hayton, *The South China Sea: The Struggle for Power in Asia* (New Haven, CT: Yale University Press, 2014), 151.

25. Yael Navaro-Yashin, *Faces of the State: Secularism and Public Life in Turkey* (Princeton, NJ: Princeton University Press, 2002), 3.

26. For more on the poetry of Hồ Xuân Hương, see Hồ Xuân Hương, *Spring Essence: The Poetry of Hồ Xuân Hương,* trans. John Balaban (Port Townsend, WA: Copper Canyon Press, 2000); and Mỹ-Vân Trần, "'Come On, Girls, Let's Go Bail Water': Eroticism in Hồ Xuân Hương's Vietnamese Poetry," *Journal of Southeast Asian Studies* 33, no. 3 (2002): 471–94.

27. The translation of the poem is my own. Neil Jamieson translates it like this: "My body is like a jackfruit on the tree / With rough skin and lots of pulp. / If a man likes it, he should poke in a stake. / Don't squeeze! You'll get juice all over your hands." For the translation and a discussion of the poem, see Neil Jamieson, "Some Things Poetry Can Tell Us about the Process of Social Change in Vietnam," *Southeast Asian Studies* 39, no. 3 (2001): 325–57.

28. This tongue-twisting phrase plays on the homonym *cả,* which can mean "all" *(cả),* "both of them" *(cả hai),* or "first," when referring to kinship relations (e.g., "first-born child," *con cả,* or "first wife," *vợ cả).*

29. Michael Herzfeld, *The Poetics of Manhood: Contest and Identity in a Cretan Mountain Village* (Princeton, NJ: Princeton University Press, 1985).

30. James Holston, *The Modernist City: An Anthropological Critique of Brasilia* (Chicago: University of Chicago Press, 1989), 107, 24.

31. Zhang, *In Search of Paradise*, 121.

32. Teresa Pires do Rio Caldeira, *City of Walls: Crime, Segregation, and Citizenship in São Paulo* (Berkeley: University of California Press, 2000); idem, "Fortified Enclaves"; D. Davis, "New Rich in China"; Douglass and Huang, "Globalizing the City in Southeast Asia"; Fraser, "Inventing Oasis"; Ghertner, "Rule by Aesthetics"; idem, "Nuisance Talk: Middle-Class Discourses of a Slum-Free Delhi," in *Ecologies of Urbanism in India: Metropolitan Civility and Sustainability*, ed. Anne Rademacher and K. Sivaramakrishnan (Hong Kong: Hong Kong University Press, 2013), 249–75; Hsing, *Great Urban Transformation*; Shatkin, "Planning Privatopolis"; Tomba, "Of Quality, Harmony, and Community"; idem, "Middle Classes in China"; Van Leeuwen, *Lost in Mall*; Zhang and Ong, *Privatizing China*.

33. Émile Durkheim, *The Division of Labor in Society*, trans. W. D. Halls (1893; New York: Free Press, 1997).

34. Marcel Mauss, "A Category of the Human Mind: The Notion of Person, the Notion of Self," trans. Ben Brewster, in Mauss, *Sociology and Psychology: Essays* (1938; London: Routledge & Kegan Paul, 1979), 59–94.

35. For an excellent study of this development among public intellectuals like journalists in colonial Saigon, see Philippe M. F. Peycam, *The Birth of Vietnamese Political Journalism: Saigon 1916–1930* (New York: Columbia University Press, 2012).

36. Habermas, "The Public Sphere," 231–36.

37. Waibel, "Production of Urban Space in Vietnam's Metropolis," 48.

4. THỦ THIÊM FUTURES PAST: A SHORT HISTORY OF
SEEING WITHOUT SEEING

1. This embankment, called Bạch Đằng Wharf since 1955, was known to the French as Quai de Donnai, later Quai de Napoléon, Quai de Commerce, Quai Francis Garnier, and finally Quai le Myre de Villers. See Nguyễn Q. Thắng and Nguyễn Đình Tư, *Đường phố Thành phố Hồ Chí Minh* [Ho Chi Minh city streets] (Ho Chi Minh City: Nhà xuất bản Văn hóa Thông tin, 2001), 106–7.

2. On the negative connotations of "outer-city districts" in Vietnam, see Harms, *Saigon's Edge*; idem, "Material Symbolism of Saigon's Edge."

3. The anthropologist Allison Truitt, visiting Thủ Thiêm in 2001, noted how the ferry ride across the river "made the district seem all the more remote" (Truitt, "Domestic Investor *[Người đầu tư trong nước]*," in *Figures of Southeast Asian Modernity*, ed. Joshua Barker, Erik Harms, and Johan Lindquist [Honolulu: University of Hawai'i Press, 2013], 54). Until quite recently, foreign study abroad programs operating in Ho Chi Minh City would explicitly warn their students not to visit District 2, based on the advice of their local partners. These negative associations about spaces across the river are not new. For a description of the conditions of the urban poor in marginal places beyond the city center in colonial Saigon, consult the arresting descriptions of poverty and disease offered by Haydon Cherry,

"Down and Out in Saigon: A Social History of the Poor in a Colonial City, 1860–1940" (Ph.D. diss., Yale University, 2011), 225–38. Thủ Thiêm was, until 2009, the site of the Thanh Bình leper colony (Trại cùi or Trại phong Thanh Bình, located on just over 7 hectares on an island within the river in Bình Khánh Ward). The colony was violently cleared by eviction forces on August 24, 2009.

4. The phrase, in Vietnamese, goes as follows: "Ăn quận năm; Chơi quận nhất, Ngủ quận ba, Quýnh nhau quận tư, Thủ Thiêm."

5. In Vietnamese urban imaginaries, "the other side of the river" has long held roughly the same connotation as the American phrase "the wrong side of the tracks." Similar connotations exist for spaces across the Red River in Hanoi, and across the Hậu River in the Mekong Delta city of Cần Thơ. Stereotypes New Yorkers hold of Jersey City across the Hudson, or that Calcutta residents hold for residents of Howrah, across the Hoogly, come to mind as similar ways of imagining such spaces. In French colonial urbanism, furthermore, urban centers tended to be placed on "high ground," "plateau" areas located within the bend of a river. However, precolonial urban centers such as Luang Prabang indicate that this was not only a colonial phenomenon. Comparing the morphology of Saigon with Shanghai is also instructive: the bend of the Saigon River looks like a smaller-scale version of the Huangpu, and the social constructions of the Pudong area of Shanghai as "empty wasteland" mirror those in Saigon.

6. For a provocative discussion of the ways formal mapmaking techniques obscure important aspects of social life in Ho Chi Minh City, see Annette Kim, *Sidewalk City*.

7. This formulation builds on the important arguments presented in James C. Scott, *Seeing Like a State: How Certain Schemes to Improve the Human Condition Have Failed* (New Haven, CT: Yale University Press, 1998). However, while Scott poses a binary distinction between state forms of legibility (i.e., juxtaposing the top-down state against the bottom-up people), my research has revealed that it is not just "the state" that does or does not see, but a range of different actors. In the case of Thủ Thiêm, state records clearly "see" the area as populated, in spite of popular perceptions that it is empty.

8. See the records recorded in Nguyễn Đình Đầu, *Nghiên cứu địa ba Triều Nguyễn*.

9. On the Thủ Thiêm market, see Tôn Nữ Quỳnh Trân, *Thủ Thiêm—Quá khứ và tương lai* [Thu Thiem: Past and future] (Ho Chi Minh City: Nhà xuất bản Tổng hợp, 2010), 12; Thạch Phương and Lê Trung Hoa, *Từ điển Thành phố Sài Gòn—Thành phố Hồ Chí Minh* [Dictionary of Saigon City—Ho Chi Minh City] (Ho Chi Minh City: Nhà xuất bản Trẻ, 2001), 384; Trịnh Hoài Đức, *Gia Định thành thông chí* [Observations of Gia Dinh] (1820; Ho Chi Minh City: Nhà xuất bản Giáo dục, 1999), 195. On the history of the Thủ Thiêm Church, see Giáo Xứ Thủ Thiêm [Thủ Thiêm Parish], *Kỷ Yếu mừng 150 năm thành lập Giáo Xứ Thủ Thiêm: 1859–2009* [Commemorative volume celebrating 150 years since the founding of Thủ Thiêm Parish: 1859–2009] (Ho Chi Minh City: Giáo xứ Thủ Thiêm, 2009.).

10. Wurster, Bernardi & Emmons, Inc., "Thu Thiem Peninsula Development Plan: Agency for International Development Contract AID/vn-101," Wurster, Bernardi & Emmons, Inc., Saigon, 1972, 25.

11. When the city was incorporated into the Nguyễn realm by Nguyễn Hữu Cảnh, in 1698, Thủ Thiêm was registered as part of Phước Long District, within dinh Trấn Biên, then part of xứ Đồng Nai, a subdivision of *phủ* Gia Định. Tôn Nữ Quỳnh Trân notes that

Vietnamese had come to settle the region well before 1623, the year when Lord Nguyễn Phước Nguyên established a tax station there, after the Cambodian king Cheyi Chétha II married Nguyễn Phúc Nguyên's daughter, making her his princess. In the years preceding, it is assumed that most of the Vietnamese settlers established themselves in fortuitous points along the banks of the Saigon and Đồng Nai rivers. See Tôn Nữ Quỳnh Trân, *Thủ Thiêm—Quá khứ và tương lai*, 11. Although the evidence for such assertions is not very descriptive, it is commonly noted in Vietnamese histories of Saigon. See, e.g.,, Trần Văn Giàu, *Địa chí văn hóa Thành phố Hồ Chí Minh*, 237.

12. John White, *Voyage to Cochin China* (London: Longman, Hurst, Rees, Orme, Brown & Green, 1824), 199. Excessive use of commas follows the original.

13. Ibid. White calls the area where they moored "Banga" but describes its location as being exactly in the spot now called Thủ Thiêm. There is no place named "Banga" in Saigon, although this term may be a corruption of the toponym "Bến Nghé." Given the unique spellings based on phonetic approximations White ascribes to other places in the book (e.g., "Canjeo" for "Cần Giờ"), it is also possible that White is referring to the place named Bến-ngự, which Pétrus Ký described as the "king's wharf" and which was located in a spot near present-day Thủ Thiêm. See Trương Vĩnh Ký, *Souvenirs historiques sur Saigon et ses environs* [Historical recollections on Saigon and its surroundings] (Saigon: Imprimerie Coloniale, 1885), 18.

14. White, *Voyage to Cochin China*, 199. A glacis is a slope running away from a fortification. The phrase in quotes is from Shakespeare's *King Lear* and is generally glossed as "pond scum."

15. Tôn Nữ Quỳnh Trân, *Thủ Thiêm—Quá khứ và tương lai*, 15. According to early documents, the *đồn* (military post) in Thủ Thiêm was commanded by Tôn Thất Mân, and this post is clearly visible in the map drawn by Le Brun in 1795. In *Gia Định thành thông chí*, by Trịnh Hoài Đức, the *đồn* Cá Trê is called Đồn Thiêm (ibid., 14).

16. For more on these forts, see Louis Malleret, "Eléments d'une monographie des anciennes fortifications et citadelles de Saïgon," *Bulletin de la Société des études indochinois, Saïgon,* 1935, plates following page 108.

17. White, *Voyage to Cochin China*, 201–3.

18. Ibid., 209–12.

19. Ibid., 232.

20. For historical descriptions of this environment, see Biggs, *Quagmire;* Nola Cooke and Li Tana, *Water Frontier: Commerce and the Chinese in the Lower Mekong Region, 1750–1880* (Lanham, MD: Rowman & Littlefield, 2004). For midcentury images of what Terry McGee describes as "aquatic urbanism" in Bangkok, Phnom-Penh, and Singapore, see the plates in T. G. McGee, *The Southeast Asian City* (New York: Praeger, 1967), 96–97.

21. Nguyễn Đình Đầu, *Nghiên cứu địa ba Triều Nguyễn;* Trịnh Hoài Đức, *Gia Định thành thông chí,* 195.

22. Such depictions are not confined to Vietnam, of course. For a compelling analysis of this phenomenon in Nepal, see Anne Rademacher, "When Is Housing an Environmental Problem? Reforming Informality in Kathmandu," *Current Anthropology* 20, no. 4 (2009): 513–33.

23. Caroline Herbelin, "Des habitations à bon marché au Việt Nam: La question du logement social en situation coloniale" [Public housing projects in Vietnam: The problem of habitation in a colonial situation], *Moussons* 13–14 (2009): 123–46.

24. The speculative etymology is recounted in Giáo Xứ Thủ Thiêm, *Kỷ Yếu mừng 150 năm thành lập Giáo Xứ Thủ Thiêm*, 16.

25. The connections between waterways and early urban form can be seen in one of the contemporary city's main boulevards, Hàm Nghi, which was formed by filling a canal in 1870. See Nguyễn Q. Thắng and Nguyễn Đình Tư, *Đường phố Thành phố Hồ Chí Minh*, 37.

26. Trương Vĩnh Ký, *Souvenirs historiques sur Saigon et ses environs*, 18, 19.

27. There is an extraordinarily sensible environmental logic to the way development in Thủ Thiêm proceeded, shying away from soft, acidic, and often inundated soils of the interior land while clustering alongside and even floating upon the river in great numbers, all while incorporating the cooling effects of the river into lived landscape.

28. Giáo Xứ Thủ Thiêm, *Kỷ Yếu mừng 150 năm thành lập Giáo Xứ Thủ Thiêm*, 21.

29. Ibid.

30. I attended many Sunday masses from 2010 to 2014, and they were always full of worshipers, even after the surrounding neighborhoods had been demolished.

31. The modern Vietnamese Catholic Church has developed politically cautious modes of interacting with the Vietnamese government, defending the faith while retaining "cordial" relations with state officials by avoiding making overtly controversial statements. See, e.g., Jacob Ramsay, "Miracles and Myths: Vietnam Seen Through its Catholic History," in *Modernity and Reenchantment: Religion in Postrevolutionary Vietnam*, ed. Philip Taylor (Lanham, MD: Lexington Books, 2007), 376.

32. The above observations about church and convent activities are a summary based on weekly visits to the church over the course of my ethnographic research, between the years 2010 and 2014.

33. For the list of religious structures, see Tôn Nữ Quỳnh Trân, *Thủ Thiêm—Quá khứ và tương lai*, 83. That list includes only twenty-eight religious structures, yet it inadvertently omits *đình* An Lợi Đông, which is however described in subsequent pages. The work also does not include family shrines built on individual household properties, of which there are many more as well.

34. For more detailed descriptions of all of these religious institutions, see ibid., 83–191.

35. Ibid., 84–87.

36. Locals say that the *đình* was established by a man named Lê Văn Đời in the year Kỷ Đậu, which locals assume to have been 1849. However, relatives of the ancestor report that this man would not have been alive at that time, so the Kỷ Đậu year in question must have been 1909, not 1849. For the full explanation, see ibid., 92.

37. Ibid., 189.

38. Ibid., 18.

39. Chapter 6 describes the demolition of one such structure.

40. Tôn Nữ Quỳnh Trân, *Thủ Thiêm—Quá khứ và tương lai*, 19.

41. Interview with Nguyễn Đình Đầu, Ho Chi Minh City, October 28, 2010.

42. Several Vietnamese scholars with a longer historical memory have expressed their concerns that the Thủ Thiêm area will be at risk of flooding, citing historic observations by the French, as well as by Vietnamese planners active during the American period, including the prodigious Ngô Viết Thụ. See Việt Hùng and Đ. Huân, "Khu đô thị mới Thủ Thiêm sẽ

ngập trong nước [The Thu Thiem New Urban Zone will be submerged under water]," *Tuổi Trẻ*, April 15, 2006.

43. Ernest Hébrard, "L'urbanisme en Indochine," *L'Architecture* 41, no. 2 (1928): 38.

44. *Xây Dựng Mới*, Oct./Nov. 1957.

45. See ibid. for plans detailing the development of Thủ Thiêm during Ngô Đình Diệm's administration. I am grateful to Matt Masur for bringing this reference to my attention.

46. Doxiadis Associates, *Saigon Metropolitan Area: Volume 1, Urban Development Program and Plan* (Athens, Greece: Prepared for the Government of the Republic of Vietnam, Ministry of Public Works, Directorate General of Reconstruction and City Planning, 1965), Preface, 1–2.

47. Ibid., Preface, 4.

48. Ibid.

49. Ibid., Preface, 5.

50. For a thoughtful discussion of Doxiadis, and an assessment of his plan's legacy in Islamabad, the capital city he designed for Pakistan in 1960, see Matthew Hull, *Government of Paper: The Materiality of Bureaucracy in Urban Pakistan* (Berkeley: University of California Press, 2012), 43–57.

51. A useful critique of high-modernist planning can be found in Scott, *Seeing Like a State*, 116.

52. Doxiadis Associates, *Saigon Metropolitan Area: Volume 1*, 250–51.

53. This was one of the defining features of Doxiadis's planning around the world. According to Hull, "Doxiadis planned for growth" (*Government of Paper*, 49).

54. Doxiadis Associates, *Saigon Metropolitan Area: Volume 3, Pilot Project* (Athens, Greece: Prepared for the Government of the Republic of Vietnam, Ministry of Public Works, Directorate General of Reconstruction and City Planning, 1965), 1. As Hull notes (*Government of Paper*, 48–49), and as Doxiadis's focus on small-scale human settlements within the larger Saigon plan also shows, Doxiadis differed from modernists like Le Corbusier in that he paid greater attention to local conditions. He did, however, plainly dislike the intermixing of functions, and endeavored to keep the planned and unplanned cities separate.

55. Doxiadis Associates, *Saigon Metropolitan Area: Volume 3*, 6, 20. The attributes quoted here were originally formatted as a list. The emphasis has been added.

56. Ibid., 8.

57. Doxiadis Associates, *Saigon Metropolitan Area: Volume 1*, 280.

58. For a description of the anthropological model of segmentary social organization, and one of the most famous diagrams in the history of social anthropology, see E. E. Evans-Pritchard, *The Nuer: A Description of the Modes of Livelihood and Political Institutions of a Nilotic People* (1940; New York: Oxford University Press, 1969), 144–47.

59. Doxiadis Associates, *Saigon Metropolitan Area: Volume 3*, 282. The schema seems to have been directly imported—if not self-plagiarized—from a similar schema used in the master plan for Islamabad. For a description of the five "classes" of urban order developed there, see Hull, *Government of Paper*, 53–57.

60. Doxiadis Associates, *Saigon Metropolitan Area: Volume 3*, 282.

61. Ibid., 284.

62. Doxiadis Associates, *Saigon Metropolitan Area: Volume 1*, 280.

63. On the notion of urban edges, cast as sites of both potential and danger, see Harms, *Saigon's Edge.*

64. Doxiadis Associates, *Saigon Metropolitan Area: Volume 1*, 118.

65. Ibid., 124. For strikingly similar examples from twenty-first-century Vietnam, see Erik Harms, "Neo-Geomancy and Real Estate Fever in Post-Reform Vietnam," *Positions: East Asia Cultures Critique* 20, no. 2 (2012): 426–28.

66. Doxiadis Associates, *Saigon Metropolitan Area: Volume 2, Administration, House Types, Land Types, Building Materials, Human Resources* (Athens, Greece: Prepared for the Government of the Republic of Vietnam, Ministry of Public Works, Directorate General of Reconstruction and City Planning, 1965), 42.

67. Wurster, Bernardi & Emmons, "Thu Thiem Peninsula Development Plan," 6. Reference to the plan is in James E. Bogle, *Dialectics of Urban Proposals for the Saigon Metropolitan Area* (Saigon: Ministry of Public Works, Republic of Vietnam, and the United States Agency for International Development, 1972), 53.

68. The fact that previous governments never actually carried out their plans for Thủ Thiêm would become significant later when residents were asked to hand their land to authorities in the first decade of 2000. Many of them doubted that the plan would ever be carried out.

69. Guy Wright, "Saigon of Tomorrow," *San Francisco Examiner,* June 22, 1973, 39.

70. Wurster, Bernardi & Emmons, "Thu Thiem Peninsula Development Plan." William W. Wurster, one of the principals in this firm, was dean of architecture (and later of the College of Environmental Design) at the University of California at Berkeley from 1950 to 1963.

71. Ibid., 18.

72. Ibid., 6.

73. Ibid.

74. Wurster, Bernardi & Emmons, Inc., "Thu Thiem Peninsula New Town, General Data, Project Statistics, Architect's Contract," Environmental Design Archives, University of California, Berkeley, Wurster/WBE Collection, Folder II.150, Thu Thiem Peninsula Plan, 1973, 1972, 3b.

75. Wurster, Bernardi & Emmons, "Thu Thiem Peninsula Development Plan," 43.

76. Ibid., 23.

77. In the Vietnamese translation running parallel to the English text, this group is called Hội Bất Động Sản Quận 9. Thủ Thiêm, at that time, was part of District 9.

78. Wurster, Bernardi & Emmons, "Thu Thiem Peninsula Development Plan," 23.

79. Wright, "Saigon of Tomorrow," 39.

## 5. BUILDING A CIVILIZED, MODERN, AND SENTIMENTAL CITY

1. Ngọc Ẩn and Bảo Ân, "Phà Thủ Thiêm nói lời chia tay" [The Thủ Thiêm ferry says goodbye], *Tuổi Trẻ,* Dec. 31, 2011.

2. P.P.H., "Dự án khu đô thị mới Thủ Thiêm: Xin áp dụng "một cửa" để đẩy nhanh tiến độ đền bù" [Thủ Thiêm New Urban Zone project: Request to use the "one-stop shop" to speed up the pace of compensation], *Tuổi Trẻ,* Jan. 26 2010.

3. Dân oan Thủ Thiêm (Danlambao), "Dân oan Thủ Thiêm bao vây công ty Hàn Quốc vì tiếp tay cho bọn cướp đất" [Thu Thiem residents surrounded Korean company to protest its support for land thieves] (2014), http://danlambaovn.blogspot.com/2014/02/dan-oan-thu-thiem-bao-vay-cong-ty-han.html; Người Thủ Thiêm, "Dự án khu Đô thị mới Thủ Thiêm: Dự án 6 không = Dự án ma" [Thu Thiem New Urban Zone project: "6 Nos" project = A ghost project] (2011), http://danlambaovn.blogspot.com/2011/12/du-khu-o-thi-moi-thu-thiem-du-6-khong.html.

4. By June 2012 a reported 522 households had not handed over their land, of which 393 had not yet agreed to the terms of settlement, while the rest were in the process of preparing to leave. For these figures, see Lê Thị Hoàng Mai, "Tình hình tiến độ thực hiện công tác bồi thường giải phóng mặt bằng các hồ sơ còn lại trong Khu đô thị mới Thủ Thiêm" [The situation of the pace of carrying out the compensation and liberation of land in the remaining dossiers in the Thu Thiem New Urban Zone], news release, June 22, 2012, www.thuthiem.hochiminhcity.gov.vn/web/guest/khudothi/cong-tac-boi-thuong.

5. Trang Bảo Sơn's statement in Vietnamese was: "Tính đến thời điểm này có thể nói công tác bồi thường hỗ trợ cho cá nhân, tổ chức bị ảnh hưởng bởi dự án cơ bản đã hoàn thành." He added the following more concrete details: by May 2014, 153 "dossiers" (hồ sơ) had yet to turn over their land; however, 14,336 out of 14,343 dossiers had received their compensation payments, indicating that they were preparing to leave. These quotes and figures are reported in Đỗ Trà Giang, "Tăng tốc thu hút đầu tư vào Thủ Thiêm" [Speed up the attraction of investment into Thủ Thiêm], Sài Gòn Giải Phóng, May 2, 2014. It is interesting to note that Mr. Sơn avoids the term eviction, but instead speaks of "the work of compensation and assistance." Residents are called "those affected" (bị ảnh hưởng) and are commonly referred to as "dossiers" in official announcements. These details recall similar language in Pakistan for "affectees" of the project to build Islamabad (Hull, Government of Paper, 163).

6. Tuổi Trẻ TV, "Cháy bãi cỏ hoang uy hiếp hầm Thủ Thiêm" [Fire in an abandoned grass field threatens the Thủ Thiêm tunnel]," Tuổi Trẻ, April 27, 2013.

7. The anthropologist Tri Phuong confirmed this as late as July 16, 2014.

8. The Vietnamese sign, printed in all capital letters, reads: "NÂNG CAO NHẬN THỨC, TRÁCH NHIỆM CỦA HỆ THỐNG CHÍNH TRỊ / TRONG PHÁT HUY SỨC MẠNH ĐẠI ĐOÀN KẾT DÂN TỘC / LẤY MỤC TIÊU 'DÂN GIÀU, NƯỚC MẠNH, DÂN CHỦ, CÔNG BẰNG, VĂN MINH' / LÀM ĐIỂM TƯƠNG ĐỒNG, ĐOÀN KẾT, TẬP HỢP CÁC TẦNG LỚP NHÂN DÂN / XÂY DỰNG, BẢO VỆ THÀNH PHỐ VÀ ĐẤT NƯỚC."

9. In Vietnamese, the sign reads: "NHÂN DÂN THÀNH PHỐ CHUNG TAY XÂY DỰNG / THÀNH PHỐ HỒ CHÍ MINH VĂN MINH, HIỆN ĐẠI, NGHĨA TÌNH."

10. Mark Sidel offers an accurate assessment of newspapers in Vietnam: "At least for some . . . editorial life existed in a complex and shifting state between autonomy and censorship," in which papers seek both to capture the interest of readers and to negotiate state limits on acceptable discourse. It is a dynamic tug of war, "rather than a slavish response to intensive external guidance from the state" (Sidel, Law and Society in Vietnam: The Transition from Socialism in Comparative Perspective [New York: Cambridge University Press, 2008], 119). Bill Hayton describes the state censorship apparatus as "a sharp knife but not too sharp" and newspaper resistance to state intervention as a form of "fence breaking" (Hayton, Vietnam: Rising Dragon [New Haven, CT: Yale University Press, 2010], 135, 45).

11. For a journalist's account of local resentment, see V. C. Mai and D. N. Hà, "Dân tiếp tục bức xúc chuyện giải tỏa, đến bù" [The people continue to be frustrated by land clearance and compensation], *Tuổi Trẻ*, June 24, 2009.

12. On this point, see Harms, "Beauty as Control in the New Saigon

13. Christina Schwenkel has also documented the ways in which residents facing eviction in Vinh City, located in north-central Vietnam, mobilized "affective claims" based on their prior service to the revolution and war effort in order to resist the terms of their dispossession. See Schwenkel, "Post/Socialist Affect," 261; idem, "Reclaiming Rights," 207.

14. My use of the term *belonging* invokes the work of Tine Gammeltoft, who eloquently shows how Vietnamese continue to assert their desire to "belong" to a larger community, despite what other scholars have recognized as an increasingly neoliberal emphasis on individualism. See Gammeltoft, *Haunting Images: A Cultural Account of Selective Reproduction in Vietnam* (Berkeley: University of California Press, 2014), 129–30.

15. See Kevin J. O'Brien, "Rightful Resistance," *World Politics* 49, no. 1 (1996): 31–55; and Kevin J. O'Brien and Lianjiang Li, *Rightful Resistance in Rural China* (New York: Cambridge University Press, 2006). For the expression of this kind of resistance in Vietnam, see Benedict J. Tria Kerkvliet, "Protests over Land in Vietnam: Rightful Resistance and More," *Journal of Vietnamese Studies* 9, no. 3 (2014): 19–54.

16. SASAKI Associates, Inc., "Thu Thiem New Urban Area," www.sasaki.com/project/139/thu-thiem-new-urban-area/ (accessed 2014).

17. Dennis Pieprz, "A Landscape Framework for Urban Sustainability: Thu Thiem, Ho Chi Minh City," in *The Ecoedge: Urgent Design Challenges in Building Sustainable Cities*, ed. Esther Charlesworth and Rob Adams (London: Taylor & Francis, 2011), 121–32.

18. Việt Hùng and Đ. Huân, "Khu đô thị mới Thủ Thiêm sẽ ngập trong nước"; Đoan Trang, "Phố Đông hiện đại bên bờ sông Sài Gòn [A modern Pudong on the banks of the Saigon River]," *Tuổi Trẻ*, March 4, 2006.

19. Li Zhang (*In Search of Paradise*, 212–15) also notes the importance of "harmony" in Chinese development projects.

20. An Nhiên and Nguyên Thảo, "Tìm kiếm vẻ đẹp cho khu vực trung tâm TPHCM" [Searching for a beautiful face for Ho Chi Minh City's central area], *Sài Gòn Giải Phóng*, Nov. 2, 2007.

21. Ban Quản lý Khu Thủ Thiêm, "Deso- First Prize in the Competition for the Central Plaza, Crescent Park, and Saigon River Pedestrian Bridge," March 27, 2009, available at www.thuthiem.hochiminhcity.gov.vn/web/english/thuthiem-new-urban-center/overview.

22. The quote, in the original French from the website of DeSo architectes, reads: "S'appuyant sur une identité affirmée des sols en terre, le projet développe de vastes espaces publics chaînés aux espaces commerciaux, et aux paysages lacustres créés." The passage was posted on the DeSo website (www.deso-architecture.com) as late as 2010, but has since been removed. The same passage is cited at two architectural news sites, both of which reference the early DeSo plan: www.lemoniteur.fr/article/deso-et-dalnoky-remportent-un-amenagement-a-ho-chi-minh-ville-629343; http://vnre.reic.vn/2008/10/french-firm-wins-urban-design-award.html.

23. For a view of corporate control over urban public spaces, see the well-known critique by Mike Davis, "Fortress Los Angeles." And for the Asian context, see the important

work of Mike Douglass, Kong Chong Ho, and Giok-Ling Ooi, "Civic Spaces, Globalisation, and Pacific Asia Cities," *International Development Planning Review* 24, no. 2 (2002): 345–61.

24. Olivier Souquet, email, June 16, 2016.

25. For negative impressions residents have of auto-urbanization, see Harms, "Civility's Footprint," 232–33.

26. For a discussion of the long history of failed attempts to implement urban plans in Ho Chi Minh City, see Du Huynh, "The Misuse of Urban Planning in Ho Chi Minh City," *Habitat International* 48 (Aug. 2015): 11–19.

27. James Holston, "The Death of the Street," in *The Modernist City: An Anthropological Critique of Brasilia* (Chicago: University of Chicago Press, 1989), 105–36.

28. Hy Hiểu, "Nhớ Ba Đình, mơ về Thủ Thiêm" [Remembering Ba Đình, dreams of Thủ Thiêm], *Tuổi Trẻ*, Sept. 8, 2009.

29. Ibid.

30. For an important example of fence breaking, and a riveting history of Vietnamese economic reformers, see Đặng Phong, *"Phá rào" trong kinh tế vào đêm trước Đổi mới.*

31. Martin Gainsborough, in "Understanding Communist Transition: Property Rights in Ho Chi Minh City in the Late 1990s" (*Post-Communist Economies* 14, no. 2 [2002]: 227–43), notes that Vietnam's equitization process allowed many connected officials to claim de facto control of property rights, often claiming resources extracted from state-owned institutions. Elsewhere (*Vietnam: Rethinking the State,* 14) he observes that "while the large landowners of the *ancien régime* have been toppled, in their place there has emerged a new landlord class, namely Communist Party cadres and government officials."

32. Karl Marx, *Capital: A Critique of Political Economy,* trans. Ben Fowkes (1867; London: Penguin Classics, 1976), 875.

33. Harvey, "Accumulation by Dispossession."

34. Shatkin, "The City and the Bottom Line"; Douglass, Ho, and Ooi, "Civic Spaces, Globalisation, and Pacific Asia Cities."

35. Thanh Nien News, "Japanese Exec Names Vietnamese Official in ODA Bribe: Report," *ThanhNienNews,* March 23, 2014.

36. Thủ Tướng Chính phủ Việt Nam [Prime Minister of Vietnam], "20/TTg: Quyết định số 20/TTg ngày 16/01/1993 của Thủ tướng Chính phủ về việc phê duyệt quy hoạch tổng thể xây dựng Thành phố Hồ Chí Minh" [Decision number 20/TTg of January 16, 1993, by the prime minister regarding approval of the Ho Chi Minh City Master Plan] (Hanoi: Chính phủ Việt Nam, 1993), art. 1.

37. Võ Văn Kiệt is one of the few heroes to emerge in the journalist Huy Đức's sensationalist exposé of the postwar period. The book, which was banned in Vietnam, repeatedly describes Kiệt as a "fence breaker." See Huy Đức, *Bên Thắng Cuộc* [The winning side] (Los Angeles: OSINBook, 2012), 315–19.

38. Labbé, *Land Politics and Livelihoods on the Margins of Hanoi,* 101.

39. Thủ Tướng Chính phủ Việt Nam, "20/TTg"; idem, "367/TTg: Quyết định số 367/TTg ngày 04/06/1996 của Thủ tướng Chính phủ về việc phê duyệt quy hoạch xây dựng Khu đô thị mới Thủ Thiêm" [Decision number 367/TTg on June 4, 1996, by the prime minister regarding the approval of the building plan for The Thu Thiem New Urban Zone] (Hanoi: Chính phủ Việt Nam, 1996).

40. This decision specified that development would proceed in the direction of Thủ Đức (the same direction specified in the Doxiadis plan detailed in chapter 4), with secondary development proceeding in the direction of Nhà Bè, Bình Chánh, and Hóc Môn. "In particular, the direction of development of the city center across to Thủ Thiêm needs to be carefully considered in relation the circumstances of land, the technical infrastructure, and the environment." For the text, see Thủ Tướng Chính phủ Việt Nam, "20/TTg," art. 1.2.

41. Quy-Toan Do and Lakshmi Iyer, "Land Titling and Rural Transition in Vietnam," *Economic Development and Cultural Change* 56, no. 3 (April 2008): 537.

42. This land market first developed around the transfer of "paper" rather than land. That is, these land use rights, which did not officially amount to land "ownership," managed to serve as a proxy for land and thus enabled a land market to develop, even though land ownership still didn't exist. Under these circumstances, context was extremely important in establishing real property values in the face of often incomplete property rights. See Annette M. Kim, "A Market without the 'Right' Property Rights," *Economics of Transition* 12, no. 2 (2004): 275–305. According to Kim, this system also made "property rights" unstable, as the interpretation of a "land use right" as "property" could be subject to volatile political shifts. For a discussion of Decree 18, of 1995, which suddenly undermined the ability of developers and banks to use land-use rights as collateral, see Gainsborough, *Vietnam: Rethinking the State,* 58–59. For an intimate portrait of the struggles over resources that emerged with new forms of property rights, as well as associated use-right fees in a Ho Chi Minh City marketplace, see Ann Marie Leshkowich, "Wandering Ghosts of Late Socialism: Conflict, Metaphor, and Memory in a Southern Vietnamese Marketplace," *Journal of Asian Studies* 67, no. 1 (2008): 5–41; and idem, *Essential Trade,* 127–49.

43. This was also just when Lawrence Ting and his associates from CD&T in Taiwan were given the approval to begin plans for the New Urban Zone development in Phú Mỹ Hưng, off in what was then derided by most city officials as "distant" Nhà Bè District (see chapters 1–3). In the course of interviews with many different developers and planning officials in Ho Chi Minh City, I was often told that Ting and his associates were themselves extremely interested in the land in Thủ Thiêm, but it was considered *"đất vàng,"* a "golden land" of opportunity: that is, Vietnamese officials wished to steward the development of this land for themselves, but they would need injections of capital to realize their ambitious proposals. Interviewees in 2010 and 2011 often chuckled when they recounted the way Ho Chi Minh City officials thought they were sending Ting and his associates to failure. Retelling the story almost twenty years later, many interviewees delighted in the irony: Thủ Thiêm was now mired in land disputes, while Phú Mỹ Hưng had become the most successful development in the entire country. Vietnamese socialist land masters, these stories implied, were clearly inferior to private Taiwanese capitalists.

44. Some of the most pressing infrastructure problems included antiquated sewers and water mains, inadequate trash collection impeded by difficult access to compact neighborhoods, clogged storm drainage, flooding, polluted canals, and narrow roads unable to accommodate traffic. Further problems included lack of green space as well as aesthetic considerations related to balancing the needs of zoning, modernization of the building stock, and heritage preservation.

45. Saigon Construction Department, "Introduction of the Projects Planned for Investment in HCM City," *Saigon Investment and Construction* 3, no. 95 (March 1995): 8, in folder 02, box 03, Walter Wylie Collection, Vietnam Center and Archive, Texas Tech University.

46. Ibid., 9–10.

47. The text describing the ban on building reads, "As fortified buildings are not allowed to be constructed here for the time being, the existing works are simple. It can be said that they are temporary" (ibid., 8).

48. "Thu Thiem is an area which has been considered suitable for the development of the city to reduce pressure on the inner city, especially the center of the old city" (ibid.).

49. As specified also in the Wurster plan before it (described in chapter 4), the entire land surface of Thủ Thiêm would be raised above sea level, only now it would be raised 1.9 meters instead of 1.5; this was well above the level of high tide, which was measured at 1.6 meters. Again borrowing from the wisdom of Wurster, the project noted that the land for building up the surface ground would come from the Đồng Nai River. Ibid., 10.

50. Chính phủ Việt Nam [Government of Vietnam], "Nghị Định của Chính Phủ Số 03-CP Ngày 06 Tháng 01 Năm 1997 về việc thành lập Quận Thủ Đức, Quận 2, Quận 7, Quận 9, Quận 12 và thành lập các phường thuộc các quận mới—Thành Phố Hồ Chí Minh" [Governmental Decision Number 03-CP of January 6, 1997, regarding the Establisment of Thủ Đức District, District 2, District 7, District 9, District 12, and the Establishment of Wards in the New Districts in Ho Chi Minh City] (Hanoi: Chính phủ Việt Nam, 1997).

51. On the concept of "fiscal socialism" in Ho Chi Minh City, see Annette Kim, *Learning to Be Capitalists: Entrepreneurs in Vietnam's Transition Economy* (Oxford: Oxford University Press, 2008), 90–99.

52. For more on the material and economic consequences of the symbolic transformation of outer-city districts into inner-city districts, see Harms, "Material Symbolism of Saigon's Edge."

53. For a balanced discussion of land conversions in periurban spaces throughout Southeast Asia, see Hall, Hirsch, and Li, *Powers of Exclusion,* 120–31.

54. As academic critics point out, with good reason, these arrangements can be risky because they offer unscrupulous officials plenty of opportunity for personal profit, graft, and corruption. But in a city with limited fiscal resources of its own, the promise of urban development offered by such financial instruments continues to have broad appeal, not just to the state, but to the people as well. See Du Huynh and Alex Ngo, "Urban Development through Land-Based Infrastructure Financing: Cases in Ho Chi Minh City" (Fulbright Economics Teaching Program, Ho Chi Minh City, 2010).

55. For a World Bank report detailing the possibilities that might be envisioned by tapping into land values, see George E. Peterson, "Unlocking Land Values to Finance Urban Infrastructure," in *Trends and Policy Options* (Washington, DC: World Bank—Public-Private Infrastucture Advisory Facility, 2009).

56. Kim, *Learning to Be Capitalists,* 56–65.

57. For a subtle and careful study of the problems that emerge with such land conversions, see Nguyen Van Suu, "Agricultural Land Conversion and Its Effects on Farmers in Contemporary Vietnam," *Focaal—European Journal of Anthropology* 54 (2009): 106–13.

58. An article, or even a dissertation, could likely be written about this tendency to blame the victims of land conversion by manufacturing stories of rural idiocy. For an example applied to Thủ Thiêm, see the three-part newspaper article series on "youth in an eviction zone": Kim Anh and Nguyễn Nam, "'Dân chơi Thủ Thiêm' thời rủng rỉnh" ["The Players of Thu Thiem" in a Time of Financial Plenty]; "Thanh niên khu đền bù giải tỏa—Bài 2: Chỉ biết hôm nay" [Youth in a Land Clearance and Compensation Zone—Part 2: Only Thinking about Today]; "TP.HCM: Thanh niên khu đền bù giải tỏa—Bài cuối: Tiền đền bù lo tương lai" [HCMC: Youth in a Land Clearance and Compensation Zone—Final Article: Compensation Money and Worries for the Future]," *Tuổi Trẻ*, May 24–26, 2009.

59. The president of the World Bank personally wrote an article for Bloomberg praising the innovations that cleaned up Ho Chi Minh City's polluted Nhiêu Lộc-Thị Nghè Canal. See Jim Yong Kim, "How Ho Chi Minh City's Filthy Canal Became a Park," *BloombergView*, Oct. 15, 2013.

60. For a short yet detailed description of one such everyday "domestic investor," see Truitt, "Domestic Investor."

61. On the injustices associated with "fuzzy property" and the assumption that land titles would bring people "rights," see Katherine Verdery, "Fuzzy Property: Rights, Power, and Identity in Transylvania's Decollectivization," in *Uncertain Transition: Ethnographies of Change in the Postsocialist World,* ed. Michael Burawoy and Katherine Verdery (Lanham, MD: Rowman & Littlefield, 1999), 53–81.

62. From the "on-the-ground" perspective of most Vietnamese I have known through this period, what developed, over the course of the 1990s and 2000s, was an economic and legal context that increasingly gave more Vietnamese people "rights" to their land, which corresponded to a period of significant and sustained economic growth that in turn led, overall, to improved standards of living and even relative wealth for many urban residents. Everyone who could was trying their hand at real estate, and many people were making impressive incomes. For most people, especially those in cities, the value of their land became a source of stability, and the general expansion of property rights seemed clearly connected to this.

63. Pieprz, "Landscape Framework for Urban Sustainability," 124.

64. Ủy ban Nhân dân Thành phố Hồ Chí Minh [Ho Chi Minh City People's Committee], "103/2001/QĐ-UB: Quyết định số 103/2001/QĐ-UB ngày 01 tháng 11 năm 2001 của UBND thành phố về thành lập Ban Quản lý Đầu tư, Xây dựng Khu đô thị mới Thủ Thiêm" [Decision number 103/2001/QĐ-UB of November 1, 2001, by the City People's Committee regarding the establishment of the Thủ Thiêm Investment and Construction Authority] (Ho Chi Minh City: Ủy ban Nhân dân Thành phố Hồ Chí Minh, 2001).

65. Ibid.

66. This operated similarly to the Saigon South Authority (Ban Quản lý Khu nam), which was authorized to do much the same thing in sections of District Seven and Nhà Bè, the site of Phú Mỹ Hưng.

67. Ủy ban Nhân dân Thành phố Hồ Chí Minh [Ho Chi Minh City People's Committee], "103/2001/QĐ-UB: Quyết định số 103/2001/QĐ-UB."

68. Hội đồng Nhân dân Thành Phố Hồ Chí Minh [Ho Chi Minh City People's Council], "21/2002/NQ-HĐ Nghị Quyết về đầu tư xây dựng trung tâm đô thị mới Thủ Thiêm"

[Resolution Regarding the Investment and Construction of the New Urban Center of Thu Thiem] (Ho Chi Minh City: Hội đồng Nhân dân Thành phố Hồ Chí Minh, 2002).

69. Ủy ban Nhân dân Thành phố Hồ Chí Minh [Ho Chi Minh City People's Committee], "135/2002/QĐ-UB: Quyết định số 135/2002/QĐ-UB ngày 21 tháng 11 năm 2002 của UBND thành phố về việc ban hành quy định về đền bù, hỗ trợ thiệt hại và tái định cư trong khu quy hoạch xây dựng Khu đô thị mới Thủ Thiêm và các khu phục vụ tái định cư tại Quận 2, Thành Phố Hồ Chí Minh" [Decision number 35/2002/QĐ-UB of November 21, 2002, by the City People's Committee regarding the issuance of regulations regarding compensation and assistance for losses and resettlement in the planned zone for building the Thu Thiem New Urban Zone and the zones serving the resettlement in District 2, Ho Chi Minh City], (Ho Chi Minh City: Ủy ban Nhân dân Thành phố Hồ Chí Minh, 2002).

70. David Brown, an independent scholar and journalist with extensive background in land issues in Vietnam, critiques this arrangement because it gives local cadres too much power in setting the terms for negotiating compensation, and often ends up shortchanging those forced to relinquish their land. For a clear discussion of this problem, see David Brown, "Vietnam's Land Law Reform: Is It Enough?," *Asia Sentinel,* Feb. 6, 2013.

71. Formerly rural land in these places on the city's edges was being paved with concrete. The demolition of Thủ Thiêm was only one part of an urbanization process extending to all corners of the city.

72. These descriptions are based on my field notes from visits in 2013 and 2014. For further descriptions of Thủ Thiêm after the demolitions, in 2013, see Trung Sơn, "Hoang vắng ở đô thị kỳ vọng đẹp nhất Đông Nam Á" [Abandonment in the urban area anticipated as the most beautiful in Southeast Asia], *VnExpress,* April 2, 2013; Xuân Thủy—Lê Nguyễn, "Thủ Thiêm cỏ mọc um tùm . . ." [Luxuriant grasses grow in Thủ Thiêm], *Tiền Phong* online, May 9, 2013.

73. Tuổi Trẻ TV, "Lộn xộn trên cầu Thủ Thiêm" [Disorderliness on the Thủ Thiêm Bridge], *Tuổi Trẻ,* June 13, 2013.

74. See note above for the quote. Astute readers will notice that the numbers of affected residents are different in the many places I cite them. Welcome to the world of "official numbers" in Vietnam! Rather than speculate on which numbers are correct, I simply use the numbers cited in each source when mentioning that source. The word *dossier (hồ sơ)* was often used by officials to refer to "those affected by the project" *(bị ảnh hưởng bởi dự* án).

75. Erik Harms, "Eviction Time in the New Saigon: Temporalities of Displacement in the Rubble of Development," *Cultural Anthropology* 28, no. 2 (2013): 344–68.

76. TN News, "Vietnam Opens First Underwater Tunnel with Hopes for Better Traffic," *Thanh Niên News,* Nov. 20, 2011.

77. Vĩnh Phú, "Đại lộ đẹp nhất TP HCM mang tên Võ Văn Kiệt" [HCMC's most beautiful boulevard carries Võ Văn Kiệt's name], *VnExpress,* April 29, 2011.

### 6. FROM THE RUBBLE

1. For a trenchant critique of Indochine chic as "the unavowed nostalgia for a bygone colonial era, which masquerades as a mandate for helping a nation preserve its historical heritage," see Panivong Norindr, "Aestheticizing Urban Space: Modernity in Postcolonial Saigon and Hanoi," *L'esprit créateur* 41, no. 3 (2001): 83.

2. For further descriptions of this house style, see Tôn Nữ Quỳnh Trân and Nguyễn Trọng Hòa, *Văn hóa hẻm phố Sài Gòn*, 94–95. According to this study, by the year 2007 there were more than 100,000 of these houses in Ho Chi Minh City. The actual number is probably much higher.

3. The figure of 14,600 households is from a January 2010 newspaper article, P.P.H., "Dự án khu đô thị mới Thủ Thiêm." It was not possible to obtain an exact figure for the number of homes demolished from the Thủ Thiêm Investment and Construction Authority. Figures on the authority's own website vary widely and are presented in a haphazard fashion. One article, written in August 2011, claims that 14,150 out of a total 14,500 households had been compensated, while another article, written in 2010, claimed that 15,500 households would ultimately be evicted. See Nguyễn Kim Đức. "Công tác bồi thường, giải phóng mặt bằng và hỗ trợ tái định cư Khu đô thị mới Thủ Thiêm tiếp tục tiến triển (24/8/2011)" [The work of compensation and liberation of land and resettlement support continues to be carried out in the Thủ Thiêm New Urban Zone], Thủ Thiêm Investment and Construction Authority website, August 24, 2011, www.thuthiem.hochiminhcity.gov.vn/web/guest/khudothi/cong-tac-boi-thuong; Thu Thiem Authority, "Thu Thiem New Urban Area Project: 12,000 Apartments for Resettlement [to] Be Built," Thủ Thiêm Investment and Construction Authority website, June 29, 2010, www.thuthiem.hochiminhcity.gov.vn/web/english/thuthiem-new-urban-center/compensation-works. It is reasonable to assume that somewhere between 14,000 and 16,000 households were ultimately evicted by the year 2014.

4. For a similar argument using different forms of evidence, see Erik Harms, "Social Demolition: Creative Destruction and the Production of Value in Vietnamese Land Clearance," in *State, Society, and the Market in Contemporary Vietnam: Property, Power, and Values*, ed. Hue-Tam Ho-Tai and Mark Sidel (New York: Routledge, 2012), 55–68.

5. Kate Jellema, "Returning Home: Ancestor Veneration and the Nationalism of *Đổi Mới* Vietnam," in *Modernity and Re-Enchantment: Religion in Post-Revolutionary Vietnam*, ed. Philip Taylor (Lanham, MD: Lexington Books, 2007), 57–89.

6. For an extended analysis of the way residents find aesthetic beauty in the Thủ Thiêm project, despite the fact that it is displacing them, see Harms, "Beauty as Control in the New Saigon." For similar examples in the Congo and India, respectively, see De Boeck, "Inhabiting Ocular Ground"; and Ghertner, "Rule By Aesthetics."

7. One *mẫu* is 4,894 square meters; an acre is approximately, 4,047 square meters. For this and more on Vietnamese agricultural measures, see Nguyễn Đình Đầu, *Nghiên cứu địa ba Triều Nguyễn*, 26.

8. For a discussion of this narrative trope, see chapter 1, as well as Harms, "Knowing into Oblivion."

9. For an example of the use of this term in Vietnamese historiography, see Nguyễn Đình Đầu, *Nghiên cứu địa ba Triều Nguyễn*.

10. The use of the term *acidic water (nước phèn)* to describe unproductive or inhospitable land is common in Vietnamese. For the connections this language has to narratives of "not yet civilized" lands occupied by Khmer people in the south, see P. Taylor, *Khmer Lands of Vietnam*, 6.

11. This idiomatic expression, translated literally, means "the place we bury each other and cut our umbilical cords."

12. Using the same idiomatic expression as above.

13. A Vietnamese idiom commonly used to celebrate the homeland, referring to the sentimental ripening of the star fruit at a rural household's garden. This is also the chorus of a popular song.

14. For a discussion of this concept, and its relation to urban transformation in the Vietnamese city of Vinh, see Schwenkel, "Post/Socialist Affect."

15. Ibid.

16. Annette M. Kim, "Talking Back: The Role of Narrative in Vietnam's Recent Land Compensation Changes," *Urban Studies* 48, no. 3 (Feb. 1, 2011): 493–508. In Kim's study, the narratives deployed are forged in resistance to low levels of compensation. What the narratives demand, in large part, is less greed and more fairness, often mobilizing stories of dire economic harship suffered by displaced residents. But these narratives are not necessarily articulated as a resistance to the privatization and commodification of property iself, nor in opposition to modernization, beautification, or "civilizing" the city.

17. Benedict Kerkvliet's analysis of over sixty land dispute cases indicate that, generally speaking, Vietnam protestors' "overall demand is to achieve justice and fairness" (Kerkvliet, "Protests over Land in Vietnam," 27). For other examples of efforts to seek justice and fairness, see Nguyen Van Suu, "Agricultural Land Conversion and Its Effects on Farmers in Contemporary Vietnam"; Nguyen Vu Hoang, "Constructing Civil Society on a Demolition Site in Hanoi," in *State, Society, and the Market in Contemporary Vietnam*, ed. Hue-Tam Ho-Tai and Mark Sidel (New York: Routledge, 2012, 87–102).

18. John Gillespie, "The Emerging Role of Property Rights in Land and Housing Disputes in Hanoi," in Ho-Tai and Sidel (eds.), *State, Society, and the Market in Contemporary Vietnam*, 113.

19. Kerkvliet, "Protests over Land in Vietnam," 27–28.

20. Ibid., 29.

21. John Gillespie, "Social Consensus and the Meta-Regulation of Land-Taking Disputes in Vietnam," *Journal of Vietnamese Studies* 9, no. 3 (2014): 91–124.

22. Ibid., 95.

23. This phrase comes from article 42.3 of the 2003 Land Law, in a section describing policies related to resettlement for land reclamation projects. For the original text, in Vietnamese and in English, see Socialist Republic of Vietnam, "2003 Luật Đất Đai" [Law on Land] (Hanoi: Nhà xuất bản Tài chính, 2010), 40, 186.

24. For useful discussions of the role of multiple currencies in Ho Chi Minh City, see Truitt, *Dreaming of Money*.

25. According to a commemorative history published by the Thủ Thiêm church, the parish was founded in 1859. See Giáo Xứ Thủ Thiêm, *Kỷ Yếu mừng 150 năm thành lập Giáo Xứ Thủ Thiêm*.

26. On the Land to the Tiller program, see Charles Stuart Callison, *Land to the Tiller in the Mekong Delta: Economic, Social, and Political Effects of Land Reform in Four Villages of South Vietnam* (Lanham, MD: University Press of America, for the Center for South and Southeast Asian Studies, University of California, 1983); and William J. Duiker, *Vietnam: Revolution in Transition*, 2nd ed. (Boulder, CO: Westview Press, 1995), 134.

27. P.P.H., "Dự án khu đô thị mới Thủ Thiêm."

28. For images of Thủ Thiêm taken during this same period, see Nicolas Lainez, "Unveiling the Invisible: Representing Transitioning Urban Space in Vietnam," EspacesTemps. net, Objects, June 28, 2012, www.espacestemps.net/articles/unveiling-the-invisible. Further images are available at http://campuspress.yale.edu/newurbanvietnam/tt-post/#ttphotos.

29. For a more detailed discussion of this point, see Harms, "Beauty as Control in the New Saigon." For confirmation of this assessment, see also Marie Gibert, "Déplacements forcés et renouvellement urbain à Hồ Chí Minh Ville" [Forced Displacement and Urban Renewal in Hồ Chí Minh City], *L'espace politique: Revue en ligne de géographie politique et de géopolitique* 22, no. 1 (2014).

## CONCLUSION: CIVILITY AND DISPOSSESSION

1. Chung Hoàng, "Thủ tướng: Làm hài hòa, đừng để thêm khiếu kiện đất đai" [Prime minister: Create harmony, don't allow more land complaints], *Vietnamnet,* May 2, 2012. Similar figures, cited from different sources, are presented in Kerkvliet, "Protests over Land in Vietnam: Rightful Resistance and More," 20, 41n.4.

2. In Vietnamese: "Trình độ hiểu biết pháp luật đất đai còn thấp." Quoted in Chung Hoàng, "Thủ tướng: Làm hài hòa, đừng để thêm khiếu kiện đất đai."

3. Ibid.

4. Socialist Republic of Vietnam, "2003 Luật Đất Đai" [Law on Land], art. 42.

5. Kerkvliet, "Protests over Land in Vietnam."

6. For a vivid account of residents coming into consciousness of their rights as they face eviction from collective housing in Vinh City, see Schwenkel, "Reclaiming Rights." Schwenkel's work is especially useful for showing the incremental process through which resident grievances proceeded in stages, from a "first round" in which they made primarily affective claims based on a sense of moral right to live in housing granted to them for service to the revolution, to a "second round" in which they made more formal claims based on legal rights to property.

7. Kerkvliet, "Protests over Land in Vietnam."

8. Gillespie, "Emerging Role of Property Rights"; Harms, "Social Demolition."

9. For a useful recent discussion of the significance of these claims, see Philip Taylor, "Introduction to the Special Issue: Contests over Land in Rural Vietnam," *Journal of Vietnamese Studies* 9, no. 3 (2014): 1–18. An earlier, but equally useful discussion, can be found in Hy Van Luong, "The State, Local Associations, and Alternate Civilities in Rural Northern Vietnam," in *Civil Life, Globalization, and Political Change in Asia: Organizing between Family and State,* ed. Robert Weller (London: Routledge, 2005), 123–46.

10. Holston, *Insurgent Citizenship.*

11. From "[A] Petition and Urgent Cry for Help" ["ĐƠN KHIẾU NẠI & KÊU CỨU KHẨN CẤP"] given to the author during field research in 2010.

12. "Cộng đồng Phú Mỹ Hưng" [Phú Mỹ Hưng Community], Title of Weblog.

13. Lê Du Phong, *Thu nhập, đời sống, việc làm của người có đất bị thu hồi* [Income, livelihood, and work of people who have had their land reclaimed] (Hanoi: Nhà xuất bản Chính trị Quốc gia, 2007), 35–36.

14. Ibid., 37.

15. Phúc Huy, "TP.HCM: nơi thiếu nơi thừa nhà tái định cư" [HCMC short of space and homes for resettlement], *Tuổi Trẻ*, Jan. 11, 2010.

16. Mahmood Mamdani, "Introduction," in *Beyond Rights Talk and Culture Talk: Comparative Essays on the Politics of Rights and Culture*, ed. Mahmood Mamdani (Cape Town, SA: David Philip Publishers, 2000), 6, 8.

17. Sidel, *Law and Society in Vietnam*, 196.

18. John Gillespie, "Exploring the Limits of the Judicialization of Urban Land Disputes in Vietnam," *Law and Society Review* 45, no. 2 (2011): 241–75.

19. Ugo Mattei and Laura Nader, *Plunder: When the Rule of Law Is Illegal* (Malden, MA: Blackwell, 2008).

20. On the concept of "talking back," see Annette Kim, "Talking Back." On the world of Vietnamese internet activism, see Patrick E. Sharbaugh and Dang Nguyen, "Make Lulz, Not War: How Online Remix and Meme Culture Are Empowering Civic Engagement in the Socialist Republic of Vietnam," *Asiascape: Digital Asia* 1, no. 3 (2014): 133–68.

21. On the shift toward rights discourse and the language of formal petitions, see Schwenkel, "Reclaiming Rights," 217. In that case, forms of paperwork conferring property ownership emboldened residents to believe in certain "fundamental rights." At the same time, in that same case, the petitions residents ultimately submitted in order to fight to defend those rights "did not achieve their desired results" (ibid., 223).

22. Jacques Rancière, "Who Is the Subject of the Rights of Man?" *South Atlantic Quarterly* 103, no. 2/3 (Spring/Summer 2004): 297–310.

23. On the notion that any claim to property is necessarily founded on exclusion, see Hall, Hirsch, and Li, *Powers of Exclusion*.

24. Rancière, "Who Is the Subject of the Rights of Man?" 302.

25. For example, the Tulane-trained lawyer Lê Công Định, a political activist, blogger, and advocate for political pluralism in Vietnam was arrested in 2009 on charges of distributing antigovernment materials at his apartment in Phú Mỹ Hưng.

26. Gillespie, "Public Land Disputes in Vietnam."

27. Sigmund Freud, *Civilization and Its Discontents* (New York: W. W. Norton, 1961), 42.

28. Lê Du Phong, *Thu nhập, đời sống, việc làm của người có đất bị thu hồi*, 45.

29. Eric Hirsch, "Property and Persons: New Forms and Contests in the Era of Neoliberalism," *Annual Review of Anthropology* 39, no. 1 (2010): 356.

30. The double-edged relationship between rights and exclusion that emerged alongside the introduction of use rights is vividly described in Leshkowich, *Essential Trade*, 127–49.

31. If the matter were a simple case of bad people grabbing land from innocent victims, the Vietnamese government would be especially well placed to solve the problem by simply turning back to socialism and collective ownership. But this is clearly not the solution in a society where most people identify socialism as the problem rather than the solution.

32. Jean-Jacques Rousseau, *On the Social Contract* (1762; Indianapolis: Hackett, 1983), 27.

33. Marx, *Capital*, 873.

34. Orlando Patterson, *Freedom*. Vol. 1: *Freedom in the Making of Western Culture* (New York: Basic Books, 1991), xiii.

35. Habermas, "Public Sphere."

# BIBLIOGRAPHY

An Nhiên and Nguyên Thảo. "Tìm kiếm vẻ đẹp cho khu vực trung tâm TPHCM" [Searching for a beautiful face for Ho Chi Minh City's central area]. *Sài Gòn Giải Phóng,* Nov. 2, 2007.

Anagnost, Ann. *National Past-Times: Narrative, Representation and Power in Modern China.* Durham, NC: Duke University Press, 1997.

Ban Quản lý Khu Thủ Thiêm. "Deso- First Prize in the Competition for the Central Plaza, Crescent Park, and Saigon River Pedestrian Bridge." March 27, 2009.

Barnes, William. "Vietnam Eager to Learn Capitalism's Lessons." FT.com [*Financial Times* online], Nov. 20, 2006.

Bhabha, Homi K. "Sly Civility." *October* 34 (1985): 71–80.

Biggs, David. *Quagmire: Nation-Building and Nature in the Mekong Delta.* Seattle: University of Washington Press, 2010.

Bogle, James E. *Dialectics of Urban Proposals for the Saigon Metropolitan Area.* Saigon: Ministry of Public Works, Republic of Vietnam, and the United States Agency for International Development, 1972.

Bradley, Mark P. "Becoming *Van Minh*: Civilizational Discourse and Visions of the Self in Twentieth-Century Vietnam." *Journal of World History* 15, no. 1 (2004): 65–83.

Brown, David. "Vietnam's Land Law Reform: Is It Enough?" *Asia Sentinel,* Feb. 6, 2013.

Butler, David. *The Fall of Saigon: Scenes from the Sudden End of a Long War.* New York: Simon & Schuster, 1985.

Caldeira, Teresa Pires do Rio. *City of Walls: Crime, Segregation, and Citizenship in São Paulo.* Berkeley: University of California Press, 2000.

———. "Fortified Enclaves: The New Urban Segregation." In *Cities and Citizenship,* ed. James Holston, 114–38. Durham, NC: Duke University Press, 1999.

Callison, Charles Stuart. *Land to the Tiller in the Mekong Delta: Economic, Social, and Political Effects of Land Reform in Four Villages of South Vietnam.* Lanham, MD: University Press of America, for the Center for South and Southeast Asian Studies, University of California., 1983.

Catton, Philip E. *Diem's Final Failure: Prelude to America's War in Vietnam.* Lawrence: University Press of Kansas, 2003.

CBRE. "Thu Thiem: The PuDong of Saigon" (market report). CBRE Vietnam, Ho Chi Minh City, 2015.

Certeau, Michel de. *The Practice of Everyday Life.* Berkeley: University of California Press, 1984.

Cherry, Haydon. "Down and Out in Saigon: A Social History of the Poor in a Colonial City, 1860–1940." Ph.D. diss., Yale University, 2011.

Chính phủ Việt Nam [Government of Vietnam]. "Nghị Định của Chính Phủ Số 03-CP Ngày 06 Tháng 01 Năm 1997 về việc thành lập Quận Thủ Đức, Quận 2, Quận 7, Quận 9, Quận 12 và thành lập các phường thuộc các quận mới—Thành phố Hồ Chí Minh" [Governmental Decision Number 03-CP of January 6, 1997, regarding the Establishment of Thủ Đức District, District 2, District 7, District 9, District 12, and the Establishment of Wards in the New Districts in Ho Chi Minh City]. Hanoi: Chính phủ Việt Nam, 1997.

Chung Hoàng. "Thủ tướng: Làm hài hòa, đừng để thêm khiếu kiện đất đai" [Prime minister: Create harmony, don't allow more land complaints]. *Vietnamnet,* May 2, 2012.

Cohen, Roger. "Status in the New Asia." *International New York Times,* May 13, 2014, 9.

Cộng đồng Phú Mỹ Hưng [Phú Mỹ Hưng Community]. "Các cơ sở pháp lý để thắng kiện tại TAND Quận 7" [Legal Bases for Winning Complaints at the District 7 People's Court]. In *Cộng đồng Phú Mỹ Hưng* [Phú Mỹ Hưng Community]. Ho Chi Minh City, 2012. (Available at https://congdongphumyhung.wordpress.com/2012/08/16/nhung-nguoi-dang-khoi-kien-can-luu-y.)

Cooke, Nola, and Li Tana. *Water Frontier: Commerce and the Chinese in the Lower Mekong Region, 1750–1880.* Lanham, MD: Rowman & Littlefield, 2004.

Crossley, Nick, and John Michael Roberts, eds. *After Habermas: New Perspectives on the Public Sphere.* Oxford: Blackwell, 2004.

Cục Thống kê Thành phố Hồ Chí Minh [Ho Chi Minh City Statistical Office]. *Niên giám Thống kê năm 2011* [Statistical yearbook 2011]. Ho Chi Minh City, 2011. (Available online at www.pso.hochiminhcity.gov.vn.)

Cumming-Bruce, Nick [Nicholas]. "Old Guard Secures the Way for Vietnam's New Rich." *Guardian,* July 17, 1996.

———. "Vietnam Learns the Way of the Market; Nick Cumming-Bruce in Hanoi Finds a Brave New World Flawed by the Emerging Gap between the New Rich and the Poor." *Guardian,* July 17, 1993.

———. "Vietnam's Communists Rely on the New Rich." *Guardian,* Jan. 1, 1990.

Dân oan Thủ Thiêm (Danlambao). "Dân oan Thủ Thiêm bao vây công ty Hàn Quốc vì tiếp tay cho bọn cướp đất" [Thu Thiem residents surrounded Korean company to protest its support for land thieves]. Danlambao, 2014. (Available at http://danlambaovn.blogspot.com/2014/02/dan-oan-thu-thiem-bao-vay-cong-ty-han.html.)

Đặng Phong. *"Phá rào" trong kinh tế vào đêm trước Đổi mới* [Economic "fence breaking" on the eve of Đổi Mới]. Hanoi: Nhà xuất bản Trí thức, 2009.

Davis, Deborah. "The New Rich in China: Future Rulers, Present Lives." *China Quarterly,* no. 196 (2008): 935–36.

———. "Urban Consumer Culture." *China Quarterly,* no. 183 (2005): 692–709.

———. "Who Gets the House? Renegotiating Property Rights in Post-Socialist Urban China." *Modern China* 36, no. 5 (2010): 463–92.

Davis, Mike. "Fortress Los Angeles: The Militarization of Urban Space." In *Variations on a Theme Park: The New American City and the End of Public Space,* ed. Michael Sorkin. New York: Hill & Wang, 1992.

De Boeck, Filip. "Inhabiting Ocular Ground: Kinshasa's Future in the Light of Congo's Spectral Urban Politics." *Cultural Anthropology* 26, no. 2 (2011): 263–86.

Dillon, David. "Honor Award Suburban Design." *Architectural Record,* May 1997, 86.

Đỗ Trà Giang. "Tăng tốc thu hút đầu tư vào Thủ Thiêm" [Speed up the attraction of investment into Thủ Thiêm]. *Sài Gòn Giải Phóng,* May 2 2014.

Đoan Trang. "Phố Đông hiện đại bên bờ sông Sài Gòn" [A modern Pudong on the banks of the Saigon River]." *Tuổi Trẻ,* March 4, 2006.

Douglass, Mike, and Liling Huang. "Globalizing the City in Southeast Asia: Utopia on the Urban Edge—The Case of Phu My Hung, Saigon." *International Journal of Asia-Pacific Studies* 3, no. 2 (2007): 1–41.

Douglass, Mike, Kong Chong Ho, and Giok-Ling Ooi. "Civic Spaces, Globalisation, and Pacific Asia Cities." *International Development Planning Review* 24, no. 2 (2002): 345–61.

Doxiadis Associates. *Saigon Metropolitan Area: Volume 1, Urban Development Program and Plan.* Athens, Greece: Prepared for the Government of the Republic of Vietnam, Ministry of Public Works, Directorate General of Reconstruction and City Planning, 1965.

———. *Saigon Metropolitan Area: Volume 2, Administration, House Types, Land Types, Building Materials, Human Resources.* Athens, Greece: Prepared for the Government of the Republic of Vietnam, Ministry of Public Works, Directorate General of Reconstruction and City Planning, 1965.

———. *Saigon Metropolitan Area: Volume 3, Pilot Project.* Athens, Greece: Prepared for the Government of the Republic of Vietnam, Ministry of Public Works, Directorate General of Reconstruction and City Planning, 1965.

Duiker, William J. *Vietnam: Revolution in Transition.* 2nd ed. Boulder, CO: Westview Press, 1995.

———. *Vietnam since the Fall of Saigon.* Monographs in International Studies, Southeast Asia Series, no. 56A. Updated ed. Athens: Ohio University Center for International Studies, 1989.

Dundes, Alan. "The Motif-Index and the Tale Type Index: A Critique." *Journal of Folklore Research* 34, no. 3 (1997): 195–202.

Durkheim, Émile. *The Division of Labor in Society.* Translated by W. D. Halls. 1893; New York: Free Press, 1997.

Earl, Catherine. *Vietnam's New Middle Classes: Gender, Career, City.* Copenhagen: NIAS Press, 2014.

Elias, Norbert. *The Civilizing Process.* 1939; Malden, MA: Blackwell, 2000.

Evans-Pritchard, E. E. *The Nuer: A Description of the Modes of Livelihood and Political Institutions of a Nilotic People.* 1940; New York: Oxford University Press, 1969.

Fraser, Davis. "Inventing Oasis: Luxury Housing Advertisements in Reconfiguring Domestic Space in Shanghai." In *The Consumer Revolution in Urban China,* ed. Deborah Davis, 25–53. Berkeley: University of California Press, 2000.

Freud, Sigmund. *Civilization and Its Discontents.* New York: W. W. Norton, 1961.

Gainsborough, Martin. "Political Change in Vietnam: In Search of the Middle-Class Challenge to the State." *Asian Survey* 42, no. 5 (Sept./Oct. 2002): 694–707.

———. "Understanding Communist Transition: Property Rights in Ho Chi Minh City in the Late 1990s." *Post-Communist Economies* 14, no. 2 (2002): 227–43.

———. *Vietnam: Rethinking the State.* London: Zed Books, 2010.

Gammeltoft, Tine M. *Haunting Images: A Cultural Account of Selective Reproduction in Vietnam.* Berkeley: University of California Press, 2014.

Ghertner, D. Asher. "Nuisance Talk: Middle-Class Discourses of a Slum-Free Delhi." In *Ecologies of Urbanism in India: Metropolitan Civility and Sustainability,* ed. Anne Rademacher and K. Sivaramakrishnan, 249–75. Hong Kong: Hong Kong University Press, 2013.

———. "Rule by Aesthetics: World-Class City Making in Delhi." In *Worlding Cities: Asian Experiments and the Art of Being Global,* ed. Ananya Roy and Aihwa Ong, 279–306. Malden, MA: Wiley-Blackwell, 2011.

Giáo Xứ Thủ Thiêm [Thủ Thiêm Parish]. *Kỷ Yếu mừng 150 năm thành lập Giáo Xứ Thủ Thiêm: 1859–2009* [Commemorative volume celebrating 150 years since the founding of Thủ Thiêm Parish: 1859–2009]. Ho Chi Minh City: Giáo xứ Thủ Thiêm, 2009.

Gibert, Marie. "Déplacements forcés et renouvellement urbain à Hồ Chí Minh Ville" [Forced displacement and urban renewal in Hồ Chí Minh City]. *L'espace politique: Revue en ligne de géographie politique et de géopolitique* 22, no. 1 (2014).

Gillespie, John. "Changing Concepts of Socialist Law in Vietnam." In *Asian Socialism and Legal Change: The Dynamics of Vietnamese and Chinese Reform,* ed. John Gillespie and Pip Nicholson, 45–75. Canberra: ANU Press, 2005.

———. "The Emerging Role of Property Rights in Land and Housing Disputes in Hanoi." In *State, Society, and the Market in Contemporary Vietnam: Property, Power, and Values,* ed. Hue-Tam Ho-Tai and Mark Sidel, 103–22. New York: Routledge, 2012.

———. "Exploring the Limits of the Judicialization of Urban Land Disputes in Vietnam." *Law and Society Review* 45, no. 2 (2011): 241–75.

———. "Public Land Disputes in Vietnam: A Multi-Actor Analysis of Five Case Studies with an East Asian Comparative." Hanoi: Transformation and Change Management Consulting Co., Ltd., for the Asia Foundation, 2014. (Available at https://asiafoundation.org/resources/pdfs/Publiclanddisputesreport.pdf.)

———. "Social Consensus and the Meta-Regulation of Land-Taking Disputes in Vietnam." *Journal of Vietnamese Studies* 9, no. 3 (2014): 91–124.

Gittings, John. "Other Worlds: Socialism Chases the Tainted Spoils of Capitalism." *Guardian,* Jan. 13, 1995, 13.

Gordillo, Gastón. *Rubble: The Afterlife of Destruction.* Durham, NC: Duke University Press, 2014.

Graw, Steve. "Nam Tien and the Development of Vietnamese Regionalism." Thesis, Cornell University, 1995.

Habermas, Jürgen. "The Public Sphere," in *Jürgen Habermas on Society and Politics: A Reader,* ed. Steven Seidman, 231–36. Boston: Beacon Press, 1989.

Hải Nam and Trung Hiếu. "Căng thẳng đối thoại về dự án Thủ Thiêm" [Tense discussion about the Thủ Thiêm project]. *Thanh Niên,* June 11, 2016, 3.

Hall, Derek, Philip Hirsch, and Tania Murray Li. *Powers of Exclusion: Land Dilemmas in Southeast Asia*. Singapore: NUS Press, 2011.

Harms, Erik. "Beauty as Control in the New Saigon: Eviction, New Urban Zones, and Atomized Dissent in a Southeast Asian City." *American Ethnologist* 39, no. 4 (2012): 735–50.

———. "The Boss: Conspicuous Invisibility in Ho Chi Minh City." *City & Society* 25, no. 2 (2013): 195–215.

———. "Civility's Footprint: Ethnographic Conversations about Urban Civility and Sustainability in Ho Chi Minh City." *SOJOURN: Journal of Social Issues in Southeast Asia* 29, no. 2 (July 2014): 223–62.

———. "Eviction Time in the New Saigon: Temporalities of Displacement in the Rubble of Development." *Cultural Anthropology* 28, no. 2 (2013): 344–68.

———. "Knowing into Oblivion: Clearing Wastelands and Imagining Emptiness in Vietnamese New Urban Zones." *Singapore Journal of Tropical Geography* 35, no. 2 (2014): 312–27.

———. "Material Symbolism of Saigon's Edge: The Political-Economic and Symbolic Transformation of Hồ Chí Minh City's Periurban Zones." *Pacific Affairs* 84, no. 3 (2011): 455–73.

———. "Modern Views, Unblocked: Looking into the Distance in Phu My Hung, a Vietnamese New Urban Zone." *Anthropological Quarterly* 89, no. 2 (2016): 369–98

———. "Neo-Geomancy and Real Estate Fever in Post-Reform Vietnam." *positions* 20, no. 2 (2012): 405–34.

———. *Saigon's Edge: On the Margins of Ho Chi Minh City*. Minneapolis: University of Minnesota Press, 2011.

———. "Social Demolition: Creative Destruction and the Production of Value in Vietnamese Land Clearance." In *State, Society, and the Market in Contemporary Vietnam: Property, Power, and Values*, ed. Hue-Tam Ho-Tai and Mark Sidel, 55–68. New York: Routledge, 2012.

———. "Urban Space and Exclusion in Asia," *Annual Review of Anthropology* 45 (Oct. 2016).

Harvey, David. "Accumulation by Dispossession." In *The New Imperialism*, 137–82. New York: Oxford University Press, 2005.

Hayton, Bill. *The South China Sea: The Struggle for Power in Asia*. New Haven, CT: Yale University Press, 2014.

———. *Vietnam: Rising Dragon*. New Haven, CT: Yale University Press, 2010.

Hébrard, Ernest. "L'urbanisme en Indochine." *L'Architecture* 41, no. 2 (1928): 33–49.

Herbelin, Caroline. "Des habitations à bon marché au Việt Nam: La question du logement social en situation coloniale" [Public housing projects in Vietnam: The problem of habitation in a colonial situation]. *Moussons* 13–14 (2009): 123–46.

Herzfeld, Michael. *The Poetics of Manhood: Contest and Identity in a Cretan Mountain Village*. Princeton, NJ: Princeton University Press, 1985.

Hickey, Gerald Cannon. *Free in the Forest: Ethnohistory of the Vietnamese Central Highlands, 1954–1976*. New Haven, CT: Yale University Press, 1982.

Hirsch, Eric. "Property and Persons: New Forms and Contests in the Era of Neoliberalism." *Annual Review of Anthropology* 39, no. 1 (2010): 347–60.

Hồ Xuân Hương. *Spring Essence: The Poetry of Hồ Xuân Hương*. Translated by John Balaban. Port Townsend, WA: Copper Canyon Press, 2000.

Hoang, Kimberly Kay. *Dealing in Desire: Asian Ascendancy, Western Decline, and the Hidden Currencies of Global Sex Work*. Oakland: University of California Press, 2015.

———. "Economies of Emotion, Familiarity, Fantasy, and Desire: Emotional Labor in Ho Chi Minh City's Sex Industry." *Sexualities* 13, no. 2 (2010): 255–72.

———. "She's Not a Dirty Low Class Girl: Sex Work in Ho Chi Minh City." *Journal of Contemporary Ethnography* 40, no. 4 (2011): 367–96.

Hội đồng Nhân dân Thành phố Hồ Chí Minh [Ho Chi Minh City People's Council]. "21/2002/NQ-HĐ Nghị Quyết về đầu tư xây dựng trung tâm đô thị mới Thủ Thiêm" [Resolution regarding the investment and construction of the new urban center of Thu Thiem]. Ho Chi Minh City, 2002.

Holston, James. "The Death of the Street." Chap. 4 in *The Modernist City: An Anthropological Critique of Brasilia*. Chicago: University of Chicago Press, 1989.

———. *Insurgent Citizenship: Disjunctions of Democracy and Modernity in Brazil*. Princeton, NJ: Princeton University Press, 2008.

———. *The Modernist City: An Anthropological Critique of Brasilia*. Chicago: University of Chicago Press, 1989.

Hsing, You-tien. *The Great Urban Transformation: Politics of Land and Property in China*. Oxford: Oxford University Press, 2010.

Hull, Matthew. *Government of Paper: The Materiality of Bureaucracy in Urban Pakistan*. Berkeley: University of California Press, 2012.

Hữu Nguyên. "Cố Thủ tướng Võ Văn Kiệt—'kiến trúc sư' đổi mới" [Former prime minister Võ Văn Kiệt—'Architect of Đổi Mới']. *VnExpress*, Nov. 17, 2012.

Huy Đức. *Bên Thắng Cuộc* [The winning side]. Los Angeles: OSINBook, 2012.

Huynh, Du. "The Misuse of Urban Planning in Ho Chi Minh City." *Habitat International* 48 (Aug. 2015): 11–19.

———. "The Transformation of Ho Chi Minh City: Issues in Managing Growth." PhD thesis, Harvard University, 2012.

Huynh, Du, and Alex Ngo. "Urban Development through Land-Based Infrastructure Financing: Cases in Ho Chi Minh City." Fulbright Economics Teaching Program, Ho Chi Minh City, 2010.

Hùynh Phú Sang. "Presentation." In *From Saigon to Ho Chi Minh City: 300-Year History*, ed. Nguyễn Đình Đầu, 5–7. Ho Chi Minh City: Land Service Science and Technics Publishing House., 1998.

Hy Hiếu. "Nhớ Ba Đình, mơ về Thủ Thiêm" [Remembering Ba Đình, dreams of Thủ Thiêm]. *Tuổi Trẻ*, Sept. 8, 2009.

IPC [Investment Promotion Company of Tân Thuận Export Processing Zone]. "Mốc sự kiện" [Milestones]. Công ty TNHH MTV Phát triển Công nghiệp Tân Thuận, www.ttipc.vn/moc-su-kien.

Jamieson, Neil. "Some Things Poetry Can Tell Us about the Process of Social Change in Vietnam." *Southeast Asian Studies* 39, no. 3 (2001): 325–57.

Jellema, Kate. "Returning Home: Ancestor Veneration and the Nationalism of Đổi Mới Vietnam." In *Modernity and Re-Enchantment: Religion in Post-Revolutionary Vietnam*, ed. Philip Taylor, 57–89. Lanham, MD: Lexington Books, 2007.

Kerkvliet, Benedict J. Tria. "Protests over Land in Vietnam: Rightful Resistance and More." *Journal of Vietnamese Studies* 9, no. 3 (2014): 19–54.

Kim Anh and Nguyễn Nam. "'Dân chơi Thủ Thiêm' thời rủng rỉnh" ["The players of Thủ Thiêm" in a time of financial plenty]. *Tuổi Trẻ,* May 24, 2009.

———. "Thanh niên khu đền bù giải tỏa—Bài 2: Chỉ biết hôm nay" [Youth in a land clearance and compensation zone—Part 2: Only thinking about today]. *Tuổi Trẻ,* May 25, 2009.

———. "TP.HCM: Thanh niên khu đền bù giải tỏa—Bài cuối: Tiền đền bù lo tương lai" [HCMC: Youth in a land clearance and compensation zone—Final article: Compensation money and worries for the future]. *Tuổi Trẻ,* May 26, 2009.

Kim, Annette. *Learning to Be Capitalists: Entrepreneurs in Vietnam's Transition Economy.* Oxford: Oxford University Press, 2008.

———. "A Market without the 'Right' Property Rights." *Economics of Transition* 12, no. 2 (2004): 275–305.

———. *Sidewalk City: Remapping Public Space in Ho Chi Minh City.* Chicago: University of Chicago Press, 2015.

———. "Talking Back: The Role of Narrative in Vietnam's Recent Land Compensation Changes." *Urban Studies* 48, no. 3 (Feb. 1, 2011): 493–508.

Kim, Jim Yong. "How Ho Chi Minh City's Filthy Canal Became a Park." *BloombergView,* Oct. 15, 2013.

Kính Cận/Viễn Đông. "Hóng mát trên cầu Phú Mỹ" [Savoring the cool air on the Phú Mỹ Bridge]. *Viễn Đông Daily,* Oct. 20, 2011.

Labbé, Danielle. *Land Politics and Livelihoods on the Margins of Hanoi, 1920–2010.* Vancouver, BC: UBC Press, 2014.

———. "Understanding the Causes of Urban Fragmentation in Hanoi: The Case of New Urban Areas." *International Development Planning Review* 33, no. 3 (2011): 273–91.

Lainez, Nicolas. "Commodified Sexuality and Mother-Daughter Power Dynamics in the Mekong Delta." *Journal of Vietnamese Studies* 7, no. 1 (2012): 149–80.

———. "Unveiling the Invisible: Representing Transitioning Urban Space in Vietnam." EspacesTemps.net, Objects, June 28, 2012, www.espacestemps.net/articles/unveiling-the-invisible.

Lan Anh Nguyen. "Battleground." *Forbes,* Sept. 19, 2008.

Lawrence S. Ting Memorial Fund. "About Us." www.lawrencestingfund.org//aboutus.

Lawrence S. Ting School Students. "Change of the Community with the Example of Phu My Hung: Submission to British Council Connecting Classroom Competition." Lawrence S. Ting School, Ho Chi Minh City, 2010.

———. "Nhà trường: MỤC ĐÍCH THÀNH LẬP" [Purpose for establishing the school]. http://lsts.edu.vn/?opt=info&act=view&id=651211d43d9caa6e02c990b0a82652dca.

Lê Du Phong. *Thu nhập, đời sống, việc làm của người có đất bị thu hồi* [Income, livelihood, and work of people who have had their land reclaimed]. Hanoi: Nhà xuất bản Chính trị Quốc gia, 2007.

Le Minh Khue. "Scenes from an Alley." In *Night, Again: Contemporary Fiction from Vietnam,* ed. Linh Dinh. New York: Seven Stories Press, 2006.

Lê Thị Hoàng Mai. "Tình hình tiến độ thực hiện công tác bồi thường giải phóng mặt bằng các hồ sơ còn lại trong Khu đô thị mới Thủ Thiêm" [The situation of the pace of carrying out the compensation and liberation of land in the remaining dossiers in the Thu Thiem New Urban Zone]. News release, June 22, 2012. (Available at www.thuthiem.hochiminhcity.gov.vn/web/guest/khudothi/cong-tac-boi-thuong.)

Leaf, Michael. "Vietnam's Urban Edge: The Administration of Urban Development in Hanoi." *TWPR* 21, no. 3 (1999): 297–315.

Lefebvre, Henri. *The Production of Space*. 1974; London: Blackwell, 1991.

Leshkowich, Ann Marie. *Essential Trade: Vietnamese Women in a Changing Marketplace*. Honolulu: University of Hawai'i Press, 2014.

———. "Finances, Family, Fashion, Fitness, and . . . Freedom? The Changing Lives of Urban Middle-Class Vietnamese Women." Chap. 6 in *The Reinvention of Distinction: Modernity and the Middle Class in Urban Vietnam*, ed. Van Nguyen-Marshall, Lisa B. Welch Drummond, and Danièle Bélanger. Dordrecht, Neth.: Springer, 2012.

———. "Standardized Forms of Vietnamese Selfhood: An Ethnographic Genealogy of Documentation." *American Ethnologist* 41, no. 1 (2014): 143–62.

———. "Wandering Ghosts of Late Socialism: Conflict, Metaphor, and Memory in a Southern Vietnamese Marketplace." *Journal of Asian Studies* 67, no. 1 (2008): 5–41.

Li, Tania Murray. *The Will to Improve: Governmentality, Development, and the Practice of Politics*. Durham, NC: Duke University Press, 2007.

Lidai Ming. "Một số phương pháp thực hiện trong việc xây dựng phát triển và quản lý khu trung tâm đô thị mới Nam Sài Gòn của công ty Phú Mỹ Hưng" [Some implementation methods for the work of building, developing, and managing the central Saigon South urban area of the Phú Mỹ Hưng Corporation]. Phú Mỹ Hưng Corp., Ho Chi Minh City, 2007.

Low, Setha. "Urban Fear: Building the Fortress City." *City & Society* 9, no. 1 (1997): 53–71.

Luong, Hy Van. "The State, Local Associations, and Alternate Civilities in Rural Northern Vietnam." In *Civil Life, Globalization, and Political Change in Asia: Organizing between Family and State*, ed. Robert Weller, 123–46. London: Routledge, 2005.

———. "Wealth, Power, and Inequality: Global Market, the State, and Local Sociocultural Dynamics." In *Postwar Vietnam: Dynamics of a Transforming Society*, 81–106. Lanham, MD: Rowman & Littlefield, 2003.

Malarney, Shaun K. *Culture, Ritual, and Revolution in Vietnam*. London: RoutledgeCurzon, 2002.

Malleret, Louis. "Eléments d'une monographie des anciennes fortifications et citadelles de Saïgon." *Bulletin de la Société des Etudes Indochinois, Saïgon*, 1935.

———. "A la recherche de Prei Nokor, note sur l'emplacement présumé de l'ancien Saïgon khmer." *Bulletin de la Société des études indochinois, Saïgon*, 1942.

Mamdani, Mahmood. "Introduction." In *Beyond Rights Talk and Culture Talk: Comparative Essays on the Politics of Rights and Culture*, ed. Mahmood Mamdani, 1–13. Cape Town, SA: David Philip Publishers, 2000.

Marx, Karl. *Capital: A Critique of Political Economy*, vol. 1. Translated by Ben Fowkes. 1867; London: Penguin Classics, 1976.

Mattei, Ugo, and Laura Nader. *Plunder: When the Rule of Law Is Illegal.* Malden, MA: Blackwell, 2008.

Mauss, Marcel. "A Category of the Human Mind: The Notion of Person, the Notion of Self," trans. Ben Brewster, in Mauss, *Sociology and Psychology: Essays,* 59–94. 1938; London: Routledge & Kegan Paul, 1979.

McElwee, Pamela. "Becoming Socialist or Becoming Kinh? Government Policies for Ethnic Minorities in the Socialist Republic of Viet Nam." In *Civilizing the Margins: Southeast Asian Government Policies for the Development of Minorities,* ed. Christopher Duncan, 182–213. Ithaca, NY: Cornell University Press, 2004.

McGee, T. G. *The Southeast Asian City.* New York: Praeger, 1967.

McHale, Shawn. "Ethnicity, Violence, and Khmer-Vietnamese Relations: The Significance of the Lower Mekong Delta, 1757–1954." *Journal of Asian Studies* 72, no. 2 (2013): 367–90.

Mỹ-Vân Trần. "'Come On, Girls, Let's Go Bail Water': Eroticism in Hồ Xuân Hương's Vietnamese Poetry." *Journal of Southeast Asian Studies* 33, no. 3 (2002): 471–94.

Navaro-Yashin, Yael. *Faces of the State: Secularism and Public Life in Turkey.* Princeton, NJ: Princeton University Press, 2002.

Ngọc Ẩn and Bảo Ân. "Phà Thủ Thiêm nói lời chia tay" [The Thủ Thiêm ferry says goodbye]. *Tuổi Trẻ,* Dec. 31, 2011.

Người Thủ Thiêm. "Dự án khu Đô thị mới Thủ Thiêm: Dự án 6 không = Dự án ma" [Thu Thiem New Urban Zone project: "6 Nos" project = A ghost project." Danlambao, 2011. (Available at http://danlambaovn.blogspot.com/2011/12/du-khu-o-thi-moi-thu-thiem-du-6-khong.html#more.)

Nguyễn Đình Đầu. *Nghiên cứu địa ba Triều Nguyễn* [Cadastral registers study of the Nguyễn dynasty]. Ho Chi Minh City: Nhà xuất bản Thành phố Hồ Chí Minh, 1994.

Nguyễn Kim Đức. "Công tác bồi thường, giải phóng mặt bằng và hỗ trợ tái định cư Khu đô thị mới Thủ Thiêm tiếp tục tiến triển" [The work of compensation and liberation of land and resettlement support continues to be carried out in the Thủ Thiêm New Urban Zone]." Aug. 24, 1011. Thủ Thiêm Investment and Construction Authority website, www.thuthiem.hochiminhcity.gov.vn/web/guest/khudothi/cong-tac-boi-thuong.

Nguyễn Q. Thắng and Nguyễn Đình Tư. *Đường phố Thành phố Hồ Chí Minh* [Ho Chi Minh City streets]. Ho Chi Minh City: Nhà xuất bản Văn hóa Thông tin, 2001.

Nguyễn Văn Kích, Phan Chánh Dưỡng, and Tôn Sĩ Kinh. *Nhà Bè Hồi sinh từ công nghiệp: Tập 1 Khu Chế xuất Tân Thuận—Bước đột phá* [Nha Be revived by industry: Volume 1, The Tan Thuan Export Processing Zone—The breakthrough step]. Ho Chi Minh City: Nhà xuất bản Tổng hợp TP. Hồ Chí Minh, 2006.

———. *Nhà Bè Hồi sinh từ công nghiệp: Tập 2 Phú Mỹ Hưng—Đô thị Phát triển bền vững* [Nha Be revived by industry: Volume 2, Phu My Hung—A sustainable urban development]. Ho Chi Minh City: Nhà xuất bản Tổng hợp TP. Hồ Chí Minh, 2006.

Nguyen Van Suu. "Agricultural Land Conversion and Its Effects on Farmers in Contemporary Vietnam." *Focaal—European Journal of Anthropology* 54 (2009): 106–13.

Nguyen Vu Hoang. "Constructing Civil Society on a Demolition Site in Hanoi." In *State, Society, and the Market in Contemporary Vietnam,* ed. Hue-Tam Ho-Tai and Mark Sidel, 87–102. New York: Routledge, 2012.

Nguyen-Marshall, Van, Lisa B. Welch Drummond, and Danièle Bélanger, eds. *The Reinvention of Distinction: Modernity and the Middle Class in Urban Vietnam*. Dordrecht, Neth.: Springer, 2012.

Ninh, Kim N. B. *A World Transformed: The Politics of Culture in Revolutionary Vietnam, 1945–1965*. Ann Arbor: University of Michigan Press, 2002.

Norindr, Panivong. "Aestheticizing Urban Space: Modernity in Postcolonial Saigon and Hanoi." *L'esprit créateur* 41, no. 3 (2001): 73–87.

O'Brien, Kevin J. "Rightful Resistance." *World Politics* 49, no. 1 (1996): 31–55.

O'Brien, Kevin J., and Lianjiang Li. *Rightful Resistance in Rural China*. New York: Cambridge University Press, 2006.

Ong, Aihwa. "Zoning Technologies in East Asia." In *Neoliberalism as Exception: Mutations in Citizenship and Sovereignty*, 97–118. Durham, NC: Duke University Press, 2006.

Ortner, Sherry B. "On Key Symbols." *American Anthropologist* 75, no. 5 (1973): 1338–46.

P.P.H. "Dự án khu đô thị mới Thủ Thiêm: Xin áp dụng "một cửa" để đẩy nhanh tiến độ đến bù" [Thủ Thiêm New Urban Zone project: Request to use the "one-stop shop" to speed up the pace of compensation]. *Tuổi Trẻ*, Jan. 26, 2010.

Patterson, Orlando. *Freedom*. Vol. 1: *Freedom in the Making of Western Culture*. New York: Basic Books, 1991.

Peterson, George E. *Unlocking Land Values to Finance Urban Infrastructure*. Trends and Policy Options, no. 7. Washington, DC: World Bank—Public-Private Infrastucture Advisory Facility, 2009. (Available at https://www.ppiaf.org/sites/ppiaf.org/files/publication/Trends Policy Options-7-Unlocking Land Values -GPeterson.pdf.)

Peycam, Philippe M. F. *The Birth of Vietnamese Political Journalism: Saigon 1916–1930*. New York: Columbia University Press, 2012.

———. "Saigon, des origines à 1859." In *Saigon, 1698–1998: Architectures/Urbanisme*, ed. Lê Quang Ninh and Stéphane Dovert, 21–51. Ho Chi Minh City: Nhà xuất bản Thành phố Ho Chi Minh, 1998.

Phu My Hung Corp. "Introduction." www.phumyhung.com.vn/eng/introduce.php?id=1.

———. "RESIDENT'S INFORMATION Customer Service Center Information." www.phumyhung.com.vn/eng/ttcudan_detail.php?id=3.

———. "Trung Tâm Phục Vụ Khách Hàng" [RESIDENT'S INFORMATION Customer Service Center Information] (Vietnamese version). www.phumyhung.com.vn/v2/gioi-thieu/trung-tam-phuc-vu-khach-hang.html.

———. *Vươn lên từ đầm lầy* [Rising from the swamps]. Ho Chi Minh City: Phú Mỹ Hưng Corp., 2005.

———. *Xin nhận nơi này làm quê hương: Những hồi ức về cố chủ tịch hội đồng Quản trị Lawrence S. Ting* [Let this place become my homeland: Recollections of the former chairman of the board Lawrence S. Ting]. Ho Chi Minh City: Phú Mỹ Hưng Corp., 2005.

Phúc Huy. "TP.HCM: nơi thiếu nơi thừa nhà tái định cư" [HCMC short of space and homes for resettlement]. *Tuổi Trẻ*, Jan. 11, 2010.

Pieprz, Dennis. "A Landscape Framework for Urban Sustainability: Thu Thiem, Ho Chi Minh City." In *The Ecoedge: Urgent Design Challenges in Building Sustainable Cities*, ed. Esther Charlesworth and Rob Adams, 121–32. London: Taylor & Francis, 2011.

Prasso, Sheridan. "Boomtown, Vietnam." *New York Times Travel Magazine*, Nov. 19, 2006.

Quy-Toan Do and Lakshmi Iyer. "Land Titling and Rural Transition in Vietnam." *Economic Development and Cultural Change* 56, no. 3 (April 2008): 531–79.

Rademacher, Anne. "When Is Housing an Environmental Problem? Reforming Informality in Kathmandu." *Current Anthropology* 20, no. 4 (2009): 513–33.

Ramsay, Jacob. "Miracles and Myths: Vietnam Seen through Its Catholic History." In *Modernity and Reenchantment: Religion in Postrevolutionary Vietnam,* ed. Philip Taylor, 371–98. Lanham, MD: Lexington Books, 2007.

Rancière, Jacques. "Who Is the Subject of the Rights of Man?" *South Atlantic Quarterly* 103, no. 2/3 (Spring/Summer 2004): 297–310.

Rodgers, Dennis, and Bruce O'Neill. "Infrastructural Violence: Introduction to the Special Issue." *Ethnography* 13, no. 4 (Dec. 1, 2012): 401–12.

Rousseau, Jean-Jacques. *On the Social Contract.* 1762; Indianapolis: Hackett, 1983.

Saigon Construction Department. "Introduction of the Projects Planned for Investment in HCM City." *Saigon Investment and Construction* 3, no. 95 (March 1995): 7–12.

SASAKI Associates, Inc. "Thu Thiem New Urban Area." www.sasaki.com/project/139/thu-thiem-new-urban-area/.

Sasges, Gerard, and Scott Cheshier. "Competing Legacies: Rupture and Continuity in Vietnamese Political Economy." *South East Asia Research* 20, no. 1 (2012): 5–33.

Schmidt, Peter. "Pleas for Civility Meet Cynicism." *Chronicle of Higher Education,* Sept. 10, 2014.

Schwenkel, Christina. "Civilizing the City: Socialist Ruins and Urban Renewal in Central Vietnam." *positions* 20, no. 2 (2012): 437–70.

———. "Post/Socialist Affect: Ruination and Reconstruction of the Nation in Urban Vietnam." *Cultural Anthropology* 28, no. 2 (2013): 252–77.

———. "Reclaiming Rights to the Socialist City: Bureaucratic Artefacts and the Affective Appeal of Petitions." *Southeast Asia Research* 23, no. 2 (2015): 205–25.

Schwenkel, Christina, and Ann Marie Leshkowich. "Guest Editors' Introduction: How Is Neoliberalism Good to Think Vietnam? How Is Vietnam Good to Think Neoliberalism?" *positions* 20, no. 2 (2012): 379–401.

Scott, James C. *Seeing Like a State: How Certain Schemes to Improve the Human Condition Have Failed.* New Haven, CT: Yale University Press, 1998.

Sharbaugh, Patrick E., and Dang Nguyen. "Make Lulz, Not War: How Online Remix and Meme Culture Are Empowering Civic Engagement in the Socialist Republic of Vietnam." *Asiascape: Digital Asia* 1, no. 3 (2014): 133–68.

Shatkin, Gavin. "The City and the Bottom Line: Urban Megaprojects and the Privatization of Planning in Southeast Asia." *Environment and Planning A* 40, no. 2 (2008): 383–401.

———. "Planning Privatopolis: Representation and Contestation in the Development of Urban Integrated Mega-Projects." In *Worlding Cities: Asian Experiments and the Art of Being Global,* ed. Ananya Roy and Aihwa Ong, 77–97. Malden, MA: Wiley-Blackwell, 2011.

Sidel, Mark. *Law and Society in Vietnam: The Transition from Socialism in Comparative Perspective.* New York: Cambridge University Press, 2008.

Simone, AbdouMaliq. *For the City Yet to Come: Changing African Life in Four Cities.* Durham, NC: Duke University Press, 2004.

Stocking, George W. *Observers Observed: Essays on Ethnographic Fieldwork*. Madison: University of Wisconsin Press, 1984.

Taylor, Keith W. "Surface Orientations in Vietnam: Beyond Histories of Nation and Region." *Journal of Asian Studies* 57, no. 4 (1998): 949–78.

Taylor, Philip. *Fragments of the Present: Searching for Modernity in Vietnam's South*. Honolulu: University of Hawai'i Press, 2001.

———. "Introduction to the Special Issue: Contests over Land in Rural Vietnam." *Journal of Vietnamese Studies* 9, no. 3 (2014): 1–18.

———. *The Khmer Lands of Vietnam: Environment, Cosmology, and Sovereignty*. Singapore: NUS Press, 2014.

———. "Poor Policies, Wealthy Peasants: Alternative Trajectories of Rural Development in Vietnam." *Journal of Vietnamese Studies* 2, no. 2 (2007): 3–56.

———. "Social Inequality in a Socialist State." In *Social Inequality in Vietnam and the Challenges to Reform*, ed. Philip Taylor, 1–40. Singapore: ISEAS, 2004.

Thạch Phương and Lê Trung Hoa. *Từ điển Thành phố Sài Gòn—Thành phố Hồ Chí Minh* [Dictionary of Saigon City—Ho Chi Minh City]. Ho Chi Minh City: Nhà xuất bản Trẻ, 2001.

Thanh Nien News. "Japanese Exec Names Vietnamese Official in ODA Bribe: Report." *ThanhNienNews,* March 23, 2014.

Thu Thiem Investment and Construction Authority. "Thu Thiem New Urban Area Project: 12,000 Apartments for Resettlement [to] Be Built." June 29, 2010. www.thuthiem. hochiminhcity.gov.vn/web/english/thuthiem-new-urban-center/compensation-works.

Thủ Tướng Chính phủ Việt Nam [Prime Minister of Vietnam]. "20/TTg: Quyết định số 20/ TTg ngày 16/01/1993 của Thủ tướng Chính phủ về việc phê duyệt quy hoạch tổng thể xây dựng Thành phố Hồ Chí Minh" [Decision number 20/TTg of January 16, 1993, by the prime minister regarding approval of the Ho Chi Minh City Master Plan]. Hanoi: Chính phủ Việt Nam, 1993.

———. "367/TTg: Quyết định số 367/TTg ngày 04/06/1996 của Thủ tướng Chính phủ về việc phê duyệt quy hoạch xây dựng Khu đô thị mới Thủ Thiêm" [Decision number 367/ TTg on June 4, 1996, by the Prime Minister regarding the approval of the building plan for the Thu Thiem New Urban Zone]. Hanoi: Chính phủ Việt Nam, 1996.

TN News. "Vietnam Opens First Underwater Tunnel with Hopes for Better Traffic." *Thanh Niên News,* Nov. 20, 2011.

Tomba, Luigi. "Middle Classes in China: Force for Political Change or Guarantee of Stability?" *PORTAL: Journal of Multidisciplinary International Studies* 6, no. 2 (2009).

———. "Of Quality, Harmony, and Community: Civilization and the Middle Class in Urban China." *positions* 17, no. 3 (2009): 591–616.

Tôn Nữ Quỳnh Trân. *Thủ Thiêm—Quá khứ và tương lai* [Thu Thiem: Past and future]. Ho Chi Minh City: Nhà xuất bản Tổng hợp, 2010.

Tôn Nữ Quỳnh Trân and Nguyễn Trọng Hòa. *Văn hóa hẻm phố Sài Gòn—Thành phố Hồ Chí Minh* [Alleyway culture in Saigon—Ho Chi Minh City]. Ho Chi Minh City: Nhà xuất bản Tổng hợp, 2007.

Trần Văn Giàu. *Địa chí văn hóa Thành phố Hồ Chí Minh* [Monograph on the Culture of Ho Chi Minh City]. Ho Chi Minh City: Nhà xuất bản Thành phố Hồ Chí Minh, 1987.

Trịnh Hoài Đức. *Gia Định thành thông chí* [Observations of Gia Dinh]. 1820; Ho Chi Minh City: Nhà xuất bản Giáo dục, 1999.

Truitt, Allison. "Domestic Investor *(Người đầu tư trong nước)*." In *Figures of Southeast Asian Modernity,* ed. Joshua Barker, Erik Harms, and Johan Lindquist, 54–56. Honolulu: University of Hawai'i Press, 2013.

———. *Dreaming of Money in Ho Chi Minh City.* Seattle: University of Washington Press, 2013.

Trung Sơn. "Hoang vắng ở đô thị kỳ vọng đẹp nhất Đông Nam Á" [Abandonment in the urban area anticipated as the most beautiful in Southeast Asia]. *VnExpress,* April 2, 2013.

Trương Vĩnh Ký. *Souvenirs historiques sur Saigon et ses environs* [Historical recollections on Saigon and its surroundings]. Saigon: Imprimerie Coloniale, 1885.

Tùng Nguyên and Trung Kiên. "Hình ảnh thành phố mang tên Bác sau 39 năm giải phóng" [Photos of the city that bears Uncle's name after 39 years of liberation]. *Dân trí,* April 30, 2014.

Tuổi Trẻ TV. "Cháy bãi cỏ hoang uy hiếp hầm Thủ Thiêm" [Fire in an abandoned grass field threatens the Thủ Thiêm tunnel]." *Tuổi Trẻ,* April 27, 2013.

———. "Lộn xộn trên cầu Thủ Thiêm" [Disorderliness on the Thủ Thiêm Bridge]. *Tuổi Trẻ,* June 13, 2013.

Ủy ban Nhân dân Quận 7 Phòng Thống kê [District 7 People's Committee Statistics Office]. *Niên giám Thống kê: 1997–2007* [Statistical yearbook: 1997–2007]. Ho Chi Minh City: Ủy ban Nhân dân Quận 7, 2006.

Ủy ban Nhân dân Thành phố Hồ Chí Minh [Ho Chi Minh City People's Committee]. "103/2001/QĐ-UB: Quyết định số 103/2001/QĐ-UB ngày 01 tháng 11 năm 2001 của UBND thành phố về thành lập Ban Quản lý Đầu tư, Xây dựng Khu đô thị mới Thủ Thiêm" [Decision number 103/2001/QĐ-UB of November 1, 2001, by the City People's Committee regarding the establishment of the Thủ Thiêm Investment and Construction Authority]. Ho Chi Minh City, 2001.

———. "135/2002/QĐ-UB: Quyết định số 135/2002/QĐ-UB ngày 21 tháng 11 năm 2002 của UBND thành phố về việc ban hành quy định về đền bù, hỗ trợ thiệt hại và tái định cư trong khu quy hoạch xây dựng Khu đô thị mới Thủ Thiêm và các khu phục vụ tái định cư tại Quận 2, Thành phố Hồ Chí Minh" [Decision number 135/2002/QĐ-UB of November 21, 2002, by the City People's Committee regarding the issuance of regulations regarding compensation and assistance for losses and resettlement in the planned zone for building the Thu Thiem New Urban Zone and the zones serving the resettlement in District 2, Ho Chi Minh City]. Ho Chi Minh City, 2002.

V. C. Mai and D. N. Hà. "Dân tiếp tục bức xúc chuyện giải tỏa, đền bù" [The people continue to be frustrated by land clearance and compensation]. *Tuổi Trẻ,* June 24, 2009.

Van Leeuwen, Lizzy. *Lost in Mall: An Ethnography of Middle-Class Jakarta in the 1990s.* Leiden: KITLV Press, 2011.

Verdery, Katherine. "Fuzzy Property: Rights, Power, and Identity in Transylvania's Decollectivization." In *Uncertain Transition: Ethnographies of Change in the Postsocialist World,* ed. Michael Burawoy and Katherine Verdery, 53–81. Lanham, MD: Rowman & Littlefield, 1999.

————. *What Was Socialism, and What Comes Next?* Princeton, NJ: Princeton University Press, 1996.

Việt Hùng and Đ. Huân. "Khu đô thị mới Thủ Thiêm sẽ ngập trong nước" [The Thu Thiem New Urban Zone will be submerged under water]. *Tuổi Trẻ*, April 15, 2006.

Vietnam, Socialist Republic of. "2003 Luật Đất Đai" [Law on land]. Hanoi: Nhà xuất bản Tài chính, 2010.

Vĩnh Phú. "Đại lộ đẹp nhất TP HCM mang tên Võ Văn Kiệt" [HCMCs most beautiful boulevard carries Võ Văn Kiệt's name]. *VnExpress*, April 29, 2011.

Vĩnh Phương and Tùng Quang. "Sống ở chung cư: Những điều được mất" [Living in an apartment building: Things gained and lost]. *Kiến trúc & đời sống* [Architecture and living], 2010, 84.

Vũ Trọng Phụng. *Dumb Luck*. Translated by Nguyễn Nguyệt Cầm and Peter Zinoman. Ann Arbor: University of Michigan Press, 2002.

Waibel, Michael. "The Production of Urban Space in Vietnam's Metropolis in the Course of Transition: Internationalization, Polarization, and Newly Emerging Lifestyles in Vietnamese Society." *Trialog* 89, no. 2 (2006): 43–48.

Waldrop, Anne. "Gating and Class Relations: The Case of a New Delhi 'Colony.'" *City & Society* 16, no. 2 (Dec. 2004): 93–116.

White, John. *Voyage to Cochin China*. London: Longman, Hurst, Rees, Orme, Brown & Green, 1824.

Wright, Guy. "Saigon of Tomorrow." *San Francisco Examiner,* June 22, 1973, 39.

Wurster, Bernardi & Emmons, Inc. "Thu Thiem Peninsula Development Plan: Agency for International Development Contract AID/vn-101." Wurster, Bernardi & Emmons, Inc., Saigon, 1972.

————. "Thu Thiem Peninsula New Town, General Data, Project Statistics, Architect's Contract." Environmental Design Archives, University of California, Berkeley, Wurster/WBE Collection, Folder II.150, Thu Thiem Peninsula Plan, 1973, 1972.

Xuân Thủy–Lê Nguyễn. "Thủ Thiêm cỏ mọc um tùm . . ." [Luxuriant grasses grow in Thủ Thiêm]. *Tiền Phong* online, May 9, 2013.

Yi-Chang, Hsiang. "The Quiet Princes—Carving Out a Kingdom in Vietnam." *China Post*, Nov. 1, 2010.

Zhang, Li. *In Search of Paradise: Middle-Class Living in a Chinese Metropolis*. Ithaca, NY: Cornell University Press, 2010.

Zhang, Li, and Aihwa Ong, eds. *Privatizing China: Socialism from Afar*. Ithaca, NY: Cornell University Press, 2008.

Zinoman, Peter. *Vietnamese Colonial Republican: The Political Vision of Vu Trong Phung*. Berkeley: University of California Press, 2013.

# INDEX

CPSIA information can be obtained
at www.ICGtesting.com
Printed in the USA
LVOW01s0850281016
510350LV00002B/6/P

9 780520 292512